Suicide through a Peacebuilding Lens

Katerina Standish

Suicide through a Peacebuilding Lens

palgrave
macmillan

Katerina Standish
National Centre for Peace
and Conflict Studies
University of Otago
Dunedin, New Zealand

ISBN 978-981-13-9736-3 ISBN 978-981-13-9737-0 (eBook)
https://doi.org/10.1007/978-981-13-9737-0

This Palgrave Macmillan imprint is published by the registered company Springer Nature Singapore Pte Ltd.
The registered company address is: 152 Beach Road, #21-01/04 Gateway East, Singapore 189721, Singapore

To those of us in the darkness and those who yearn to bring light.

Foreword

In this extraordinarily well-researched book, Katerina Standish provides a veritable wealth of data and analysis. Interspersed in the statistics she posits, with deeply moving insight, the profoundly challenging nuances, complexities and mysteries of understanding suicide. While utterly impressive in its scholarly presentation, this is not a book for scholars alone. Dr. Standish demonstrates an exquisitely intuitive response to the current statistical reality of suicide, a reality so shocking and yet so little attended to within the peacebuilding community.

Its value to students and scholars across virtually all of the social and medical science disciplines (and into the humanities) is immense for not only has she provided insight into how disciplines currently regard and respond to suicide she has with clarity and courage provided a template and an urging for closer professional collaboration in the future.

The urgency of her call is beautifully articulated in her enigmatically titled final chapter, *Peacebuilding Suicide*. Here is outlined, in perfectly accessible detail, not only the rationale for collaboration but the enduring prescription for treasuring human connection, human relationships especially that of friendship. *We are the community that is needed, we are the connections that need to be reconnected and we are the tribe that needs to come back together.*

This book is both personal and political and it is the way in which both are openly declared and infused throughout the text that makes this, such an incredibly precious, indeed compelling literary *taonga*. This is a scholarly and deeply personal heartfelt response to the staggering statistical truth about the global prevalence of suicide as the leading cause of violent death worldwide.

Hers is an irresistible cry from the heart for us all to notice those in the neighbourhood for whom the blessings of friendship, deep and loving filial relationality, positive reciprocal connectedness may well be either tenuous or non-existent and an irresistible appeal for us all to act more intentionally in building the beloved community of which Dr. Martin Luther King spoke so eloquently. A community within which all might know an unconditional sense of belonging and within which all might experience the unconditional right to human flourishing. In this spirit, her final sentence is thus seminal, *[suicide] is a global and pressing issue and there is not a moment to lose.*

Dunedin, New Zealand

Dr. Jenny Te Paa Daniel
Te Mareikura
National Centre for Peace and
Conflict Studies
The University of Otago

Preface

I wrote this book to help myself to understand suicide, to assist my field to engage with life-ending acts from a more conceptually stable position and to imagine how peacebuilders can incorporate suicide into our work.

In this preface, I would like to step in front of the Mac keyboard for a moment and introduce myself. I understand the person who chooses to remain a question mark behind their work and not place themselves in the research. So much of the academic world leaves the author a shadow behind the page (my brilliant sister, who is a professor of Art History will likely read these words and tell me to cut them, and that it is 'not scholarly' to be revelatory). And I confess I do feel the risk of identity signalling, as if my humanity is about to be separated into 'tribally aligned' or 'unworthy outsider'. However, I wonder if you might be curious to know why I have written this, and why I am venturing into an arena that has stretched my scholarship farther than ever before.

I write this as a straight, neurotypical Canadian cis-gender woman of Mediterranean and British descent (Greek-Canadian). I identify myself as a progressive social democrat and critical peace pedagogue. I am deeply committed to humanization and well-being on our planet. I practise yogic discipline and my *maha* yoga is Feminist Kundalini Tantra. I do not follow an Abrahamic, Philosophical or Pagan ideology but embrace holisticism—a metaphysics or interconnectivity of body, mind and spirit (physical, mental, supraconscious) that views existence as a combination of matter and energy. I am a person who has experienced insecurity, vulnerability and personal trauma and I am now a middle-aged woman approaching the halfway point of my centennial. I have a job that is deeply meaningful to me, I have a family that loves me and I live in a small cottage with neighbours who smile at me over the fence.

But someone I love deeply wants to die, or at least not exist anymore, and the realization that there was a person in my life who did not want to be here with me has shaken me utterly. I have never been suicidal; indeed, the thought of harming myself has never arisen in my mind. So I come to this topic without personal experience of attempting suicide and without an inclination to ever do so. I am here because now that I know what I know, that my loved one is just one of so many more, I want to understand this human phenomenon and I want to *peacebuild* it—to intervene and transform the potential violence of self-killing via relationship: connection, positive reciprocity, interconnection and friendship. I may fail utterly, but I offer this attempt for your perusal.

Writing a 'hierarchy of harm' for medical students was the intention of the original research that led to the writing of this book. But the *motive* for the *intent* relates to the fact that suicide surrounds me now and it is a form of violence that surrounds many of us. There are few people I have met since I began this journey in 2016 not touched by suicide or at risk and from my personal and professional vantage point PACS may have something to offer. An oft-repeated maxim echoes in suicide literature that intones 'despite thousands of studies about suicide we still don't know how to stop it'. This book seeks to unearth what 'it' is and invites PACS scholar/practitioners to add suicide to our peacebuilding work and research.

My exploration has undoubtedly made mistakes (all my own) and bypassed important and perhaps pivotal voices in research, which I sincerely apologize for, but in the last 16 years my field has only marginally addressed the leading cause of violent death in many, many nations and I had to start somewhere. I write this to be of service to those who come after me and to elevate the contributions of the scholar/practitioners, advocates, health professionals, community peer support workers, suicide prevention donors and fellow travellers from individuals to institutions who already recognize this important work. If this book became an introductory textbook for scholar/practitioners of PACS interested in exploring suicide, I genuinely hope it aids in beginning to close the gap in our knowledge. If it inspires our interdisciplinary friends to consider *peacebuilding* suicide in addition to their common interventions, then I will have succeeded in adding to the global response of millions in this widespread and preventable form of violence. And for those who simply want to understand more about the world around you (as I did) here is a small part of the puzzle we need, together, to discern, if we want to understand and transform the violence of suicide in our families, communities and the world.

Thank you, sincerely, for venturing into this content with me.

Dunedin, New Zealand[1]

Katerina Standish
Deputy Director
National Centre for Peace
and Conflict Studies

Reference

World Population Review. 2019. *Suicide Rate by Country*. World Population Review. Accessed March 16, from: http://worldpopulationreview.com/countries/suicide-rate-by-country/.

[1] Country #49 out of 176 for rate of suicide according to the World Population Review (2019).

Acknowledgements

Firstly, this book would not have been possible without the trail of breadcrumbs I began to follow as a direct result of the work of two incredibly insightful and extraordinary research assistants: Russell Hunter and Katherine Scott. For your work and wonder, I am in your debt.

To my friend and colleague Dr. Heather Devere who heard about this idea years ago and has been a never-ending fount of support and incredibly intelligent reflection, thank you. To Professor Tony Ballantyne for generously enabling this work, thank you. To colleagues at the National Centre for Peace and Conflict Studies for encouragement, consideration and material support, especially Dr. Jenny Te Paa Daniel for your kind foreword and Dr. Rachel Rafferty for resources for Chapter 2, thank you.

Thanks to Dr. Christina Smylitopoulos for encouragement and daily succour and to my peeps in PACS all over the world who is in this with me!

Finally, and, enduringly, to my husband Corey who has never NOT helped me with everything that I have ever tried to do. I thank for consistently challenging my thinking and understandings, for all your skills and capabilities with all things digital and technical, for keeping the home fires burning (literally…it's Dunedin) and emptying the dishwasher that time.

PRAISE FOR *SUICIDE THROUGH A PEACEBUILDING LENS*

"Suicide through a peacebuilding lens not only fills a significant gap in our wider understanding of conflict transformation around the challenges of suicide, too often placed in narrow perspectives of individual mental health—Katerina offers us a significant step forward in how building peace requires a praxis of friendship and developing better imagination about our wider social well-being. This careful exploration, moving fluidly across disciplines and approaches, masterfully inspires us to more inclusively and adeptly develop what long has been known—that caring for each other ultimately requires both personal and social courage and vision. A book well worth the read that echo into many spheres of our peacebuilding development."

—Professor John Paul Lederach, *Professor Emeritus, University of Notre Dame, USA*

"Innovative and clear, Suicide through a Peacebuilding Lens by peace scholar, Dr. Katerina Standish, is an honest and constructive engagement with the issue of suicide as an act of violent self-harm. Standish highlights that, although suicide is a leading cause of violent death worldwide, it has been barely covered in the Peace and Conflict Studies literature. In applying a peacebuilding lens, Standish illuminates this topic with an insightful analysis, providing an encouraging and hopeful 'Encounter Theory' that has practical application. She argues convincingly that bringing together concepts of connection, interconnection, reciprocity and friendship can help prevent suicide and save lives."

—Dr. Heather Devere, *Director of Practice, National Centre for Peace and Conflict Studies, University of Otago and Executive Editor of AMITY the Journal of Friendship Studies, New Zealand*

"Suicide Through a Peacebuilding Lens is a ground-breaking study. Meticulously researched, this book throws new light on the nature & prevalence of suicide. It is a 'must' read for peace-building practitioners and a pioneering work of scholarship."

—Professor Padraig O'Malley, *The John Joseph Moakley Distinguished Professor of Peace and Reconciliation, University of Massachusetts Boston, USA*

"In her new book, *Suicide through a Peacebuilding Lens*, Katerina Standish opens wide a conversation about a subject that has been taboo across cultures and disciplines. Peace and Conflict Studies (PACS) as a new discipline prides itself in addressing the world through different lenses; however, PACS scholarly journals and books are only beginning to look at mental health as a crucial aspect of strong, inclusive communities. This book opens the doors and windows on a subject that is painful and important to all citizens of the world. With her meticulous research and strong, clear voice, Standish candidly begins a global conversation that is imperative to true peace. This book will be a "must read" for all peace scholars and it is an encouraging, eye-opening resource for practitioners and scholars across disciplines interested in community health in general and mental health in particular."

—Dr. Maureen P. Flaherty, *Associate Professor Peace & Conflict Studies, Acting Director, Centre for Ukrainian Canadian Studies, University of Manitoba, Canada*

"*Suicide through a Peacebuilding Lens* transcends the 'traditional' explorations in the field of Peace and Conflict Studies. In an original move, carefully argued and empirically grounded, Standish shows us how an exploration of suicide through a peacebuilding lens does not merely address another lacuna in the field. Rather, she offers many unique insights into how Peace and Conflict Studies may enrich—as well as be enriched by—paying attention to the stunning realization that the leading cause of violent death worldwide is suicide. Standish displays an excellent command of the complex material that she uses to develop her analysis and presents an excellent balance between theoretical analysis on the one hand, and practical implications, on the other."

—Dr. Michalinos Zembylas, *Professor of Educational Theory and Curriculum Studies, The Open University of Cyprus. Co-author of* Psychologized Language in Education: Denaturalizing a Regime of Truth, *Cyprus*

"*Suicide through a Peacebuilding Lens* is a path-breaking book that starts a necessary conversation about suicide in the field of peace and conflict studies. Dr. Katerina Standish examines perspectives on suicide across disciplines, throughout the world, and through history. She makes important interdisciplinary linkages to show where insights and skills from peacebuilding can be useful toward strengthening and scaling up established approaches to suicide prevention. This well-researched and accessibly written book brings suicide into a more mainstream discussion so that as peacebuilders and as a society, we can better understand and respond to the prevalence of suicide throughout the world."

—Dr. Jessica Senehi, *Arthur V. Mauro Centre for Peace and Justice Studies, University of Manitoba, Canada*

"This book is the first comprehensive exploration of suicidal violence from a PACS perspective. It is original, insightful and a call to action. In this accomplished scholarship, Katerina Standish has written a must-read primer for anyone seeking to understand suicide (from any field) and the unique opportunity to peacebuild suicide via relationship. This book is not solely a thoughtful exploration of suicidal violence, it is a rationale and means for recognizing and eradicating suicidal violence, one person at a time. As Standish says: *suicide is a global and pressing issue and there is not a moment to lose.*"

—Professor Sean Byrne, *Foundational Director and Director of the PACS Graduate Program at the Arthur V. Mauro Centre for Peace and Justice Studies, University of Manitoba, Canada*

"While scholars of Peace Education and Peace and Conflict Studies seek to understand how various forms of violence—direct, cultural, and structural—operate and manifest in our communities and societies at large, Katerina Standish deftly illustrates how self-harm and self-violence is an equally, if not more pressing, global phenomenon, one that has been largely ignored by theorists in these fields. *Suicide through a Peacebuilding Lens* is a must read for those truly concerned with the eradication of violence, and is a ground-breaking and welcome account of the necessary role of peacebuilding in the understanding and prevention of suicide."

—Dr. Maria Hantzopoulos, *Professor of Education, Vassar College, USA*

"Suicide through a peacebuilding lens is a convincing and empathetic inquiry into a topic that has been almost completely ignored in Peace and Conflict Studies (PACS) literature—the problem of suicide. Even though PACS scholars have busied themselves with exploring conflict, terrorism or homicide, it turns out rates of suicide are significantly higher than all forms of violent and preventable death across the globe. This surprising fact illustrates the great need for a book such as this. This book will be of great interest to students in multiple disciplines, scholars, policy-makers and a wide variety of practitioners."

—Dr. Chuck Thiessen, *Centre for Trust, Peace and Social Relations, Coventry University, UK*

"*Suicide through a Peacebuilding Lens* is a comprehensive, thorough, informative, highly readable, and thought provoking multidimensional exploration of a very personal and interpersonal issue that multiple professions have grappled to decipher. Dr. Standish highlights the complexity helping us blend a wealth of knowledge while illuminating new possibilities. By bringing a peacebuilding voice and emphasizing the centrality of relationship, our attention and our vision are shifted. The transformative potential of interconnection is emphasized under the introduction of encounter theory. The possibilities of peacebuilding relationships expand our thinking about addressing, minimizing, and preventing the violence of suicide."

—Professor Cathryne Schmitz, *Emeritus Social Work, University of North Carolina Greensboro, USA*

"Katerina Standish's book *Suicide through a Peacebuilding Lens* provides a very insightful exploration into the phenomenon of suicide from within the perspective of peacebuilding. Her book deeply informs our understanding of suicide and, given that the leading cause of violent death in the world is suicide and that the core problematic of peace and conflict studies is violence in all its forms, it uncovers a very important neglected area of study in the field: suicide. Standish's book makes a very significant contribution to both the study of suicide and peacebuilding. It should be widely read."

—Dr. Dale T. Snauwaert, *Professor of Educational Theory and the Social Foundations, The University of Toledo, Founding Editor of* In Factis Pax: Journal of Peace Education and Social Justice, *USA*

"Dr. Katerina Standish has written an exhaustive treatise on suicide that makes an important and extraordinary contribution to the field of Peace and Conflict Studies. In our sphere we are so often focused on the interpersonal and international that we forget that the greatest threat from violence is actually the intrapersonal—that which the self-experiences with itself. This volume promises to ignite an important discussion in the field and should lead to a greater exploration of how peacebuilders can help to combat this most pervasive form of direct violence."

—Dr. Heather Kertyzia, *Head of Peace and Conflict Studies Department at University for Peace, Costa Rica*

"Many of our hearts have been wrenched by the isolation and pain that accompanies proximity to suicide. I was shocked to learn from this book that globally, suicide is the number one killer of human life. Nestled in the deeply compassionate, candid, and comprehensive scholarship that characterizes Katerina Standish, this important book provides information about suicide while exploring the explanations offered by six traditional academic disciplines. True to herself, Standish responds with hope for meaningful transformation of our approaches to suicide by engaging the lens of peacebuilding to help guide our understandings, responses, and the shared experiences that surround suicide."

—Dr. Laura E. Reimer, *Research Associate, The Arthur V. Mauro Institute for Peace and Justice, University of Manitoba, Canada*

"Standish offers a multi-faceted exploration of instrumental and medical suicide, tracing how it is perceived across disciplinary lines. The peacebuilding lens adds the imperative to be attentive to those who are vulnerable to suicide, using analogical strategies to negative and positive peace to prevent it from happening. At the heart of these strategies are encounters leading to relationships. Given the correlation of suicide with personal challenges associated with mental ill-health along with the reality of trauma, including PTSD, in the wake of violent conflict, this book could enable peacebuilders to not only prevent suicide in their own 'worlds' but to devise more effective strategies for holistic healing in post violent conflict context."

—Vern Neufeld Redekop, *Professor Emeritus of Conflict Studies, Saint Paul University, Canada*

Contents

List of Figures

List of Tables

CHAPTER 1

The Suicide Gap

Serendipity: finding something good without looking for it. (N.A.)

This exploration into *suicide through a peacebuilding lens* began when I decided I would attempt to create a *hierarchy of harm* for a unit I was teaching at the medical school at the University of Otago in Dunedin, New Zealand.[1] I knew the 3rd year med students were quite keen for stats and hard data (as opposed to narrative forms of research) and so I thought I would look at the world statistics on forms of violence and death and then present it to the students assigned to my class. I was, at the time, teaching a course called *Social, Cultural and Political Violence* to students who had six weeks, in four years, to consider the social sciences and/or humanities and I wanted to support them to recognize violence from an expansive platform—not just a *punch* at the bar but a process and outcome of dehumanization which takes myriad form. I am a scholar/practitioner of Peace and Conflict Studies (PACS) and I was teaching into the University of Otago's Medical Humanities programme when I decided to look a little closer at violence from a demographic viewpoint.

What I found was a nugget of information that stunned me: the leading cause of violent death worldwide was suicide.[2] Not murder, or 'terrorism', not ethnic conflict, or child neglect, not domestic violence or forced deprivation but self-harming to the point of death. I knew the med students needed to consider rates of violence not merely

K. Standish, *Suicide through a Peacebuilding Lens*,
https://doi.org/10.1007/978-981-13-9737-0_1

incarnations of the same so I found a site that let you look at violence worldwide from either cause or context to entertain notions of 'risk' and 'tendency' from a population perspective. From this research, it became clear to me that the greatest threat to humans isn't homicidal gun violence or home-grown radical 'terrorists' or even environmental hazards—it is the self.[3] Statistically speaking, the greatest threat to you—is *you*.

Originally set up to chart the United Nations' Sustainable Development Goals (SDGs), the University of Oxford compiles a meta-database of health indicators (https://ourworldindata.org/about) to show global trends. The site is open source and the below 'world' graphic was the first analysis I looked at.[4] You will notice that among the top ten causes of death, there are two forms of non-medical death: road accidents and suicide. In this graphic, the first one I drew up on the website, there were roughly double the amount of road accidents to suicide. Considering I was intending to show my students a *hierarchy of harm*, not illness, I was looking for forms of intentional violence, not accidental death or death from disease (Fig. 1.1).

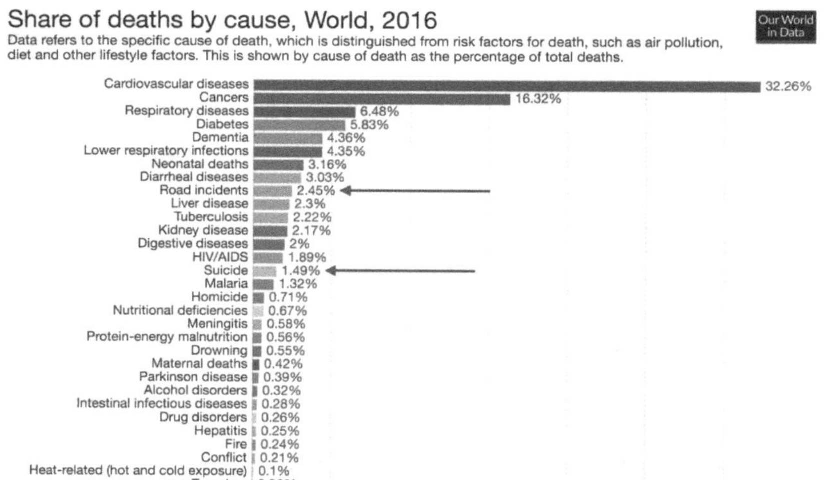

Fig. 1.1 What the world dies from 2016 (*Source* https://ourworldindata.org/what-does-the-world-die-from)

But when I did a country-by-country analysis, it became clear that it was suicides, not road accidents, that were the number one cause of violent death in many, many nations. As I was working at the University of Otago in New Zealand (a country with a suicide epidemic),[5] New Zealand was my first *country* pull (Fig. 1.2).

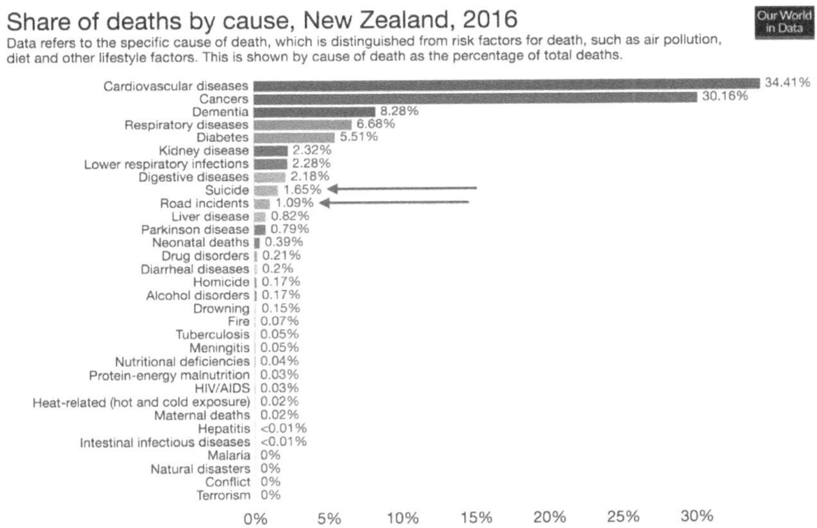

Fig. 1.2 What New Zealand dies from 2016 (*Source* https://ourworldindata.org/what-does-the-world-die-from)

And I am Canadian, so my next pull was the country of my birth (Fig. 1.3).

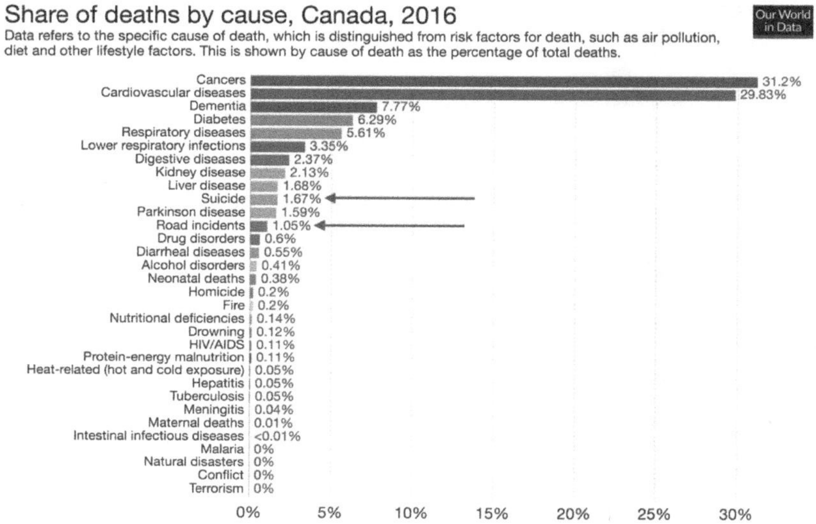

Fig. 1.3 What Canada dies from 2016 (*Source* https://ourworldindata.org/what-does-the-world-die-from)

The net went wider as I began to see this trend in the next chart (Fig. 1.4).

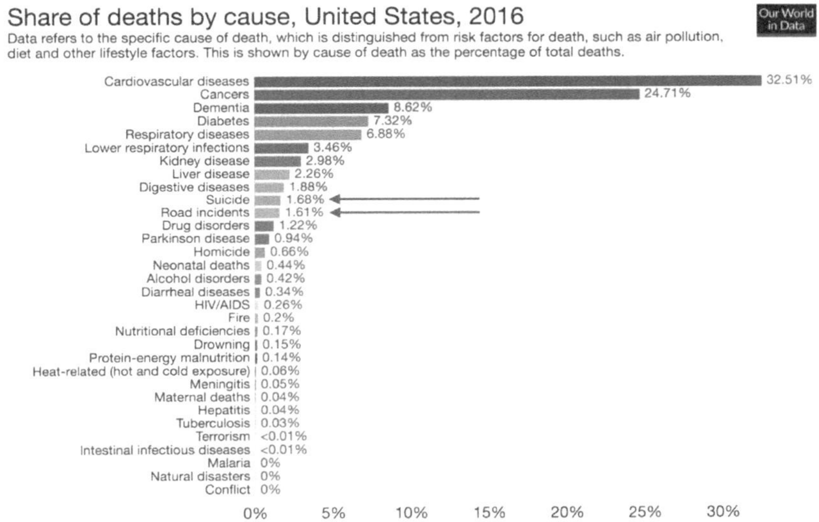

Fig. 1.4 What the USA dies from 2016 (*Source* https://ourworldindata.org/what-does-the-world-die-from)

And it was not just in North America. It was in Russia too (Fig. 1.5).

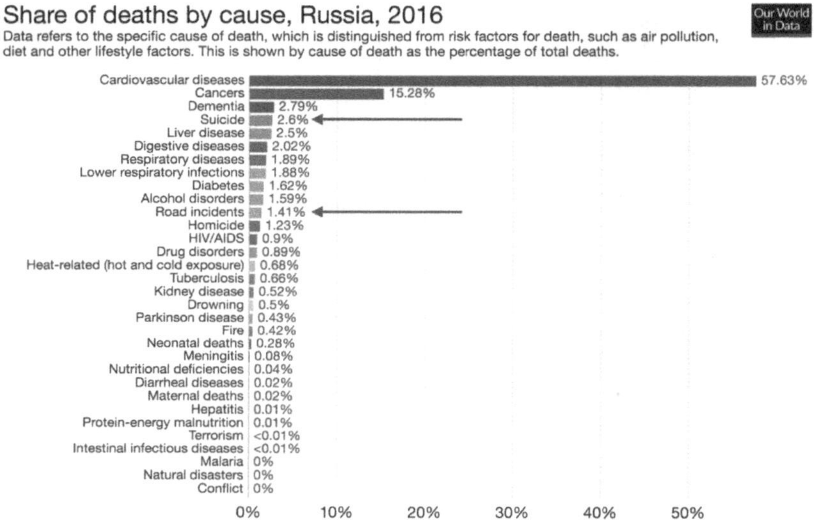

Fig. 1.5 What Russia dies from 2016 (*Source* https://ourworldindata.org/what-does-the-world-die-from)

And South Korea (Fig. 1.6),

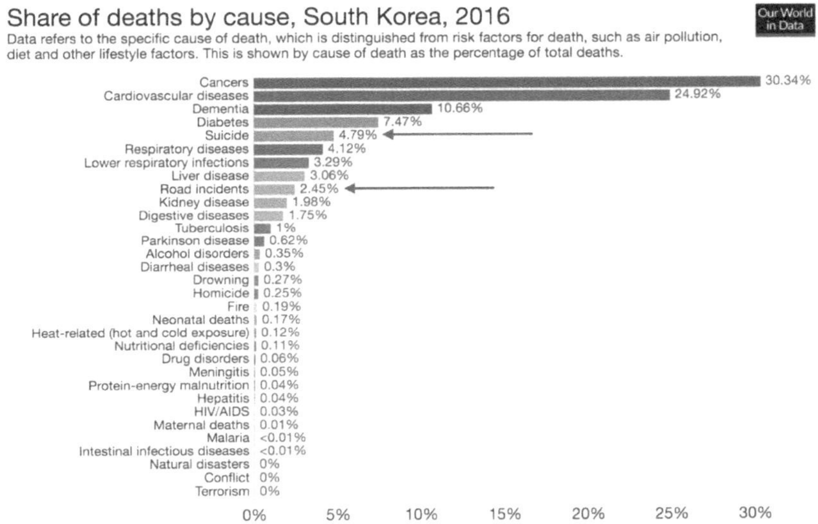

Fig. 1.6 What South Korea dies from 2016 (*Source* https://ourworldindata.org/what-does-the-world-die-from)

In Australia (Fig. 1.7),

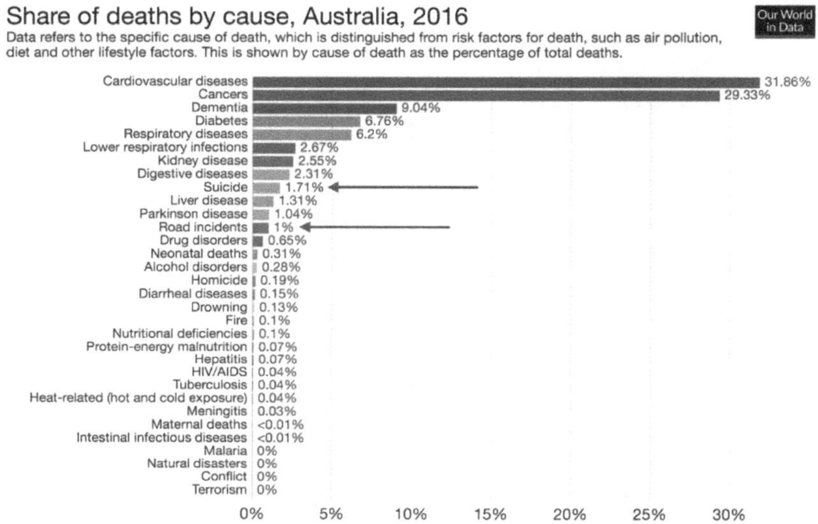

Fig. 1.7 What Australia dies from 2016 (*Source* https://ourworldindata.org/what-does-the-world-die-from)

And in European nations (Figs. 1.8, 1.9, 1.10, 1.11, 1.12, 1.13, and 1.14),

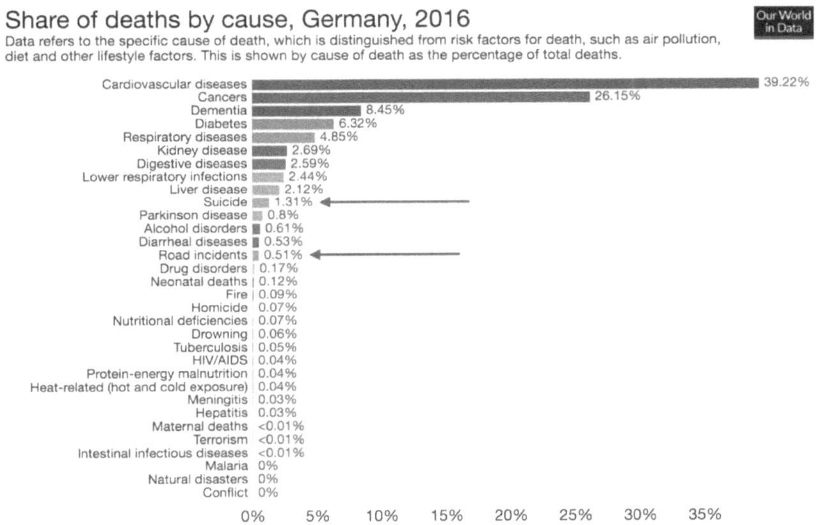

Fig. 1.8 What Germany dies from 2016 (*Source* https://ourworldindata.org/what-does-the-world-die-from)

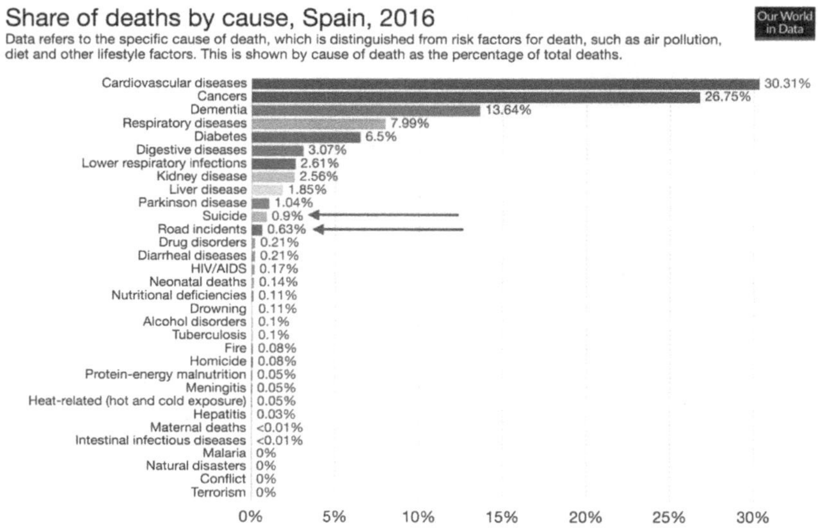

Fig. 1.9 What Spain dies from 2016 (*Source* https://ourworldindata.org/what-does-the-world-die-from)

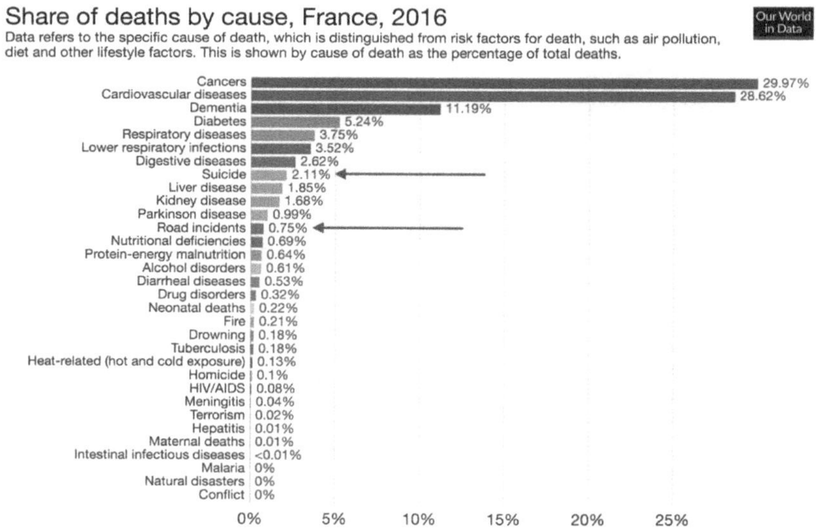

Fig. 1.10 What France dies from 2016 (*Source* https://ourworldindata.org/what-does-the-world-die-from)

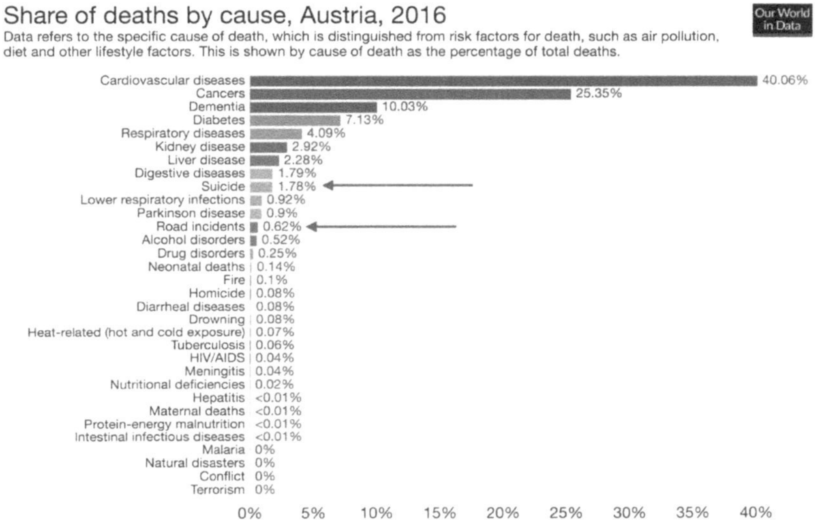

Fig. 1.11 What Austria dies from 2016 (*Source* https://ourworldindata.org/what-does-the-world-die-from)

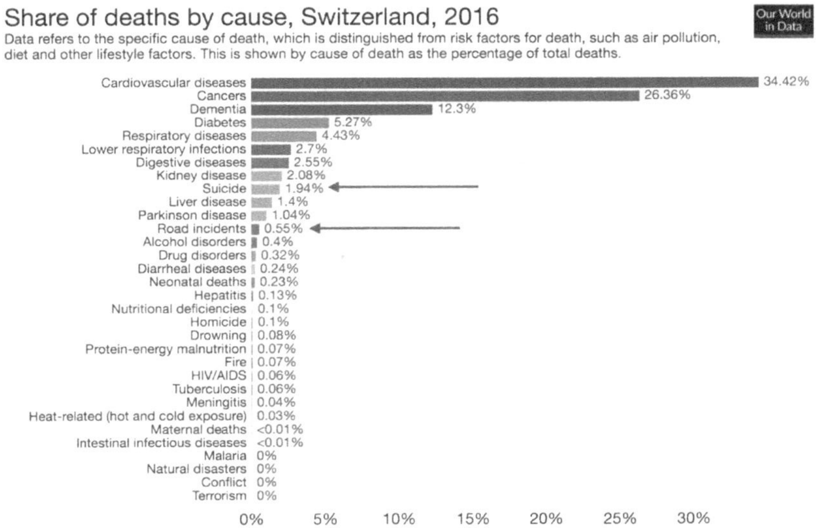

Fig. 1.12 What Switzerland dies from 2016 (*Source* https://ourworldindata.org/what-does-the-world-die-from)

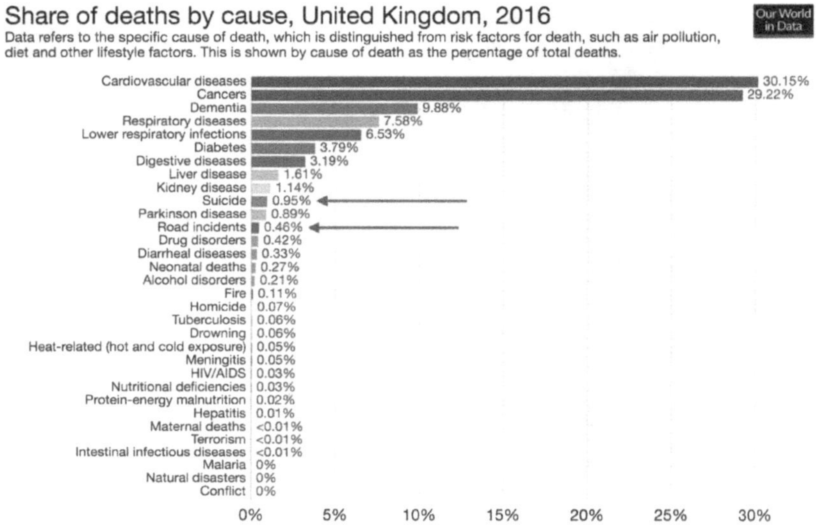

Fig. 1.13 What the UK dies from 2016 (*Source* https://ourworldindata.org/what-does-the-world-die-from)

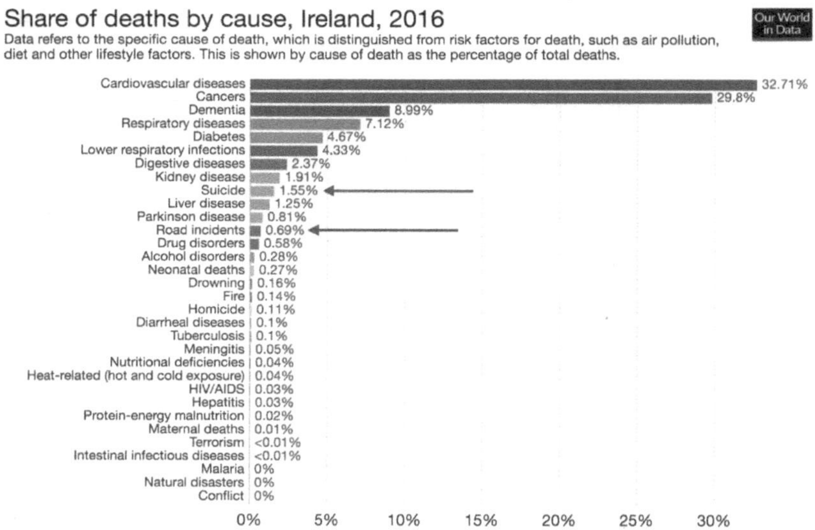

Fig. 1.14 What Ireland dies from 2016 (*Source* https://ourworldindata.org/what-does-the-world-die-from)

And I am a PACS scholar so I decided to look at some *so-called* post-conflict nations such as Sri Lanka, Serbia and Bosnia-Herzegovina (Figs. 1.15, 1.16, and 1.17).

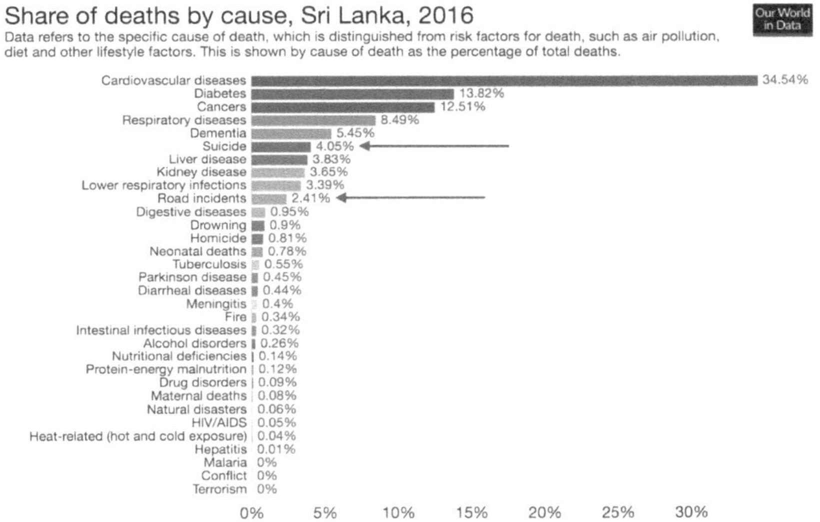

Fig. 1.15 What Sri Lanka dies from 2016 (*Source* https://ourworldindata.org/what-does-the-world-die-from)

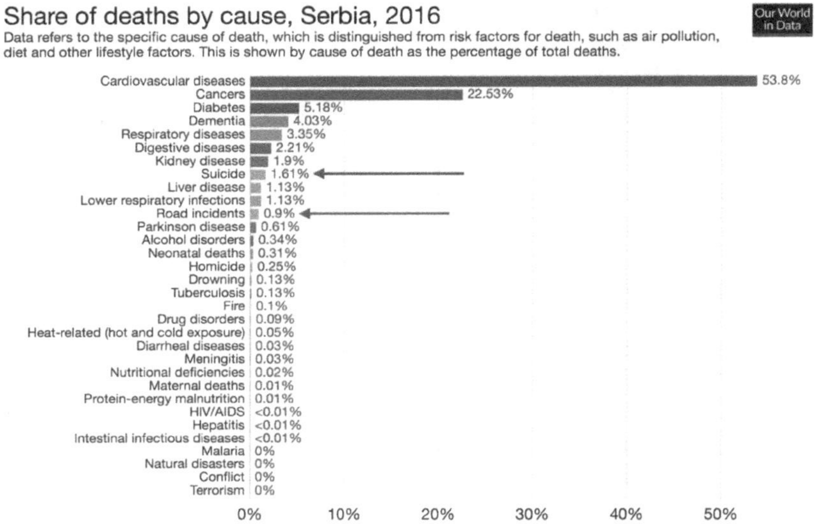

Fig. 1.16 What Serbia dies from 2016 (*Source* https://ourworldindata.org/what-does-the-world-die-from)

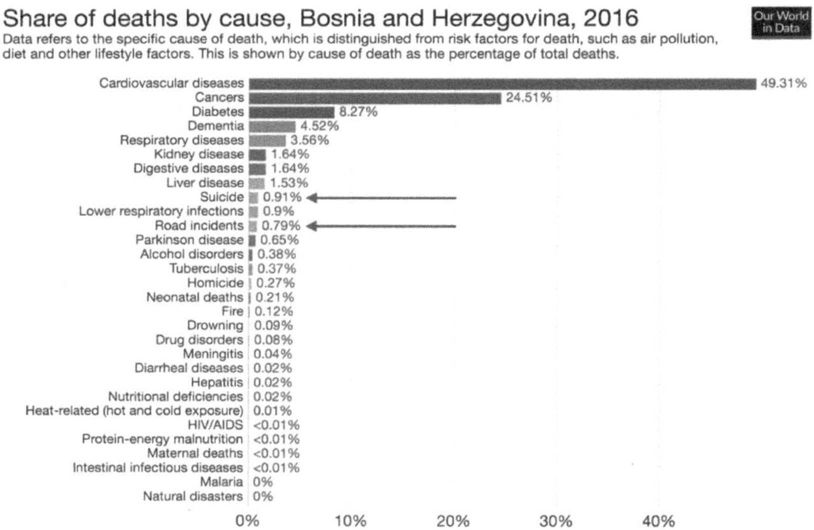

Fig. 1.17 What Bosnia and Herzegovina dies from 2016 (*Source* https://ourworldindata.org/what-does-the-world-die-from)

And even in huge nations such as India and China, where road accidents were listed higher than suicide, the rates of *Suicide* compared to *Homicide*, *Conflict* and *Terrorism* were staggering (Figs. 1.18 and 1.19).

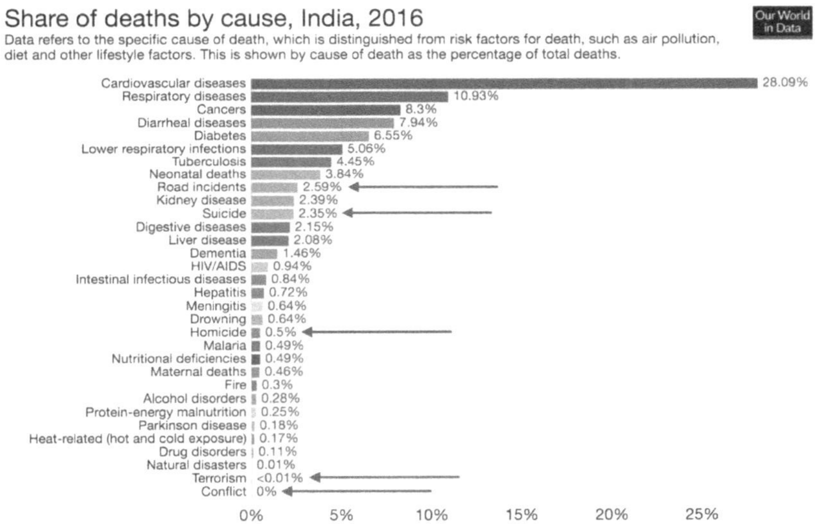

Fig. 1.18 What India dies from 2016 (*Source* https://ourworldindata.org/what-does-the-world-die-from)

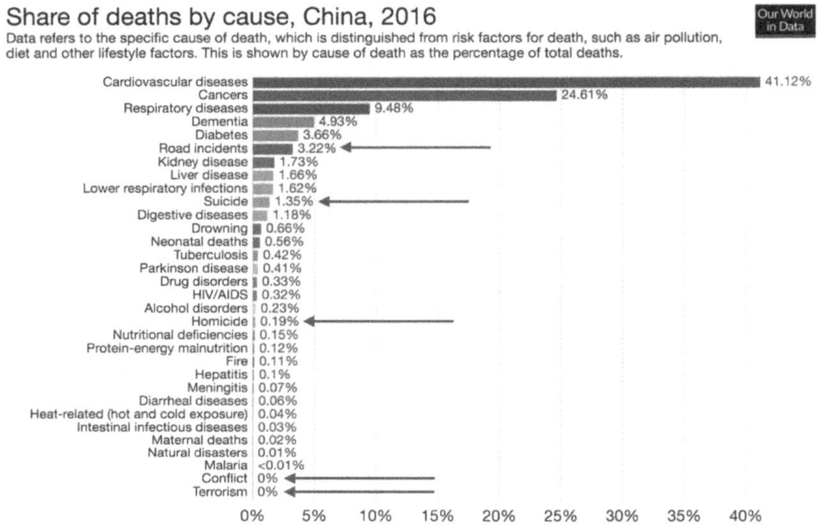

Fig. 1.19 What China dies from 2016 (*Source* https://ourworldindata.org/what-does-the-world-die-from)

And in nations with religious inhibitions that dampen suicide stats and where underreporting of suicide is routine, suicide was still the leading cause of non-accidental violent death (Figs. 1.20, 1.21, 1.22, and 1.23).

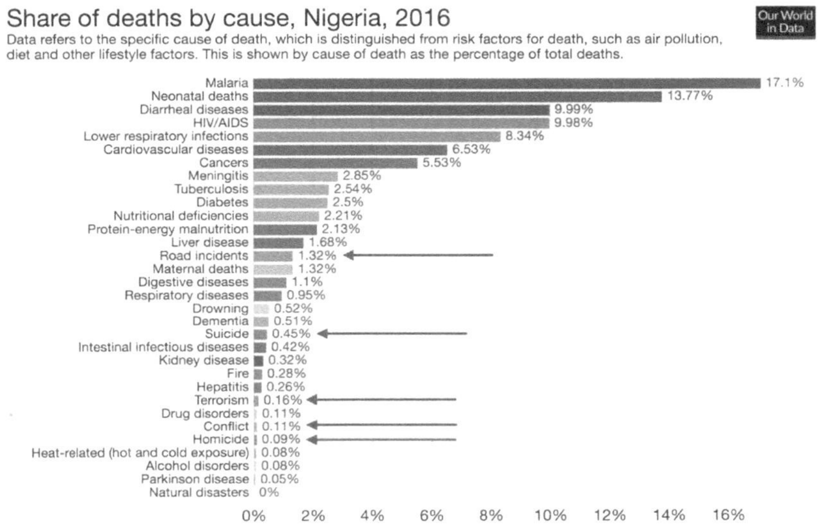

Fig. 1.20 What Nigeria dies from 2016 (*Source* https://ourworldindata.org/what-does-the-world-die-from)

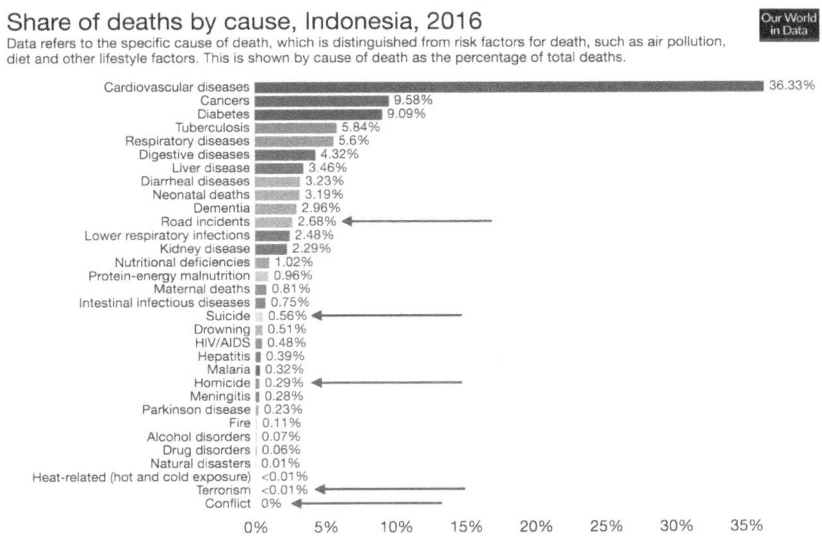

Fig. 1.21 What Indonesia dies from 2016 (*Source* https://ourworldindata.org/what-does-the-world-die-from)

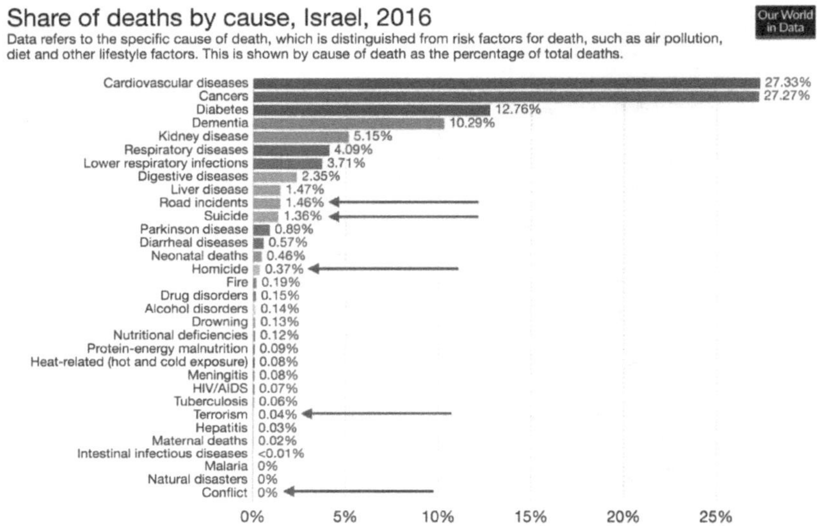

Fig. 1.22 What Israel dies from 2016 (*Source* https://ourworldindata.org/what-does-the-world-die-from)

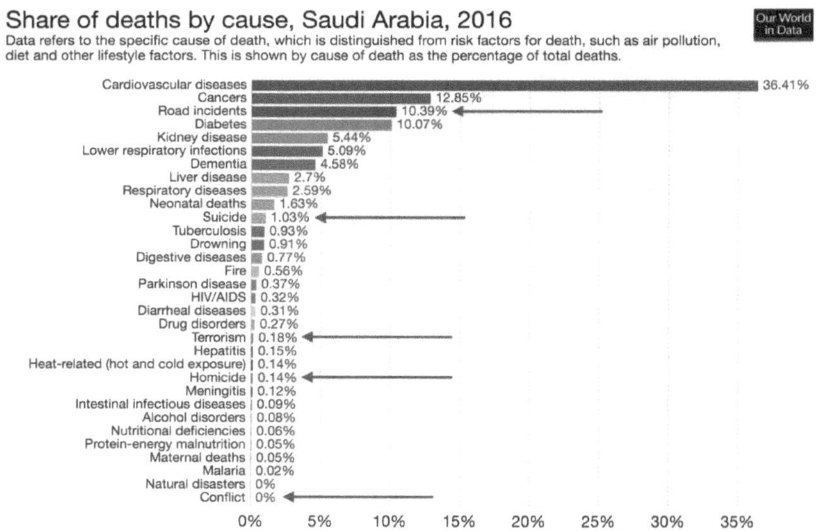

Fig. 1.23 What the Kingdom of Saudi Arabia dies from 2016 (*Source* https://ourworldindata.org/what-does-the-world-die-from)

There were dozens of countries with higher levels of road accidents to be sure, but all of the charts I pulled had higher suicide rates than other listed violent forms of *preventable* and *deliberate death:* conflict, 'terrorism' or homicide. Every single chart I pulled, in the developed or developing world, had *higher rates of suicide* than other forms of violent death—every, single, one.

Grasping this new knowledge, I began to question what this information might mean to my field, and to my understanding of violence as a PACS scholar. PACS has many different avenues of inquiry and agency, at a PACS disciplinary dinner you are just as likely to find a development professional, an intercultural dialogue specialist, a Gandhian scholar, a human rights lawyer or a third-party intervention expert at your table. And when you get up to mingle after the keynote, you will likely meet a few peace educators (like me), conflict analysts and pragmatic nonviolence practitioners on your way to the bathroom. It was entirely possible that I was simply out of the loop—stuck in my critical peace pedagogy bubble. So I decided to look closer, to take a broader view of the PACS discipline. Just because suicide had not surfaced as salient in my sub-discipline that did not mean that others were not fervently attending this prevalent form of violence in their research and activism.

So I looked. In 2017, I conducted empirical research that revealed *how* and *how often* suicide is considered in my field by surveying the prevalence of 'suicide' as a topic in the top six PACS journals. From January 2002 until March 2017, I looked for content associated with suicide in *Journal of Peace Research*, *Journal of Conflict Resolution*, *Peace Review*, *Journal of Peace and Conflict Studies*, *Peace and Conflict: Journal of Peace Psychology* and *Peace and Change.* The journals were searched using the term 'suicide' and analysis found that only 16 of the 3261 articles (0.49%) contained information related to the phenomena of suicide; after closer inspection, I found only four of the six journals had positive results from the search including 8 entries in the *Journal of Conflict Resolution*, five entries in the *Journal of Peace Research*, two entries in *Peace Review* and only one article in *Journal of Peace and Conflict Studies* (Table 1.1).

Table 1.1 Number of articles found in PACS journals in 2017

Journal name	*Total articles*	*Articles related to suicide*
Journal of Conflict Resolution	676	8
Journal of Peace Research	709	5
Peace Review	948	2
Journal of Peace and Conflict Studies	155	1
Peace and Change	300	0
Peace and Conflict: Journal of Peace Psychology	473	0
Totals	3261	16

Of the 16 articles found, two were book reviews and 14 were research articles that utilized the topic of suicide (Table 1.2).

And of the 14 articles that did incorporate suicide in their work, 13 were found to relate to what I will typologize as *instrumental*[6] suicide and only 1 out of a total of 3261 articles, in fifteen years, related to *medical* suicide—the leading cause of violent death worldwide.[7]

This led me to a crisis of theoretical (missed)understanding in my work, an obvious gap in the literature that was so huge you could drive the United Nations through it. A tiny question then filled my mind but quickly began to influence all of my disciplinary understandings was PACS—a field focused on understanding conflict[8] and violence and transforming conflict nonviolently—skipping over *the* universal variety of violent death worldwide to concentrate on forms of violence that were particular, minimal and overwhelmingly characterized as *deviant*, *extraneous* or *symbolic* (including sectarian conflict and 'terrorism')? As so-called experts in *peacebuilding*—recognizing and ameliorating conflict—were we neglecting a chance to add our social scientific standpoint to this global phenomenon? As a field, were we focusing on international conflict, ethnic conflict, religious conflict and war (civil, conventional or asymmetrical) when the leading cause of death was something no individual in the world was safe from? Were we focusing on minor, even inconsequential violence but missing a violence that is all around us? *Were we missing a whole forest for a few trees?*

I began to educate myself about suicide, I began to look at the theories and circumstances of life-ending acts, to listen to those who had thought about suicide (ideation), attempted suicide and those left behind. I began

Table 1.2 List of journal articles by publication from 2017

Journal name	*Articles related to suicide*	*Citations*
Journal of Conflict Resolution	8	Benmelech, Efraim, Claude Berrebi, and Esteban F. Klor. 2010. "The Economic Costs of Harboring Terrorism." *The Journal of Conflict Resolution* 54 (2): 331–353 Ferrero, Mario. 2006. "Martyrdom Contracts." *The Journal of Conflict Resolution* 50 (6): 855–877 Wade, Sara J., and Dan Reiter. 2007. "Does Democracy Matter? Regime Type and Suicide Terrorism." *The Journal of Conflict Resolution* 51 (2): 329–348 Choi, Seung-Whan, and James A. Piazza. 2017. "Foreign Military Interventions and Suicide Attacks." *The Journal of Conflict Resolution* 61 (2): 271–297 Najeeb, Shafiq M., and Abdulkader H. Sinno. 2010. "Education, Income, and Support for Suicide Bombings: Evidence from Six Muslim Countries." *The Journal of Conflict Resolution* 54 (1): 146–178 Collard-Wexler, Simon, Constantino Pischedda, and Michael G. Smith. 2014. "Do Foreign Occupations Cause Suicide Attacks?" *The Journal of Conflict Resolution* 58 (4): 625–657 Braun, Robert, and Michael Genkin. 2014. "Cultural Resonance and the Diffusion of Suicide Bombings: The Role of Collectivism." *The Journal of Conflict Resolution* 58 (7): 1258–1284 Jacobson, Daniel, and Edward H. Kaplan. 2007. "Suicide Bombings and Targeted Killings in (Counter-) Terror Games." *The Journal of Conflict Resolution* 51 (5): 772–792

continued

Table 1.2 continued

Journal name	*Articles related to suicide*	*Citations*
Journal of Peace Research	5	Acosta, Benjamin. 2016. "Dying for Survival: Why Militant Organizations Continue to Conduct Suicide Attacks." *Journal of Peace Research* 53 (2): 180–196 Wolfsfeld, Gadi, Paul Frosh, and Maurice T. Awabdy. 2008. "Covering Death in Conflicts: Coverage of the Second Intifada on Israeli and Palestinian Television." *Journal of Peace Research* 45 (3): 401–417 Hoffman, Aaron M. 2010. "Voice and Silence: Why Groups Take Credit for Acts of Terror." *Journal of Peace Research* 47 (5): 615–626 Book Review Bloom, Mia M. 2006. "Book Note: Making Sense of Suicide Missions." *Journal of Peace Research* 43 (4): 494 Book Review Biggs, Michael. 2006. "Dying to Kill: The Allure of Suicide Terror." *Journal of Peace Research* 43 (2): 228
Peace Review	2	Nahid, Aziz. 2011. "What Self-Immolation Means to Afghan Women." *Peace Review* 23 (1): 45–51 Niva, Steve. 2003. "Bombings, Provocations and the Cycle of Violence." *Peace Review* 15 (1): 33–38
Journal of Peace and Conflict Studies	1	Huffman, Tim. 2016. "You Have Atomic Bombs, We Have the Martyrdom-Seekers: Ayman Al-Zawahiri's Narrative Arc of the Martyr." *Peace and Conflict Studies* 23 (1): Article 3

to formulate a platform of understanding based on much of what I had read and heard from people who had actually 'lost' someone and those whose life work it was to combat suicide in community, profession and scholarship. This book is the result of this work and my attempt to share with you what I have found. I learned that the number one cause of suicide is mental illness (by a landslide) and that in combatting suicide related to mental illness there are three approaches: (1) awareness raising, gatekeeper training and means restriction, (2) medication and cognitive counselling (altering the way the brain worked and/or how thinking could be changed to change thinking patterns and affirm life) and a third one that rang like an enormous 'gong' in my mind, (3) *relationship building*.

It seemed to me that whereas the first category of remedy involved societal response: awareness raising (to make suicide more visible), professional development of medical and social work personnel (to spot potential suicides who come into the system) and consumer protection (to take dangerous substances and methods away as well as opportunities), and the second category of remedy (medication and counselling) included psycho-medical approaches from medical and therapeutic professionals, the third approach was not only something many of us can and should do (connect with others) but something those in my field were actually trained for. PACS has spent the last 70 years building a discipline that studies and transforms conflict via relationship (Lederach 2005), what if some of us turned our gaze away from considering Track I and II deliberations between warring groups to consider a far larger incarnation of violence? And, more, what if the work of this was *a bridge* between other fields as well, between people who work on *relationship* in other disciplines too? (Fig. 1.24).

The word relationship comes from the LATIN *relationem* 'a bringing back and restoring…a sense or state of being related'. After we separate out purely academic scholars who measure, count and register aspects or facets of conflict or peace (read: bombs, guns, votes or dead bodies),[9] much of my field is filled with so-called *pracademics*, scholar-practitioners who pair their peacebuilding with reflection and theory. For peacebuilding pracademics to contribute to a more connected world, to repair broken relationships, foster new ones, build trust using kindness and positive reciprocity and be of service to others who are unable to build such relationships for themselves (for reasons related to history, personality, culture and circumstances), we have to look closely at obstacles and barriers, but crucially, opportunities for understanding, too.

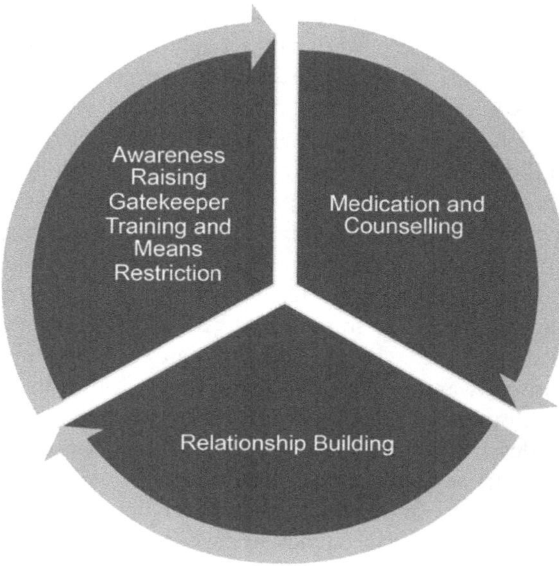

Fig. 1.24 Three approaches to suicide

This book seeks to offer a potential corrective to this unmistakable lacuna in the field through an exploration of suicide through a peacebuilding lens.[10] It does not intend to cover everything important to know about life-ending acts (self-death, auto-homicide, *autothanasia*, self-killing, self-annihilation, killing yourself, self-murder, *felo de se,* etc.) but it does intend to emphasize a critical perception: a leading cause of violent death worldwide (whether extremist, radical or mundane) is *almost completely ignored* in the peacebuilding field: *suicide*.

There are many forms of violence in the world, and the PACS field habitually conceptualizes them through the aperture of *direct*, *indirect* (structural) and *cultural* violence (Galtung 1990). This allows for violence related to *worldviews* such as sexism and racism to be considered as well as *institutional* forms of violence that mobilize discrimination against individuals or groups. More *tangible* forms of violence such as physical harm and threats are contemplated via the construct of 'direct' violence but in all of these formulations and characterizations one form of violence is frequently absent: *suicide*, the most frequent form of violence in human society. The PACS field is concerned with understanding, preventing, intervening and transforming conflict, and a key feature of our field is the foundational methodology of *peacebuilding*[11] an action that transforms violence. Just as a medical professional becomes an expert in disease in order to facilitate health, we in PACS develop proficiency in 'violence' to foster *nonviolences*,[12] methods of engaging with conflict that are life-affirming, non-harming and productive. As scholar/practitioners, we are uniquely placed to perceive and interact with violence nonviolently (via peacebuilding), and we are a normative field that declares wholeheartedly that violence is an unnecessary response to conflict.[13]

This book illustrates that the leading cause of violent death in many human communities[14] is a multifaceted phenomenon that needs to be fully comprehended and appreciated as a significant and *frequently preventable* form of violence. This manuscript will supply a theoretical framework for assessing suicide as *medical* or *instrumental* and suggests future lines of inquiry that challenge the categorization of suicide as *only* pathology or *always* tragedy. It asks how intention, motivation and intervention affect our considerations if we investigate suicide as a component of social, cultural and political violence. The book proposes a counter-argument against the suicide-as-catastrophe assumption and then offers a potential address of suicide via peacebuilding.

This introductory chapter is an empirical exploration of suicide in the top six PACS journals. This chapter will also include disciplinary encounters with suicide to include considerations from psychology, medicine, sociology, anthropology, social work, criminal justice, anthropology, political studies and philosophy. This introductory chapter will present an evidentiary platform for the argument that PACS has incorporated the subject of suicide in the literature only to a minor extent over the past 16 years, show what trends are exhibited and define typical encounters with suicide in nine common fields. The chapter concludes with a book summary of the remaining 8 chapters and their theoretical contributions.

Inconsiderable Suicide

This section presents the research findings of the analysis of six PACS journals from January 2002 to December 2018. Content associated with suicide in *Journal of Peace Research*, *Journal of Conflict Resolution*, *Peace Review*, *Journal of Peace and Conflict Studies*, *Peace and Conflict: Journal of Peace Psychology* and *Peace and Change*. The journals were searched using the term 'suicide' and analysis found that only 17 of the

Table 1.3 PACS journal analysis 2002–2018

Journal name	*Total articles*	*Articles related to suicide*
Journal of Conflict Resolution (JCR)	807	8
Journal of Peace Research (JPR)	780	5
Peace Review (PR)	993	2
Journal of Peace and Conflict Studies (PACS)	178	1
Peace and Change (P&C)	328	1
Peace and Conflict: Journal of Peace (JPP) Psychology	538	0
Totals	3624	17

364 articles (0.46%) contained information related to the phenomena of suicide; on further review, I found only five of the six journals had positive results from the search including eight entries in the *Journal of Conflict Resolution*, five entries in the *Journal of Peace Research*, two entries in *Peace Review* and a single article each in *Journal of Peace and Conflict Studies* and *Peace and Change*.

This journal analysis (updated from the original 2017 research presented previously in this chapter) surveyed entries from January 2002 to December 2018 and located a total of 3624 articles, over 16 years, that referred to suicide (see Table 1.3).

The 2018 content analysis located a total of 17 'hits' related to suicide and included 15 full-length research articles and two book reviews.

As can be seen in Fig. 1.25, the majority of articles that included the topic suicide were in the *Journal of Conflict Resolution*, with five in the *Journal of Peace Research*, two in the *Peace Review* and one in the *Journal of Peace and Conflict Studies* and *Peace and Change*, respectively. The journal *Peace and Conflict: Journal of Peace Psychology* (ironically, I thought considering the medicalization of suicide) has none.

When the content was further analysed, the 17 articles located were divided by type into either *medical* or *instrumental* suicide (Fig. 1.26).

All eight articles located in the *Journal of Conflict Resolution* concerned what I term *instrumental* suicide (see Chapter 5) as did all five of those found in the *Journal of Peace Research*. Articles from the *Journal of Peace and Conflict Studies* and *Peace and Change* also related to *instrumental* suicide, whereas the single article in the *Peace Review* encountered both *medical* and *instrumental* suicide.[15]

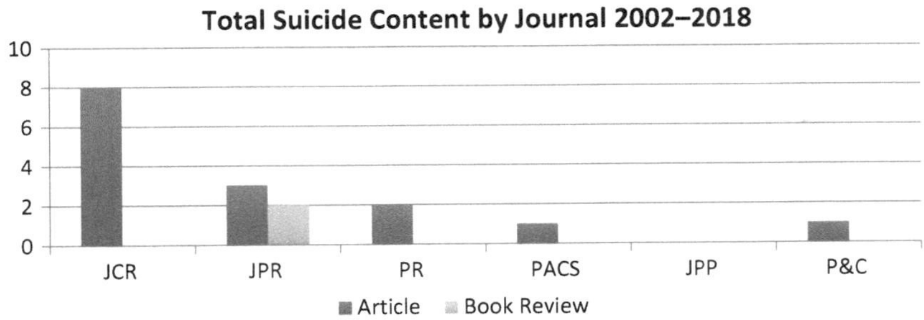

Fig. 1.25 Suicide content by journal (This 2018 table added to the original data from 2017 which identified 16 items [see Fig. 1.2] to show 17 items [15 research articles and two book reviews] and includes the following article from *Peace and Change*: Coburn, Jon. 2018. "'I Have Chosen the Flaming Death': The Forgotten Self-Immolation of Alice Herz." *Peace and Change* 43 (1): 32–60.)

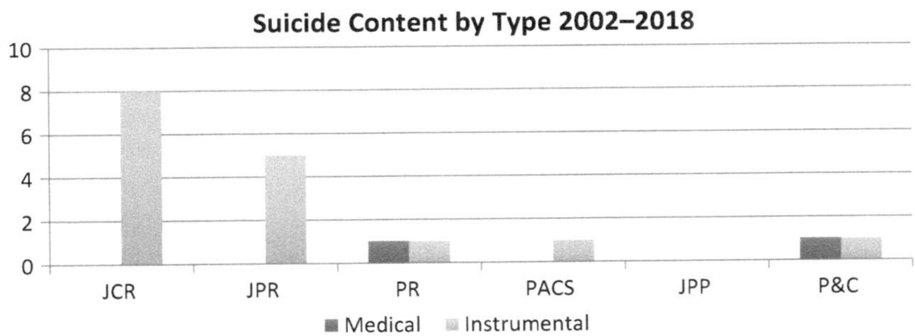

Fig. 1.26 Suicide content by type

From this view of the discipline (from the last 16 years), 'suicide' is an inconsiderable topic and one that speaks to a lacuna or at least blind spot in our field. We will learn later on in this book (in Chapter 4) that the majority of suicides are found in the category of *medical* suicide. We see from this content analysis of the top six journals in PACS that when suicide is considered, at all, it is not the dominant form. If the number one form of violent death in most places is self-death, then why isn't my discipline turning its transformative gaze to suicide? I think we should, and this book seeks to offer both a rationale and methodology for peace-building suicide that might assist.

The Suicide Kaleidoscope

There are many ways of looking at the phenomena of suicide. The term, even the sentiment, of 'suicide' is not in dispute (it refers to an act of self-killing) and the *definition* of suicide is widely agreed on within the academic community, yet despite this singularity of understanding of the term, perceptions of suicide vary greatly between different disciplines of study. There is no alternative translation of 'suicide'; it does not mean a 'small fruit' in one field and a 'viscous liquid thrown on the wall' in another. It means a personal act that leads to death (of *self* for certain, but also, in certain circumstances, *others* too). This diversity or kaleidoscope of perception means that there is a wide way of looking at, communicating about and engaging with the phenomena of deliberate individual life-ending acts.[16]

Varying perceptions of suicide occur due to the differing contexts from which disciplines approach suicide. These differences in perception can lead to diverging views on the causes of suicide and on means of prevention. This is not to say that all disciplines have contradictory views; similarities in perception of suicide also occur, particularly as some disciplines have adopted multidisciplinary views in recent decades. Throughout this section, perceptions of suicide will be explored in relation to the fields of medicine, psychology, sociology, anthropology, social work, criminal justice, political studies and philosophy. This exploration will underline the varying perceptions of suicide and the key focuses of suicide research in each field, contextualizing these within the disciplines. As the causes of suicide in relation to different disciplines are discussed in greater detail elsewhere in this publication (see Chapter 7), these will be mentioned but will not be greatly expanded on within this section.

Psychology

The first discipline to be explored within this chapter is psychology. The field of psychology seeks to understand mental processes and behaviour. Henriques (2004) outlines that psychology is a discipline that is both a science and a practice, which adds a practical approach to much study within this field. This means that the study of suicide has been both theoretical and practical, with much research being focused on causes and means of prevention of suicide. The literature makes it evident that perceptions of suicide within psychology have greatly changed over the decades, with psychological practice changing in turn. Wray et al. (2011) highlighted that psychology originally concentrated on the psychodynamics of suicide, which perceived suicide to be the result of the internal conflict of individuals surrounding their emotional and primal drives and their struggles with the meaning of life. These perceptions were set aside in the 1980s due to lack of empirical accuracy (Wray et al. 2011). The next phase of perception of suicide for psychology was the medical model of considering suicide (Sommers-Flanagan and Shaw 2017). This medical model perceived suicide as a deviant act and emphasized the importance of medically driven evaluation, diagnosis and intervention. Such intervention typically took place in the form of psychotherapy, hospitalization or medication, with the aim of eradicating suicide ideation (Sommers-Flanagan and Shaw 2017). Dazzi et al. (2014) highlight that individuals who have considered or attempted suicide have decreases in suicidality when this suicidality was frequently discussed with them, whether the other discussant was a counsellor or a researcher. Psychological practice still follows this medical model, though the importance of psychodynamic social factors has also been recognized (Van Orden et al. 2010).

A more recent perception of suicide within psychology has been through the lens of interpersonal theories of suicide. Interpersonal theories of suicide are based on the foundation that individuals die by suicide because they can and because they want to (Joiner 2005; Van Orden et al. 2010). Three factors are key to individuals completing suicide according to an interpersonal theory of suicide; two of which relate to suicidal desire—thwarted belongingness and perceived burdensomeness—and one which relates to capability—the acquired capability for suicide (Van Orden et al. 2010). Basic interpersonal research highlights that an unmet need to belong has a highly negative effect on psychological well-being, while feelings of being a burden on family members have been a strong predictor of suicide in adults and youth (Van Orden et al. 2008). The need for the acquired capability to complete suicide is explained as suicidal desire alone is insufficient to cause suicide—this is why not everyone with suicide ideation dies by suicide (Van Orden et al. 2008). This demonstrates a perception that there are not only social factors but a loss of fear of suicide involved in suicidal behaviour. Loss of fear of suicide is a concept discussed relatively little within other psychological literature. Van Orden et al. (2010) explain the need for interpersonal theories as current biological, psychosocial and cognitive-behavioural theories can each only explain aspects of suicidal behaviour and cannot predict suicide.

Psychology's approach to studying suicide notably leads to the development of the psychological autopsy, which has become invaluable to researchers not only within psychology but also in other disciplines (Wray et al. 2011). The psychological autopsy is a retrospective case study method that includes investigation of medical and police records as well as in-depth interviews with the friends and families of those who have completed suicide, ultimately aiming to construct a wider perspective of such individuals than a forensic autopsy could provide (Pridmore 2015). Although there is criticism of psychological autopsies as a method, with Pridmore (2015) noting many theoretical, methodological and analytical flaws, this method has continued to be employed throughout many disciplines.

Medicine

The next discipline to be discussed within this chapter is medicine. Medicine as a field of study surrounds the prevention, diagnosis and treatment of disease, and, similarly to psychology, is both a science and a practice. Suicide has garnered increasing attention from medical professionals and public health researchers, with several instrumental reports surrounding the reduction in suicide being released in the late 1990s and early 2000s (Wray et al. 2011). Psychiatry, a subfield of medicine specializing in the prevention, diagnosis and treatment of mental disorders, tends to lead medical research into suicide. The medical field has traditionally held the perception that suicide is the result of mental illness (Pridmore and Pridmore 2016). Due to the esteem that medical science generally holds within communities, this has led to the majority of funds allocated for suicide prevention being directed to medical undertakings (Pridmore 2015). Other biomedical factors have also been shown to play a causal role in suicide, with genetic factors increasing the likelihood of both mental illness and suicidal behaviour (Goldney 2015; Bondy et al. 2006).

While the perception of mental illness leading to suicide continues to be held by the majority of the medical field, the adoption of multidisciplinary approaches has led to the inclusion and acknowledgement of other factors being related to suicide. For example, Rajalin et al. (2017)

utilized psychology alongside psychiatry in research and concluded that suicide can occur due to factors other than mental health, such as in individuals that are undergoing serious interpersonal problems. Colpe and Pringle (2014) also highlight that suicide is the result of complex interplay between many factors, which may include poor mental health, substance abuse and/or negative life experiences. Pierre (2015) also distinguishes that there are forms of suicide that are not related to mental illness but rather to circumstances of cultural frameworks that sanction suicide, such as martyrdom. The medical field's approach to suicide and suicide prevention is ultimately driven by the underlying perception that suicide is related to mental illness, though a biopsychosocial model has been utilized in recent years. This model emphasizes the multidisciplinary approach as it can include assessment of medical conditions as well as social issues that may be affecting patients (Farre and Rapley 2017). There are two main approaches within the medical field that have been developed in order to prevent suicides, the first of which is the treatment of mental illness with medication and/or counselling. The second approach is gatekeeper training for those likely to come across suicidal individuals to educate individuals to recognize signs of mental illness and psychological distress, such as general practitioners, nurses, teachers and caregivers (Mann et al. 2005). This approach is partially in response to studies that highlight there is a high chance that individuals that complete suicide will have contact with their primary care provider in the month before their suicide (Pearson et al. 2009; Luoma et al. 2002). There are also public health approaches to suicide prevention, the most effective of which is means restriction that results in common means of completing suicide being difficult for individuals to access (Yip et al. 2012) like putting high fences on bridges where suicides typically fenestrate (jump) to their death.

Though the necessity of multidisciplinary research has become clear within medicine, the majority of medical research into suicide still underlines mental health and biological causal factors for suicide. This has drawn some criticism, with Pridmore and Pridmore (2016) arguing that suicides are being medicalized, with suicides being reclassified to be a medical problem even where there is no indication of mental illness. These authors also argue that psychiatry has reclassified experiencing *sadness* into a depressive disorder within the current medical climate, further skewing perceptions that suicide is caused by mental illness. They surmise that perceiving suicide to be caused only by mental illness has placed the responsibility for suicide prevention solely on the shoulders of medical professionals. Fitzpatrick and River (2018) further underline that the medical approach to suicide prevention may not be appropriate for all individuals, with some interventions being experienced as discriminatory and culturally inappropriate, and call for alternative models that could provide effective and sensitive care.

There are two forms of suicide in particular that have led to recent, passionate and ongoing discussion among the medical field—assisted suicide and euthanasia. These forms of suicide, due to the input of medical services, have led to much debate (see Chapter 8) within the medical field and thus the medical field holds mixed perceptions of them. Seale (2009) highlights several studies demonstrating that different medical specialties have varying opinions of assisted suicide/euthanasia, with the medical professionals of specialties that have greater experience with end-of-life care such as oncologists, palliative care doctors and geriatricians being more opposed to these forms of suicide. Seale also highlights that public opinion tends to favour legalization of assisted suicide/euthanasia more than medical opinions do. In brief, the arguments made by the medical field include not only whether assisted suicide/euthanasia is morally/medically appropriate for the patient, but also whether it is ethically and morally correct for doctors to actively take the lives of patients or assist them to take their own lives (Grewal et al. 2012; Vaughn 2010). Fenigsen (2012) argues that the legalization of assisted suicide/euthanasia could fundamentally alter the practice of medicine. As assisted suicide and/or euthanasia are now available in a number of countries, research continues to be ongoing and medical perceptions on this issue continue to be mixed.

Sociology

The third discipline to be discussed in relation to perceptions of suicide is sociology. Lee (2016) defines sociology as a field that explores human society and social behaviour, and underlines that the focus of sociology is to contextualize individual actions within society. This focus informs sociologists' research into suicide, of which there has been much. Sociology's perception of suicide is that suicide is not a matter of individuals so much as a social phenomenon (Wray et al. 2011; Pridmore and Pridmore 2016). This perception is heavily influenced by Émile Durkheim's prominent work on suicide from 1897 (Scourfield et al. 2012). Durkheim examined the relationship between suicide and social factors, particularly social integration and regulation (Wray et al. 2011). Durkheim's research demonstrated that social integration, the sense of social belonging resulting from social ties, and social regulation, the monitoring and external restraints that also result from social ties, can lead to increased vulnerability to suicide if out of balance (Durkheim 1897, cited in Wray et al. 2011). Durkheim also developed a theory known as the social-environmental approach, which highlighted that change to social, political, religious or economic environmental factors could alter social roles, values and relationships and lead to a greater risk of suicide (1897, cited in Milner et al. 2013). Durkheim's theories are renowned both in sociology and in other disciplines, and modern academics continue to expand on his notions of social integration and regulation as the primary social forces leading to suicide (Mueller and Abrutyn 2015).

Sociology has also perceived the importance of the relationship between social factors and suicide. Stack (2000) listed gender roles, race, alcohol consumption, inequality and unemployment as factors that have been shown to interact with and increase the risk of suicide. The link between gender and race, and suicide is clear due to disparities of suicide rates; men are three to four times more likely to complete suicide than women, and there is much discrepancy between suicide rates of differing races (Wray et al. 2011). Relationship status, fertility, migration, dwelling location, modernization and access to suicide methods have also been shown to influence the risk of suicide (Milner et al. 2013). Interestingly, there is relatively little reference to mental illness as a cause of suicide within sociological literature.

A further perception of suicide within sociology is that suicide is socially contagious. Social contagion of suicide has been demonstrated by much research and has also been shown to occur in a number of circumstances (Mueller and Abrutyn 2015). Individuals, particularly youth, are at increased risk of suicidal behaviour and suicide if they experience the suicide death or attempt of a role model (Baller and Richardson 2009). Mueller et al. (2015) underline that social relationships can impact suicidal behaviour. This is explained to occur in situations such as individuals being exposed to unhealthy behaviours, stress or negative emotions from other individuals significant in their lives, and can negatively impact mental health and well-being. Increased suicidality as a result of exposure to a suicide also could be explained by social learning theory, which states that behaviour is learned through social interaction that reinforces positive and negative behaviour (Mueller and Abrutyn 2015). Suicide contagion is not only limited to exposure to individuals that are personally known to each other, but can also take place on a societal and global scale. There are clear links between the suicide deaths of entertainment celebrities and increases in national suicide rates in several countries, including the USA, Germany, Japan, Taiwan and Austria (Mesoudi 2009). Such suicides are known within the literature as imitation suicides (Wray et al. 2011). Further sociological studies have shown that females are more likely than males to complete suicide after the death of entertainment or political figures (Milner et al. 2013).

Anthropology

The next discipline to be discussed in this chapter is anthropology. Anthropology is the social/cultural and physical study of humanity, and investigates the workings of societies globally with comparative and cross-cultural methods (Lee 2016). Anthropology has had somewhat limited engagement with the concept of suicide, and the methods of anthropological research have resulted in a lack of comprehensive theories (Münster and Broz 2015; Staples and Widger 2012). However, there have been some anthropological perceptions of suicide made evident through the research that has been carried out. The first perception of suicide that is tangible in the literature of anthropology is that suicide is a universal issue. Anthropology seeks not only to carry out in-depth research into different cultures, but also to find the commonalities between different cultures (Lee 2016). Suicide is one of these commonalities and has been witnessed as an issue in a large variety of cultures and contexts. Though anthropological research is carried out ethnographically, Münster and Broz (2015) highlight that there is a challenge for anthropologists to think beyond the widespread Western conceptualization of suicide as a pathological and individual act that is carried out wilfully. These authors underline that they are cynical about a universal definition of suicide, due to the variation that can occur in self-destructive actions and contested interpretations of these actions. Staples and Widger (2012) agree highlighting the lack of a clear line between suicide and extreme risk-taking behaviour or wilful self-neglect.

Anthropological research has also perceived that suicide is interpreted differently in different cultures. Cultures construct different understandings of suicide through the social narratives surrounding suicide. These narratives are broadly categorized into two groups: monologue suicides that are inwardly focused acts intended to end persistent pain and dialogue suicides that are expressive and intended to communicate a message (Marecek and Senadheera 2012). European and North American cultures usually have a narrative of monologue suicide, with mental illness playing a prominent role (Marecek and Senadheera 2012). Social narratives around suicide can also be seen in the case of martyrdom[17]; interestingly, however, the suicide of an individual can be perceived as martyrdom even if that was not the individual's intention (Dabbagh 2012). This can also occur in relation to suicides that are essentially monologue in nature but are cast as politically charged dialogue suicides due to the context that they are completed in.[18] This has been exemplified in the context of farmer suicides in India (Münster 2015). Staples and Widger (2012) also demonstrate that different cultures have different terminology for suicide, which can in turn guide social and cultural narratives of suicide.

A final perception of suicide visible within the anthropological research is that suicide has a tense relationship with agency. As aforementioned, the common Western conceptualization is that suicide is carried out wilfully, and although there may be a pathological basis for this action that undermines genuine agency suicide can also be communicative (Münster and Broz 2015). Münster (2015) provides an example of the tension between agency and suicide in the context of high rates of politicized farmer suicides in India[19] due to desperate economic and environmental circumstances. He argues that farmers could be viewed as victims of their overwhelming debt and the structures behind it; however, this view denies farmers' any agency. Furthermore, Münster points out that farmers' suicides cannot be conceived of as public or political acts if there is no agency involved. This example demonstrates that the relationship of suicide and agency within anthropology is such that those that complete suicide can have agency if the suicide is carried out for a communicative purpose, but also that suicide can occur without individuals having agency. Though suicide is defined in other disciplines as an intentional act, anthropology perceives that there are complications in simplifying and assuming the intentions and agency of suicide victims.

Social Work

The fifth discipline to be discussed within this chapter is social work. Similarly to psychology and medicine, social work is an inherently practical field where theory influences and is influenced by the practice of professional social work. This field of research seeks to develop social work responses and frameworks for the circumstances of vulnerable individuals, but there has been limited practical response carried out on suicide despite suicidal behaviour being common among individuals that social workers work with (Joe and Niedermeier 2006). Social work perceives suicide to be the result of mental disorder and/or psychosocial issues such as substance abuse, physical illness, unemployment, negative life events and marital problems (Feldman and Freedenthal 2006; Joe and Niedermeier 2006). This shows that social work perceives suicide to be socially related as well as related to mental illness. As such, this brings suicide into the realm of social work as a social problem to solve, with consequent responsibilities for social workers.

It is observable within social work literature that there is an importance placed on social workers preventing and intervening in suicide. Feldman and Freedenthal (2006) underline that while suicide is most visible to social workers providing mental health services, it is prominent in nearly all locations of social work. These authors make it clear that social workers should be trained in suicide intervention, as social workers are on the frontlines in regard to discerning suicidal ideation in vulnerable individuals that they are involved with. Joe and Niedermeier (2006) also highlight the importance of the role that social workers have in preventing suicide within society, mentioning that social workers are the largest occupational group of mental health professionals in the USA. Furthermore, studies have shown that approximately one-third of social workers will face a client completing suicide throughout their career (Jacobson et al. 2012). Unfortunately, several authors point out that social workers receive varied and limited training on suicide, which may impact the quality of service that social workers can provide (Feldman and Freedenthal 2006; Osteen et al. 2014).

The perceptions of suicide visible within social work literature and the practical aspect of social work lead to the importance of patterns and trends of suicide in relation to suicide prevention and intervention efforts. Joe and Niedermeier (2006) believe prevention/intervention should be based on demographic patterns and trends of suicide, which can predict and prioritize where social support should be increased. This includes focusing suicide risk and management of patients who face significant social stress, such as divorce, a move into a nursing home, being jailed or unemployed for a substantial period, and reducing factors that increase suicide risk such as hopelessness, mental disorders, childhood trauma and physical violence. Manthorpe and Iliffe (2011) argue that common methods of suicide should be removed from society insofar as is possible, underlining that prevention should occur on a society-wide scale as well as an individual scale. Joe and Niedermeier (2006) likewise mention that common means of suicide should be confiscated, particularly limiting access to firearms for men and access to poison for women as these have been shown to be gender-specific means of suicide. Another suggestion surrounding suicide prevention in social work literature is taking into account culturally based social stigma when working with clients (Joe and Niedermeier 2006). Al-Krenawi and Graham (2000) further highlight the importance of cultural sensitivity while dealing with clients, including working within family and gender hierarchies and utilizing different means of relationship building in order to construct culturally appropriate interactions. It is evident that more research on social work prevention and intervention of suicide needs to be carried out, with both Manthorpe and Iliffe (2011) and Maple et al. (2017) underlining the importance of this research being carried out in order to provide evidence for future practice.

Criminal Justice

The sixth discipline to be explored in relation to perception of suicide is criminal justice. The field of criminal justice concentrates on exploring criminal behaviour and the response of society to criminal behaviour, and aims to find explanations for this relationship (Bernard and Engel 2001). Perceptions of suicide within the criminal justice discipline thus are limited to suicide among individuals that have been through criminal justice systems. Suicide has been an increasingly prevalent issue for criminal justice for the past few decades, as research has demonstrated that suicide rates are greater than general population averages for both individuals in correctional institutes and individuals that have been processed within the criminal justice system and reside in the community (Gupta and Girdhar 2012; Webb et al. 2011). Hakansson et al. (2011) highlight that suicide is one of the main causes of death of those associated with the criminal justice system. Though the rates of suicide within criminal justice populations are already high, suicide could also be chronically underreported due to circumstantial events such as victims dying in hospitals rather than in their cells, or through records not counting the post-release suicides of individuals who have recently finished prison sentences (Gupta and Girdhar 2012).

The perception of suicide within the criminal justice field is that suicide is a consequence of vulnerable individuals in high-stress situations and/or mental illness. Liebling (2001) highlights that correctional institutes have populations where individuals are quite likely to be at risk of suicidal behaviour. This is due to large groups within prison populations who have characteristics that are generally associated with an increased suicide risk, such as poor interpersonal relationships, addiction, social and/or economic disadvantage and adverse life events. Criminal justice literature also creates strong links between mental illness and suicide, but Liebling (2001) notes that a high proportion of those at risk have psychological difficulties that don't quite meet the grounds for a psychiatric diagnosis. Such difficulties may include alcohol or drug problems, anxiety and depression, and personality disorders. Marzano et al. (2016) carried out an extensive literature review that also emphasized the role of mental health issues, including depression, previous self-harm and hopelessness, as well as other factors such as relationship issues and prison problems. These prison problems could be issues such as bullying or social isolation, which have been shown to be associated with suicidal behaviour within prisons (Marzano et al. 2016). This has implications for prevention strategies that traditionally treat suicide as an exclusively medical problem.

With the underlying perception that suicide is a consequence of vulnerable individuals in stressful situations and/or mental illness, criminal justice research has shifted some focus from identifying at-risk individuals to identifying situations that put vulnerable individuals at risk. Such situations include times early in custody, being in seclusion or in circumstances following bad news or a relationship breakdown (Liebling 2001). This demonstrates the importance of both individual and situational factors in relation to suicide risk. Marzano et al. (2016) underline the importance of reducing access to means of suicide and increasing training for prison officers and staff so they have the ability to identify those at risk and provide better treatment. As the immediate contact points of those within prisons, prison officers are highly important in the effort to reduce suicide. Patterson and Greifinger (2010) further highlight the importance of mental health screening of all inmates on arrival, with suicide risk assessments carried out and appropriate treatment given to those in need. This demonstrates the focus and perception of the field that suicide is related to mental health and/or vulnerable individuals.

Political Studies

The seventh discipline to be explored in this chapter is political studies, which is the study of government, power, authority and conflict at local, national and international levels. The context of political studies has led to discussion of suicide being limited to *instrumental* forms of suicide[20] such as martyrdom,[21] as these types of suicide often communicate political messages or intentions and involve other people in addition to the individual suicide themselves. The main area of focus in political studies related to suicide is suicide 'terrorism', where suicides intend or commit violence to other individuals as a tactic to incite fear (Pierre 2015). Given the global climate since 2001, such research has been increasing in quantity and scope. The main focus of this research has been on 'terrorist' individuals, 'terrorist' organizations and the communities that these things happen within. There are two key perceptions of suicide visible within the literature. The first perception is that suicide, in the context of suicide 'terrorism', is used as a weapon and political statement in intra-state warfare. 'Terrorist' organizations are increasingly reliant on suicide attacks to achieve their political objectives (Pape 2003). The main objective of suicide attacks is to stop foreign occupation and regain control of areas that non-state groups consider to be their territory (Pape 2003). The *Global Terrorism Index* (2017) indicated that of 25,673 deaths from 'terrorism' in 2017, 54% of them were a result of bombs or explosions (many in suicide attacks) (GTI 2017). Pierre (2015) underlines that suicide 'terrorists' utilize death to show the extent of their commitment to their cause. Suicide 'terrorism' is seen to have many strategic benefits to 'terrorists' as it enables an opportunity to balance power in an asymmetrical conflict as well as providing relative efficiency and flexibility in planning and committing attacks (Gill 2007). It is also inexpensive, with one operation potentially costing as little as US$150 (Sheehan 2014). Furthermore, 'terrorism' creates interactions with political actors at different levels, from political leaders to civilians, which enables the spread of awareness of the terrorist groups' goals and criticisms (Gill 2007). This makes suicide appear an effective weapon.

The second key perception of suicide in political science literature is that many factors can lead to suicide 'terrorism' and thus suicide. Suicide 'terrorists' differ from other individuals that complete suicide, as suicide 'terrorists' are not necessarily suicidal (Sheehan 2014). As suicide is being engaged as a weapon rather than an opportunity to die, suicide 'terrorists' may have a wide range of personal and/or political motivations. A culture of martyrdom is perceived to be key to suicide 'terrorism', as it places individual suicide 'terrorists' in positions of honour that may not be reached without death (Pierre 2015). As the cultural and religious aspects of martyrdom will be discussed in more detail later (see Chapters 2, 5 and 6), they will not be expanded on here. It is worth noting, however, that some 'terrorist' groups consciously cultivate cultures of martyrdom in order to attract recruits (Sheehan 2014).

There are several other factors that may play a role in motivating suicide 'terrorism', including social networks, rational choice, religious fanaticism, cognitive dissonance, revenge for personal suffering, altruism and despair (Gill 2007). Relative deprivation, humiliation, social rejection and exclusion, injustice and personal loss and trauma have also been demonstrated to be factors of individuals becoming suicide 'terrorists' (Speckhard 2005). This highlights not only that a wide range of individuals may become suicide 'terrorists', but also that within political science suicide is perceived as something that is caused by social, economic and emotional circumstances.

Philosophy

The final discipline to be discussed in this chapter is philosophy. Philosophy seeks to examine the fundamental nature of knowledge and existence, and thus suicide is of central interest. Western philosophers have discussed suicide since Classical Greek times and continue to do so in modern times (Pridmore and Pridmore 2016). As a discipline, philosophy perceives suicide as an ethical quandary with the vast majority of research concentrating on the morality and rationality of suicide. Albert Camus, a renowned French philosopher, asserted in 1955 that suicide was the one truly serious philosophical question, with the judgement of whether life is worth living being the answer to the fundamental question that philosophy poses (cited in Staples and Widger 2012).

Due to the nature of philosophy as a discipline, perceptions of suicide within philosophy continue to be debated. The main argument surrounding the perception of suicide relates to whether or not suicide can be considered an immoral or morally permissible death. These arguments have implications for ethical positions on euthanasia and assisted suicide. There are three main ethical positions on this topic, and each position leads to a different perception of suicide (Khan and Mian 2010). The first ethical position is the moralistic perspective, which perceives suicide as unacceptable due to the overriding moral obligation to protect life. Key figures in philosophy including Plato and Aristotle considered suicide to be an offence against society, though Plato did make exceptions in cases of moral corruption of an individual's mind, suicide by order of law, as a response to adverse events and due to shame of carrying out unjust actions (Khan and Mian 2010). Kant, a central figure in modern philosophy, argued that suicide is never morally permissible or rational as life is inherently more important than avoiding or ending pain (Cholbi 2010). Those who hold this perception of suicide view euthanasia and assisted suicide as morally inappropriate; Velleman (1999) asserts that while there may be a moral justification for death by suicide in some cases, there is no right of self-determination in order to carry out suicide.

The second ethical position on suicide within philosophy is the libertarian perspective. The libertarian perspective places importance on freedom of choice and as such perceives suicide as a reasonable act to carry out to avoid pain (Khan and Mian 2010). Libertarian perspectives follow Hume's (1784) logic that the morality of an act is ascribed by humans, not inherent in the act (cited in Khan and Mian 2010). As such, the libertarian perception of suicide highlights the importance of the circumstances surrounding suicide in deciding the moral permissibility and rationality of suicide. Suicides perceived to be morally permissible due to the likelihood of the individuals' future being significantly more unhappy than happy are known as prudential suicide (Cholbi 2010). Khan and Mian (2010) highlight that tendencies towards libertarian perspectives on suicide may be reflected in many countries where suicide has been decriminalized and/or euthanasia and assisted suicide is legalized.

The final ethical position on suicide within philosophy is the relativist perspective, which perceives suicide to be right or wrong through consideration of relevant circumstances and consequences (Khan and Mian 2010). While this is a similar perception to the libertarian perspective, there is not an inherent belief in the value of freedom of choice regarding suicide. It is suggested that clinicians who decide on euthanasia and/or assisted suicide may utilize this approach, as they must weigh societal and family needs against individual needs (Khan and Mian 2010). While clinicians, and indeed all individuals including academics, may not fall exactly into one of these three ethical positions, the positions act as general guidelines for perceptions of suicide and associated principles within philosophy.

Summarizing Academic Diversity

Throughout this section, perceptions of suicide have been explored in relation to psychology, medicine, sociology, anthropology, social work, criminal justice, political studies and philosophy (Table 1.4).

The diversity in sensitivities of suicide both within and between disciplines demonstrates the extent to which perception is affected by the context of the discipline. This diversity could be positively utilized to create greater shared knowledge of suicide and more accurate suicide prevention techniques if an interdisciplinary approach to perceptions of suicide was utilized. To this rubric of understanding, this book offers a further theorization of suicide in PACS to include (Table 1.5).

Table 1.4 Suicide by discipline

Discipline	*Perceptions of suicide*
Psychology	Internal conflict of individuals Suicide as a deviant act Thwarted belongingness and perceived burdensomeness Acquired capability
Medicine	Result of mental illness With genetic factors increasing
Sociology	Social phenomenon Related to gender, race, inequality, alcohol consumption and unemployment Contagious Social integration and regulation
Anthropology	Universal issue *Monological* (inward act) *Dialogical* (communicative act) Related to social/cultural narratives
Social Work	Mental disorder and/or psychosocial issues Demographic patterns Hopelessness, mental disorders, childhood trauma and physical violence Means of suicide should be confiscated Gender-specific

continued

Table 1.4 continued

Discipline	*Perceptions of suicide*
Criminal Justice	Suicide is a consequence of vulnerable individuals in high-stress situations and/or mental illness Related to poor interpersonal relationships, addiction, Social and/or economic disadvantage and adverse life events Bullying or social isolation
Political Studies	Used as a weapon and political statement Strategic benefits Inexpensive Creates interactions
Philosophy	Ethical quandary regarding suicide as a moral or immoral act Moralistic (suicide *mostly* unacceptable) Libertarian (suicide reasonable) Relativist (right or wrong according to context)

Table 1.5 Suicide by discipline plus peace and conflict studies

Discipline	*Perception of suicide*
Peace and Conflict Studies	*Medical* (Involves *individual*) mental illness, assisted suicide or euthanasia *Instrumental* (Involves *others*) homicide-suicide, martyrdom/altruistic suicide, daredevil suicide or protest suicide

Notes

1. I didn't fully realize this initiative in the end but got sidetracked with the matter that has contributed to this book.
2. The world dies of medical forms of death such as cancer or heart disease and road accidents (which are lethal but mostly accidental) but the number one form of *violent death*: deliberate, intentional but also avoidable and preventable is *suicide* (https://ourworldindata.org/what-does-the-world-die-from).

3. Although hazards can threaten life, they are circumstances and *not* forms of violence.
4. My original research used the 2016 analysis but figures from 2017 were available June 2019. Visit 'Our World in Data' and change the country in the bottom left corner to see how your nation fairs: https://ourworldindata.org/what-does-the-world-die-from.
5. What's behind New Zealand's shocking youth suicide rate? Andreas Illmer, *BBC News*, https://www.bbc.com/news/world-asia-40284130.
6. Suicide through a peacebuilding lens typologizes acts of self-killing into *medical* or *instrumental* forms of suicide.
7. Updating my original research to add analysis from April 2017 to December 2018 contributed another 363 research articles to the tally (for a total of 3624) but yielded only a single article related to 'suicide', an essay about the use of self-immolation by Alice Herz and Norman Morrison during the Vietnam conflict in the USA (Coburn, Jon. 2018. "'I Have Chosen the Flaming Death': The Forgotten Self-Immolation of Alice Herz." *Peace and Change* 43 (1): 32–60). Updated results: from January 2002 to December 2018 (16 years) 17 articles contained information relevant to suicide or 0.46%.
8. Conflict is not violence, conflict can be productive and creative and emerge from a sense of inequity or injustice and be a transformative force for change (think voting rights for women or the civil rights movement) but *violent* conflict is conflict that is destructive—it seeks to subdue with force discordant views, or worse, eradicate people or peoples who symbolically register difference.
9. Magnus Haavelsrud's (1996) *intellectual* approach.
10. Although *peacebuilding* is a term associated with the PACS field, many other disciplines seek to intervene and ameliorate conflict and violence when they encounter it and this exploration seeks to be inclusive wherever possible.
11. Peacebuilding is a term that refers to techniques of 'intervention' that transform conflict nonviolently and can be delineated into negative peacebuilding (stopping violence) and positive peacebuilding (preventing violence).
12. Professor Gene Sharp famously listed 198 nonviolences in his 1973 work *The Politics of Nonviolent Action*. Boston: Porter Sargent.
13. PACS adheres to the Gandhian *ends-means* maxim that posits that one cannot use violence to achieve peace but the field has both pacifist and non-pacifist contingents who nevertheless concur that violence begets more violence and should be avoided at all costs. Whether you consider violence a human abomination (ideological pacifists) or simply inefficient (agents of pragmatic nonviolence), violence can be and should be avoided.
14. Developing countries list suicide as the #2 cause of violent death but in Western countries, the rate of suicide to road death is roughly 2:1 (https://ourworldindata.org/what-does-the-world-die-from).

15. Nahid, Aziz. 2011. "What Self-Immolation Means to Afghan Women."
16. Life-ending acts in this book refer to *medical* and *instrumental* suicide, not acts of homicide alone.
17. Martyrdom operations are termed suicide attacks in the West and are acts of deliberate self-killing that can also include injury or homicide of others. Martyrdom is considered a form of altruistic suicide or self-sacrifice suicide and will be discussed more fulsomely in Chapter 5, *Instrumental* Suicide.
18. So-called protest will be discussed more fully in Chapter 5.
19. Farmer suicides are discussed in more depth in Chapter 5.
20. This field of study frequently characterizes acts of aggression considered forms of asymmetric warfare as 'terrorism'. The term 'terrorism' is conceptually unstable but is used frequently in academic discourse, the media and popular culture to delegitimize acts of violence by non-state groups or individuals (see Chapter 5) and while acts of violence can be described by their characteristics, the terms 'terrorism', 'terrorist', 'terroristic', etc., do not relate to the act under assessment so much as the actors who embark on such acts and their perceived intentions, perceived motivations and perceived legitimacy. In 2009, in the *British Journal of Sociology*, theorist Richard Felson created a typology of *legitimate* or *illegitimate* violence to include legitimate acts: violent acts of self-defense, or violent acts done by the military or police and illegitimate violent acts: violent acts of interpersonal harm, violent acts of belligerency or violent acts termed militant (by non-state actors), to show how the same acts are culturally established as permissible or not. Using terms related to 'terrorism' is a discursive act of *delegitimizing* acts and actors of violence, not *describing* them. This book is not here to destabilize or unpack the phenomenon of using language (discourse) as a form of power and/or how disciplines have normalized such language and will elect to problematize such terms in scare quotes.
21. Martyrdom operations as a form of *instrumental* suicide will be explored more deeply in Chapter 5.

References

Acosta, Benjamin. 2016. "Dying for Survival: Why Militant Organizations Continue to Conduct Suicide Attacks." *Journal of Peace Research* 53 (2): 180–196.

Al-Krenawi, Alean, and John Graham. 2000. "Culturally Sensitive Social Work Practice with Arab Clients in Mental Health Settings." *Health and Social Work* 25 (1): 9–22.

Baller, Robert, and Kelly Richardson. 2009. "The 'Dark Side' of the Strength of Weak Ties: The Diffusion of Suicidal Thoughts." *Journal of Health and Social Behavior* 50: 261–276.

Benmelech, Efraim, Claude Berrebi, and Esteban F. Klor. 2010. "The Economic Costs of Harboring Terrorism." *The Journal of Conflict Resolution* 54 (2): 331–353.

Bernard, Thomas, and Robin Engel. 2001. "Conceptualizing Criminal Justice Theory." *Justice Quarterly* 18 (1): 1–30.

Biggs, Michael. 2006. "Book Note: Dying to Kill: The Allure of Suicide Terror." *Journal of Peace Research* 43 (2): 228.

Bloom, Mia M. 2006. "Book Note: Making Sense of Suicide Missions." *Journal of Peace Research* 43 (4): 494.

Bondy, B., A. Buettner, and P. Zill. 2006. "Genetics of Suicide." *Molecular Psychiatry* 11 (4), 336–351.

Braun, Robert, and Michael Genkin. 2014. "Cultural Resonance and the Diffusion of Suicide Bombings: The Role of Collectivism." *The Journal of Conflict Resolution* 58 (7): 1258–1284.

Choi, Seung-Whan, and James A. Piazza. 2017. "Foreign Military Interventions and Suicide Attacks." *The Journal of Conflict Resolution* 61 (2): 271–297.

Cholbi, Michael. 2010. "A Kantian Defense of Prudential Suicide." *Journal of Moral Philosophy* 7 (4): 489–515.

Coburn, Jon. 2018. "'I Have Chosen the Flaming Death': The Forgotten Self-Immolation of Alice Herz." *Peace and Change* 43 (1): 32–60.

Collard-Wexler, Simon, Pischedda Constantino, and Michael G. Smith. 2014. "Do Foreign Occupations Cause Suicide Attacks?" *The Journal of Conflict Resolution* 58 (4): 625–657.

Colpe, Lisa, and Beverly Pringle. 2014. "Data for Building a National Suicide Prevention Strategy: What We Have and What We Need." *American Journal of Preventive Medicine* 47 (3): 130–136.

Dabbagh, Nadia. 2012. "Behind the Statistics: The Ethnography of Suicide in Palestine." *Culture, Medicine and Psychiatry* 36 (2): 286–305.

Dazzi, T., R. Gribble, S. Wessely, and N. T. Fear. 2014. "Does Asking About Suicide and Related Behaviors Induce Suicidal Ideation? What Is the Evidence?" *Psychological Medicine* 44 (16): 3361–3363.

Farre, Albert, and Tim Rapley. 2017. "The New Old (and Old New) Medical Model: Four Decades Navigating the Biomedical and Psychosocial Understandings of Health and Illness." *Healthcare* 5 (4): 88–97.

Feldman, Barry, and Stacey Freedenthal. 2006. "Social Work Education in Suicide Intervention and Prevention: An Unmet Need?" *Suicide and Life-Threatening Behavior* 36 (4): 467–480.

Felson, Richard B. 2009. "Is Violence Natural, Unnatural, or Rational?" *The British Journal of Sociology* 60: 577–585. https://doi.org/10.1111/j.1468-4446.2009.01257.x.

Fenigsen, Richard. 2012. "Other People's Lives: Reflections on Medicine, Ethics and Euthanasia." *Issues in Law and Medicine* 28 (2): 95–359.

Ferrero, Mario. 2006. "Martyrdom Contracts." *The Journal of Conflict Resolution* 50 (6): 855–877.

Fitzpatrick, Scott, and Jo River. 2018. "Beyond the Medical Model: Future Directions for Suicide Intervention Services." *International Journal of Health Services* 48 (1): 189–203.

Galtung, Johan. 1990. "Cultural Violence." *Journal of Peace Research* 27 (3): 291–305.

Gill, Paul. 2007. "A Multi-Dimensional Approach to Suicide Bombing." *International Journal of Conflict and Violence* 1 (2): 142–149.

Goldney, Robert. 2015. "The Importance of Mental Disorders in Suicide." *Australian and New Zealand Journal of Psychiatry* 49 (1): 21–23.

Global Terrorism Index. 2017. *Global Terrorism Index 2017.* Institutes for Economics and Peace, Department of Homeland Security, USA. Accessed March 16 from http://visionofhumanity.org/app/uploads/2017/11/Global-Terrorism-Index-2017.pdf.

Grewal, Bhajneek, Jennifer Harrison, and David Jeffrey. 2012. "Licensed to Kill—The Impact of Legalizing Euthanasia and Physician Assisted Suicide on the Training of UK Medical Students." *Scottish Universities Medical Journal* 1 (1): 6–13.

Gupta, Anju, and N. K. Girdhar. 2012. "Risk Factors of Suicide in Prisoners." *Delhi Psychiatry Journal* 15 (1): 45–49.

Haavelsrud, Magnus. 1996. *Education in Developments.* Norway: Arena Publishers.

Hakansson, Anders, Louise Bradvik, Frans Schlyter, and Mats Berglund. 2011. "Variables Associated with Repeated Suicide Attempt in a Criminal Justice Population." *Suicide and Life-Threatening Behavior* 41 (5): 517–531.

Henriques, Gregg. 2004. "Psychology Defined." *Journal of Clinical Psychology* 60 (12): 1207–1221.

Hoffman, Aaron M. 2010. "Voice and Silence: Why Groups Take Credit for Acts of Terror." *Journal of Peace Research* 47 (5): 615–626.

Huffman, Tim. 2016. "You Have Atomic Bombs, We Have the Martyrdom-Seekers: Ayman Al-Zawahiri's Narrative Arc of the Martyr." *Peace and Conflict Studies* 23 (1): Article 3.

Jacobson, Daniel, and Edward H. Kaplan. 2007. "Suicide Bombings and Targeted Killings in (Counter-) Terror Games." *The Journal of Conflict Resolution* 51 (5): 772–792.

Jacobson, Jodi, Phillip Osteen, Tanya Sharpe, and Jennifer Pastoor. 2012. "Randomized Trial of Suicide Gatekeeper Training for Social Work Students." *Research on Social Work Practice* 22 (3): 270–281.

Joe, Sean, and Danielle Niedermeier. 2006. "Preventing Suicide: A Neglected Social Work Research Agenda." *The British Journal of Social Work* 38 (3): 507–530.

Joiner, Thomas. 2005. *Why People Die by Suicide.* Cambridge, MA: Harvard University Press.

Khan, Murad, and Ayesha Mian. 2010. "'The One Truly Serious Philosophical Problem': Ethical Aspects of Suicide." *International Review of Psychiatry* 22 (3): 288–293.

Lederach, Jean Paul. 2005. *The moral imagination: The art and soul of building peace*. Oxford: Oxford University Press.

Lee, Bandy. 2016. "Causes and Cures V: The Sociology and Anthropology of Violence." *Aggression and Violent Behaviour* 27: 158–163.

Liebling, Alison. 2001. "Suicides in Prison: Ten Years On." *Prison Service Journal* 138: 35–41.

Luoma, Jason, Catherine Martin, and Jane Pearson. 2002. "Contact with Mental Health and Primary Care Providers Before Suicide: A Review of the Evidence." *American Journal of Psychiatry* 159 (6): 909–916.

Mann, J. John, Alan Apter, Jose Bertolote, Annette Beautrais, Diane Currier, Ann Haas, Ulrich Hegerl, Juoko Lonnqvist, Kevin Malone, Andrej Marusic, Lars Mehlum, George Patton, Michael Phillips, Wolfgang Rutz, Zoltan Rihmer, Armin Schmidtke, David Shaffer, Morton Silverman, Toshitomo Takahashi, Airi Varnik, Danute Wasserman, Paul Yip, and Herbert Hendin. 2005. "Suicide Prevention Strategies: A Systematic Review." *Journal of the American Medical Association* 294 (16): 2064–2074.

Manthorpe, Jill, and Steve Iliffe. 2011. "Social Work with Older People—Reducing Suicide Risk: A Critical Review of Practice and Prevention." *British Journal of Social Work* 41 (1): 131–147.

Maple, Myfanwy, Tania Pearce, Rebecca Sanford, and Julie Cerel. 2017. "The Role of Social Work in Suicide Prevention, Intervention and Postvention: A Scoping Review." *Australian Social Work* 70 (3): 289–301.

Marecek, Jeanne, and Chandanie Senadheera. 2012. "'I Drank It to Put an End to Me': Narrating Girls' Suicide and Self-Harm in Sri Lanka." *Contributions to Indian Sociology* 46 (1–2): 53–82.

Marzano, Lisa, Keith Hawton, Adrienne Rivlin, E. Naomi Smith, Mary Piper, and Seena Fazel. 2016. "Prevention of Suicidal Behavior in Prisons: An Overview of Initiatives Based on a Systematic Review of Research on Near-Lethal Suicide Attempts." *Crisis* 37 (5): 323–334.

Mesoudi, Alex. 2009. "The Cultural Dynamics of Copycat Suicide." *PLoS One* 4 (9): e7252, viewed 20 September 2018. https://doi.org/10.1371/journal.pone.0007252.

Milner, Allison, Heidi Hjelmeland, Ella Arensman, and Diego De Leo. 2013. "Social-Environmental Factors and Suicide Mortality: A Narrative Review of over 200 Articles." *Sociology Mind* 3 (2): 137–148.

Mueller, Anna, and Seth Abrutyn. 2015. "Suicidal Disclosures Among Friends: Using Social Network Data to Understand Suicide Contagion." *Journal of Health and Social Behaviour* 56 (1): 131–148.

Mueller, Anna, Seth Abrutyn, and Cynthia Stockton. 2015. "Can Social Ties Be Harmful? Examining the Spread of Suicide in Early Adulthood." *Sociological Perspectives* 58 (2): 204–222.

Münster, Daniel. 2015. "Farmers' Suicides as Public Death: Politics, Agency and Statistics in a Suicide-Prone District (South India)." *Modern Asian Studies* 49 (5): 1580–1605.

Münster, Daniel, and Ludek Broz. 2015. "The Anthropology of Suicide: Ethnography and the Tension of Agency." In *Suicide and Agency: Anthropological Perspectives on Self-Destruction, Personhood and Power*, edited by Ludek Broz and Daniel Münster, 1st ed., 3–23. London: Ashgate.

Nahid, Aziz. 2011. "What Self-Immolation Means to Afghan Women." *Peace Review* 23 (1): 45–51.

Najeeb, Shafiq M., and Abdulkader H. Sinno. 2010. "Education, Income, and Support for Suicide Bombings: Evidence from Six Muslim Countries." *The Journal of Conflict Resolution* 54 (1): 146–178.

Niva, Steve. 2003. "Bombings, Provocations and the Cycle of Violence." *Peace Review* 15 (1): 33–38.

Osteen, Philip, Jodi Jacobson, and Tanya Sharpe. 2014. "Suicide Prevention in Social Work Education: How Prepared Are Social Work Students?" *Journal of Social Work Education* 50 (2): 349–364.

Pape, Robert. 2003. "The Strategic Logic of Suicide Terrorism." *American Political Science Review* 97 (3): 343–361.

Patterson, Raymond, and Robert Greifinger. 2010. "Treatment of Mental Illness in Correctional Settings." In *Public Health Behind Bars: From Prisons to Communities*, edited by Robert Greifinger, 347–367. New York: Springer.

Pearson, Anna, Pooja Saini, Damian Da Cruz, Caroline Miles, David While, Nicole Swinson, Alyson Williams, Jenny Shaw, Louis Appleby, and Navneet Kapur. 2009. "Primary Care Contact Prior to Suicide in Individuals with Mental Illness." *British Journal of General Practice* 59 (568): 825–832.

Pierre, Joseph. 2015. "Culturally Sanctioned Suicide: Euthanasia, Seppuku, and Terrorist Martyrdom." *World Journal of Psychiatry* 5 (1): 4–14.

Pridmore, Saxby. 2015. "Mental Disorder and Suicide: A Faulty Connection." *Australian and New Zealand Journal of Psychiatry* 49 (1): 18–20.

Pridmore, William, and Saxby Pridmore. 2016. "Suicide Is Not the Exclusive Domain of Medicine." *American Journal of Medical Research* 3 (1): 174–187.

Rajalin, Mia, Tatja Hirvikoski, Ellinor Salander Renburg, Marie Asberg, and Jussi Jokinen. 2017. "Family History of Suicide and Interpersonal Functioning in Suicide Attempters." *Psychiatry Research* 247: 310–314.

Scourfield, Jonathan, Ben Fincham, Susanne Langer, and Michael Shiner. 2012. "Sociological Autopsy: An Integrated Approach to the Study of Suicide in Men." *Social Science and Medicine* 74 (4): 466–473.

Seale, Clive. 2009. "Legalisation of Euthanasia or Physician-Assisted Suicide: Survey of Doctors' Attitudes." *Palliative Medicine* 23 (3): 205–212.

Sharp, Gene. 1973. *The Politics of Nonviolent Action*. Boston: Porter Sargent.
Sheehan, Ivan. 2014. "Are Suicide Terrorists Suicidal? A Critical Assessment of the Evidence." *Innovations in Clinical Neuroscience* 11 (9–10): 81–92.
Sommers-Flanagan, John, and Sidney L. Shaw. 2017. "Suicide Risk Assessment: What Psychologists Should Know." *Professional Psychology: Research and Practice* 48 (2): 98–106.
Speckhard, Anne. 2005. "Understanding Suicide Terrorism: Countering Human Bombs and Their Senders." In *Towards a Transatlantic Consensus on the Nature of the Threat*, edited by Jason Purcell and Joshua Weintraub, 158–175. Washington, DC: Atlantic Council Publication.
Stack, Steven. 2000. "Suicide: A 15-Year Review of the Sociological Literature. Part I: Cultural and Economic Factors." *Suicide and Life-Threatening Behavior* 30 (2): 145–162.
Staples, James, and Tom Widger. 2012. "Situating Suicide as an Anthropological Problem: Ethnographic Approaches to Understanding Self-Harm and Self-Inflicted Death." *Culture, Medicine and Psychiatry* 36 (2): 183–203.
Van Orden, Kimberly, Tracy Witte, Kathryn Gordon, Theodore Bender, and Thomas Joiner Jr. 2008. "Suicidal Desire and the Capability for Suicide: Tests of the Interpersonal-Psychological Theory of Suicidal Behavior Among Adults." *Journal of Consulting and Clinical Psychology* 76 (1): 72–83.
Van Orden, Kimberly, Tracy Witte, K. C. Cukrowicz, S. R. Braithwaite, E. A. Selby, and Thomas Joiner Jr. 2010. "The Interpersonal Theory of Suicide." *Psychological Review* 117 (2): 575–600.
Vaughn, Lewis. 2010. *Bioethics: Principles, Issues and Cases*. New York: Oxford University Press.
Velleman, J. David. 1999. "A Right of Self-Termination?" *Ethics* 109 (3): 606–628.
Wade, Sara J., and Dan Reiter. 2007. "Does Democracy Matter? Regime Type and Suicide Terrorism." *The Journal of Conflict Resolution* 51 (2): 329–348.
Webb, Roger, Ping Qin, Hanne Stevens, Preben Mortensen, Louis Appleby, and Jenny Shaw. 2011. "National Study of Suicide in all People with a Criminal Justice History." *Archives of General Psychiatry* 68 (6): 591–599.
Wolfsfeld, Gadi, Paul Frosh, and Maurice T. Awabdy. 2008. "Covering Death in Conflicts: Coverage of the Second Intifada on Israeli and Palestinian Television." *Journal of Peace Research* 45 (3): 401–417.
World Population Review. 2019. *Suicide Rate by Country*. World Population Review. Accessed March 16 from http://worldpopulationreview.com/countries/suicide-rate-by-country/.
Wray, Matt, Cynthia Colen, and Bernice Pescosolido. 2011. "The Sociology of Suicide." *Annual Review of Sociology* 37 (1): 505–528.
Yip, Paul, Eric Caine, Saman Yousuf, Shu-Sen Chang, Kevin Chien-Chang Wu, and Ying-Yeh Chen. 2012. "Means Restriction for Suicide Prevention." *The Lancet* 379 (9834): 2393–2399.

CHAPTER 2

Understandings of Suicide

> There is but one truly serious philosophical problem, and that is suicide. (Albert Camus)

This chapter begins by looking at how the phenomena included in the term 'suicide' are conceptualized, encountered and understood in different groups—in the past and in the contemporary world. Recognizably, beliefs about the nature and acceptability of suicide vary across cultures and across history. Culture and religious or philosophical worldviews often inform how suicide is conceptualized and understood within a society or social group and in addition to group held perceptions, how the individual self is conceptualized, including the relation of self to community and self to nature/spirit, also shapes how suicide is understood. Many cultures have socially acceptable (even desirable) usages of suicide but also injunctions against forms of suicide. Suicide is a multifaceted phenomenon and our understanding benefits from a comprehensive appreciation of life-ending actions in personal and cultural/social context.

This book is going to argue that there is no such thing as 'one' suicide that suicide can be broadly categorized into *medical* or *instrumental* suicide and that regardless of how we understand the term suicide, these violent life-ending acts of self-killing, lethal self-harm, self-sacrifice or self/other-killing, Peace and Conflict Studies (PACS), a field fittingly positioned to recognize and reveal suicide as a preventable act of violence (whether *medical* or *instrumental*) largely leaves this form of harm

K. Standish, *Suicide through a Peacebuilding Lens*,
https://doi.org/10.1007/978-981-13-9737-0_2

to other disciplines such as medicine, social work, psychology, strategic studies and terrorism studies. This book is an appeal to the interdisciplinary field of PACS to engage with Suicide Studies as a sub-discipline of PACS and to turn our attentive gazes—who are ever watchful for violence and nonviolent transformation of violence—to a form of harm that, as-yet; we do not seem to be incorporating into our work. I applaud all of my colleagues (those in my field or comfortably adjacent to and in partnership with it) for shining light on a world with violence and to imagine, initiate and future vision a way of being that eschews violence for nonviolence. I think we can do more. This book is a platform of understanding we can use that may help facilitate that onus.

Culture contours suicide. Our shared symbolic landscape of acts termed suicide relates intimately with our perception of self, society and surroundings, and one of the primary facets of understanding this project holds is that there can be no singular appreciation of suicide (no absolute standard) because the phenomenon of suicide is social/cultural. As the 'social environment of the person, who voluntary ends his [or her] life usually dictates the behaviour' (Lykouras et al. 2013, 548), cultural context is vitally important in understanding the overall prevalence of suicide, perceptions of suicide, forms of self-killing employed and legitimized and possible intervention and prevention.

Culture relates to myriad human domains. Which leads to research questions that are not easily answered such as *is suicide an act of individuals, of groups, of ethnic, religious or secular collectives?* Results reveal *yes/and* answers where *yes/no* might be anticipated (and desirable). Studies show that the effects of different religious or philosophical beliefs can determine how socially acceptable suicide is (ranging from prohibited to honourable) and that such understandings can correlate with overall suicide rates (Gearing and Lizardi 2009; Nelson et al. 2012; Stompe and Ritter 2011). Major religions and cultural traditions hold concepts of voluntary death that are condoned—not only acceptable but portrayed as heroic self-sacrifice or spiritual achievement. How can researchers perceive of suicide as a tragedy in cultural spaces where it is seen as triumph?

In the West, White et al. (2016) remind us that the study of suicide is 'narrowly focused on questions of individual pathology and deficit' (2) and that, similar to conflict analysis in PACS, the identification and management of 'risk has dominated the professional and research conversations' for decades (3). Western cultural conceptions of suicide seem to be influenced by two strands of thought. One is the (secular) philosophy of individual autonomy and freedom while the other is the Judeo-Christian tradition that emphasizes the value and sacredness of individual life. There is significant debate between these two positions in the area of assisted suicide and euthanasia (examined in more detail in Chapters 4 and 8) while self-killing is usually agreed to be a tragedy resulting from mental illness and/or a psychological breakdown in the face of severe life stresses. Orthodox Judaism takes a stronger position against self-killing than modern Christianity seeing it as an offence against God whereas many modern Christians consider it tragic but acceptable (Gearing and Lizardi 2009). But a West defined by the Judeo-Christian tradition has seen significant changes in attitudes about suicide (in particular in Europe) in the early modern period, as the cultural dominance of the Catholic Church waned and new philosophies such as humanism emerged (Ferngren 1989). The rise of humanistic philosophies contributed to a transformation of the evaluation of life-ending acts that can be seen today in many parts of the world.

In other cultures, religion (or spiritual worldviews) continues to play a strong role in how suicide is comprehended. The major religions of Islam, Hinduism and Buddhism all have texts that contain an injunction against suicide. That said, some forms of self-killing are not classified as individual acts of self-killing but as noble self-sacrifice, an act that increases personal and familial prestige and honour (at least by some within the religion). Examples of this include *istishhad*/martyrdom operations in Islam (Abdel-Khalek and Ahmed 2004), *suttee/sati*/widow suicide and *jauhar/johar*/self-destruction in Hinduism (Vijayakumar 2004), *sallekhana/santhara*/self-starvation in Jainism (Koveleskie 2015; Laidlaw 2005) and *bonzo/bonze*/self-immolation (political, altruistic or religious) in Buddhism (Park 2004; Benn 2001). While there may be a substantial overall difference in attitude to suicide between Abrahamic faiths (Judaism, Christianity, Islam) that view the individual life as belonging to God, Eastern religions/spiritual traditions believe in rebirth (Stompe and Ritter 2011) which may contribute to some permissible or legitimate (indeed desirable) perceptions of suicide. However, Eastern religions do have injunctions against suicide, usually understood in terms of self-pollution and its negative consequences for rebirth (Nimbalkar 2007; Werner 2008), and there are instances of Abrahamic suicide (usually involving self-sacrifice) that escape the preciousness of life maxim.

Peoples in the Anglosphere are experiencing heightened rates of suicide, but Indigenous peoples experience the 'highest suicide rates in North America' (White et al. 2016, 8; Leenaars 2006). Explanations vary, but some authors point to the effects of colonial history (Hunter and Harvey 2002; Lawson-Te Aho and Liu 2010) that include cultural models of illness and intervention whereby particular Western beliefs, practices and modes of service disable local and Indigenous contexts in dynamic and destructive ways. There is a strong case for adapting suicide prevention initiatives to local culture and context (Tighe et al. 2015; Wexler and Gone 2012), but simply inserting Indigenous content into imperial prevention strategies will not result in a decolonization of suicide. Although Indigenous peoples (especially young males) have the highest rate of self-killing in the world, troublingly, Western suicide prevention techniques that mobilize social support and integration do not always see similar success levels in Indigenous settings where 'Aboriginal individuals seem immune to the protective factors believed to be preventative of suicide' (Keast-O'Donovan 2017, 2). Culture, is more than content, it shapes the container that holds culture and in instances of past cultural trauma, attempting to fill a damaged or broken vessel is evidence that there is no single solution to the multitudinous dilemmas that can result in suicide.

From the literature, we can see that cultural understanding slides the perception of suicide from tragic deed to selfless act. Suicide as self-sacrifice (in English termed martyrdom or altruistic suicide) is seen very positively in a number of cultures. Abrahamic faiths, as we will see, have categories of self-death that are considered virtuous and some South Asian religions have a concept of suicide as a form of spiritual attainment—the ultimate renunciation of attachment to the material world. Certain methods of self-killing have gained particular legitimacy within a culture, e.g. self-immolation in Buddhism or Hinduism, suicide attacks (martyrdom operations) among some sections of the Islamic world or the IRA Hunger Strikes in Irish Catholicism. A common theme is that these acts of self-killing are understood to be done to benefit the group rather than to alleviate personal suffering, which makes them different from individual suicide, which makes them permissible.

Regarding illegitimate forms of suicide—when religious injunctions against self-killing are strong—this seems to correlate with lessened rates of suicide (especially in more monocultural places) but not to the extent of a complete absence of suicide. The reduction in the suicide rate may also relate to social stigma around illegitimate suicide as an undesirable by-product of life-ending acts. The reality that how a culture views suicide may correlate with under-reporting of suicide is a concern the world over; many studies indicate gender rates of suicide that vary across cultures—with more men than women completing suicide in almost all cultures, populations and age cohorts—yet higher rates of self-killing among women in rural China that relate to social stigma and reporting of suicide. There is, as has hopefully been suggested, no easy or standard understanding of the human utilization and conceptualization of suicide, which may speak to a unique aperture of understanding that this book and PACS may be able to offer.

Yes, the scientific model linking the likelihood of a suicide to precursors such as mental illnesses (especially depression), family history of suicide (the so-called suicide gene) and life stresses such as family conflict, unemployment and trauma seems to hold up cross-culturally when it has been investigated empirically. However, cultural factors can certainly help to explain why someone becomes depressed—for example, according to what is considered shameful in a given society or the ability for a person, as a part of a greater group (such as the Indigenous), to experience culture in the wake of group trauma—or the relative willingness or reluctance of individuals to consider suicide as an option to end suffering of some kind. Culturally glorified forms of self-killing for communal or spiritual reasons—which do not fit the pattern of suicide-as-a-result-of-mental-illness that predominates in Western discussions—are further argument for a social/cultural perspective on this form of self-violence. Having presented an overview of the phenomena included in various groups or worldviews in relation to suicide, the remainder of this chapter will elucidate on how suicide is conceptualized culturally, temporally and demographically. The following three sections will examine suicide in the Western, Indigenous, Islamic, Judeo-Christian, Hindu, Jain, Sikh, Buddhist and the Confucian world; suicide in the ancient civilizations of Rome, Greece, India and China; and then consider how age, gender and urban/rural geography relate to suicide.

Author's Note

I am a Canadian cisgender female with ancestry from Greece, northern Europe and Britain. I practise Yogic Science and do not hold a creed, religion or philosophical standpoint; I consider myself a progressive feminist and political social democrat. I am going to survey a number of cultural groups and collectivities in the following chapter to which I do not belong, and do not intimately, understand. I know this. I encourage readers of this work to glean snippets of information that I have tried to collate without prejudice, as my goal is not to speak for these cultures but to survey literature about the phenomenon of suicide from the kaleidoscope of human perception.

Importantly, I am, to the best of my knowledge, not Indigenous. I am very aware of the fact that for hundreds of years, Western scholars have been doing research 'on' the Indigenous as if they could/should speak about peoples in communities as if they were studying 'things' or 'objects' and not full humans who deserve dignity and to define their own 'knowledge(s)' for themselves.

There is great variation in the Indigenous (and non-Indigenous) world. I urge readers to resist the temptation to distil the material in this chapter into stereotypes. I am writing this unit with caution and respect, and I sincerely understand that one of the social-scientific pits of describing groups to whom you do not belong is to solidify into a mass a group of individuals who may share membership in one or more collective but live (and die) in vastly different ways. I want to state that I am using a Western approach in this book that I do not claim to be using decolonizing pedagogy or Indigenous methodology. As I am using a case study methodology in this chapter, I am relying on the work of other scholars to investigate this chapters' research question: *How can suicide be described in different human groups?* Finally, I am a PACS scholar, not a suicidologist, historian, psychologist, anthropologist or theologian. To readers interested in suicidal mentality and methods, please see other sources. And if you are interested in comprehensive descriptions and classifications of the cultures and religions surveyed in the following section, I wholeheartedly encourage you read other works more suitable to enlighten your understandings than this book. As my goal in this chapter is to illuminate how different cultural groups characterize suicide, I have concentrated on content suitable to that end. I apologize in advance for lacunae.

In humility, Katerina Standish.

Suicide in the Modern Era

Western Culture

The West is not a geographical position so much as a shared cultural landscape that includes a variety of political, social, economic, racial, gendered, philosophical and historical dimensions. Individuals, collectives and countries can be considered part of the 'Western World' despite location and a primary feature of Western culture involves notions of equality, democracy and hybrid economic systems that combine market economy with aspects of social welfare. The following section looks at how suicide is described in the West.

Aside from the influence of Judeo-Christian theology that is dealt with separately below, suicide culture tends to draw on scientific (clinical) or philosophical (ethical) analysis. From a clinical perspective, self-killing is largely believed to be the result of mental illness and empirical evidence from the World Health Organization (WHO) has supported this finding since 1948. In the West, mental illness is considered the primary risk precursor in suicidology where it is generally acknowledged that '98% of those who committed suicide had a diagnosable mental disorder' at the time of their death (Bertolote and Fleischmann 2002, 183).[1] Indeed, Critical Suicide Studies highlights this scientific bias to illuminate that three assumptions dominate the field of suicidology in the West: 'Suicide is pathological [suicide occurs when individuals are mentally unwell] … Suicidology is science [suicide is best understood through a Western medical lens] … [and] Suicide is individual [the person commits suicide untethered to their exteriority]' (Marsh 2016, 16–17). These dominant assumptions are possible reasons that despite decades of empirical studies about suicide, there is little evidence about how to actually stop suicide as a violent, life-ending act (De Leo 2002).

Philosophically, Western culture viewed suicide from a strict moral lens from the time of Augustine of Hippo (fifth century) until the seventeenth century. This derived from a contention that life was sacred and that suicide was a violation of the sixth Christian commandment 'thou shall not kill' relayed to believers in the Old Testament (in the book of Exodus 20:13). In the hundreds of years that followed, there was limited philosophical challenge to the assertion that life was given (and taken) only by God and that human suicide was imagined to defy

God's righteous dominion and was therefore an abomination. Suicide, to the Christian church, was a sin that affected numerous life rites including burial but also a crime whose repercussions could include seizure of property (Ferngren 1989).

It was later, during the early modern period that the assessment of suicide became rationalized 'that suicide was not an offence against God just merely a matter of personal choice unencumbered by theological or dogmatic consideration and devoid of blame or disgrace' (Ferngren 1989, 155). Suicide then gained a cultural focus on the individual instead of the divine engaging with ethical conundrums that consider the value of 'life' versus the right of the individual to 'choose death'. This discussion is particularly prevalent with regard to assisted suicide and euthanasia (see Chapters 4 and 8) where a tension inhabits the space between life and the right to end life—at least for the individual (Chapple et al. 2006; Szasz 2002). There is no clear cultural theme in the West where self-killing is condoned, but, in some instances (e.g. the military or to protect a child), self-sacrifice can be viewed as heroic as though the willingness to sacrifice personal safety for another is a sign of potent honour and/or affection (Takeda 2010). Overall, in the West, suicide is viewed with an appreciation for individual well-being and is understood in clinical terms as separate from the relationship of the suicidal individual to wider culture or community.

Indigenous Culture

Most authors who engage with suicide in Indigenous cultures seek to understand why these communities exhibit much higher rates than any other social groups globally (see Leenaars 2006 for statistics). Indigenous peoples living in the Anglosphere generally understand suicide differently from the individual-clinical approach of mainstream society, which is creating a demand for culturally grounded knowledge and prevention programs—termed Aboriginal Suicidology (Wexler and Gone 2012; Elliott-Farrelly 2004). The connection of the Indigenous individual to their traditional culture/worldview can have a protective effect against suicide whereas the opposite is a contributing factor in the risk of suicide and experiences of illness (Chandler and Lalonde 2008; Garroutte et al. 2003).

Indigenous psychologists focus on the link between individual well-being and cultural well-being at the group level (Lawson-Te Aho and Liu 2010), and many authors assert that the colonial experience is an important determinant of self-harm. In Canada, First Nations peoples were systematically targeted by Christian churches from the 1840s until 1990 on behalf of the government (TRC Canada 2015). This annihilation of culture (disputes continue whether the genocide was meant to destroy the peoples or merely their Indigeneity) has had a miserable legacy; Aboriginal youth in Canada have the highest suicide rate 'than that of any culturally identifiable group in the world' (Chandler and Lalonde 2004, 111) putting the many descendants of Indian residential schools at risk of abuse, cultural marginalization and suicide.

Indigeneity (membership in an Indigenous group) is multifaceted, and while there are similarities in the experience of encountering violent empire in the Indigenous world, the degree of cultural destruction (up to and including genocide) has a reverberant impact on the well-being of Indigenous peoples in the contemporary world. This is supported by empirical investigations of the effects of Indian Residential School System on Canadian Aboriginals (Elias et al. 2012) where the targeting of natives did not simply eradicate First Nations peoples throughout Canada (through forced sterilization, deliberate disease transmission and widespread abuse and neglect) but also deliberately and systematically destroyed their ways of being in the world. While the exact experiences of Canadian First Nations, Aborigines in Australia, Native Americans or the Māori peoples in New Zealand (just to name the most studied groups) are diverse, similar colonial tactics were employed—destroy the individual and/or the individuals' place in their world. That Indigenous people suffer suicide at higher rates than the non-Indigenous should not come as a large surprise. Wexler and Gone (2016) remind us that, today, suicide in the Indigenous world can be comprehended as 'a way of expressing communal distress and despair in response to historical circumstances shaped by violent domination and colonial power. [Such]...trauma has been defined as the communal stress and collective grief associated with shared experiences of genocide and racism' (60), experiences shared all over the world by dominated peoples.

The Māori are the Indigenous peoples of New Zealand. In traditional Māori culture:

> Individual well-being is sourced and tied to the well-being of the collective cultural identity. Therefore, individual pain is inseparable from collective pain and the role of the collective becomes that of carrying individuals who are suffering. The state of kahupo … [spiritual blindness] is characterized by a loss of hope, meaning, and purpose and an enduring sense of despair…the symptoms of chronic dissociation or separation of the physical from the spiritual…. (Lawson-Te Aho and Lui 2010, 125)

In Indigenous groups in Canada, 'the self is relationally defined and suicide is seen as a social and spiritual problem tied to family, community and the cultural context…poor communications across generations has left many youths feeling alone' (Kral and Idlout 2016, 232). While there are some similarities to how Māori and First Nations peoples conceptualize suicide (relational-spiritual), Indigenous groups as a whole do not have a single way of understanding suicide due to the great diversity of their cultures. Past scholarship-related information about suicide in Inuit communities in what is now Canada and Greenland affirming that life-ending acts were 'positively sanctioned in the culture' (Krauss cited in Hicks 2007, 31) when linked to illness, mourning or advanced age. Modern suicide follows a very different pattern: Inuit suicide is affecting youth-aged children (mostly males or in suicide clusters), tends to involve alcohol and impulsivity (Hicks 2007) and is negatively viewed in the community. While some Indigenous groups are documented to have a form of self-killing that is viewed as acceptable or heroic (Andriolo 1998), one group is not the same as the next and there is a need for understanding the cultural meaning of suicide among young Indigenous people within their specific cultural contexts today (Chandler and Lalonde 2004; Hunter et al. 1999).

Notably, there is nuance in new scholarship that is asking whether there is any difference between suicide and Indigenous suicide (Goldney 2002) and more detailed investigations of cultural continuity and suicide in various aboriginal groups (Chandler and Lalonde 2008) that show vast disparities in the utilization of self-harm leading to death correlated to cultural facets such as native language use (Hallett et al. 2007). Despite specificities and increasing empirical knowledge, a general consensus in the literature is that Indigenous suicide is a critical concern and that prevention programs will be more effective when they consider Indigenous cultural meanings, historic context and spiritual worldviews.

Islamic Culture

This section seeks to gain some understanding of suicide in an Islamic context while cautioning readers not to assume that Islam is monolithic, that every Muslim (follower of Islam) is the same or that every Muslim is Arab (a group that includes persons from a multitude of faiths). In addition, although Islam has been associated with suicide attacks since the early 2000s globally, it needs to be recognized that while suicide attacks by some Muslims are a modern incarnation of violence, Islam, a religion hundreds of years old, has actually exhibited such acts in limited amounts. Further, throughout history there are numerous secular 'suicide attacks' and attacks by a variety of non-Islamic groups or individuals (Pedahzur 2006) leaving religion, alone, a poor explanatory base for understanding suicide attacks in modern conflict (Gambeta 2005).

Self-killing is prohibited in Islam as a means to end individual suffering. Islamic theology views human life as belonging to God (El Azayem and Hedayat-Diba 1994). This prohibition can be seen to contribute to the fact that Muslim-majority countries have much lower rates of documented suicides compared to others (Ineichen 1998; Lester 2006; Shah and Chandia 2010). The exception to the theological prohibition on voluntarily seeking death is *istishhad*/martyrdom a part of Jihad (Holy War) (Khashan 2003; Lester and Akande 1994). There are various sub-groupings in Islam, but in general, martyrdom is considered legitimate and condoned and the *Shia* sect, in particular, has a robust concept of self-sacrifice in the face of tyranny or humiliation (Khashan 2003). Despite sanctioned forms of suicide, actual non-martyrdom rates of suicide have been seen as lower than other ethnic or religious groups (such as Hindus in the UK, Malaysia and Singapore) but not dissimilar in regard to attempts at suicide (Ineichen 1998; Kamal and Loewenthal 2002). Lester (2006) writes that:

> Despite the possible under-reporting of suicidal behaviour in countries where such behaviour is illegal, suicide rates do appear to be lower in Muslims than in those of other religions, even in countries which have populations belonging to several religious groups. Rates of attempted suicide, on the other hand, do not appear to be lower in Muslims as compared to non-Muslims. (77)

In addition, the status of non-martyrdom suicide in the Islamic world as both a sin and a crime leads to a dampening statistically in reported deaths. Notwithstanding, a 2000 study used newspaper suicide reports in Pakistan to 'challenge the widely held belief that suicide is a rare phenomenon in an Islamic country' (Khan and Reza, 31) and found that 306 suicides (the majority by single males under 30 years of age) were completed in a two-year period using (mostly) pesticides. Pritchard and Amanullah conducted a study in 2007 that investigated what are termed Other Violent Deaths (OVD) by the WHO a type of death classified as a non-suicide. They found that 'OVD rates in 10 Islamic countries were considerably higher than the western average and eight had OVD rates considerably higher than their suicide rates' leading Pritchard and Amanullah to conclude that '...high OVD rates, especially the Middle Eastern, may be a repository for hiding culturally unacceptable suicides' (2007, 421). The notion that the 'very grave sin' of suicide is mostly proscribed in Islam is challenged by *instrumental* suicide such as suicide attacks/martyrdom operations (Kamal and Loewenthal 2002, 111).

Growth in the employment of suicide attacks (using suicide bombs or suicide vehicles) by some Muslims in both Islamic and non-Islamic countries has received substantial attention. Islamic scholars do not necessarily consider suicide attacks as martyrdom operations (Anees 2006), but it seems that the individuals who carry out such acts of suicide-homicide do view it as such (Khashan 2003; Kushner 1996). The decision to carry out a suicide attack may involve multiple factors in a particular context, and in many instances, psychological pathology has not been found to be a factor motivating suicide attacks as most are carried out on behalf of a group by an individual seeking to make a positive difference in the world (Reuter 2004). While suicide attacks are not unique to Islam or are an inevitable result of adherence to Islamic theology (Gambetta 2005; Pedahzur 2006), *medical* suicide related to mental illness or debilitating affective states are staunchly prohibited.

Judeo-Christian Culture

There is both overlap and difference between Jewish (Judaism) and Christian perspectives on self-killing (Kaplan et al. 2012). Unsurprisingly, and similar to the other Abrahamic faith, Islam, Jewish and Christian traditions emphasize the sanctity of human life viewing suicide as an offence against God (Engelhardt 2013; Gearing and Lizardi 2009; Keown and Keown 1995). On the issue of assisted suicide and euthanasia (see Chapters 4 and 8), all three of the Abrahamic faiths are opposed, citing theological reasons (Colucci and Martin 2008; Stomp and Ritter 2010; Kaplan et al. 2012), yet each tradition has some concept of martyrdom or noble voluntary death. In Judaism, 'heroic suicide is praised…from the suicide of Samson and the collective suicide in Masada, to the collective readiness of Jews in Medieval times and during the Holocaust to kill themselves rather than succumb to their enemies' (Witztum and Stein 2012, 725). Early Christian martyrs considered that dying for their faith gained them automatic entry into Heaven and burial beside the grave of a martyr was considered a chance to 'tag-along' on the martyr's trip to the afterlife (Moss 2012). From this, it can be considered that in Judeo-Christian traditions, self-killing is differentiated between self-sacrifice and deliberate life-ending acts to end physical or psychic pain (Constantelos 2004; Sweeney 1993; Witztum and Stein 2012). While one act was revered (even desirable), suicide for self was considered deeply illegitimate.

Orthodox Judaism and Orthodox Christianity are clearly and strongly opposed to self-harm as an act against God (Bresnahan 1995; Colucci and Martin 2008; Gearing and Lizardi 2009). But, the history of Non-Orthodox Christianity and Reform Judaism are less definitive. In Reform Judaism (similar to Conservative, Orthodox and Ultra-Orthodox Judaism), suicide is banned and considered incompatible with Judaic teachings but a person who completes suicide can be buried in a Jewish cemetery. As assisted suicide and euthanasia hasten death and Reform Judaism maintains that all life must be cherished until its final moments, suffering, of any kind, does not permit life-ending action (Kaplan and Schoeneberg 1988 cited in Bailey and Stein 1995). Non-Orthodox Christians in Western Europe viewed self-killing at the beginning and end of the medieval period in less absolute terms, and Christians began to view self-killing as tragic, but acceptable. Theologians argue strongly against assisted suicide and euthanasia as a failure of the ethic of care (Cohen 1996; Schotsmans 2003; Witztum and Stein 2012), but there is a greater permissibility of life-ending acts being acceptable from the twentieth century onward (Engelhardt 1998).

Peterson (2014) attributes the injunction against suicide in Abrahamic religious movements not to faith but to sovereignty. Peterson considers that although the literal prohibition against suicide in the Judeo-Christian world is theological (coming from both scripture and practice), the intentional prohibition relates to religious nationalism and an alliance between politics and religion that reveals that 'taking personal life' is considered an affront not to God but to the state that requires 'bodies' for war. The ethical and historical rationales for theological doctrine devised several thousand years ago in both Judaism and Christianity are beyond the scope of this section; however, it can be surmised that in the contemporary world, Judaism and Christianity largely forbid life-ending acts.

The phenomenon of suicide exists in all cultural groupings, but despite the variability of human experience, there can be some general conclusions regarding religion and suicide. While 'none of the world religions argue for suicide', Abrahamic traditions have specific injunctions against self-killing whereas Eastern religions 'with a concept of transmigration and rebirth' show a much broader encounter with the phenomenon of suicide (Stompe and Ritter 2010, 118). In the next section, the Eastern religions of Hinduism, Jainism, Sikhism, Buddhism and Confucianism will be examined to describe how suicide is conceptualized from within eastern religious culture.

Hindu Culture

Hinduism is substantially different, in theological terms, from the Abrahamic faiths, which affects how suicide is understood and how self-killing is practised in Hindu cultures. Suicide is more prevalent among Hindus than, for example, Muslims, for reasons already suggested (Ineichen 1998) because the Hindu belief in rebirth principally understands suicide in terms of how a good or bad death will have karmic consequences for future reincarnation (Lakhan 2008). *Karma* is the basis for Hindu religious objection to suicide, which is then viewed as a failure to show adequate gratitude for the achievement of human form in this lifetime (Agoramoorthy and Hsu 2017). That said, there is a tradition of voluntary death by fire as a form of spiritual achievement in Hinduism (Warshall 1999) and of fasting to death as an end to suffering (or culmination of ascetic practice known as *Prayopavesa* which must be done with community approval and according to community rules) (Agoramoorthy and Hsu 2017). Euthanasia by caregivers can be perceived in Hinduism as an act of compassion (Lakhan 2008) and is therefore acceptable. The overall moral concern in Hindu cultures is to die an enlightened death, not for selfish reasons, and this may or may not involve a voluntary end to life.

Voluntary death is problematized in Hindu cultures regarding two practices: widow burning (*suttee*) and assisted suicide (termed physician-assisted suicide [PAS] in India)/euthanasia. Hindus historically viewed the traditional practices of widows sacrificing themselves on their husband's funeral pyres, such as *suttee*, favourably despite not being explicitly condoned or recommended in Hindu scriptures (Agoramoorthy and Hsu 2017; Nrugham 2015). Although these practices are outlawed in India today, a new phenomenon of honour suicides relating to dowry payments (Kumar 2003; Nrugham 2015; Shurei 1997) has emerged highlighting a gendered dimension to suicide in Hindu culture. Although suicide in India is still more prevalent among men, there is a rising incidence of female suicide today that has economic roots (Agoramoorthy and Hsu 2017). Self-immolation is currently being associated with disputes over female dowries, a series of gifts (often monetary) given before and immediately after a marriage in Hindu culture; 'when dowry expectations are not met, the young bride may be killed or compelled to commit suicide, most frequently by burning' (Kumar 2003, 31). Regarding PAS/euthanasia, in Hindu culture it is an offence to take another's life (it is considered murder) but PAS, where the patient takes his or her own life with assistance from either a doctor or a third-party, is gaining legitimacy but with consideration surrounding wellness, illness and whether maladies are physical or mental (Kahn and Tadros 2013). Although 'it has been suggested that Hindu tradition is relatively tolerant of suicide', it can be seen in this limited exploration that there is significant nuance between types of suicide in the Hindu world and its acceptability and/or prohibition (Kamal and Loewenthal 2002, 111).

Buddhist Culture

Similar to Hinduism, Buddhism is strongly concerned with the cycle of rebirth and karmic consequences. Buddhists view suicide as motivated by cravings and desire and therefore do not consider suicide as a 'good death' (where the consciousness of the dying person is in an enlightened state) but a 'bad death' which can lead to rebirth on a plane of endless suffering (Becker 1990; Disayavanish and Disayavanish 2007). Suicide as a means to end suffering is, therefore, highly illogical according to Buddhist philosophy as it leads to future and perpetual suffering.

There is some debate among scholars about whether euthanasia might be compatible with Buddhist teaching as early Buddhist texts contain stories where the Buddha accepted some suicides (when the individual was suffering greatly and irreversibly ill) (Becker 1990), but the Buddha's key concern was that the mind of a suicide victim was in a good condition to achieve equanimity—being selfless and wantless at the moment of their death. Buddhism principally judges an action by the intention behind it and having an aim of causing death for self or other can be seen as contrary to Buddhist teaching to preserve life (Keown 1998).

Multiple forms of Buddhist culture exist (*Mahayana*, *Theravada* and *Vajrayana* traditions) in Asia, Southeast Asia and outside Asia with various traditions of religious suicide, particularly through self-immolation, that are viewed very differently from self-killing to alleviate one's own suffering (Lamotte 1987; Warshall 1999). There seems to be significant debate among different scholars and different strands of Buddhist philosophy on whether voluntary self-immolation marks a spiritually admirable transcendence of the self or whether it is contrary to the precept of nonviolence (see Keown 1998; Kleine 2006; Kovan 2013; Wiltshire 1983). Self-immolation as a method of drawing attention to mercilessness is an ancient tradition in both Hindu and Buddhist traditions that is thought to lead to 'transmigration into a new body' (Warshall 1999, 76). As 'the Buddha declared that the crucial variable governing rebirth was the nature of the consciousness at the moment of death', Buddhist considerations of life-ending acts such as suicide, assisted suicide or euthanasia tend to relate to the mentality of the individual when their life ends (Becker 1990, 543). Buddhism does not have a formal, single view on many forms of suicide (including passive suicide/euthanasia) (Kovan 2013) but rather expects individuals to read the scriptures and formulate their own understanding (Barnes 1996). While it would be doctrinally neat to assume that suicide is forbidden in Buddhist cultures, the widespread incidences of self-immolation (hundreds of Buddhist monks, nuns and laypersons have self-immolated) and honourable self-killing (to evade capture or shame) show a variability in how such tenets are understood leaving room for more acceptability in Buddhism for certain types of suicide (Benn 2001; Kovan 2013). While the major Eastern religions have been covered in the previous two sections (Hinduism and Buddhism), the next sections will briefly explore what limited content exists regarding suicide in Jain and Sikh culture.

Jainism

Jainism is an Indigenous Indian religion with areas of overlap with Hinduism and Buddhism but recognized legally as a distinct religious group. Regarding suicide, the Jains have a practice of the voluntary acceptance of death at the end of life through fasting (*sallekhana*), which they view as a high form of spiritual achievement and distinct from suicide (Bilimoria 1992; Laidlaw 2005). This practice of 'fasting to death' is viewed very highly by Jains as the culmination of an individuals' commitment to asceticism and worldly renunciation. In *sallekhana*, an individual fasts to death voluntarily and the decision—considered ethical, honourable and nonviolent—is free from either coercion or compulsion (Kazuyoshi 2009). There was consternation from Jains when the Indian government outlawed the practice as a form of suicide in 2015 (Bhatt 2015), but nevertheless, completing suicide by denying oneself nutrition is both condoned and revered in the Jain tradition.

Sikhism

The Sikh religion also emerged from the Indian subcontinent but much more recently (in the 1600s), but its position on suicide largely mirrors that of Islam and Christianity.

> Sikhs have a high respect for life, which they see as a gift from God. Most Sikhs are against euthanasia, as they believe that the timing of birth and death should be left in God's hands…the Sikh Gurus rejected suicide (and by extension, euthanasia) as an interference in God's plan. Suffering, they said, was part of the operation of karma, and human beings should not only accept it without complaint but act so as to make the best of the situation that karma has given them. (BBC 2009, October 27, 4–5)

While there is limited literature available on their attitude to suicide in English-language academic literature, Sikh teachings are opposed to euthanasia and self-killing (BBC 2009) but not martyrdom, which is seen as part of a glorious tradition of self-sacrifice and courage (Dhillon 1992). The Sikh religion focuses on submitting the individual human will to God and from this stem the objection to self-skilling and also the valorization of martyrdom (Singh 2015). Despite the elevation of the martyr's death in Sikhism, other forms of suicide are deftly forbidden (Nesbitt 2015).

Confucian Culture

Confucian ethics tend to understand suicide in terms of interpersonal relationships and duties (Park and Lester 2012; Ping-Cheung 1999). In Confucian ethics, preservation of biological life is a good, but it is not the supreme good—rather the decision of living or dying should be based on upholding virtues known as '*ren*' (benevolence) and '*yi*' (justice). Suicide that is completed in order to uphold these values is therefore morally permissible and even praiseworthy. In addition, it is considered morally wrong to prolong one's life at the expense of these two virtues (Ping-Cheung 1999).

Confucian society is the only cultural group in the world with a higher rate of suicide for females than males. An empirical study in rural China found that Confucian ethics of filial piety and harmony reduced the willingness of young people to consider suicide but that the ethic of female subordination (to males and superior females) was positively correlated with suicide (Zhang and Liu 2012). Zhang's further research findings relate suicide to Confucianism in a study of suicide in men and women in rural China (2014).

> In rural China, 392 suicides (both men and women) aged 14–35 years consecutively sampled from 16 counties of three provinces were studied with 416 community living controls of the same age range and from the same locations…It is found that believing in Confucianism and being married are both protecting the rural young men from suicide, while the two same variables are either risk or nonprotecting factors for the Chinese rural young women's suicide. (146)

Gendered aspects of the Confucian tradition influence males differently than they effect females. Concern with duty, mercy and upholding human dignity means that Confucian philosophy can accommodate the assisted suicide and euthanasia forms of suicide as a moral act in circumstances where palliative care is failing to relieve severe physical and psychological suffering (Ping-Cheung 2010) but that social forces may also contribute to the obvious gendering of suicide in rural China.

Suicide in the Ancient World

Overview

> Historical analysis can contribute to the study of suicide as a form of human behaviour by providing perspective. Examining suicide in relation to changing social conditions, value systems, institutions and ideologies at different periods and in various societies may suggest ways of looking at suicide in our society. (Rosen 1971, 267)

Modern human populations are the descendants of dozens of globalizing empires and the inheritors of a number of cultural/social/political traditions. In this section, an attempt is being made to trace connections or departures between modern cultural groups and ancient empires. While the previous section looked at contemporary cultural groups, the following section will briefly examine how suicide was considered in some parts of the ancient world. While a survey of pre-history would have delighted the embryonic archaeologist in me, I listened to the counsel of others and truncated my investigations to sources I could reasonably write about with some weight. While a definitive guide to suicide in antiquity is not the goal of this section, the following information produces a partial understanding of the civilizations examined.

And, though there were ancient civilizations in the Arctic, Asia, Southeast Asia, the Americas and Africa that are not surveyed in this section, a global survey of ancient cultures in regard to suicide proved very difficult. Most sources regarding Africa (particularly sub-Saharan) are contemporary studies, and the search for other cultures in other parts of the world did not garner enough scholarship to supply content here.[2] If I have missed something vital in the English language, it is not that it does not exist but that my research skills must have failed me. Nevertheless, optimistically, relevance may be established from looking into how suicide is characterized in ancient Rome, Greece, India and China.

In the following section, more substantial attention has been given to Rome and Greece and less to India and China (where suicide information was particularly difficult to find). Despite the unequal nature of the information garnered, it can be established that different societies in ancient times viewed self-killing very differently from one another. Overall, the literature suggests that contemporary views on suicide (including secular and religious perspectives) have unquestionably changed from the attitudes prevalent thousands of years ago. This suggests that conceptualizations of suicide are not fixed over time but change with changing cultural norms.

> In the history of these attitudes, we can observe continuities and breaches, reserving a special place in cases of mental diseases. The delayed emergence of a generally accepted term for the voluntary exit from life (the term suicidium established during the 17th century), is connected to reactions triggered by the act of suicide...[not] frequency...[or] the extent of the phenomenon. (Lykouras et al. 2013, 548)

Reactions triggered by the act of suicide relate to cultural and historical understandings of voluntary exit. Some influence of ancient ideas—especially Greco-Roman philosophy and Judeo-Christian doctrine—are still seen regarding current thinking about suicide in the West (Droge and Tabor 1992). And contemporary Confucian, Hindu and Buddhist cultures in China and India show the influence of ancient religious and philosophical texts.

The moral acceptability of suicide seems to have occupied philosophers and theologians in several ancient cultures (Droge and Tabor 1992). Considering the fact that all who live, eventually die, the concept of death (good death, bad death or desirable death) is a natural (cultural) human concern. Within ancient cultures (as with modern ones), prominent thinkers often disagreed and there was substantial debate about life-ending acts.

Broadly speaking, self-killing (*autothanasia*) seems to have been viewed as acceptable in Greco-Roman and Judeo-Christian thinking in the ancient world, provided the act was believed to be committed for noble rather than selfish purposes (Amundsen 1989; Droge 1988; Droge and Tabor 1992). In the ancient Greco-Roman world,

> Suicide was regularly practiced throughout antiquity and was justified by many as an obvious means of deliverance from all sorts of affliction and oppression. In general, ancient society did not discriminate against suicide, nor did it attach any particular disgrace to it, provided there was sufficient justification for the act. (Droge 1988, 263)

The Hebrew and Christian Bibles do not proscribe suicide (excepting the sixth commandment to 'not kill', which is part of the debate), and the early Christian church (pre-Constantine) did not forbid suicide (Droge and Tabor 1992). The beginning of Christian objections to suicide is attributed to St Augustine (Droge and Tabor 1992) although this assertion has been challenged (Petersen 2011). And, despite widespread contemporary proscription of suicide in the modern medical profession, the ancient Greek physicians' creed—the Hippocratic Oath—did not prohibit euthanasia (van Hooff 2004). Further information on how some ancient groups conceptualized self-killing is included under the subheadings below.

Ancient Greece

There is a false separation between Ancient Greece and Ancient Rome as the two empires were enmeshed in many ways (and therefore termed Greco-Roman). There is some overlap in the next two subsections, but effort has been made to separate out the Greco from the Roman wherever possible. Hellenic, Roman and Near East scholars are likely to see great gaps in my research (apologies), but for those who are new to this material, some useful information may be garnered.

The ethics around voluntary death were of great interest to ancient Greek philosophers such as Socrates, Plato and Aristotle. Literary sources—concerning both mythology and history—from the period are a useful source for estimating popular attitudes towards self-killing as the sense prevails that inclusion of suicide in literature indicated a social reality that existed at the time (Laios et al. 2013). Overall, Ancient Greeks (similar to most modern groups) distinguished sharply between what they saw as cowardly self-killing and honourable voluntary death (Garrison 1991). As suicides were often completed in response to social pressures and expectations of honour, discourses of validity permeated notions of support or suppression of life-ending acts (Garrison 1991). As Garrison remarks, 'the punishment of the corpses of suicides raises significant questions about the typical ancient attitude towards suicide' (1991, 1) but the emerging social consensus of the time is that very few were repulsed by life-ending acts despite behaviour that would be viewed as irreverent and undignified (for the corpse) today.

Socrates, Plato and Aristotle each ruminated on suicide. Socrates disagreed with the act of suicide and found it an affront to the authority of God—although he is purported to have drunken Hemlock poison himself to avoid execution which is arguably a form of suicide although not exactly voluntary (Rist 1969), while Plato and Aristotle distinguished between acceptable and unacceptable forms of self-killing (Garrison 1991). Plato believed suicide was acceptable when ordered by the state as a punishment (or in the face of an unbearable disgrace beyond remedy) but not when completed out of what he viewed as laziness or cowardice (Miles 2001). Aristotle mostly condemned suicide in view of its political and social ramifications, but he did qualify this by writing that self-killing was acceptable when it was intended to seek the good (Papadimitriou et al. 2007).

There is substantial discussion of euthanasia in Greek sources (Mystakidou et al. 2005). The concept of dying a good death—painless, in old age, occurring naturally—existed in ancient Greek culture and is the origin of the term 'euthanasia' which originally meant a 'good' death and now refers to (hopefully) compassionate life-ending. Greek dramas provide an exploration of popular attitudes towards the notion of tragic/compassionate suicide (Garrison 1991) where multiple characters in the tragedies kill themselves. While different authors vary in their depiction of suicide, it was clearly a way for characters to resolve an inner conflict or an otherwise irresolvable dilemma.

Greeks saw the debilitation of old age as humiliating, denying them the posthumous fame they desired, so suicide was contemplated to restore honour. Plato was in favour of abandoning deformed individuals to death for the good of the wider republic, a practice that is known today as 'passive euthanasia'. The rise of Orthodox Christianity in Greece, unsurprisingly, led to a substantial change in attitudes where suicide and euthanasia were concerned as both came to be seen as immoral and eventually outlawed in medieval Greece.

Ancient Rome

How Romans understood death and suicide was linked to wider social concerns such as gender, national and personal identity, politics, legality and social differentiation (Edwards 2007). Self-killing is very prevalent in written sources from Ancient Rome (Edwards 2007; Griffin 1986), which may reflect the fascination of elites with political suicide or a widespread prevalence of suicide in the general population (Griffin 1986; Hill 2004). Edwards (2007) writes of the pervasiveness of suicide in ancient Rome leaving one writer to conclude 'it is difficult to avoid thinking of suicide as the characteristic Roman way of death' (Griffin 1986, 64). There is multitude of reasons for suicide in Roman civilization involving aspects of despair, grief, devotion, old age, the degradation of rape, finances, erotic dissatisfaction, shame and defiance as death was ubiquitous in ancient Rome and life was very short (Hope 2009; Laios et al. 2013).

Roman writers have tended to describe suicide dispassionately as a reasoned reaction to events—defeat by an enemy or an accusation of treason—rather than the outcome of some kind of psychological torment (Hill 2004). Some suicides tended to be dramatically public in character while others took place in intimate privacy (Hill 2004). In addition, in Ancient Rome the state could require an individual to kill him or herself as a form of capital punishment—choosing between suicide and execution—elites (and non-elites) would often choose suicide as a less disreputable death (Hill 2004). The fall of the Roman Empire did not lead to a territorial inheritor but many attribute the widespread contention that there are 'good' and 'bad' deaths to cultural facets of Ancient Rome (Beard 2016).

Ancient India

The Indian subcontinent has, over the course of history, been home to many cultures and civilizations and has produced the major religions of Hinduism, Buddhism, Jainism and Sikhism. While each has a slightly distinct perspective on suicide, except in certain sanctioned cases, all of these religions are opposed to suicide. In particular, self-immolation as a form of self-sacrifice has been seen as spiritually worthy among Hindus and Buddhists, and *suttee* and *jauhar* have been practised since ancient times until the British Colonial period (Vijayakumar 2004).

The first reports of suicide in India are found in Vedic texts dating from 4000 BCE, and early Buddhist sources indicate that self-immolation was viewed positively in at least some traditions well over two thousand years ago (Halkias 2015). In various Tamil literary sources, references to suicide include widow self-immolation, fasting to death and suicide as a response to bereavement (Somasundaram et al. 1989).

> In Ancient India, two forms of altruistic suicide were practiced. One was Jauhar, a kind of mass suicide by women of a community when their menfolk suffered defeat in battle; the other was Sati, a suicide of a widow on the funeral pyre of her husband or after the cremation. (Vijayakumar 2004, 73)

Despite these two forms of common suicide, Ancient Hindu texts did not encourage the practice of self-death, termed *Pranatyaga* or *Atmahatya* in Sanskrit, meaning 'abandoning the life force'. While suicide for selfish reasons was discouraged, some forms of ritualistic suicide (considered altruistic) were religiously sanctioned (Agoramoorthy and Hsu 2017; Vijayakumar 2004). This suggests that in ancient India, as in so many other societies in both the past and today, there was a distinction between acceptable and unacceptable forms of self-killing, with, in the case of Ancient India, those undertaken on behalf of the community and involving women, seen as most honourable.

Ancient China

Suicide was a prevalent part of ancient China (Lee and Kleinman 2000) leading some scholars to declare suicide a tell-tale sign of Chinese culture (Lin 1990 cited in Perry and Selden 2000). Confucian philosophy regarded suicide that was done for the sake of others as both ethical and praiseworthy but did not condone suicide that would lead to the harm of others (Ping-Cheung 1999). Suicide among women seems to have been quite widespread although explanations for this vary (see Fong 2001; Meng 2002; Yang and Lu 2008).

> Suicide was connected...with wars, corrupt emperors and inauspicious family situations...an act of ardent loyalty towards an emperor... as a moral protest, and as a strategy for dealing with exploitative and oppressive social relations...when transposed into the female life world, suicide was available to women as a way of defending their loyalty and chastity...[escape] from life situations they found to be more unbearable than death [such as]...brutal bondage as a kind of slave and producer of sons in miserably oppressive family situations, accusations of adultery or incest, marriage to abusive husbands who squandered the family fortune, took concubines and other wives [or] abuse by in-laws. (Lee and Kleinman 2000, 296)

Suicide could be seen as a form of resistance to oppressive authority or a pathway to glorious martyrdom in Ancient China (Lee and Kleinman 2000). The attraction to suicide for women may relate to the subservient position of women in Chinese culture at least in the ancient periods (Meng 2002). Similar to the Confucian culture of today, while suicide was a typical exit to life in Ancient China there were less or more honourable forms of these acts.

Approaching a Geography and Demography of Suicide

Overview

When I embarked on a demographic and geographical analysis of global suicide, there was a deluge of statistics before me that sometimes concurred and other times limited my ability to make substantial conclusions (just perusing the WHO stats is a staggering research journey). There are always exceptions when you try to collapse data or extrapolate findings outside of a research study, and this section unquestionably exhibits epistemological discrepancy.

This section will seek to briefly parse out from a multitude of empirical data a tangible takeaway regarding the people who engage with life-ending acts and where they live. This section, obviously, is seeking to harness knowledge gained by researchers working all over the world, many in the investigation of *medical* suicide, others looking more closely at *instrumental* suicide and some looking at both. There are gaps in the data—big gaps—and this short section will join the oft-repeated entreaty ending many of the studies I surveyed that call for 'more', the need for more studies, more temporality, more widespread investigations and more comparative research so that adequate conclusions can be made.

Suicide is found in all regions of the world (Retterstøl 1993; Hirsch 2006). Despite an assertion that 'suicide rates are highest among relatively more prosperous countries' which would most obviously include the West (Vijayakumar et al. 2008, 19), the suicide rate is highest in Indigenous communities worldwide (and highest in Canadian Indigenous groups see Chandler and Lalonde [2004]). Country data by the WHO (2015) listed Sri Lanka, Guyana, Mongolia and Kazakhstan as the top four nations who record suicidal deaths. As of 2005, China accounted for 30% of suicides globally (Yip et al. 2005) and Belarus was found to have one of the highest rates of suicide in the world (Razvodovsky and Stickley 2009).

But, as has been mentioned, not all countries in the world record suicides or recognize suicides and these figures only relate to successful[3] suicides, not suicidal attempts or suicidal ideation (imaging suicide). As these stats do not partition out suicides related to mental illnesses or aggression, only limited conclusions can be drawn regarding tendency or risk factors, but in Sri Lanka—the country with the most suicides globally according to the WHO—risk of unnatural death (suicide) relates to migration (Cheng and Lee 2008). As we will see, this connection between suicide and human mobility is seen in other parts of the globe as well.

The WHO notes that Southeast Asian rates of suicide are the highest in the world followed by Africa, Europe, the Western Pacific and then the Americas. The Eastern Mediterranean region held last place, and each of these regions is further declined by country in data graphs that compare rates in 2000, 2005, 2010 and 2015. A quick glance at the country data shows many decreasing rates since the year 2000 but multiple countries whose rates are clearly on the rise (2017b).

There is limited data from Islamic countries regarding suicide (Demirel et al. 2008), and though in the past ten years, suicide rates in the Islamic world have tended to be lower than in many Western countries—the suicide rate is rising (Hami et al. 2010). This West-Islam difference is attributed frequently to the protective effect of Islamic teachings (see Moradi and Ali 2002; Morad et al. 2005; Eskin 2004), but it may also signal 'hidden suicides' where deaths are not officially recognized as such due to social stigma and the fact that suicide, in Muslim countries is unwaveringly illegal (see Hami et al. 2010). The insulation effect of religion in Muslim nations is seen in some research to be highly selective as in multiple studies the suicide rate of non-Muslims living in Muslim countries is significantly higher. In Dubai, 'the suicide rate among expatriates…was seven times higher than the rate among the nationals' (Dervic et al. 2012, 652); Elfawal (1999) found that in Damman, Saudi Arabia, 'immigrants formed 77%' of suicides (163) and in a 2007 study of the Arab World authors Karam et al. (2008) found that 'females who were displaced or refuges were significantly more likely to report suicide ideation' (359).

These results have an echo is European data. Suicide attempt rates (SARs) were calculated in one study that found that of 54 immigrant groups studied 27 groups showed significantly higher SARs rates than country nationals (Lipsicas et al. 2012) and such 'higher rates among immigrants' were attributed to 'difficulties in acculturation and integration' (244). In a Swiss study from Yilmaz and Riecher-Rössler (2012), immigrants from Turkey (especially women) showed a suicide rate of 38.6% compared to 14% in Swiss Nationals, attributed by the authors to 'cultural and immigration-specific issues' including being socially isolated (366). The crisis of suicide in asylum seekers for many years in many parts of the world shows high levels of 'self harm', hundreds of attempted suicides and high levels of successful suicide (Cohen 2008, 235). A Netherlands study shows much higher rates of suicide mortality in immigrants (Garssenet al. 2006) showing 'young adult males of non-western origin...much more likely to commit suicide than native Dutch' (2143). A study that compared immigrant and non-immigrant groups in Europe and distribution of suicide attempts concluded that higher immigrant suicide rates 'may be indicative of difficulties in the acculturation process in Europe' (Lipsicas et al. 2012, 279). And a systematic review of suicide in immigrant populations in Europe from 2014 states that 'immigrants from non-Western countries are often socioeconomically disadvantaged relative to the majority populations... [facing] socio-psychological stressors like discrimination and marginalization' (Spallek et al. 2014, 63). Interestingly, Scandinavian data showed higher rates of suicide in first-generation immigrants implying a carry-over effect of migration that may increase risk of suicide for the children of migrants (Hjern and Allebeck 2002). It is, of course, not surprising that immigrant populations are facing challenges not faced in native populations. Many people become migrants because of unsafe or unsustainable circumstances in their home countries. As has been suggested in Chapter 1 of this book, PACS should be present in looking at how violence connects to the experience of human mobility globally and it isn't. At least not yet.

This chapter has so far sought to unpack suicide from cultural, historical and geographical perspectives. As stated previously, the goal of this chapter has not been to present the combined knowledge of decades of suicide research but to elucidate how suicide is conceived of and what its parameters might be in future interdisciplinary PACS analysis. The final section of this exploration will briefly survey three facets of humanity that seem prevalent in suicidology. As there is significant overlap in the cultural, historical and epidemiological literature, this section concludes with a short deliberation on age, gender and urban vs. rural living in relation to suicide.

Age

Suicide rates vary according to age, but not to the same degree across all cultural groups. While generally, worldwide, the likelihood of completing suicide increases with age, suicide rates seem to be intensifying at a higher rate among male and female youth (Chandler and Lalonde 2004; Beautrais and Fergusson 2006; Bertolote and Fleischmann 2015). Despite age being a factor in increasing incidence of suicide (particularly in ageing males), youth is a risk factor for suicide attempts in many contexts including Belgium, France, Germany, Italy, the Netherlands, Spain, Pakistan (Bernal et al. 2007; Khan and Reza 2000) and among Indigenous groups (see next paragraph). Furthermore, completed[4] suicide among young men is often higher than among women, while suicide ideation can be more prevalent among young women. This suggests that age intersects with culture and gender to imply why some individuals attempt suicide (see, e.g., Zhang 2014).

In particular, a number of Indigenous groups in post-colonial Western countries have an incredibly high rate of suicide among young people, usually young men. These groups include Māori in New Zealand (Beautrais and Fergusson 2006; Lawson-Te Aho and Liu 2010), Inuit in Canada (Hicks 2007; Kral 2012), Australian Aborigines (McCoy 2007) and people of the Western Pacific—who along with Southeast Asia comprised over 50% of global suicides in 2008 (WHO 2008). A common theme in this literature is how later generations have been affected by colonial legacies, in particular the breakdown of traditional relationships and rituals that used to offer a structure and support to the adolescent experience. WHO fact sheets claim that suicide is the number two cause of death in 15–29 year old's (WHO 2017). In the Middle East, suicide is more prevalent among older adults (Pritchard and Amanullah 2007) while in Pakistan it seems to be more predominant among the young (Khan and Reza 2000). And, in instances of suicide attack, young Muslim men and women carry out most suicide attacks motivated by a vision of how they will be remembered by others (Reuter 2004).

Gender

There is substantial evidence of global gender differences in suicide rates (especially rates of completed suicide rather than suicide ideation or attempts). A widespread pattern is that males are more likely than females to complete suicide (Khan and Reza 2000; Payne et al. 2008; Wexler 2006). However, the example of rural China demonstrates that this can be reversed in specific cultural circumstances (Yip et al. 2000; Zhang 2014). This suggests that higher levels of male suicide in other contexts may relate more to cultural and sociological factors than to some biological predisposition, but cultural concepts of suicide do affect females in China[5] in dissimilar patterns to the rest of the globe. Indeed, it is suggested that gender and culture interact to shape the relative likelihood of males and females completing suicide that relate to vulnerability, responsibility and the opportunity for life-ending acts (Canetto and Sakinofsky 1998; Joe et al. 2008; Langhinrichsen-Rohling et al. 2009). Gender can interact with cultural concepts of maleness and femaleness when influencing suicidal behaviour (Payne et al. 2008) and in certain cultures, particularly Hinduism, forms of self-killing are reserved especially for women that relate to how female roles are culturally conceived (Andriolo 1998; Bhugra 2005). In other cultures, the erosion of traditional understandings and experiences of maleness may be implicated in high suicide rates among young men (McCoy 2007; Wexler 2006) where weakening social bonds correlate to migration and dislocation.

In most countries and regions, the suicide rate is much higher for young men (Amami et al. 2013; Mekaoui et al. 2016; Turhan et al. 2011; Yasan et al. 2008) and suicide attempts by young men are also seen as significantly more likely to result in death (Hanna et al. 2011; Mahir et al. 2012). Rates of *medical* suicide (see Chapter 4) attempts among young Muslim males and females are rising in the Middle East (Rezaeian 2010) as well as *instrumental* suicide (see Chapter 5) or suicide attacks which, when enacted, is considered to be a form of agency, especially for women, on behalf of salient group identity (Alvanou 2007).

Gender differences affect methods of attempting suicide (Ben et al. 2016; Hanna et al. 2011) and sociocultural factors link the greatest risk of suicide to unemployment among men and unmarried status among women (Hanna et al. 2011). The WHO maps trends in suicide methods and find less and less difference in the methods used by men and women to complete suicide. While historically men tend to use hanging and firearms to complete suicide whereas women typically choose poison (in particular, drug overdoses), the top three methods now used overall, globally, are hanging, pesticides and firearms (2017). The WHO states:

> There is a much larger difference in suicide methods between countries than between genders. Where a suicide method is particularly popular in men, it will often also be popular in women, and vice versa. In general, underlying suicide patterns tell us more about the availability and acceptability of suicide methods than about gender disparities. (2017, 25)

Overall, it seems that both culture and opportunity shape how men and women conceive of and complete suicide at different rates, for different reasons and using (at times) different methods. And, as we have seen, culture also affects how the act of self-killing by men or women is perceived by others in their society or social group.

Urban–Rural

There is no doubt that some countries have greater incidences of suicide than others and this may relate to settlement patters such as whether individuals live in the city or the country. A number of studies have examined differences in urban and rural rates of suicide, often also in relation to age groups and gender. A sampling of some of the more up-to-date studies is found below. Overall, it seems that urban–rural distinctions also apply in explaining suicide rates alongside age, gender and cultural factors.

Despite the myth of the loneliness of urban living, most studies found suicide is more prevalent in rural areas (McCarthy et al. 2012; Park and Lester 2012; Yip et al. 2000). Reasons put forward for higher rates of suicide in rural areas include socio-economic factors (Hirsch 2006; Vijayakumar et al. 2008; Yip et al. 2000, 2005), lack of provision of mental health services and suicide prevention programs (Judd et al. 2006; Razvodovsky and Stickley 2009), social isolation (Hirsch 2006; Razvodovsky and Stickley 2009) and rural cultural norms (Judd et al. 2006; Zhang 2014). The marginalization of rural living combined with isolation puts rural at risk residents in a similar position to several other groups who engage with life-ending acts—desolate.

Conclusion

This chapter has sought to establish cases of suicide in history and the contemporary world with an aim to both illuminate the diverse characterizations of life-ending acts and highlight some notable similarities. The research shows men, women, the aged and the young practice suicide all over the world. There are no groups of people who do not engage with suicide, and in many cases, there are strict cultural, social or theological proscriptions regarding life-ending acts. There are two families of suicide that can be identified in the literature: suicide related to self-suffering and suicide as a noble or heroic act. The motivations for both forms of suicide (characterized in detail in Chapters 4 and 5) can be broadly connected to cultural understandings, stress, trauma, societal stigma, geographical isolation and social dislocation. While this chapter sought to explore global and historical descriptions of suicide, the next chapter outlines the twenty-first-century field of PACS and presents a rationale for suggesting that PACS needs to pay attention to suicide. The next chapter will argue that PACS contains tools that can be used to transform how we engage with the phenomena of suicide that relate to the transformation of suicidal violence and regard for those who imagine, anticipate or participate in life-ending acts.

Notes

1. Joiner (2010) posits it is closer to 95% and has argued that the number could be as high as 100% if you consider 'subclinical variants of mental disorders' (89).
2. For an older source on suicide in Africa, see Bohanna, Paul. 1960. *African Homicide and Suicide*. Princeton, NJ: Princeton University Press. For a more recent publication, see Snyder, Terri L. 2015. *The Power to Die: Slavery and Suicide in British North America*. Chicago: University of Chicago Press.
3. These are also termed 'completed' suicides.
4. Also termed 'successful' suicide.
5. And perhaps Bangladesh (see Arafat 2018).

References

Abdel-Khalek, Ahmed M. 2004. "Neither Altruistic Suicide, nor Terrorism but Martyrdom: A Muslim Perspective." *Archives of Suicide Research* 8 (1): 99–113.

Agoramoorthy, Govindasamy, and Minna J. Hsu. 2017. "The Suicide Paradigm: Insights from Ancient Hindu Scriptures." *Journal of Religion and Health* 56 (3): 807–816.

Alvanou, Maria. 2007. "Palestinian Women Suicide Bombers: The Interplaying Effects of Islam, Nationalism and Honor Culture." National Defense College Working Paper 3: 20.

Amami, Othman, Jihene Aloulou, Monia Elleuch, and Lobna Aribi. 2013. "Attempted Suicide in High School and University Students: A Tunisian Case Study of 61 Cases." *La Tunisie Medicale* 91 (3): 175–178.

Amundsen, Darrel W. 1989. "Medical Ethics, History of Europe: I. Ancient and Medieval. B. Early Christianity." Encyclopedia of Bioethics. *Encyclopedia.com*. Accessed March 12, 2019. https://www.encyclopedia.com/science/encyclopedias-almanacs-transcripts-and-maps/medical-ethics-history-europe-i-ancient-and-medieval-c-medieval-christian-europe.

Andriolo, Karin. 1998. "Gender and the Cultural Construction of Good and Bad Suicides." *Suicide and Life-Threatening Behavior* 28 (1): 37–49.

Anees, Munawar A. 2006. "Salvation and Suicide: What Does Islamic Theology Say?" *Dialog* 45 (3): 275–279.

Arafat, S. M. Yasir. 2018. "Females Are Dying More Than Males by Suicide in Bangladesh." *Asian Journal of Psychiatry*. https://doi.org/10.1016/j.ajp.2018.10.014. Accessed March 20, 2018. https://ac-els-cdn-com.ezproxy.otago.ac.nz/S1876201818307834/1-s2.0-S1876201818307834-main.pdf?_tid=0adc89b8-f8f2-43db-9b3c-f0eab4766c32&acdnat=1553039169_44b93b499362912ae8b5c818b9a5a293B.

Bailey, William T., and Lawrence B. Stein. 1995. "Jewish Affiliation in Relation to Suicide Rates." *Psychological Reports* 76 (2): 561–562.

Barnes, Michael. 1996. "Euthanasia: Buddhist Principles." *British Medical Bulletin* 52 (2): 369–375.

BBC. 2009. "Euthanasia, Assisted Dying, and Suicide." Accessed June 26, 2017. http://www.bbc.co.uk/religion/religions/sikhism/sikhethics/euthanasia.shtml.

Beard, Mary. 2016. *SPQR: A History of Ancient Rome*. New York: Liveright Publishing Corporation.

Beautrais, Annette L., and David M. Fergusson. 2006. "Indigenous Suicide in New Zealand." *Archives of Suicide Research* 10 (2): 159–168.

Becker, Carl B. 1990. "Buddhist Views of Suicide and Euthanasia." *Philosophy East and West* 40 (4): 543–556.

Ben, Khelil M., Amine Zgarni, Malek Zaafrane, Youssef Chkribane, Meriem Gharbaoui, Hana Harzallah, Ahmed Banasr, and Moncef Hamdoun. 2016. "Suicide by Self-Immolation in Tunisia: A 10 Year Study (2005–2014)." *Burns: Journal of the International Society for Burn Injuries* 42 (7):1593–1599.

Benn, James Alexander. 2001. *Burning for the Buddha: Self-Immolation in Chinese Buddhism*. Los Angeles: University of California.

Bernal, M., Josep Maria Haro, Sebastian Bernert, T. de Graaf, Brugha Ron, Ronny Bruffaerts, and J. P. Lépine. 2007. "Risk Factors for Suicidality in Europe: Results from the ESEMED Study." *Journal of Affective Disorders* 101 (1): 27–34.

Bertolote, José Manoel, and Alexandra Fleischmann. 2002. "Suicide and Psychiatric Diagnosis: A Worldwide Perspective." *World Psychiatry* 1 (3): 181–185.

Bertolote, José Manoel, and Alexandra Fleischmann. 2015. "A global perspective in the epidemiology of suicide." *Suicidologi* 7 (2).

Bhatt, Yesha. 2015. "Santhara Is Not Suicide; It's the Pathway to God!; Amdavadi Jains React on the Ban on the Age-Old Practice in Jainism, by Rajasthan HC." *DNA (Daily News & Analysis)*, August 11.

Bhugra, Dinesh. 2005. "Sati: A Type of Nonpsychiatric Suicide." *Crisis* 26 (2): 73–77.

Bilimoria, Purushottama. 1992. "The Jaina Ethic of Voluntary Death." *Bioethics* 6 (4): 331–355.

Bresnahan, James F. 1995. "Observations on the Rejection of Physician-Assisted Suicide: A Roman Catholic Perspective." *Christian Bioethics* 1 (3): 256–284.

Canetto, Silvia Sara, and Isaac Sakinofsky. 1998. "The Gender Paradox in Suicide." *Suicide and Life-Threatening Behavior* 28 (1): 1–23.

Chandler, Michael J., and Christopher E. Lalonde. 2004. "Transferring Whose Knowledge? Exchanging Whose Best Practices? On Knowing About Indigenous Knowledge and Aboriginal Suicide." *Aboriginal Policy Research: Setting the Agenda for Change* 2: 111–123.

Chandler, Michael J., and Christopher E. Lalonde. 2008. "Cultural Continuity as a Protective Factor Against Suicide in First Nations Youth." *Horizons* 10 (1): 68–72.

Chapple, A., S. Ziebland, A. McPherson, and A. Herxheimer. 2006. "What People Close to Death Say About Euthanasia and Assisted Suicide: A Qualitative Study." *Journal of Medical Ethics* 32 (12): 706–710.

Cheng, Andrew T., and Chau-Shoun Lee. 2008. "Suicide in Asia and the Far East." In *The International Handbook of Suicide and Attempted Suicide*, edited by Keith Hawton and Kees van Heeringen, 29–48. New York: Wiley.

Cohen, Cynthia B. 1996. "Christian Perspectives on Assisted Suicide and Euthanasia: The Anglican Tradition." *The Journal of Law, Medicine & Ethics* 24 (4): 369–379.

Colucci, Erminia, and Graham Martin. 2008. "Religion and Spirituality Along the Suicidal Path." *Suicide and Life-Threatening Behavior* 38 (2): 229–244.

Constantelos, Demetriosj. 2004. "Altruistic Suicide or Altruistic Martyrdom? Christian Greek Orthodox Neomartyrs: A Case Study." *Archives of Suicide Research* 8 (1): 57–71.

De Leo, Diego. 2002. "Why Are We Not Getting Closer to Preventing Suicide?" *British Journal of Psychiatry* 181: 372–374.

Demirel, Birol, Taner Akar, Aslihan Sayin, Selçuk Candansayar, and Antoon A. Leenaars. 2008. "Farewell to the World: Suicide Notes from Turkey." *Suicide and Life-Threatening Behavior* 38 (1): 122–127.

Dervic, Kanita, Leena Amiri, Thomas Niederkrotenthaler, Yousef Said, Mohamed O. Salem, Martin Voracek, and Gernot Sonneck. 2012. "Suicide Rates in the National and Expatriate Population in Dubai, United Arab Emirates." *International Journal of Social Psychiatry* 58 (6): 652–656.

Dhillon, Gurdarshan Singh. 1992. *India Commits Suicide*. Chandigarh: Singh & Singh Publishers.

Disayavanish, Chamlong, and Primprao Disayavanish. 2007. "A Buddhist Approach to Suicide Prevention." *Journal of the Medical Association of Thailand = Chotmaihet thangphaet* 90 (8): 1680–1688.

Droge, Arthur J. 1988. "Mori Lucrum: Paul and Ancient Theories of Suicide." *Novum Testamentum* 30 (3): 263–286.

Droge, Arthur J., and James D. Tabor. 1992. *A Noble Death: Suicide and Martyrdom Among Christians and Jews in Antiquity*. San Francisco: Harper.

Edwards, Catharine. 2007. *Death in Ancient Rome*. New Haven: Yale University Press.

El Azayem, Gamal A., and Zari Hedayat-Diba. 1994. "The Psychological Aspects of Islam: Basic Principles of Islam and Their Psychological Corollary." *The International Journal for the Psychology of Religion* 4 (1): 41–50.

Elfawal, Mohamed A. 1999. "Cultural Influence on the Incidence and Choice of Method of Suicide in Saudi Arabia." *The American Journal of Forensic Medicine and Pathology* 20 (2): 163–168.

Elias, Brenda, Javier Mignone, Madelyn Hall, Say P. Hong, Lyna Hart, and Jitender Sareen. 2012. "Trauma and Suicide Behaviour Histories Among a Canadian Indigenous Population: An Empirical Exploration of the Potential Role of Canada's Residential School System." *Social Science & Medicine* 74 (10): 1560–1569.

Elliott-Farrelly, Terri. 2004. "Australian Aboriginal Suicide: The Need for an Aboriginal Suicidology?" *Australian e-journal for the Advancement of Mental Health* 3 (3): 138–145.

Engelhardt Jr., H. Tristram. 1998. "Physician-Assisted Suicide Reconsidered: Dying as a Christian in a Post-Christian Age." *Christian Bioethics* 4 (2): 143–167.

Engelhardt Jr., H. Tristram. 2013. "Orthodox Christian Bioethics: Medical Morality in the Mind of the Fathers." In *Religious Perspectives on Bioethics*, edited by John F. Peppon, Mark J. Cherry, and Ana Iltis, 21–30. London: Taylor & Francis Group.

Eskin, Mehmet. 2004. "The Effects of Religious Versus Secular Education on Suicide Ideation and Suicidal Attitudes in Adolescents in Turkey." *Social Psychiatry and Psychiatric Epidemiology* 39 (7): 536–542.

Ferngren, Gary B. 1989. "The Ethics of Suicide in the Renaissance and Reformation." In *Suicide and Euthanasia*, edited by Baruch A. Brody, 155–181. Dordrecht: Springer.

Fong, Grace S. 2001. "Signifying Bodies: The Cultural Significance of Suicide Writings by Women in Ming-Qing China." *Nan nü* 3 (1): 105–142.

Gambetta, Diego. 2005. *Making Sense of Suicide Missions.* Oxford: Oxford University Press on Demand.

Garrison, Elise P. 1991. "Attitudes Toward Suicide in Ancient Greece." *Transactions of the American Philological Association (1974–2014)* 121: 1–34.

Garroutte, Eva Marie, Jack Goldberg, Janette Beals, Richard Herrell, Spero M. Manson, and AI-SUPERPFP Team. 2003. "Spirituality and Attempted Suicide Among American Indians." *Social Science & Medicine* 56 (7): 1571–1579

Garssen, M. J., J. Hoogenboezem, and A. J. Kerkhof. 2006. "Suicide Among Migrant Populations and Native Dutch in The Netherlands." *Nederlands tijdschrift voor geneeskunde* 150 (39): 2143–2149. PMID: 17059089.

Gearing, Robin E., and Danwhite A. Lizardi. 2009. "Religion and Suicide." *Journal of Religion and Health* 48 (3): 332–341.

Goldney, Robert D. 2002. "Is Aboriginal Suicide Different? A Commentary on the Work of Colin Tatz." *Psychiatry, Psychology and Law* 9 (2): 257–259.

Griffin, Miriam. 1986. "Philosophy, Cato, and Roman Suicide: I." *Greece and Rome (Second Series)* 33 (01): 64–77.

Halkias, Georgios T. 2015. "The Self-Immolation of Kalanos and Other Luminous Encounters Among Greeks and Indian Buddhists in the Hellenistic World." *Journal of the Oxford Centre for Buddhist Studies* 8: 163–186.

Hallett, Darcy, Michael J. Chandler, and Christopher E. Lalonde. 2007. "Aboriginal Language Knowledge and Youth Suicide." *Cognitive Development* 22 (3): 392–399.

Hami, Hinde, Abdelmajid Soulaymani, Maria Windy, Abdelrhani Mokhtari, and Rachida Soulaymani. 2010. "Young Men and Suicide in Morocco." *Journal of Men's Health* 7 (3): 327.

Hanna, Morid M., Etemad A. A. El-Shereef, and Azza H. Griew. 2011. "Study of Pattern and Outcome of Suicidal Methods Used in Benghazi City–Libya." *Egyptian Journal of Forensic Sciences* 1 (3): 124–132.

Hicks, Jack. 2007. "The Social Determinants of Elevated Rates of Suicide Among Inuit Youth." *Indigenous Affairs* 4: 30–37.

Hill, Timothy D. 2004. *Ambitiosa Mors: Suicide and the Self in Roman Thought and Literature*. New York: Routledge.

Hirsch, Jameson K. 2006. "A Review of the Literature on Rural Suicide." *Crisis* 27 (4): 189–199.

Hjern Anders, and Peter Allebeck. 2002. "Suicide in First-and Second-Generation Immigrants in Sweden a Comparative Study." *Social Psychiatry and Psychiatric Epidemiology* 37 (9):423–429. https://doi.org/10.1007/s00127-002-0564-5. PMID: 12242618.

Hope, Valerie. 2009. *Roman Death: The Dying and the Dead in Ancient Rome*. London: Continuum.

Hunter, Ernest M., and Desley Harvey. 2002. "Indigenous Suicide in Australia, New Zealand, Canada and the United States." *Emergency Medicine* 14 (1): 14–23.

Hunter, Ernest M., Joseph Reser, Mercy Baird, and Paul Reser. 1999. *An Analysis of Suicide in Indigenous Communities in North Queensland: The Historical, Cultural and Symbolic Landscape*. Brisbane: Department of Social and Preventive Medicine, University of Queensland.

Ineichen, Bernard. 1998. "The Influence of Religion on the Suicide Rate: Islam and Hinduism Compared." *Mental Health, Religion & Culture* 1 (1): 31–36.

Joe, Sean, Silvia Sara Canetto, and Daniel Romer. 2008. "Advancing Prevention Research on the Role of Culture in Suicide Prevention." *Suicide and Life-Threatening Behavior* 38 (3): 354–362.

Joiner, Thomas. 2010. *Myths About Suicide*. Cambridge: Harvard University Press.

Judd, Fiona, Anne-Marie Cooper, Caitlin Fraser, and Julian Davis. 2006. "Rural Suicide—People or Place Effects?" *Australian and New Zealand Journal of Psychiatry* 40 (3): 208–216.

Kamal, Zein, and Kate Miriam Loewenthal. 2002. "Suicide Beliefs and Behaviour Among Young Muslims and Hindus in the UK." *Mental Health, Religion & Culture* 5 (2): 111–118.

Kaplan, K. J., M. Innamorati, E. Piacentini, M. Battuello, D. Lester, R. Tatarelli, and M. Pompili. 2012. "Religiosity and Suicide: A Selective Overview of Abrahamic Religions (Judaism, Christianity and Islam) Versus Greek Narratives." In *Exploring the Phenomenon of Suicide,* edited by Maurizio Pompili, 445–462. London: Nova Science Publishers

Karam, Elie G., Ranja V. Hajjar, and Mariana M. Salamoun. 2008. "Suicidality in the Arab World Part II: Community Studies." *Arab Journal of Psychiatry* 19 (1): 1–24.

Kazuyoshi, H. 2009. "Fasting unto Death: Holy Ritual or Suicide?" The 3rd BESETO Conference of Philosophy. University of Tokyo, Komaba and Hongo,

Tokyo, Japan, January 10–11, Accessed June 3, 2017. http://utcp.c.u-tokyo.ac.jp/events/pdf/017_Hotta_Kazuyoshi_3rd_BESETO.pdf.

Keast-O'Donovan, Kona. 2017. "Social and Cultural Factors Contributing to Aboriginal Suicide Rates: A Critical Analysis." *Undergraduate Awards* 10: 1–12. http://ir.lib.uwo.ca/undergradawards_2017/10.

Keown, Damien. 1998. "Suicide, Assisted Suicide and Euthanasia: A Buddhist Perspective." *Journal of Law and Religion* 13 (02): 385–405.

Keown, Damien, and John Keown. 1995. "Killing, Karma and Caring: Euthanasia in Buddhism and Christianity." *Journal of Medical Ethics* 21 (5): 265–269.

Khan, Murad Moosa, and Hashim Reza. 2000. "The Pattern of Suicide in Pakistan." *Crisis: The Journal of Crisis Intervention and Suicide Prevention* 21 (1): 31.

Khan, Farooq, and George Tadros. 2013. "Physician-Assisted Suicide and Euthanasia in Indian Context: Sooner or Later the Need to Ponder!" *Indian Journal of Psychological Medicine* 35 (1): 101.

Khashan, Hilal. 2003. "Collective Palestinian Frustration and Suicide Bombings." *Third World Quarterly* 24 (6): 1049–1067.

Kleine, Christoph. 2006. "'The Epitome of the Ascetic Life': The Controversy Over Self-Mortification and Ritual Suicide as Ascetic Practices in East Asian Buddhism." In *Asceticism and Its Critics: Historical Accounts and Comparative Perspectives*, 153–177. Oxford: Oxford University Press.

Kovan, Martin. 2013. "Thresholds of Transcendence: Buddhist Self-Immolation and Mahāyānist Absolute Altruism Part One." *Journal of Buddhist Ethic* 20: 775–812.

Koveleskie, Michaela. 2015. "The Spirituality of the Vow of Sallekhana: Not All Decisions to Die Are Suicidal." Accessed June 24, 2017. https://www.iup.edu/WorkArea/DownloadAsset.aspx?id=193211.

Kral, Michael J. 2012. "Postcolonial Suicide Among Inuit in Arctic Canada." *Culture, Medicine and Psychiatry* 36 (2): 306–325.

Kral, Michael J., and Idlout, Lori. 2016. "Indigenous Best Practices" In *Critical Suicidology: Transforming Suicide Research and Prevention for the 21st Century*, edited by Jennifer White, Ian Marsh, Michael, J. Kral and Jonathan Morris, 229–243 Vancouver: UBC Press.

Kumar, Virendra. 2003. "Burnt Wives—A Study of Suicides." *Burns: Journal of the International Society for Burn Injuries* 29 (1): 31–35.

Kushner, Harvey W. 1996. "Suicide Bombers: Business as Usual." *Studies in Conflict & Terrorism* 19 (4): 329–337.

Laidlaw, James. 2005. "A Life Worth Leaving: Fasting to Death as Telos of a Jain Religious Life." *Economy and Society* 34 (2): 178–199.

Laios, K., G. Tsoukalas, M. I. Kontaxaki, M. Karamanou, and G. Androutsos. 2013. "Suicide in Ancient Greece." *Psychiatrike = Psychiatriki* 25 (3): 200–207.

Lakhan, Shaheen. 2008. "Hinduism: Life and Death." *Student British Medical Journal* 16: 310–311.

Lamotte, Etienne. 1987. "Religious Suicide in Early Buddhism." *Buddhist Studies Review* 4 (2): 105–118.

Langhinrichsen-Rohling, Jennifer, John Friend, and Ashley Powell. 2009. "Adolescent Suicide, Gender, and Culture: A Rate and Risk Factor Analysis." *Aggression and Violent Behavior* 14 (5): 402–414.

Lawson-Te Aho, Keri, and James H. Liu. 2010. "Indigenous Suicide and Colonization: The Legacy of Violence and the Necessity of Self-Determination." *International Journal of Conflict and Violence* 4 (1): 124–133.

Lee, Sing, and Arthur Kleinman. 2000. "Suicide as Resistance in Chinese Society." In *Chinese Society: Change, Conflict and Resistance*, 2nd ed., edited by Elizabeth J. Perry and Mark Selden, 289–311. London: Routledge.

Leenaars, Antoon A. 2006. "Suicide Among Indigenous Peoples: Introduction and Call to Action." *Archives of Suicide Research* 10 (2): 103–115.

Lester, David. 2006. "Suicide and Islam." *Archives of Suicide Research* 10 (1): 77–97.

Lester, David, and Adebowale Akande. 1994. "Attitudes About Suicide Among the Yoruba of Nigeria." *The Journal of Social Psychology* 134 (6): 851–853.

Lipsicas, Cendrine Bursztein, Ilkka Henrik Mäkinen, Danuta Wasserman, Alan Apter, Ad Kerkhof, Konrad Michel, Ellinor Salander Renberg, Kees van Heeringen, Airi Värnik, and Armin Schmidtke. 2012. "Gender Distribution of Suicide Attempts Among Immigrant Groups in European Countries—An International Perspective." *European Journal of Public Health* 23 (2): 279–284.

Lykouras, Lefteris, Effie Poulakou-Rebelakou, Costas Tsiamis, and Dimitri Ploumpidis. 2013. "Suicidal Behaviour in the Ancient Greek and Roman World." *Asian Journal of Psychiatry* 6 (6): 548–551.

Mahir, Siham, Abdelmajid Soulaymani, Hind Hami, Abdelrhani Mokhtari, Doha Benali, Lahcen Ouammi, Maria Windy, and Rachida Soulaymani Benchekh. 2012. "Suicide by Poisoning in the Souss-Massa-Draa Region of Morocco." *Sante publique* (Vandoeuvre-les-Nancy, France) 25 (3): 343–350.

March, Ian. 2016. "Critiquing Contemporary Suicidology." In *Critical Suicidology: Transforming Suicide Research and Prevention for the 21st Century*, edited by Jennifer White, Ian Marsh, Michael J. Kral, and Jonathan Morris, 15–30. Vancouver: UBC Press.

McCarthy, John F., Frederic C. Blow, Rosalinda V. Ignacio, Mark A. Ilgen, Karen L. Austin, and Marcia Valenstein. 2012. "Suicide Among Patients in the Veterans Affairs Health System: Rural–Urban Differences in Rates, Risks, and Methods." *American Journal of Public Health* 102 (S1): S111–S117.

McCoy, Brian. 2007. "Suicide and Desert Men: The Power and Protection of kanyirninpa (Holding)." *Australasian Psychiatry* 15 (Suppl. 1): S63–S67.

Mekaoui, Nour, Lamiae Karboubi, Fatima Zahra Ouadghiri, and Badr Sououd Benjelloun Dakhama. 2016. "Epidemiological Aspects of Suicide Attempts Among Moroccan Children." *Pan African Medical Journal* 24: 112.

Meng, Liu. 2002. "Rebellion and Revenge: The Meaning of Suicide of Women in Rural China." *International Journal of Social Welfare* 11 (4): 300–309.

Morad, Mohammed, Efrat Merrick, Amir Schwarz, and Joav Merrick. 2005. "A Review of Suicide Behavior Among Arab Adolescence." *The Scientific World Journal* 5: 674–679.

Moradi S., and A. Khademi. 2002. "Evaluation of Suicides Resulting in Death in Iran, Comparing with the World Rates." *Legal Medicine* 8 (27): 16–21 [In Persian].

Moss Candida, R. 2012. *Ancient Christian Martyrdom: Diverse Practices, Theologies, and Traditions.* London: Yale University Press.

Murray, Miles. 2001. "Plato on suicide ('Phaedo' 60C-63C)." *Phoenix* 55 (3/4): 244–258.

Mystakidou, Kyriaki, Efi Parpa, Eleni Tsilika, Emmanuela Katsouda, and Lambros Vlahos. 2005. "The Evolution of Euthanasia and Its Perceptions in Greek Culture and Civilization." *Perspectives in Biology and Medicine* 48 (1): 95–104.

Nelson, Graham, Ryan Hanna, Alaa Houri, and Bonnie Klimes-Dougan. 2012. "Protective Functions of Religious Traditions for Suicide Risk." *Suicidology Online* 3: 59–71.

Nesbitt, Eleanor. 2015. "Sikhism: A Guide for the Perplexed." *British Journal of Religious Education* 37 (2): 213–215.

Nimbalkar, Namita. 2007. "Euthanasia: The Hindu Perspective." National Seminar on Bio Ethics, 24–25 January.

Nrugham, Latha. 2015. "Sati-Suicide by Widows Sanctioned by Hindu Scriptures and Society?" *Suicidologi* 18 (1):19–22.

Papadimitriou, John D., Panayiotis Skiadas, Constantinos S. Mavrantonis, Vassilis Polimeropoulos, Dimitris J. Papadimitriou, and Kyriaki J. Papacostas. 2007. "Euthanasia and Suicide in Antiquity: Viewpoint of the Dramatists and Philosophers." *Journal of the Royal Society of Medicine* 100 (1): 25–28.

Park, B. C. 2004. "Sociopolitical Contexts of Self-Immolations in Vietnam and South Korea." *Archives of Suicide Research* 8 (1): 81–97.

Park, B. C., and Lester David. 2012. "Rural and Urban Suicide in South Korea." *Psychological Reports* 111 (2): 495–497.

Payne, Sarah, Viren Swami, and Debbi L. Stanistreet. 2008. "The Social Construction of Gender and Its Influence on Suicide: A Review of the Literature." *Journal of Men's Health* 5 (1): 23–35.

Pedahzur, Ami, ed. 2006. *Root Causes of Suicide Terrorism: The Globalization of Martyrdom.* New York: Routledge.

Perry Elizabeth J., and Mark Selden. 2000. *Chinese Society: Change, Conflict and Resistance.* New York: Routledge.

Petersen, Nils Arne. 2011. "Contextualising Early Christian Martyrdom." In *Early Christianity in the Context of Antiquity*, edited by Jakob Engberg, Uffe Holmsgaard Eriksen, and Anders Klostergaard, 276. Frankfurt-am-Main: Peter Lang.

Peterson, Lucy. 2014. "This Is My Body: Exploration of Sexuality, Christianity, and Suicide." *Senior Theses*. Paper 853. http://digitalcommons.bard.edu/sr-theses/853.

Ping-Cheung, Lo. 1999. "Confucian Views on Suicide and Their Implications for Euthanasia." In *Confucian Bioethics*, 69–101. Dordrecht: Springer.

Ping-Cheung, Lo. 2010. "Euthanasia and Assisted Suicide from Confucian Moral Perspectives." *Dao* 9 (1): 53–77.

Pritchard, Colin, and Siraj Amanullah. 2007. "An Analysis of Suicide and Undetermined Deaths in 17 Predominantly Islamic Countries Contrasted with the UK." *Psychological Medicine* 37 (3): 421–430.

Razvodovsky, Yury, and Andrew Stickley. 2009. "Suicide in Urban and Rural Regions of Belarus, 1990–2005." *Public Health* 123 (1): 27–31.

Retterstøl, Nils. 1993. *Suicide: A European Perspective*. Cambridge: Cambridge University Press.

Reuter, Christoph. 2004. *My Life Is a Weapon: A Modern History of Suicide Bombing*. Princeton: Princeton University Press.

Rezaeian, Mohsen. 2010. "Suicide Among Young Middle Eastern Muslim Females." *Crisis* 31 (1):36–42.

Rist, J. M. 1969. *Stoic Philosophy*. Cambridge: Cambridge University Press.

Rosen, George. 1971. "History in the Study of Suicide." *Psychological Medicine* 1 (4): 267–285.

Schotsmans, Paul T. 2003. "Relational Responsibility, and Not Only Stewardship: A Roman Catholic View on Voluntary Euthanasia for Dying and Non-dying Patients." *Christian Bioethics* 9 (2): 285–298.

Shah, Ajit, and Mahmood Chandia. 2010. "The Relationship Between Suicide and Islam: A Cross-National Study." *Journal of Injury and Violence Research* 2 (2): 93.

Shurei, Shai. 1997. *Don't Burn the Brides*. Delhi: Ajanta.

Singh, Gurmuhk. 2015. "Sikh View About Euthanasia and Suicide: Not Assisted Dying, but Guru-Guided Living, Is the Sikh Way." Accessed June 23, 2017. https://www.sikhnet.com/news/sikh-view-about-euthanasia-and-suicide.

Somasundaram, O. S., C. Kumar Babu, and I. Aruna Geethayan. 1989. "Suicide Behaviour in the Ancient Civilizations with Special Reference to the Tamils." *Indian Journal of Psychiatry* 31 (3): 208.

Spallek, Jacob, Anna Reeske, Marie Norredam, Signe Smith Nielsen, Jessica Lehnhardt, and Oliver Razum. 2014. "Suicide Among Immigrants in Europe—A Systematic Literature Review." *European Journal of Public Health* 25 (1): 63–71.

Stompe, Thomas, and Kristina Ritter. 2010. "Religion and Suicide-Part 1: The Attitudes of Religions Towards Suicide." *Neuropsychiatrie: Klinik, Diagnostik, Therapie und Rehabilitation: Organ der Gesellschaft Osterreichischer Nervenarzte und Psychiater* 25 (3): 118–126.

Sweeney, George. 1993. "Irish Hunger Strikes and the Cult of Self-Sacrifice." *Journal of Contemporary History* 28 (3): 421–437.

Szasz, Thomas Stephen. 2002. *Fatal Freedom: The Ethics and Politics of Suicide.* Syracuse: Syracuse University Press.

Takeda, Arata. 2010. "Suicide Bombers in Western Literature: Demythologizing a Mythic Discourse." *Contemporary Justice Review* 13 (4): 455–475.

Tighe, Joe, Kathy McKay, and Myfanwy Maple. 2015. "'I'm Going to Kill Myself If You Don't …': Contextual Aspects of Suicide in Australian Aboriginal Communities." *International Journal of Culture and Mental Health* 8 (1): 1–12.

Truth and Reconciliation Commission of Canada. 2015. *Canada's Residential Schools: Reconciliation: The Final Report of the Truth and Reconciliation Commission of Canada.* Vol. 6. Montreal: McGill-Queen's University Press.

Turhan, Ebru, Tacettin Inandi, Mustaffa Aslan, and Cem Zeren. 2011. "Epidemiology of Attempted Suicide in Hatay, Turkey." *Neurosciences* 16 (4): 347–352.

van Hooff, Anton. 2004. "Paetus, It Does Not Hurt: Altruistic Suicide in the Greco-Roman World." *Archives of Suicide Research* 8 (1): 43–56. https://doi.org/10.1080/13811110490243859.

Vijayakumar, Lakshmi. 2004. "Altruistic Suicide in India." *Archives of Suicide Research* 8 (1): 73–80.

Vijayakumar, Lakshmi, Jane Pirkis, Tran Thanh Huong, Paul Yip, Rohini De A. Seneviratne, and Herbert Hendin. 2008. "Socio-Economic, Cultural and Religious Factors Affecting Suicide Prevention in Asia." In *Suicide and Suicide Prevention in Asia,* edited by Herbert Hendin, Michael Phillips, Lakshmi Vijayakumar, Jane Pirkis, Hong Wang, Paul Yip, Danuta Wasserman, Jose Bertolote, and Alexandra Fleischmann, 19–30. Geneva: World Health Organization.

Warshall, Peter. 1999. "Holy Suicide." *Whole Earth* 99: 76.

Werner, Karel. 2008. "Death, Rebirth and Personal Identity in Buddhism." *International Journal* 10: 19–39.

Wexler, Lisa Marin. 2006. "Inupiat Youth Suicide and Culture Loss: Changing Community Conversations for Prevention." *Social Science & Medicine* 63 (11): 2938–2948.

Wexler, Lisa Marin, and Joseph P. Gone. 2012. "Culturally Responsive Suicide Prevention in Indigenous Communities: Unexamined Assumptions and New Possibilities." *American Journal of Public Health* 102 (5): 800–806.

White, Jennifer, Ian Marsh, Michael, J. Kral, and Jonathan Morris. 2016. *Critical Suicidology: Transforming Suicide Research and Prevention for the 21st Century.* Vancouver: UBC Press.

WHO. 2008. "Suicide and Suicide Prevention in Asia Overview." Accessed June 25, 2017. http://www.who.int/mental_health/publications/suicide_prevention_asia/en/.

WHO. 2015. "Suicide Rates, Age Standardized—Data by Country." Accessed June 28, 2017. http://apps.who.int/gho/data/view.main.MHSUICIDEASDRREGv?lang=en.

WHO. 2017a. "Methods of Suicide: International Suicide Patterns Derived from the WHO Mortality Database." Accessed June 28, 2017. http://www.who.int/bulletin/volumes/86/9/07-043489/en/.

WHO. 2017b. "Suicide: Fact Sheet." Accessed June 28, 2017. http://www.who.int/mediacentre/factsheets/fs398/en/.

Wiltshire, Martin G. 1983. "The 'Suicide' Problem in the Pāli Canon." *Journal of the International Association of Buddhist Studies* 6 (2): 124–140.

Witztum, Eliezer, and Daniel Stein. 2012. "Suicide in Judaism with a Special Emphasis on Modern Israel." *Religions* 3 (3): 725–738.

Yang, Guo, and Xi Lu. 2008. "The Weapon of the Weak: A Tentative Study on the Reasons Why Women in Song Dynasty Committed Suicide." *Journal of Lanzhou University* 5: 20.

Yasan, Aziz, Ramazan Danis, Lut Tamam, Sehmus Ozmen, and Mustafa Ozkan. 2008. "Socio-Cultural Features and Sex Profile of the Individuals with Serious Suicide Attempts in Southeastern Turkey: A One-Year Survey." *Suicide and Life-Threatening Behavior* 38 (4): 467–480.

Yilmaz, Tarik A., and Anita Riecher-Rössler. 2012. "Attempted Suicide in Immigrants from Turkey: A Comparison with Swiss Suicide Attempters." *Psychopathology* 45: 366–373. https://doi.org/10.1159/000337266

Yip, Paul S. F., Chris Callanan, and Hok Pan Yuen. 2000. "Urban/Rural and Gender Differentials in Suicide Rates: East and West." *Journal of Affective Disorders* 57 (1): 99–106.

Yip, Paul S. F., Ka Y. Liu, Jianping Hu, and X. M. Song. 2005. "Suicide Rates in China During a Decade of Rapid Social Changes." *Social Psychiatry and Psychiatric Epidemiology* 40 (10): 792–798.

Zhang, Jie. 2014. "The Gender Ratio of Chinese Suicide Rates: An Explanation in Confucianism." *Sex Roles* 70 (3–4): 146–154.

Zhang, Jie, and Eric Y. Liu. 2012. "Confucianism and Youth Suicide in Rural China." *Review of Religious Research* 54 (1): 93–111.

CHAPTER 3

Why Peace and Conflict Studies?

> Conflict is ubiquitous. That ubiquity stems from the basic fact of human individuality and difference in the context of limited physical and social resources. [But] conflict itself should not be confused with violence… intentional harming (Boulding 2000, 89).
>
> Although we live in a world of many grave problems, oppression, and violence, we also live in a world of much good and great potential for a better future. While we are unable to transform this world overnight, we can take important steps to change it, to solve its problems, lift its oppression, and minimize the many applications of violence (Sharp 2005, 1).
>
> We must set our feet deeply into the geographies and realities of what destructive relationships produce, what legacies they leave, and what breaking their violent patterns will require. Second, we must explore the creative process itself, not as a tangential inquiry, but as the wellspring that feeds the building of peace. In other words, we must venture into the mostly uncharted territory of the artist's way as applied to social change, the canvases and poetics of human relationships, imagination and discovery, and ultimately the mystery of vocation for those who take up such a journey (Lederach 2005, 5).

Peace and Conflict Studies (PACS) is a field of study that seeks ultimately to construct and disseminate knowledge about both the causes of conflict and violence and the means to transform violent conflict into nonviolent conflict. While this field is relatively young in the realm of academia having only developed post-World War II, PACS is a growing

K. Standish, *Suicide through a Peacebuilding Lens*,
https://doi.org/10.1007/978-981-13-9737-0_3

field within both developed and developing countries (Bartolucci and Gallo 2011). Suicide has rarely been studied within PACS, despite being a form of violence and global phenomenon that kills over 800,000 individuals every year (World Health Organization 2014). This chapter seeks to review the existing literature to explore the background and normative goal of conflict transformation of PACS as a field to highlight the problematic lack of suicide research within PACS. This chapter will begin by exploring PACS as a field of study and will then briefly explore the ways in which other disciplines, including psychology, medicine, sociology, anthropology, social work, criminal justice, political studies and philosophy, are compatible with PACS research. Following this, the chapter will explore PACS' normative goal surrounding the transformation of violence before examining the parameters of the transformation of violence in relation to suicide. While this chapter will briefly encapsulate what the field of PACS entails the primary goal of this chapter is to create a rationale for why the field should focus on suicide with an eventual aim to posit peacebuilding suicide as a viable and valuable avenue of violence eradication via peace praxis (explored in Chapter 9).

Peace and Conflict Studies as a Field of Study

Origins of Peace and Conflict Studies

In order to examine PACS as a field of study, it is important to contextualize PACS within history. PACS emerged as a field of study in reaction to global politics and the way in which global politics were studied in the context of the post-World War II world (Ryan 2003). Drago (2012) highlights that most academics viewed the introduction of PACS to be an emotional reaction to events such as the Vietnam War. Some academics assert that the roots of PACS extend to the post-World War I decades, when the devastation caused by industrial warfare led to the creation of the League of Nations and many questions surrounding how to avoid war again (Robben and Ferrándiz 2007). Stephenson (1999) identifies Quincy Wright and Lewis Fry Richardson as the forefathers of the field as they carried out separate quantitative analyses of causes of war in the 1930s. Perceptions of PACS from academics outside the field have historically been varied and continue to be divided. The field is global and growing and includes a variety of alternatively designated fields such as peace research, peace and conflict research, conflict studies and studies in nonviolence.

PACS has developed through several waves of progress since its conception as the study of Alternative Dispute Resolution (Byrne 2015). The first wave of progress was the Conflict Management and Peace Studies wave of the 1960s/1970s (Byrne 2015; Reimer et al. 2015). This was followed by the Conflict Analysis and Resolution wave of the 1980s and the Conflict Transformation wave of the 1990s. The most recent wave of progress has been the PACS wave of the twenty-first century, which places importance on peacebuilding, human rights and social justice (Byrne 2015; Reimer et al. 2015). Ryan (2003) underlines that developments in PACS have been directly linked to the context of global affairs, with the Cold War, the end of the Cold War and the ethnic-based conflicts of the 1990s having large impacts on the direction of the field's research.

Defining Peace and Conflict Studies

There has been much difficulty in defining PACS within the literature due to the diversity of the field, which has subfields including but not limited to peace education, peacebuilding and restorative justice (Reimer et al. 2015). Further confusion is also created due to the range in names from Peace Studies to Conflict Research that are utilized to denote the landscape of PACS, and the occurrence of fields with similar titles such as Conflict Resolution that are separate disciplines. This can, understandably, lead to confusion when trying to define PACS. Andrew Mack (1985, 23) highlighted that it may be easier to conceive of PACS as a 'syndrome', by which he meant as a collection of characteristics that tend to group together. He identified the most important characteristics of PACS as optimism, broad definitions of peace and violence, policy-oriented research, commitment to particular values and interdisciplinarity. Stephenson (1999) identifies similar characteristics of PACS, highlighting that PACS is value explicit, policy-oriented, international and interdisciplinary. These are four characteristics of PACS on which the PACS field generally agrees, thus these four characteristics will be expanded on to create a clearer image of PACS as a discipline.

Key Characteristics of Peace and Conflict Studies

The first key characteristic of PACS is that PACS is value explicit, which means that there are basic values that all within the field share and embody. Galtung asserted that without commitment to values, there is little difference between PACS and social studies (cited in Ryan 2003).

The value that is most explicit within PACS is a commitment to peace as a value in itself (Stephenson 1999; Galtung 1985). This value essentially denotes the negativity of violence and guides academics and practitioners within the field to prevent or stop violence wherever possible. A related value of PACS is the belief that violence is not inherent to human nature. This value is a fundamental aspect of the normative goal of PACS to transform violence into nonviolent conflict, as it results in recognition of violence as intentional and thus unnecessary as a form of conflict (Ryan 2003). Discovering and addressing the roots of violent conflict is highly important to effective conflict transformation and sustainable peace (Galtung 2007).

There are some concerns, however, that the optimistic inclinations of PACS researchers create scepticism of theories of natural aggression and lead these researchers to focus on avoidable causes of violence in order to sidestep other root causes of violent conflict (Ryan 2003). Further criticism concerns the ability of PACS to create unbiased knowledge while being value explicit (although this could be lodged as a criticism of all research standpoints, not just the one held in PACS) (Ryan 2003). Regardless, PACS as a field is explicit about the entrenched values regarding the importance of peace and the lack of necessity of violence. Developing intervention tools and techniques that can transform violence is the natural application of these values and is the major peace technology of the field: *peacebuilding*.

The second characteristic that defines PACS is that PACS is policy-oriented. Stephenson (1999) describes PACS as procedural as it aims to describe, explain and recommend policy surrounding the conditions of peace to governments and social movements. This is differentiated from International Relations research, which is characteristically limited to description and explanation. The practical nature of PACS is the basis of this characteristic of policy orientation, as PACS was developed to answer questions and develop tools surrounding violent conflicts (Ryan 2003). There is an intrinsic link thus between practice, theory and research within PACS (Reimer et al. 2015). As Graf et al. (2007, 128) state, 'better theory leads to better practice', a major aim of the field. Reimer et al. (2015) highlight that research has provided significant alternatives to the typical pattern of responding to conflict with violence and asserts that conflict is being transformed around the world as theory guides practice and practice in turn guides further inquiry.

The third characteristic of PACS evident within the literature is that PACS utilizes an international (rather than state-centric) perspective. In establishing this international perspective, academics highlight that the protection of national interests that results from a state-centric viewpoint does not enhance peace (Jeong 2000). Jeong (2000) underlines that state institutions are unwilling and unable to respond to the basic needs of populations, which is a major barrier to achieving peace. Stephenson (1999) further distinguishes PACS from fields such as International Relations by highlighting that PACS considers violence and peace from an individual level to a global level, rather than being limited to examining issues from a single-state perspective as other disciplines can be. Furthermore, Stephenson emphasizes that PACS is not limited to accepting the nation state as a given and can thus focus on other systems of organization. As Byrne (2015) points out, conflict occurs on multiple levels of human engagement including local, regional, national and/or global and can be interpersonal, community-based or both. In order to create comprehensive theories surrounding conflict that apply in a multitude of contexts, PACS therefore has adopted not only an international perspective but also an interdisciplinary perspective.

The final characteristic defining PACS as a field is interdisciplinarity. As a field, PACS has a broad disciplinary base (Stephenson 1999; Bartolucci and Gallo 2011). Ryan (2003) underlines that an interdisciplinary approach allows for academics in the field to avoid state-centric focuses and enables effective responses to more complex situations, such as the ethnic conflicts of the 1990s. Johan Galtung (2010) also strongly advocates the importance of the interdisciplinary approach of PACS, likening the necessity of including other disciplines to the way in which medical research needs disciplines such as chemistry, anatomy and pathology. Bartolucci and Gallo (2011) emphasize that problems cannot be classified by disciplines and that PACS should be viewed as a thematic area that other disciplines can contribute to.

There are some complications that emerge from the 'interdisciplinary' approach. This interdisciplinarity has led to so much diversity within PACS, that, as mentioned, it can be quite challenging for people from both within and without to define the field. Galtung (2010) raises another issue; the human and social sciences that are utilized in the PACS interdisciplinary approach are the product of the post-Westphalian state system and harmfully reify the state and state system. However,

Galtung sees globalization as the long-term remedy to this issue as the state system may be replaced by systems of regions. Galtung stresses that the definitive test of validity is not objective knowledge but intersubjective knowledge, with principles and conclusions that are agreed on by a wide range of observers. As such, interdisciplinarity is not only beneficial in allowing for multifaceted approaches to complex situations but also for creating and validating shared knowledge.

The Compatibility of Peace and Conflict Studies

PACS' interdisciplinarity can be appreciated in two ways: the first relates to the prevalence of training in the discipline where many if not most of its practitioners hold academic education outside the field. It is typical in any PACS department to have individuals with advanced degrees and training in, for example, social work, education, political studies and sociology and, despite increases in academic minors, majors, masters and doctoral programs worldwide, limited if not *no* individuals with academic training exclusively in PACS. This may change in the coming generations but for now, one of the reasons PACS is so interdisciplinary is that it has to be. The second relates to the fertile collaborative and attentive nature of the field that seeks to communicate and perceive circumstances and dispositions from holistic and multifaceted positions. PACS is filled with people who presume they need others to understand and manifest change and this leads them to instinctively reach out and partner with people. In the following section, eight fields will briefly be explored to elucidate their complementarity with the PACS platform.

Psychology

Psychology is the study of behaviour and mental processes, and the compatibility of psychology and PACS is such that the field of peace psychology already exists (Christie 1999). Christie (1999) states that there is much value in peace psychology, not least due to the ability to develop theories surrounding peaceful or violent behaviours that are sensitive on both a micro-level and a macro-level. Galtung (2010) highlights that psychology may help in understanding the intricacies of intrapersonal and interpersonal conflict. The aim of peace psychology is to mitigate and prevent episodes of violence at all levels of society, as well as to promote the constant pursuit of social justice (Cohrs et al. 2013).

Medicine

Medicine is the study and practice of the prevention, diagnosis and treatment of disease. There are several areas where medicine and PACS are compatible in regards to research, such as the effects of conflict on physical, mental and population health and the role that health initiatives can play in peacebuilding (MacQueen and Santa-Barbara 2000). As war has been framed within the medical discipline as a public health problem, medicine has an opportunity and ability to address issues of conflict and peacebuilding (Santa-Barbara 2006; MacQueen and Santa-Barbara 2000).

Sociology

Sociology is the study of human society and social behaviour and seeks to contextualize behaviour within societies (Lee 2016). While sociology has generally concentrated the study of violence on social and criminal violence, there is much potential for interdisciplinary work with PACS in this area (Lee 2016). Sociology's perspectives on social and structural violence, and concepts such as social belonging, may provide significant insight within PACS. The sociological concentration on the link between social structures and behaviour may additionally aid understanding of how violent structures and relations produce further violent relations (Galtung 2010).

Anthropology

Anthropology is a discipline that studies humanity worldwide (Lee 2016) and can be separated into cultural (social) and physical domains. Galtung (2010) suggests that cultural anthropology could aid in PACS through enabling understanding of how violent cultures represent themselves and what peace cultures for individuals and groups might look like and cultural anthropology may be able to highlight gender perspectives on war, violence and peace (Hydle 2006). As humans are cultural creatures, we learn violence (or nonviolence) the same way we learn language. Cultural anthropology can provide many insights into how humans transmit and symbolically enshrine certain norms and values related to conflict, violence, nonviolence and peace whereas physical anthropology can contribute understandings about how we, as greater apes, are similar or distinct from other primates in our social and biological compositions and behaviour.

Social Work

Social work is fundamentally a practice-based field where academics and practitioners seek to develop responses and frameworks for supporting vulnerable individuals. Kafula (2016) highlights the need for social work literature and practice to engage with the concepts of peace, human rights and development, as social workers are often situated where they can advance tangible outcomes of human rights and social justice. Moreover, social workers and social work research often deal with the violence of all types, which is a fundamental issue of PACS. The similarity in the policy-oriented nature of PACS and social work may also aid in compatibility to unearth systematic forms of violence or conflict transformation.

Criminal Justice

Criminal justice as a field concentrates on criminal behaviour and societal responses to criminal behaviour (Bernard and Engel 2001). There is much compatibility between the criminal justice field and PACS, particularly surrounding issues of transitional justice, restorative justice and reconciliation. Further areas of compatible study also include the responses to and rehabilitation of those who have committed crimes, such as in situations of disarmament, demobilization and reintegration that relate to the relationship between victim/perpetrator in the aftermath of violent conflict.

Political Studies

Political studies is the study of power, authority, governments and conflict at local, national and international levels. This has obvious crossovers with PACS, as these are foundational issues of PACS. However, unlike PACS political studies is ultimately bound to the state system (Stephenson 1999). The inclusiveness of PACS means that studying state systems and their roots and responses to violence and conflict (not to mention their efforts to foster and sustain positive peace) are complementary concerns. Political studies is highly compatible with PACS research and may be able to illuminate issues surrounding the use and abuse of power, processes of legitimization and contestation and the reality of institutions that hold and reproduce power over time (Galtung 2010).

Philosophy
With a focus on the fundamental nature of knowledge and existence, philosophy concentrates on questions of ethics and logic. Violence, conflict and peace have long been concerns of philosophy alongside issues of power and governance, which demonstrates mutual points of interest and compatibility with PACS. Webel (2007) highlights that in some locations, progressive and peace-oriented philosophers have created organizations such as 'Concerned Philosophers for Peace' and the field has inherited philosophies of nonviolence from both Eastern and Western philosophical traditions. To list just one example, the Eastern concept of *ahimsa* is considered one of the foundational tenets of the PACS field and is interpreted as nonviolence or non-harming. The philosophical roots of PACS include dozens of works but none challenge or dismiss the original philosophical foundation of the field appreciated in the Eastern concept of *ahimsa*: violence is intolerable.

The Normative Goal of Peace and Conflict Studies: Transformation of Violence

Defining Violence and Peace Within PACS

The ultimate goal of PACS as a field is to achieve the transformation of violent conflict into nonviolent conflict. In order to understand the goal of transforming violence, it is important to first distinguish between conflict and violence. The easiest way to define conflict is: discord. Conflict can be considered a disagreement that causes one or more parties involved in a specific circumstance to perceive threats to their needs, concerns or interests (Reimer et al. 2015) but also an inherent aspect of life that can be a valuable tool for social change (Bartolucci and Gallo 2011). Webel confirms that conflict can be constructive and valuable and promote and increase peace where involved parties utilize nonviolent means to reach compromises and create achievable solutions.

Conflict can be contrasted now with violence: a deliberate harm that is destructive. Galtung (1969, 168) defines violence as 'the cause of the difference between the potential and the actual', where violence prevents an individual from reaching their full human potential. Galtung breaks violence down into three categories: direct, indirect (structural) and cultural. Direct violence is violence that can be traced back to an actor/ actors and is an event; indirect (structural) violence is systemic violence that is built into the structures of society and results in power inequality and ultimately unequal life chances via discrimination; and cultural violence is violence that is legitimized through aspects of human culture (Galtung 1990) that, importantly, is a root of direct and indirect forms of violence. These theories of violence have been highly impactful and utilized within the literature of PACS (Gleditsch et al. 2014).

When discussing the definition of violence, it is also important to discuss the definition of peace. The definition of peace differs between disciplines, which can impact the aims and means of conflict transformation. Galtung (1969) distinguished peace to exist in two categories, which are widely accepted within PACS. The first category is *negative peace*, which is achieved by an absence of direct violence. This is the understanding of peace that is most common, both within the context of international politics and within the interdisciplinary debates of war and peace (Gleditsch et al. 2014; Bartolucci and Gallo 2011; Webel 2007). The second category of peace is *positive peace*, and positive peace is achieved by the negation of structural/cultural violence too (Gleditsch et al. 2014). Positive peace is the only sustainable form of peace, as negative peace allows for structural and cultural violence to continue. Concepts such as social justice respect for human rights and ecological balance are included in the conceptualization of positive peace, as these things are necessary for humanity and the presence of these conditions diminishes structural and cultural violence (Ryan 2003). Webel (2007) depicts the concept of negative and positive peace by placing peace on a spectrum, with negative peace representing weak peace at one end of the spectrum and positive peace at the other representing a strong, durable peace. Webel underlines that positive peace demonstrates the need for 'active individual and collective self-determination and emancipatory empowerment' (2007, 8). This is because he conceives that positive peace is not something that can be provided externally, instead requiring the active participation of those who wish to attain peace. This notion is supported by Graf et al. (2007), who assert that peace must be organic. This means that peace should be developed from within, rather than imposed on a society or imported into a society and highlights the importance of ownership over peace of those who actually live within conflicted societies.

The conceptualization of positive peace has progressed from Galtung's (1969) premise that negative peace was comprised of non-aggression or the cessation of direct violence whereas positive peace included the absence of cultural and structural forms of violence and conditions needed to maintain full humanity. Harris (2004) conceptualized positive peace as a triangulation between social justice, ecological sustainability and nonviolence and later scholarship has expanded on Harris' tenet to include (positive) relationship (Standish et al. forthcoming) envisioning positive peace as a quadrant of four interconnected value/practices.

The separation between negative and positive peace is a key feature of PACS research and scholarship. Where negative peace research, scholarship and practice is aligned with militaries and/or paramilitaries and notions of direct or potential direct violence, positive peace research, scholarship and practice is concerned with fostering peace technologies that prevent or inhibit all forms of violence.[1]

Transforming Violence Within PACS

The normative basis of PACS is to discover tools and techniques for transforming violent conflict so that societies can become self-reliant in dealing with conflicts using nonviolent means (Graf et al. 2007). The normative commitment of PACS to transform violent conflict is based on PACS' central values of the importance of nonviolence and the negativity of violence (Reimer et al. 2015). Galtung (2007) underlines that violence is seen as the result of untransformed conflict, with Graf et al. (2007) recognizing that violent responses to conflict have the impact of further engraining conflict and preventing possible solutions. Academics within PACS recognize that conflict is an inherent part of life, thus individuals, groups and societies need to develop tools so that they can respond to conflict positively and nonviolently (Bartolucci and Gallo 2011).

The term conflict transformation was first used within the field by John Paul Lederach and is a framework for both describing and understanding the root causes of and responses to conflict (Reimer et al. 2015). Conflict transformation ultimately aims to change responses to conflict so that no violence is involved (Reimer et al. 2015). Graf et al. (2007) highlight that the transformation of violence is a dynamic process as it requires not only changes to the institutions and structures of society, but also requires changes of attitudes, relationships, the culture of peace and the way in which conflicts are approached so that circumstances are conducive to peace. These changes are ongoing and must be adjusted to suit developing contexts. A network of academics and practitioners belonging to TRANSCEND International, including Johan Galtung, have developed the TRANSCEND approach in relation to conflict transformation (Ryan 2003; Graf et al. 2007). TRANSCEND have held workshops, produced training manuals and run courses surrounding this topic. This approach outlines that conflict transformation must occur to prevent violence and operationalizes academic approaches to conflict transformation. These approaches set out the importance of identifying, transforming and transcending attitudes, behaviours and contradicting desires that lead to conflict (Galtung 2007). The importance of dialogue in conflict transformation is highlighted repeatedly, both within the TRANSCEND model and in unrelated literature. The role of PACS practitioners in transforming violence is to have dialogue with participants that will support self-reflection processes, increase the capacity for empathy, enable creativity in imagining a new reality and empower the use of nonviolent strategies. Furthermore, PACS practitioners must recognize their own biases so that these can be taken into account (Graf et al. 2007).

Transforming Violence Relative to Suicide in Peace and Conflict Studies

While there is much research surrounding the transformation of conflict within PACS, there is very little research addressing suicide (see Chapter 1). This lack of research of suicide is in relation to conflict transformation as well as the field of PACS in general, which has not engaged with the concept of suicide. Within this section, the current parameters of the field in relation to the transformation of suicidal violence will be explored.

Suicide as a Form of Violence

The first parameter surrounding the transformation of violence within PACS is that all forms of violence should be transformed. As previously discussed, this normative goal is based on the explicit values surrounding peace that are characteristic of PACS. As the transformation of violence in relation to suicide has not been addressed within PACS, it must be assumed that this is either an oversight or a denial that suicide is a form of violence. Following Galtung's (1990) definitions of violence, suicide definitely classifies under at least one category. All suicide is direct violence as it is violence being carried out by an individual that will result in the loss of potential. There is space for debate here, as some academics may argue that in the case of euthanasia and/or assisted suicide there may not be clear loss of potential when the quality of life is already low. However, as there is choice to end life inherent in decisions relating to euthanasia and/or assisted suicide, this should still be classified as loss of potential. Further debate may occur surrounding the fact that there is autonomy in completing suicide, at least in some cases. There may also be structural and cultural violence associated with suicide however, with social factors having been shown to impact the likelihood of suicide (Stack 2000). As such, this parameter of transforming violence highlights that the transformation of suicide as a form of violence should be viewed as important within PACS, particularly where there are high rates of suicide.

An Obligation to Research Suicide—The Seville Statement

Another parameter surrounding the transformation of conflict is not related solely to PACS but applies to all fields of study. In 1986, twenty leading scientists from around the globe wrote the Seville Statement for UNESCO, which states that violence and war are not inherent within human nature but are products of culture (cited in Adams 1989). This statement also highlighted that as violence and war were of human creation, so could be peace. This places the onus of achieving peace on humans as individuals and as a group. While suicide is not directly mentioned in the Seville Statement it follows that, as a form of violence, suicide is not an inherent biological behaviour. This is a key notion because, as the Seville Statement notes, if individuals believe that violence is biologically determined then there is less likelihood that they will engage in activities that encourage peace (1986, cited in Adams 1989).

As well as acknowledging that there is a social rather than biological basis for violence, the Seville Statement highlights that it is the responsibility of scientists within academic disciplines to address the most dangerous and destructive activities of our species (1986, cited within Adams 1989). This includes the responsibility of studying issues that are divisive or tricky to navigate, such as suicide. As such, PACS academics and practitioners have a responsibility to engage in suicide research. Given the strong link between research, theory and practice within PACS, a focus on suicide could lead to the transformation of a form of violence that is a global issue.

Conclusion

Throughout this chapter, the literature of PACS has been reviewed in order to examine PACS as a field, as well as the key concept of violence transformation. This examination was then used to highlight the current parameters of the PACS field in relation to suicide. PACS aims to study the causes and transformation of all types of violence at all levels that it occurs, but very little research has been carried out surrounding suicide. Though it has not been recognized as such within PACS, suicide is a form of violence. Furthermore, academics have a recognized obligation to research all topics regardless of difficulty. These factors highlight that PACS has a problematic research gap surrounding suicide, particularly in relation to research that explores tools for transforming suicidal violence.

Note

1. The separation between negative and positive peace will be revisited in Chapter 9 when the proposal of peacebuilding suicide via relationship is explored more in depth.

References

Adams, David. 1989. "The Seville Statement on Violence: A Progress Report." *Journal of Peace Research* 26 (2): 113–121.

Bartolucci, Valentina, and Giorgio Gallo. 2011. "Beyond Interdisciplinarity in Peace Studies: The Role of System Thinking." *SSRN Electronic Journal*: 1–34, viewed August 20, 2018. https://www.researchgate.net/publication/256009105_Beyond_Interdisciplinarity_in_Peace_Studies_The_Role_of_System_Thinking.

Bernard, Thomas, and Robin Engel. 2001. "Conceptualizing Criminal Justice Theory." *Justice Quarterly* 18 (1): 1–30.

Boulding, Elise. 2000. *Cultures of Peace: The Hidden Side of History*. Syracuse: Syracuse University Press.

Byrne, Sean. 2015. "Foreword: Peace and Conflict Studies—The Cutting Edge." In *Transformative Change: An Introduction to Peace and Conflict Studies*, edited by Laura Reimer, Cathryne Schmitz, Emily Janke, Ali Askerov, Barbara Strahl, and Thomas Matyók, vii–ix. London: Lexington Books.

Christie, Daniel. 1999. "Peace Studies: The Multidisciplinary Foundations of Peace Psychology." *Peace and Conflict: Journal of Peace Psychology* 5 (1): 95–99.

Cohrs, J. Christopher, Daniel J. Christie, Mathew P. White, and Chaitali Das. 2013. "Contributions of Positive Psychology to Peace Towards Global Wellbeing and Resilience." *American Psychologist* 68 (7): 590–600.

Drago, Antonino. 2012. "Peace Studies and the Peace Movement." *Peace Research* 44 (2): 163–191.

Galtung, Johan. 1969. "Violence, Peace and Peace Research." *Journal of Peace Research* 6 (3): 167–191.

Galtung, Johan. 1985. "Twenty-Five Years of Peace Research: Ten Challenges and Some Responses." *Journal of Peace Research* 22 (2): 141–158.

Galtung, Johan. 1990. "Cultural Violence." *Journal of Peace Research* 27 (3): 291–305.

Galtung, Johan. 2007. "Introduction: Peace by Peaceful Conflict Transformation—The TRANSCEND Approach." In *Handbook of Peace and Conflict Studies*, edited by Charles Webel and Johan Galtung, 14–23. New York: Routledge.

Galtung, Johan. 2010. "Peace Studies and Conflict Resolution: The Need for Transdisciplinarity." *Transcultural Psychiatry* 47 (1): 20–32.

Gleditsch, Nils Petter, Jonas Nordkvelle, and Håvard Stran. 2014. "Peace Research: Just the Study of War?" *Journal of Peace Research* 51 (2): 145–158.

Graf, Wilfried, Gudrun Kramer, and Augustin Nicolescou. 2007. "Counselling and Training for Conflict Transformation and Peace-Building: The TRANSCEND Approach." In *Handbook of Peace and Conflict Studies*, edited by Charles Webel and Johan Galtung, 123–142. New York: Routledge.

Harris, Ian. 2004. "Peace Education Theory." *Journal of Peace Education* 1 (1): 5–20.

Hydle, Ida. 2006. "An Anthropological Contribution to Peace and Conflict Research." *Contemporary Justice Review* 9 (3): 257–267.

Jeong, Ho-Won. 2000. *Peace and Conflict Studies: An Introduction*. New York: Ashgate.

Kafula, Chilala S. 2016. "The Role of Social Work in Peace, Human Rights and Development in Africa." *Journal of Education and Social Policy* (5): 115–121.

Lederach, John Paul. 2005. *The Moral Imagination: The Art and Soul of Building Peace*. Oxford: Oxford University Press.

Lee, Bandy. 2016. "Causes and Cures V: The Sociology and Anthropology of Violence." *Aggression and Violent Behaviour* 27: 158–163.

Mack, Andrew. 1985. *Peace Research in the 1980s*. Canberra: Australian National University.

MacQueen, Graeme, and Joanna Santa-Barbara. 2000. "Peace Building Through Health Initiatives." *British Medical Journal* 321 (7256): 293–296.

Reimer, Laura, Cathryne Schmitz, Emily Janke, Ali Askerov, Barbara Strahl, and Thomas Matyók. 2015. "Introduction to the Field of Peace and Conflict Studies." In *Transformative Change: An Introduction to Peace and Conflict Studies*, edited by Laura Reimer, Cathryne Schmitz, Emily Janke, Ali Askerov, Barbara Strahl, and Thomas Matyók, 1–18. London: Lexington Books.

Robben, Antonius, and Francisco Ferrándiz. 2007. *Multidisciplinary Perspectives on Peace and Conflict Research*. Spain: University of Deusto.

Ryan, Stephen. 2003. "Peace and Conflict Studies Today." *The Global Review of Ethnopolitics* 2 (2): 75–82.

Santa-Barbara, Joanna. 2006. "Medicine, Peace and Public Policy." *Croation Medical Journal* 47 (2): 352–355.

Sharp, Gene. 2005. *Waging Nonviolent Struggle: 20th Century Practice and 21st Century Potential*. Boston: Porter Sargent Publishers, Inc.

Stack, Steven. 2000. "Suicide: A 15-Year Review of the Sociological Literature Part I: Cultural and Economic Factors." *Suicide and Life-Threatening Behavior* 30 (2): 145–162.

Standish, Katerina, Heather Devere, Adan Suazo, and Rachel Rafferty. Forthcoming. *The Springer Handbook of Positive Peace*. Singapore: Springer.

Stephenson, Carolyn. 1999. "Peace Studies, Overview." In *The Encyclopedia of Violence, Peace and Conflict*, edited by L. Kurtz and J. Turpin, 2809–2820. San Diego: Academic Press.

Webel, Charles. 2007. "Introduction: Toward a Philosophy and Metapsychology of Peace." In *Handbook of Peace and Conflict Studies*, edited by Charles Weber and Johan Galtung, 3–13. New York: Routledge.

World Health Organization. 2014. *Preventing Suicide: A Global Imperative*. Geneva: World Health Organization.

CHAPTER 4

Medical Suicide

> It is a safe assumption that virtually everyone who desires death also simultaneously desires life. (Joiner 2010, 64)

This book seeks to comprehensively engage with the phenomena of suicide so that the interdisciplinary field of Peace and Conflict Studies (PACS) can appreciate and incorporate this form of violence in our research, our practice and our peacebuilding. In order to facilitate such an inclusive perspective, this book engages with the phenomena collected under the rubric of 'suicide' from a variety of standpoints that include disciplinary, cultural, historical and terminological. To this end, this chapter, along with the following chapter, aims to explore the numerous forms of suicide that have been identified within existing literature. It is hoped that through such a broad terminological appreciation that scholar/practitioners will approach the work of violence eradication and intervention in the realm of 'suicide' in a meaningful and intentional manner.

In the social sciences, health sciences and humanities, different apertures of observance, reflection and action are appropriate and normalized. In the interdisciplinary field of PACS, there may be several approaches to the work of conflict recognition, transformation and intervention that require a wide-ranging appreciation of a form of addressed violence.[1] This book argues that suicide, as a form of violence, is an appropriate subject matter for our field to address. But what is suicide, how do we appreciate the phenomena included in what is collapsed

K. Standish, *Suicide through a Peacebuilding Lens*,
https://doi.org/10.1007/978-981-13-9737-0_4

into the word suicide? And, when we conceive of an act of suicide can we grasp the conduct, the drive and/or circumstances that led to the behaviour so we, as a field, can work towards intervention? Intervention (action that seeks to help, assist or improve a situation) does not occur without recognition first so how we perceive of an issue or activity greatly affects our ability to comprehend and encounter it (Lederach 2005). Ideally, a well-defined demarcation has to happen in our minds before the important work of transformation[2] begins—our capacity to meaningfully understand suicide will affect our perception of what suicide is. So how do we see it? Do we imagine a depressive person committing self-harm or a suicide bomber using their violent death as an assault on innocent bystanders? We instinctively know these two incarnations of suicide are dissimilar but do we also consider other forms of suicide violent acts?

Medical Suicide vs. Instrumental Suicide

Suicide occurs due to the existence and interaction of genetic, psychological, social and cultural risk factors combined with experiences of trauma and loss (Zalsman et al. 2016). This book will outline and describe a suicide typology that includes seven types of suicide distinguished in the contemporary literature. These typologies can be separated into two categories: those that are medically related, including mental illness, assisted suicide and euthanasia; and those that are instrumental, not medically related and notably less typical, including homicide-suicides, martyrdom operations (altruistic suicide), daredevil suicides and protest suicides. In *Myths About Suicide*, Joiner averred:

> Should suicide terrorism be analysed along with what one might term more conventional suicide-related deaths? Few in any suicide theorists have confronted this issue head-on; those who have commented state fairly emphatically and from the outset that these kinds of phenomena are beyond their scope. Yet the phenomenon of suicide terrorism can be viewed as one of the key geopolitical challenges of our time and a phenomenon like suicide terrorism obviously does have suicidal elements. Therefore, it seems to me incumbent on the theorist either to explain why it is "out of bounds" or else to take in on directly. (2010, 99–100)

This book endeavours to do the latter because it is of great importance to explore the differing typologies of suicide from a PACS perspective as the differences between typologies greatly impact recognition, research and intervention strategies. The goal of such an exploration is to nuance our appreciation of this form of violence (self-violence that can also include the harming of others) so we can engage more meaningfully with this prevalent form in our conceptualizations and our peacebuilding.[3] As peacebuilding is an intervention (we discussed the morality of intervention in Chapter 3) it is critical that we use appropriate perceptions as a foundation for action. The goal of separating *medical* and *instrumental* suicide in this book is to firmly establish our perch in our peacebuilding work. Similar to the separation of the terms cultural genocide and instrumental genocide in the last century, the separation of *medical* suicide and *instrumental* suicide in PACS will aid scholars to cease ignoring or bypassing this phenomenon of violence due to terminological instability (Fig. 4.1).

Throughout this chapter, the medically related typologies of mental illness, assisted suicide and euthanasia will be explored. This exploration includes definitions, patterns of the forms and themes within the relevant literature included, in order to highlight not only the realities of different types of suicides but also to illustrate the key areas of relevant research that have been and are being undertaken.

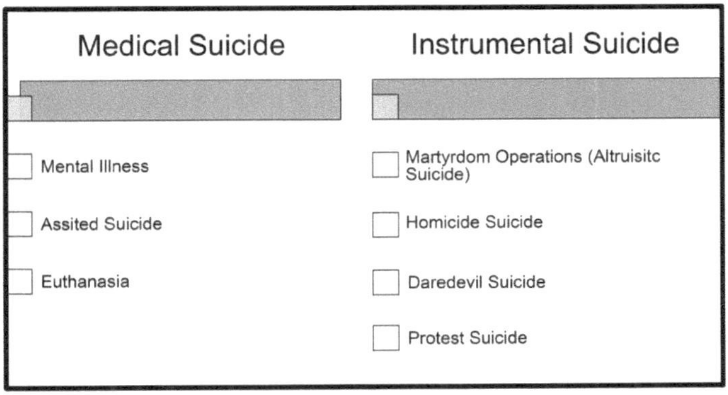

Fig. 4.1 *Medical* and *instrumental* suicide

Mental Illness and Suicide

The first form of suicide to be discussed within this chapter is suicide related to mental illness. Mental illnesses, also known as mental disorders or psychiatric disorders within the literature, include but are not limited to mood disorders such as depression, anxiety and bipolar disease, alcohol and substance abuse problems and schizophrenia. Psychological autopsy studies in the developing world have consistently discovered that 90% (Phillips 2010) of suicides suffered from a mental disorder at the time of their death.[4] These figures are not necessarily reflected in the developing world: while similar associations have been found in India, researchers have found that mental illness has much less significance in relation to suicide in China (Hawton and van Heeringen 2009). Mental illness, often greatly stigmatized in developing countries where mental health is not prioritized, may impact the reported and recognized levels of mental illness in suicides.

Different countries having different suicide rates have been related to variance in cultural factors as well as differences in reporting suicides. However, there is similarity in the suicide rates between countries with comparable sociocultural and socio-economic experiences, which Goldney (2015) suggests is due to a base rate of suicide that is essentially related to mental illness. Goldney (2013, cited in Goldney 2015) explains the variations from this base rate between countries as due to differing psychosocial factors: how the mind functions and the impact of the surrounding social environment. This base rate of mental illness highlights a strong connection between mental illness and suicide and suggests that mental illness is not being adequately treated in order to prevent suicides. The prevalence of mental illness in cases of suicide must also be noted in relation to the forms of suicide—such prevalence means that mental illness is likely to be present in individuals whom complete suicides that can be classified under a different type—while suicides occur in individuals who suffer from mental illnesses, the mental state of individuals who endure physical disability or physiological illness is not necessarily considered, i.e. a terminal cancer patient of advanced age request physician-assisted suicide does not preclude mental illness but the physical illness may mask a mental illness that goes unaddressed because of the circumstances. This demonstrates the complexity of suicide especially in double-diagnosis situations so that appropriate violence intervention (and suicide prevention) measures can be used in relation to mental illness.

Patterns of Suicide Relating to Mental Illness

While nearly all forms of mental illness are strongly associated with an increased risk of suicide, the patterns of suicide surrounding different types of mental illness demonstrate that there are forms of mental disorder that dominate this experience (Panczak et al. 2013). Mood disorders or affective disorders, the main types of which are depression, bipolar disorder and anxiety, are the leading mental illnesses of those individuals that complete suicide (Hawton and van Heeringen 2009). Of these affective disorders, depression, also known as major depressive disorder, is the most commonly experienced mental disorder by those that complete suicide. Although depression is a medical diagnosis of mental unwellness it can stem from myriad factors that relate to everything from our physiological instrument (the mind, the body) as well as our environments, living conditions and life experiences of loss, trauma and abuse. Depression (in many forms) is experienced by an estimated 300 million people worldwide and includes symptoms of low moods including misery and melancholy, a lack of interest and enjoyment in life as well as reduced energy, fatigue, sleep difficulties, inability to concentrate and feelings of worthlessness and despair. Depressive symptoms can range from mild to severe and can last for several weeks or years (WHO 2017). During severe depressive episodes, it is unlikely that the sufferer is able to function in regard to social, employment or domestic activities and such circumstances of incapacity can exacerbate the condition further. Depression results from complex social, psychological and biological factors but fortunately can often be treated with combinations of psychotherapy and medication. Despite the hopeful information that treatment is possible, worldwide, less than half of those who suffer from depression receive treatment. The heavy burden of mental illness is something that is born globally and without widespread attention and intervention the base rate of mental illness is unlikely to shrink (WHO 2017). The good news is that the majority of people who suffer with depression do not complete suicide and while depression is present in more than half of the individuals that do complete suicide (highlighting depression's prevalence) only about 4% of individuals who suffer from depression take their own lives (Hawton and van Heeringen 2009).

Bipolar disorder, another of the mood disorders, is less prevalent than depression globally but is more lethal. Bipolar disorder combines depression with episodes of mania where self-esteem and mood are heightened, creating great highs and very low lows. Suicide attempts are very common among those whom suffer from bipolar disorder, with 25–56% attempting suicide at least once in their lifetime and 11–19% completing suicide (de Abreu et al. 2009). Anxiety disorders, the last of the mood disorders, include panic disorders and post-traumatic stress disorder, and, similar to depression, are strongly linked to an increase in suicidal behaviour. The existing literature however is unclear whether this increase is solely due to anxiety disorders or if this increase is the result of the coexistence of other mental illnesses that may also be present (Fawcett 2013). There has been some evidence of anxiety disorders being implicated in completed suicides, but further study is needed to overcome methodological drawbacks that have been experienced thus far (Nepon et al. 2010).

Following mood disorders, substance abuse disorders are the next most dominant factor for suicide in relation to mental illness. A substance abuse disorder is defined as abuse or dependence on alcohol or another drug (Ilgen and Kleinberg 2011). While it is difficult to separate substance abuse disorders from other mental illnesses, particularly depression, individuals with substance abuse disorders are nearly six times more likely to attempt suicide in their lifetime (Ilgen and Kleinberg 2011). This can be broken down by gender—men with a substance abuse disorder are around 2.3 times more likely to die by suicide, while such a disorder among women results in suicide being 6.5 times as likely. A recent study of 6000 adults in addiction treatment that emphasized participants who had committed acts of serious violence such as rape, murder or assault resulting in serious injury found that individuals who had committed grave harm were more than twice as likely to attempt suicide multiple times that those whose actions were nonviolent (Ilgen and Kleinberg 2011). This connection between substance abuse, violence and suicide is backed up by other studies that demonstrate a link between domestic violence, alcohol abuse and a greater likelihood of completing suicide (Connor et al. 2001).

Another two patterns have arisen in relation to mental illness and suicide: co-morbidity and gender. Co-morbidity, or the co-occurrence of more than one mental illness in an individual, is common in individuals that complete suicide (Effinger and Stewart 2012). Such co-morbidity is likely to create a dramatically greater risk for suicide than would be experienced by an individual with just one mental illness. In adolescents that complete suicide, co-occurrence of depression and substance abuse disorders is seen more commonly than either of the mental disorders alone (Effinger and Stewart 2012). Similarly, co-morbidity of anxiety and depression also created stronger association with suicide risk (Mykletun et al. 2007). The second further pattern relates to the gendered component of mental illness and suicide. In high-income countries, women are reported more likely to have depression than men, but male suicide rates are three to four times greater than female suicide rates (Bjerkeset et al. 2008). This has several possible explanations, including greater stigmatization of depression in men which leads to a decrease in male willingness to seek help (especially in older males), men choosing far more lethal methods to end their lives (firearms) than women choose (poison) but ultimately underlines a gendered difference in mental illness and suicide that is frequently seen worldwide (Oliffe et al. 2016). This difference requires further study as there are cultural differences that impact such explanations including religion and spirituality but a gendered component is clearly established within the literature.

Key Themes of Mental Illness/Suicide Literature

Two predominant themes have been identified within the literature of mental illness and suicide: biomedical factors and predisposition to complete suicide, and intervention strategies that have been developed in response to suicides. The next section will explore these topics and their association with medical suicide.

Biomedical Factors and Predisposition to Complete Suicide

This theme explores the link between biomedical factors and the predisposition to complete suicide. A landmark study carried out by Statham et al. in 1998 examined this link by scrutinizing 5995 respondents from an Australian twin registry and discovered that genetic factors accounted for around 45% of differences in suicidal thoughts and behaviours, the other 55% being due to environmental factors (cited in Goldney 2015). Goldney (2015) concludes from this study that this 45% of variation is due to genetically linked biochemical differences that can be connected to mental illness. However, Bondy et al. (2006) dispute that transmission of mental disorders alone is responsible for the link between suicide and genetics, and argue that some individuals have a genetic liability to complete suicide that is related instead to impulsive aggression and other similar personality traits. There is a distinguished connection between familial history and suicide rates with family history of suicide at least doubling the likelihood of an individual completing suicide independently of family history of mental illness (Hawton and Heeringen 2009). As genes interact not only with each other but also with the environment (including nature, culture, and society), the research needed to determine the connection between genetics and suicide is complex and fraught with challenges. Further research is needed on this topic in order to gain further insight into the biological basis of suicidal behaviour and could have great implications on intervention and treatment strategies. Simply put, a genetic marker for suicide could provide valuable and targeted interventions in populations (groups and individuals) that hold such markers and this could lead to environmental inhibitors that deter suicidal gene expression in persons at risk.

The Prevention of Suicide in Those Suffering from Mental Illness
The next theme within mental illness and suicide literature is the prevention of suicide of those suffering from mental illnesses. With the individual ramifications, familial affliction and the burden that suicide places on society, prevention strategies are an integral part of suicide research. The complex nature of suicide has made prevention highly challenging, but increased recognition of suicide as a public health issue has encouraged research, detection, treatment and management of those at risk of suicide (Zalsman et al. 2016). As high-quality treatment has been shown to fail in reducing repetition of self-harm prevention, early intervention of suicide is essential (Kaess 2012). Suicide prevention strategies are complicated, as a multi-level, multifactorial strategy must be applied simultaneously and systematically to a society in order to reduce suicide rates (Krysinska et al. 2016). This is no easy feat.

At an individual level, those who have been diagnosed with a mental illness, those who suffer from suicidal ideation, those who have attempted suicide or self-harm are targets of suicide prevention strategies. While social interventions are essential, the prominence of medical professionals in suicide prevention at the individual level is highly evident within the literature. In regard to those with a mental illness, suicide prevention mainly takes place in the form of treatment such as medication and therapy, both of which have been shown to reduce suicide risk (Zalsman et al. 2016). Two independent studies, the first by Burgess et al. in 2000 and the second by the National Confidential Inquiry in 2001, established that approximately 20% of suicides completed by individuals who had previously received care for mental illness could have been prevented, had a number of issues been overcome (cited in Goldney 2015). These issues include the management of depression and other mental disorders, poor staff-patient relationships and inadequate continuity of care, each of which has implications for the manner in which mental illness is handled by medical professionals at an individual level. For individuals who have attempted suicide or carried out self-harm, the likelihood of completing suicide is majorly increased (Bostwick et al. 2016). Prevention of suicide in such individuals is inherently more difficult, as the period following hospital discharge poses an extremely high risk of suicide. While follow-up mental health care is shown to decrease this risk, gaps between inpatient and outpatient treatment and lack of research surrounding the effectiveness of different clinical interventions for high-risk individuals pose significant barriers to suicide prevention (Olfson et al. 2014).

On a societal level, key suicide prevention methods include community awareness raising, gatekeeper training and restricting access to common means of suicide. Societal suicide prevention is essential, as 30–50% of those who complete suicide do not have medical contact in the year before their death (Schaffer and Sinyor 2016). Leaving suicide prevention to the medical community means that up to half of the individuals who successfully kill themselves are going without treatment. A failure rate of (up to) 50% is the same survival rate as pneumonic plague so absent medical treatment is associated with dire outcomes, which makes societal prevention crucial.

Community awareness raising differs between societies, but is often carried out in schools and through responsible media. However, there is limited evidence of the efficacy of these methods decreasing suicide rates (Zalsman et al. 2016). In one study constraining access to common means of suicide involved restricting access to firearms, which had varying success—there were no great decreases in suicide rates, and evidence instead that individuals were merely finding alternatives to using a firearm to complete suicide (Zalsman et al. 2016). Other restrictions however such as packaging analgesics in smaller packages in the UK and erecting barriers at sites such as bridges where suicide by jumping is common have been shown to reduce suicides, by 43 and 86% respectively (Zalsman et al. 2016). In developing countries where pesticides are the main way of completing suicide, restricting pesticide availability and safer storage of pesticides is seen as the key to reducing deaths, but data is not yet available to demonstrate this (Zalsman et al. 2016). With the importance of suicide prevention, both at an individual level and at societal level, further research on modes, effectiveness and coordination of prevention is essential. From this short exploration, there is no 'single' solution to prevention of medical suicide involving mental illness and a diverse array of possibilities with differing success.

Assisted Suicide and Euthanasia

The second and third suicide forms highlighted within the literature concern assisted suicide and euthanasia. While these are two separate forms of life-ending acts, the similarities of assisted suicide and euthanasia in circumstance, pattern of incidence and literature themes are great enough to discuss the two within the same space. These two typologies are often grouped together both within social discussion and the literature on suicide and medical practice, and individuals that oppose assisted suicide generally also oppose euthanasia. Assisted suicide and euthanasia are greatly controversial practices that are being debated worldwide in regard to legalization and related implications, and are a key topic of contemporary bioethics. Suicide is not illegal in most countries, but aiding and abetting suicide has been widely illegalized and punished, setting the scene for extreme tension in relation to assisted suicide and euthanasia debates (Mishara and Weisstub 2013). The following section will include a definition of both concepts, an exploration of the patterns of individuals whom utilize assisted suicide or euthanasia, and a discussion of themes found within the literature that relate to assisted suicide and euthanasia.

Assisted Suicide

Assisted suicide, also known as physician-assisted suicide (PAS), occurs when a doctor supplies the medical means to end an individual's life, with the individual themselves then self-administering such medical means to end their life (Emanuel et al. 2016). The medical means is typically a prescription for a lethal dose of a muscle-relaxant drug (Marcuccio and McCollum 2015). The World Federation of the Right to Die Societies (2017) accentuates that assisted suicide must be distinguished from euthanasia which involves terminal sedation (where a terminally ill patient is sedated until their eventual death from disease or dehydration), withholding or withdrawing from life-sustaining treatments or utilizing pain medication that quickens death due to side effects. While many other nations are currently debating legalization, as of 2018, assisted suicide was legal only in the Netherlands, Belgium, Luxembourg, Switzerland, Germany, Colombia, and Canada, as well as eight states in the USA: Oregon, Colorado, Hawaii, Washington, Montana, Vermont, Washington, DC, and California. Switzerland was early with assisted suicide where assisted suicide was decriminalized in 1942. In Switzerland, assisted suicide does not require a physician to 'assist' and it is legal given that the assisting individual (not necessarily a doctor) is not doing so for selfish purposes (Gauthier et al. 2015). The legalization of assisted suicide in North America has been relatively recent, with the first official legalization occurring in the US state of Oregon in 1994, and the latest in Canada in 2016. This possibly demonstrates the ongoing and relevant nature of suicide concerns and procedures and perhaps an increasing prevalence due to an ageing population.

Assisted suicide requests and procedures have varying guidelines depending on geographic location. The USA, Canada and Luxembourg require patients to be at least 18 years old, whereas the Netherlands allow patients to participate in assisted suicide from 12 years of age. Belgium has no age limit, but requires the patient to have the capacity to understand the circumstances (Emanuel et al. 2016). Interestingly, all US states require patients to be terminally ill and have a survival prognosis of six months or less but patients do not have to be in unbearable pain or show any symptoms. In comparison, Netherlands, Belgium and Luxembourg do not require patients to be terminally ill but do require that patients have unbearable physical or mental pain with no outlook of improvement (Emanuel et al. 2016). Switzerland has become known as a destination for 'suicide tourism' due to the relaxed laws surrounding assisted suicide, and there are six official organizations that offer suicide assistance—four of which cater to individuals who are not Swiss residents (Gauthier et al. 2015). These relaxed laws mean that individuals don't have to meet any criteria for assisted suicide, other than the assistant being unselfishly involved, and the growth of suicide tourism has been noted with numbers doubling in Switzerland between 2009 and 2012 (Gauthier et al. 2015). As a significant portion of individuals seek and gain assisted suicide as a result of physical illnesses there may be ethical and procedural ramifications of administering lethal assistance to individuals who are experiencing mental illness that need further consideration.

While the scope of this chapter does not permit an exhaustive exploration of mental illness in association with assisted suicide a problematique that is well articulated contends that some mental illnesses are cyclical or temporary and will respond favourably to treatment which places an additional concern for advocates, individuals and professionals regarding making permanent decisions in circumstances that are quite possibly temporary (Biggs and Diesfeld 1995).

Euthanasia

While the term 'assisted suicide' is often used interchangeably with euthanasia in society and in some literature, there is a fundamental difference in the two concepts. Euthanasia is defined as the intentional termination of a patient's life by a physician at the patient's request and ultimately differs from assisted suicide in the procedure proceeding death—assisted suicide includes the patient taking their own life by administering supplied medicine, whereas euthanasia involves the physician ending the patients' life on their behalf (Emanuel et al. 2016). Shekhar and Goel's (2012) classification of euthanasia includes three key criteria: firstly, it must be voluntary on the patient's behalf; secondly, there must be active termination of the patient's life; and finally, the act of euthanasia must be deliberate. Euthanasia is commonly carried out by lethal injections of muscle relaxants, but is not limited to this method. In countries where euthanasia is not legal such behaviour is considered homicide, though punishment is dependent on the circumstances of the death (Mishara and Weisstub 2013).

It is important to note that when discussing euthanasia in this text, active-voluntary euthanasia is being referred to, as there are several variations of euthanasia's definition within the literature. Vaughn (2010) usefully identifies four kinds of euthanasia—active-voluntary, active-involuntary, passive-voluntary and passive-involuntary. Active euthanasia is clarified to be euthanasia where death is caused directly by a physician, as opposed to passive euthanasia where the patient is 'let die' by the ending of life-sustaining treatment. Passive euthanasia is often viewed not as a form of euthanasia but rather as a circumstance of medical practice.[5] There is a clear difference visible between active and passive euthanasia in that passive euthanasia is generally legal provided certain criteria are met, and in that it is seen as a moral and legal right of the patient to refuse treatment even if this treatment is life-sustaining (Vaughn 2010). Moral and legal debate thus surrounds not whether it is right to allow a patient to die, but rather if it is right to deliberately take a patient's life if consent is given. Voluntary euthanasia, the main subject of euthanasia debate, takes place with the consent of the patient while involuntary euthanasia takes place without the patient's consent (usually due to incapacitation or other medical inabilities) and is widely illegalized (Vaughn 2010).

As with assisted suicide, active-voluntary euthanasia is legal in the Netherlands, Belgium, Luxembourg, Switzerland, Colombia and Canada. However, unlike assisted suicide, euthanasia is illegal everywhere in the USA (Emanuel et al. 2016). As such, if euthanasia is carried out in the USA, doctors can be charged with homicide. There is an exception made for passive euthanasia in the USA however, and in many other countries, as it does not involve active termination of a patient's life. End-of-life procedures also differ between countries in relation to euthanasia, with only Colombia requiring a review of the euthanasia process before the final act of euthanasia is actually completed (Emanuel et al. 2016).

Patterns of Individuals Utilizing Assisted Suicide and Euthanasia

As assisted suicide and euthanasia are linked to the ill health of individuals and often occur through official medical channels, there are some patterns that can be observed in relation to the individuals who utilize these options.

Patterns of Assisted Suicide

Unfortunately, there is little research available from developing countries of assisted suicide or euthanasia, which limits these patterns to the few developed states where studies have occurred. Emanuel et al. (2016) utilize an Oregon study from 1998 to 2015 and a further study in Washington from 2009 to 2015 to highlight that individuals typically utilizing assisted suicide are older, white and well educated. A Canadian assessment reports that in 2016 there were almost 1000 assisted deaths (almost 50% of which took place in the Province of Quebec) at the average age of 72 and while there was an even gender balance between recipients of assisted suicide medical causes were split between cancer (56.8%), multiple sclerosis (MS) amyotrophic lateral sclerosis (ALS) (23.2%), and heart and lung diseases (10.5%) (Grant 2017). Similar studies carried out in Belgium gave further evidence of the advanced age of assisted suicide recipients with individuals typically being older (but younger than eighty) and with greater levels of education related to a greater likelihood of an individual completing assisted suicide (cited in Emanuel et al. 2016). The studies carried out in the USA underlined that approximately 75% of individuals that are granted assisted suicides suffer from cancer, with a small minority, generally less than 15%, suffering from neurodegenerative diseases such as MS or ALS (Emanuel et al. 2016). While one might assume that pain is the main motivation behind desiring assisted suicide, less than a third of such individuals have insufficient control over their pain. Instead, in Emanuel et al.'s (2016) study, motivations for assisted suicide are predominantly loss of autonomy and dignity, and being less able to enjoy life's activities.

Patterns of Euthanasia

Individuals utilizing euthanasia follow similar patterns to assisted suicide. Dierickx et al. (2015) carried out a comparison of the expression and granting of euthanasia requests in Belgium, highlighting that the number of euthanasia requests granted grew significantly between 2007 and 2013, going from 55.4 to 76.7% of requests granted. Within the data of these granted requests, trends can be viewed: the dominant users of assisted suicide are patients with cancer, those with college/university education and those who die before reaching 80 years of age; however, patients with diseases other than cancer, those older than 80 years of age and individuals that reside in nursing homes are showing an increase in both requests and granted requests for euthanasia. The authors highlight an overarching development of acceptance of euthanasia within the population for the increase in both the number of requests submitted and the requests granted. Other studies show that individually, loss of dignity and pain are the main motivations behind euthanasia in both the Netherlands and Belgium, again echoing the trend seen of assisted suicides (Emanuel et al. 2016). The 'loss of dignity' factor for individuals who seek either assisted suicide or euthanasia is a critical observation and one that links *medical* suicide with *instrumental* suicide as will be seen in Chapter 5.

Key Themes of Assisted Suicide and Euthanasia Literature

There are certain, shared, themes of assisted suicide and euthanasia within the literature pertaining to the ethical and social ramifications of legalization of assisted suicide and/or euthanasia. The ethical ramifications will be discussed first within this section and include the degree of personal autonomy in choosing assisted suicide/euthanasia and the position of physicians in assisted suicide/euthanasia. Following this, the social ramifications will be covered, such as the devaluation of disability in society and the 'slippery slope' that is presented by assisted suicide and euthanasia. These ramifications are communal to assisted suicide and euthanasia as they centre on the theme of offering death as a medical option within society.

The Existence of Personal Autonomy in Choosing Death

The first ethical ramification of assisted suicide/euthanasia is the existence of personal autonomy in choosing death as a medical option. Personal autonomy is the fundamental argument of assisted suicide/euthanasia advocates, who promote the right for individuals to make decisions that are predominantly their own business (George 2006). This is also referred to within the literature as the 'right to die' with dignity: the ability of an individual to determine their own death if faced with debilitating or terminal illness (Kelly and McLoughlin 2009). As such, some advocates see forcing such individuals to continue their lives if they do not wish to as constituting a lack of respect for their dignity and their independence (George 2006).

Opponents of assisted suicide/euthanasia argue that assisted suicide and euthanasia do not simply allow self-determination but instead create actual dangers that may ultimately undermine personal autonomy of some individuals in selecting these options (Golden and Zoanni 2010; George 2006). This argument is based on the pressures that individuals from vulnerable populations, especially the disabled, ill and elderly, might face while choosing assisted suicide or euthanasia. Such pressures include altruistic concern about burdening their families or worry about going into or remaining in an extended care facility. Disabled individuals may face societal/medical pressures, which will be expanded on later in this chapter in relation to the devaluation of disability that assisted suicide/euthanasia could create. Golden and Zoanni (2010) highlight that instead of being a valid choice, selecting assisted suicide/euthanasia is often viewed as the *only choice*, particularly in situations of where there is a lack in healthcare/care facilities or financial issues. As such, legalization and normalization of assisted suicide/euthanasia may endanger vulnerable populations pressured to end their lives. An alternative proposed is to both increase the quality of aged and palliative care and access to such care.

The Position of Physicians Within Assisted Suicide and Euthanasia

The second ethical ramification identified as a theme within the literature is the position of physicians within assisted suicide and euthanasia practices. Given that the foremost duty of a physician is to promote healing and preserve life, the legalization of assisted suicide and/or euthanasia is a highly contentious issue in the field of medical ethics. The arguments for the ethicalness of assisted suicide/euthanasia are based on a physician's duty to remove pain and have mercy on patients when they are clearly and capably requesting it (Kelly and McLoughlin 2009). In instances where pain management is suitable or irrelevant ethical arguments for life-ending procedures reside in tension with ethics of care.

The fundamental argument for assisted suicide and euthanasia being unethical is that it is ultimately a physicians' duty is to promote healing and preserve life, and, importantly, not to inconvenience, harm or kill for any reason (Vaughn 2010). Yang and Curlin (2016) highlight that for millennia, the Hippocratic Oath has been sworn to protect and heal patients. Opponents of assisted suicide/euthanasia argue that pain can be removed without causing/permitting death and that palliative care can alleviate certain indignities making more drastic (read: permanent) procedures unnecessary (Yang and Curlin 2016). This clashes with the TINA factor: TINA stands for 'there is no alternative' and relates in medicine to exhausting potential avenues of care (Shekhar and Goel 2012). In relation to assisted suicide/euthanasia, this means that there are no sufficient options in regard to palliative care and pain management opening up alternative possibilities such as life-ending procedures. Opponents of assisted suicide/euthanasia deride the existence of the TINA factor and argue that the legalization of life-ending procedures actually undermines and inevitably lowers the quality of palliative services (Schafer 2013). This argument requires further development, as proponents note that territories where assisted suicide and/or euthanasia is available have generally sustained good palliative care systems, and in some places, such as the US state of Oregon, palliative services have actually expanded (Schafer 2013).

Some academics recognize a decreased moral responsibility of physicians in relation to some forms of assisted suicide, due to not ultimately completing the act of inducing patients' death (Vaugh 2010). This is visible in society as assisted suicide is often viewed as a safeguard to euthanasia, demonstrating that euthanasia (at least involuntary forms) is seen as more unethical and amoral (Schafer 2013). This is a disputed point however, as many within both academia and societies do not make any differentiation between the ethicalness of assisted suicide and euthanasia. For many physicians, carrying out assisted suicide/euthanasia processes is both demanding and highly stressful. For some physicians, it is outside of their personal principles to make such a decision and can be fraught with moral trauma (Shekhar and Goel 2012). The experience of administering to patients in life-ending scenarios is distinctive to each instance (and each physician) and due to the uniqueness of every case; it is unwise to make generalizations about how physicians should/could/would handle assisted suicide/euthanasia cases. In practice and in relation to legalization and standardization of assisted suicide/euthanasia procedures however, lack of generalization becomes problematic. The debates surrounding the ethical notion of physicians aiding in assisted suicide and euthanasia continue in many streams and show no consensus on rights, responsibilities or professional (mis)conduct.

The Devaluation of Disability

In regard to the social ramifications of the legalization of assisted suicide and euthanasia, key debates in the literature surround the depreciation or devaluation of living with a disability in society and the 'slippery slope' that is presented by assisted suicide and euthanasia to eliminate the less able from society. The first of these social ramifications of assisted suicide/euthanasia, the devaluation of disability, concerns the idea that normalizing the choice of death (over the choice of living with disability) develops a depreciation of the human experience and an outright danger for those suffering from a disability of suicide. Golden and Zoanni (2010) link studies showing that the vast majority of those completing suicide in both the US state of Oregon and the Netherlands do so out of reasons associated with disability—*with the devaluation of disability*. Such motives include feelings of loss of dignity, and/or the loss of control over various bodily functions. These views connect the choice of suicide to a fear of disability, driven by a society full of prejudices about the dignity and reality of being a person living with a disability, and envisaging a two-tiered system that is dangerous to those with existing disabilities that may be generated from positions that normalize death as preferable to living with a disability (Golden and Zoanni 2010). The first tier of this system includes nondisabled individuals interested in suicide that receive suicide prevention advice/treatment, while the second tier of this scheme involves individuals with existing disabilities that paternalistically receive assisted suicide prescriptions (instead of treatment), ultimately resulting in the diminishment of disabled individuals as a social group as this second tier would result in the possible eradication of a segment of society. For obvious reasons, the normalization (or inclination) of death over disability has far-reaching implications and may influence personal autonomy and agency in decision-making surrounding life-ending processes such as assisted suicide and euthanasia.

Obviously, legalization of assisted suicide and euthanasia change medical practice and could possibly accentuate a subconscious bias that medical professionals could hold towards individuals living with disabilities that may be reinforced and potentially acted on with further legalization (Gill 2010). Some academic literature has shown that in some instances disabled individuals were pressured to sign 'Do Not Resuscitate' forms, or were continuously asked to sign in a manner that suggested this option was in their best medical interest (Heyer 2011). These actions demonstrate a devaluation of disability giving evidence to the predicted 'second tier' of Golden and Zoanni and can be correlated to the 'slippery slope' argument about assisted suicide/euthanasia discussed in the following paragraph. These ongoing debates within the literature continue to be played out in society in places where assisted suicide is legal or may be legalized and, similar to other facets of medical suicide, an ethical consensus is far from tangible.

The Slippery Slope of Assisted Suicide and Euthanasia

The second social ramification highlighted within the assisted suicide/euthanasia literature is the 'slippery slope' that assisted suicide and euthanasia could create within medical practice, judicial processes, and ultimately, society. Slippery slope arguments are frequently utilized in circumstances of morally contested social change and assume that some or all of the consequences of permitting a particular practice are morally unacceptable (Lewis 2007). In relation to assisted suicide and euthanasia, the slippery slope involves the legalization of assisted suicide leading to the approval of voluntary euthanasia, then consequently to the acceptance of involuntary euthanasia. Golden and Zoanni (2010) emphasize the existence of this slippery slope by highlighting that assisted suicide and euthanasia have now become the norm in the Netherlands for individuals suffering from terminal illness. These authors identify a remarkable shift in Dutch policies regarding life-ending procedures: from assisted suicide to euthanasia in terminally ill patients; then to euthanasia for chronically ill patients; to euthanasia for psychological distress; and finally to involuntary euthanasia justified by the medical incompetence of patients to make their own decisions.

There is a counter to this slippery slope theory held by proponents of assisted suicide and euthanasia who utilize available statistics to highlight that there has been no notable rise in involuntary euthanasia in places where assisted suicide/euthanasia is legal. In the Netherlands, where euthanasia has been legal for since 2001, there are 1000 deaths per year comprising 0.8% of all Dutch deaths classed as active-involuntary euthanasia (Vaughn 2010) and in Switzerland, where assisted suicide has been legal since 1942 the rate has actually been dropping since the early 1980s (Francis 2017). While opponents of euthanasia point to this as proof of the slippery slope, proponents highlight that many of these individuals were near death, had become incompetent after initially requesting euthanasia or that the euthanasia was passive rather than active, involving withholding or ending of treatments as opposed to deliberate measures (Vaughn 2010). Although there have been relatively few empirical studies on this issue the studies seem to demonstrate that there is limited evidence that legalization of euthanasia significantly impacts the number of active-involuntary euthanasia cases. This may underline the perception that while social attitudes may have become more positive towards assisted suicide/euthanasia, this is having a limited impact on the established parameters of medical practice thus far. Concerns and considerations surrounding assisted suicide and euthanasia will be expanded and critiqued in Chapter 8.

Conclusion

The three forms of *medical* suicide discussed within this chapter—suicide related to mental illness, assisted suicide and euthanasia—are the forms of suicide experienced most typically (predominantly mental illness) within society. As such, these three types are surrounded by much stigma and controversy and debates continue both in academia and in society around the many related issues, from prevention of suicide in patients with mental illnesses to the devaluation of disability that assisted suicide/euthanasia can generate. The exploration of debates within suicide is continued in the following chapter, which outlines the *instrumental* forms of suicide that occur less often in society; homicide-suicide, martyrdom/altruistic suicide, daredevil suicide, and protest suicide.

Notes

1. While all forms of violence are a form of conflict (discord) not all forms of conflict are violent. Conflict can be productive and creative whereas violence (deliberate harm) is always destructive.
2. Transformation is an act that changes a circumstance of violence into a circumstance of nonviolence.
3. Peacebuilding encompasses acts of intervention that seek to reduce or eliminate harm and support living systems that contribute to full humanity.
4. We recall that in developed nations this number was 98% (Bertolote and Fleischmann 2002) to 100% (Joiner 2010).
5. See the 'doctrine of double effects' in Chapter 8.

References

Bertolote, José Manoel, and Alexandra Fleischmann. 2002. "Suicide and Psychiatric Diagnosis: A Worldwide Perspective." *World Psychiatry* 1 (3): 181–185.

Biggs, Hazel, and Kate Diesfeld. 1995. "Assisted Suicide or People with Depression: An Advocate's Perspective." *Medical Law International* 2: 23–37.

Bjerkeset, Ottar, Pål Romundstad, and David Gunnell. 2008. "Gender Differences in the Association of Mixed Anxiety and Depression with Suicide." *The British Journal of Psychiatry* 192 (6): 474–475.

Bondy, Brigitta, Andreas Buettner, and P. Zill. 2006. "Genetics of Suicide." *Molecular Psychiatry* 11 (4): 336–351.

Bostwick, J. Michael, Chaitanya Pabbati, Jennifer Geske, and Alistair McKean. 2016. "Suicide Attempt as a Risk Factor for Completed Suicide: Even More Lethal Than We Knew." *The American Journal of Psychiatry* 173 (11): 1094–1100.

Connor, Kenneth, Christopher Cox, Paul Duberstein, and Lili Tian. 2001. "Violence, Alcohol and Completed Suicide: A Case Control Study." *The American Journal of Psychiatry* 158 (10): 1701–1705.

De Abreu, Lena, Beny Lafer, Enrique Baca-Garcia, and Maria Oquendo. 2009. "Suicidal Ideation and Suicide Attempts in Bipolar Disorder Type I: An Update for the Clinician." *Revista Brasileria de Psiquiatria* 31 (3): 271–280.

Dierickx, Sigrid, Luc Deliens, Joachim Cohen, and Kenneth Chambaere. 2015. "Comparison of the Expression and Granting of Requests for Euthanasia in Belgium in 2007 vs. 2013." *Journal of the American Medical Association* 175 (10): 1703–1706.

Effinger, Jenell, and David Stewart. 2012. "Classification of Co-occurring Depression and Substance Abuse Symptoms Predicts Suicide Attempts in Adolescents." *Suicide and Life Threatening Behaviour* 42 (4): 353–358.

Emanuel, Ezekiel, Bregje Onwuteaka-Philipsen, John Urwin, and Joachim Cohen. 2016. "Attitudes and Practices of Euthanasia and Physician-Assisted Suicide in the United States, Canada and Europe." *Journal of the American Medical Association* 316 (1): 79–90.

Fawcett, Jan. 2013. "Suicide and Anxiety in DSM-5." *Depression and Anxiety* 30 (10): 898–901.

Francis, Neil. 2017. "Professor Margaret Somerville Should Retract Her Indefensible 'Suicide Contagion' Claim." *Dying for Choice*, April 13. Accessed June 29, 2017. http://www.dyingforchoice.com/docs/SomervilleIndefensibleSCclaimApr2017.pdf.

Gauthier, Saskia, Julian Mausbach, Thomas Reisch, and Christine Bartsch. 2015. "Suicide Tourism: A Pilot Study on the Swiss Phenomenon." *Journal of Medical Ethics* 41 (8): 611–617.

George, Katrina. 2006. "Autonomy and Vulnerability at the Death Bed." *University of Western Sydney Law Review* 10 (1): 139–155.

Gill, Carol. 2010. "No, We Don't Think Our Doctors Are Out to Get Us: Responding to the Straw Man Distortions of Disability Rights Arguments Against Assisted Suicide." *Disability and Health Journal* 3 (1): 31–38.

Golden, Marilyn, and Tyler Zoanni. 2010. "Killing Us Softly: The Dangers of Legalizing Assisted Suicide." *Disability and Health Journal* 3 (1): 16–30.

Goldney, Robert. 2015. "The Importance of Mental Disorders in Suicide." *Australian & New Zealand Journal of Psychiatry* 49 (1): 21–23.

Grant, Kelly. 2017. "At Least 970 People Received an Assisted Death in Canada in 2016: Report." *The Globe and Mail*, April 26. Accessed June 25, 2017. https://www.theglobeandmail.com/news/national/at-least-970-people-received-an-assisted-death-in-canada-in-2016-report/article34823863/?click=sf_globe.

Hawton, Keith, and Kees van Heeringen. 2009. "Suicide." *The Lancet* 373 (9672): 1372–1381.

Heyer, Katharina. 2011. "Rejecting Rights: The Disability Critique of Physician Assisted Suicide." *Studies in Law, Politics and Society* 54: 77–112.

Ilgen, Mark, and Felicia Kleinberg. 2011. "The Link Between Substance Abuse, Violence and Suicide: Implications and Interventions." *Psychiatric Times* 28 (1): 25–27.

Joiner, Thomas. 2010. *Myths About Suicide*. Cambridge: Harvard University Press.

Kaess, Michal. 2012. "Suicide Prevention." *British Medical Journal* 345 (7873): 5.

Kelly, Brendan, and Declan McLoughlin. 2009. "Physician-Assisted Suicide and Psychiatry." *Psychiatry* 8 (7): 276–279.

Krysinska, Karolina, Philip Batterham, Michelle Tye, Fiona Shand, Alison Calear, Nicole Cockayne, and Helen Christensen. 2016. "Best Strategies for Reducing the Suicide Rate in Australia." *Australian and New Zealand Journal of Psychiatry* 50 (2): 115–118.

Lederach, John Paul. 2005. *The Moral Imagination: The Art and Soul of Building Peace*. Oxford: Oxford University Press.

Lewis, Penney. 2007. "The Empirical Slippery Slope from Voluntary to Non-voluntary Euthanasia." *The Journal of Law, Medicine and Ethics* 35 (1): 197–210.

Marcuccio, Elizabeth, and Joseph McCollum. 2015. "Physician-Assisted Suicide: Moral, Ethical and Legal Considerations." *International Journal of Arts & Sciences* 8 (5): 177–187.

Mishara, Brian, and David Weisstub. 2013. "Premises and Evidence in the Rhetoric of Assisted Suicide and Euthanasia." *International Journal of Law and Psychiatry* 36 (5–6): 427–435.

Mykletun, Arnstein, Ottar Bjerkeset, Martin Prince, Simon Overland, and Robert Stewart. 2007. "Anxiety, Depression and Cause-Specific Mortality: The HUNT Study." *Psychosomatic Medicine* 69 (4): 323–331.

Nepon, Josh, Shay-Lee Belik, James Bolton, and Jitender Sareen. 2010. "The Relationship Between Anxiety Disorders and Suicide Attempts: Findings from the National Epidemiological Survey on Alcohol and Related Conditions." *Depression and Anxiety* 27 (9): 791–798.

Olfson, Mark, Steven Marcus, and Jeffrey Bridge. 2014. "Focusing Suicide Prevention on Periods of High Risk." *The Journal of the American Medical Association* 311 (11): 1107.

Oliffe, John, John Ogrodniczuk, Susan Gordon, Genevieve Creighton, Mary Kelly, Nick Black, and Corey Mackenzie. 2016. "Stigma in Male Depression and Suicide: A Canadian Sex Comparison Study." *Community Mental Health Journal* 52 (3): 302–310.

Panczak, Radoslaw, Adrian Spoerri, Marcel Zwahlen, Matthias Bopp, Felix Gutzwiller, and Matthias Egger. 2013. "Religion and Suicide in Patients with Mental Illness or Cancer." *Suicide and Life Threatening Behaviour* 43 (2): 213–222.

Phillips, Michael. 2010. "Rethinking the Role of Mental Illness in Suicide." *American Journal of Psychiatry* 167 (7): 731–733.

Schafer, Arthur. 2013. "Physician-Assisted Suicide: The Great Canadian Debate." *International Journal of Law and Psychiatry* 36 (5–6): 522–531.

Schaffer, Ayal, and Mark Sinyor. 2016. "Building an Evidence Base for National Suicide Prevention Strategies." *Australian & New Zealand Journal of Psychiatry* 50 (2): 175–176.

Shekhar, Skand, and Ashish Goel. 2012. "Euthanasia: India's Position in the Global Scenario." *American Journal of Hospice & Palliative Medicine* 30 (7): 628–631.

The World Federation of Right to Die Societies. 2017. *Is Physician-Assisted Suicide the Same as Euthanasia*. Accessed April 14, 2017. http://www.worldrtd.net/qanda/physician-assisted-suicide-same-euthanasia.

Vaughn, Lewis. 2010. *Bioethics: Principles, Issues and Cases*. New York: Oxford University Press.

World Health Organization. 2017. *Depression: Fact Sheet*. Accessed April 10, 2017. http://www.who.int/mediacentre/factsheets/fs369/en/.

Yang, Tony, and Farr Curlin. 2016. "Why Physicians Should Oppose Assisted Suicide." *The Journal of the American Medical Association* 315 (3): 247–248.

Zalsman, Gil, Keith Hawton, Danuta Wasserman, Kees van Heeringen, Ella Arensman, Marco Sarchiapone, Vladimir Carli, Cyril Höschl, Ran Barzilay, Judit Balazs, György Purebl, Jean Pierre Kahn, Pilar Sáiz, Alejandra Lipsicas, Cendrine Bursztein, Julio Bobes, Doina Cozman, Ulrich Hegerl, and Joseph Zohar. 2016. "Suicide Prevention Strategies Revisited: 10-year Systematic Review." *Lancet Psychiatry*, 3 (7): 646–659.

CHAPTER 5

Instrumental Suicide

> No one really knows why they are alive until they know what they'd die for. (Martin Luther King Jr.)
>
> If you're not ready to die for it, take the word "freedom" out of your vocabulary. (Malcolm X)
>
> Let us all be brave enough to die the death of a martyr. (Mahatma Gandhi)

This chapter explores the second PACS typology of suicide identified: *instrumental suicide*. As the interdisciplinary field of PACS engages with self-killing as a form of violence in future research and practice, it is hoped that pracademics will begin to locate their inquiries in *medical* suicide, *instrumental* suicide (or both), but with nuance and a platform of thoughtfulness that makes visible the diverse forms of this self-directed violence. This may seem simple to say (or ridiculous even) but the idea behind creating gathering spaces for phenomena is to differentiate and focus energy in such a way that does not assume, collapse, manipulate or erase facets of understanding derived from one form of inquiry to another instance (dissimilar in nature) of phenomena. It is not to presume that there are not elements of both kinds of suicide in an act but to deliberately position our inquiries to exclude understandings that are inappropriate, unsuitable or nonchalant. It is not far-fetched (as this chapter will present) to assume that individuals who engage in homicide-suicide, suicide attacks, daredevil actions or suicide protests are not also under some form of psychological stress. It is inappropriate to

K. Standish, *Suicide through a Peacebuilding Lens*,
https://doi.org/10.1007/978-981-13-9737-0_5

conclude that all *instrumental* suicides relate to mental unwellness (or that all forms of euthanasia or assisted suicide are also 'tragic' instances of an un-well mind).

This chapter will identify forms of suicide that are *instrumental*, i.e. life-ending acts connected to a particular aim that involve others. The major difference between *medical* and *instrumental* suicide identified in this study is that *medical* suicide is largely an *act of individuals* (or on behalf of individuals) and instrumental suicides are generally *acts that include or engage other people*. This is not to imply that acts of suicide do not impact others (the average medical suicide is said to affect a minimum of six people intimately) but to present information that supports the conclusion that in *instrumental* suicide the goal of the act tends to involve *others* while in contrast, in *medical* suicide the goal of suicide tends to involve *the self*.

The majority of suicides, globally, relate to mental illness but this chapter will focus on less typical forms of suicide: *homicide-suicide*, *martyrdom*/altruistic suicide, *daredevil* suicide and *protest* suicide. While *instrumental* suicides are demonstrably different to the *medical* typology of suicide (mental illness, assisted suicide and euthanasia), the prevalence of mental illness in those who complete life-ending acts often gives homicide-suicide, martyrdom/altruistic suicide, daredevil and protest suicide a bouquet of illness (either physical, psychological or both). The suicides classified into the two typologies in this book seek to uncover not simply disparate acts but the multitude of motivations that can lead to suicide which may present opportunities for intervention. In this chapter, homicide-suicide, martyrdom/altruistic suicide, daredevil suicide and protest suicide will be explored with definitions, patterns of the forms, investigations of the dominant themes within the surrounding literature as well as their idiosyncrasies. The terms altruistic suicide (collapsed in this chapter into martyrdom operations) and daredevil suicide are contentious terms, which will be further discussed below. The notion of suicide as an act of protest (we will later see) is even more convoluted but needs to be tackled attentively. The rarity of these forms of suicide conceptually and materially limits the literature surrounding these forms of suicide but in every instance I have tried to encapsulate the foundation of understanding for these forms without any claim to being comprehensive. My goal is to illustrate the breadth of phenomena that can (and often are) be collapsed into the catch-all: *suicide* and to distinguish *instrumental* forms from *medical*.

Homicide-Suicide

The first kind of suicide to be covered in this chapter is homicide-suicide. Homicide-suicide is defined as an incident in which an individual kills one or more people and then takes their own life, immediately or within 24 hours (Roma et al. 2012). Though also frequently known as 'murder-suicide', the term homicide-suicide is increasingly preferred in research communities as 'murder' has a specific legal definition that can be determined only after a criminal trial whereas 'homicide' is a term that relates to the act of taking life itself regardless of legal determination (Saint-Martin et al. 2008). While homicide-suicides, at minimum, involve at least two individuals, incidents where only one individual is killed by the perpetrator of a homicide-suicide are frequently referred to as dyadic death (du Plessis and Hlaise 2012). For purposes of clarity, this chapter will not refer separately to dyadic death and homicide-suicide but use the latter term to all forms of deliberate life-taking acts.

Comparisons have shown that homicide-suicide events have different characteristics to both homicides (the killing of one person by another person) and suicide (self-killing), which suggests that homicide-suicide is a distinct behaviour that creates challenges for theories of both homicide and suicide (Manning 2015). A characterization of homicide-suicides would include the fact that such acts are more likely than typical homicide to involve multiple victims, female victims and child victims, and furthermore, are considerably more likely to occur in the home between family members and intimate partners (Manning 2015). Global stats for intentional death that include homicide-suicide are very difficult to come by (Fridel and Zimmerman 2018). Many databases include homicide or suicide stats but not always both. In the USA, homicide-suicides are considered very uncommon with estimates suggesting it affects between 0.2 and 0.38 per 100,000 persons annually (Burgess et al. 2015). The distinctiveness of homicide-suicide as a behaviour (and the generally horrifying nature of these incidences) drives interest and need for further research into this area especially in how it relates to driving or motivating self-killing.

Types of Homicide-Suicides

As is common in various suicide forms, a significant number of individuals who commit homicide-suicides are believed to be mentally ill (Roma et al. 2012), and people who commit homicide (killing others) are also prone to suicide (killing self) (Dayan 2018; Saleva et al. 2007). James Knoll IV (2016) has conceived of five major patterns of homicide-suicides, utilizing a classification system that assesses the victim-perpetrator relationship and the perpetrator's motivation. His classification system was based on Marzuk et al.'s (1992) development of a foundational clinical typology of homicide-suicide classification that has since been proven to be globally consistent (cited in Knoll IV 2016). Homicide-suicides are recorded as occurring across all demographics of society, but are rare in relation to other, much more prevalent kinds of violent death (Eliason 2009). Interestingly, several studies show that in the USA about 75% of homicide-suicides are carried out by white individuals, which must be considered in profiling people at risk of homicidal behaviour and homicide-suicide (Riedel 2010).

The first of the five patterns identified by Knoll IV is intimate-possessive homicide-suicide—this is termed uxoricide in other sources meaning *a man who kills his wife* or domestic homicide meaning *murders that occur between intimate partners*—and this form of homicide-suicide accounts for between 50 and 75% of all homicide-suicide cases; 1/3 of all women killed in the USA and two women a week in the UK die from this form of violence, much of it spontaneous in nature (Gray 2015). The perpetrator of these cases is typically a male who kills their female partner after estrangement. Such men usually exhibit characteristics including being aged between 30 and 40 years old and having a history of jealousy, domestic abuse and prior estrangement occurring in their relationship with their victims (Knoll IV 2016). These men commonly also suffer from mental illness, including depression and/or substance abuse (Roma et al. 2012). Manning (2015) highlights that while it is a common idea that suicide after homicide is committed out of the guilt associated with the original rage killing, suicide might also be an act of protest against injustice—something explored more later in this chapter—a method of avoiding justice or to seek revenge on someone. These motivational factors are not only typical in the first homicide-suicide pattern but may be relevant for other patterns of homicide-suicide as well (Fig. 5.1).

The second pattern Knoll IV identified is intimate-physically ailing homicide-suicide. These homicide-suicides are also termed mercy-killing suicides or sometimes as altruistic homicides, and they occur when a suicidal individual kills one or more close dependents in order to spare them from deprivation or shame (Manning 2015). Elderly men with poor health and/or ailing spouses are the typical executor of intimate-ailing homicide-suicides. Similar to intimate-possessive suicide, the

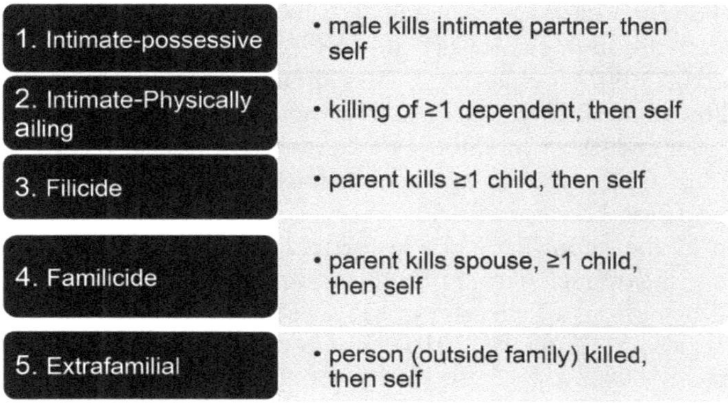

Fig. 5.1 Five patterns of homicide-suicide (Knoll IV 2016)

perpetrator of the homicide-suicide is usually male and the object of his violence is habitually a female though the acts are motivated in different ways. Knoll IV (2016) highlights that there are often financial difficulties (resulting from poor health and depression) that can be linked to the despairing motives visible within this pattern of homicide-suicide.

The third pattern of Knoll IV's homicide-suicide typology is filicide-suicide, instances where a parent kills their children and then themselves (Ateriya et al. 2018). Filicide is also termed infanticide, prolicide, feticide, neonaticide or child homicide. In one 26-country study, the Centre for Disease Control (CDC) found that in children aged 0–14 years child homicide was one of the top five causes of death (top three for ages 1–4) and researchers have noted that filicide rates have tripled since the twentieth century (West 2007). Filicide rates are highest in El Salvador, Guatemala and Venezuela (UNICEF 2014) and victims of filicide (whether committed by mothers or fathers) are commonly (51–57%) male (Liem and Koenraadt 2008; Friedman et al. 2005). Motives for this pattern of suicide range from psychosis to altruism to revenge that relate to distinct subcategories of this form of homicidal violence. Knoll IV's research illustrated that infants are more likely to be killed by their mothers, but that women who kill their newborns are less likely to complete suicide. Burgess et al. (2015) highlight that while women are more likely than men to kill children in early childhood father's or stepfathers are the typical perpetrator of child homicide in later childhood (Liem and Koenraadt 2008). Logan et al.'s (2008) study found that although there were a nearly equivalent number of men and women who kill their children 'fathers are more often perpetrators of filicide followed by suicide' (Liem and Koenraadt 2008, 166).

The fourth pattern in Knoll IV is termed familicide-suicide; in familial-suicide, a perpetrator kills their spouse and at least one of their children. These homicide-suicides, very rare, are almost exclusively perpetrated by the senior male of a household. Common triggers of familial homicide-suicide include marital, financial or work-related issues, which can lead to notions of altruism in the sense of relieving family from sustained suffering (Knoll IV 2016). There are two main forms of familial homicide—type one (murder by proxy) targets the spouse (killing the kids to affect the spouse) and type two (suicide by proxy) targets the whole family including the spouse and the children (Shackelford and Weekes-Shackelford 2012). The Violence Policy Centre demonstrated that as women are unlikely to kill both their intimate partner and their children they are therefore less likely to commit this type of homicide-suicide (2002, cited in Riedel 2010).

Knoll IV's fifth and final pattern is extrafamilial homicide-suicide, which can range from single-victim homicide-suicides to mass murder, or aggrieved, homicide-suicides. To clarify, extrafamilial homicide-suicides involve the killing of a person (or people) from outside of one's family followed by the self. Unfortunately, there are actually few well-ranged statistical studies that have been carried out on this pattern of homicide-suicide, due to the wide range of incidents that can be included within this category. For example, mass murder homicide-suicide could range from a school shooting to vehicle-assisted suicide (using a car, truck or airplane) and can have very divergent features—in many instances, too, the perpetrator may not deliberately take his or her life (and it is almost always a he) but not expect to live through the acts either (think of a mass shooter getting gunned down, waiting for authorities to stop a truck rampage using firearms [the so-called suicide by cop], or knowing that ditching a plane into a mountain range means that you are almost certainly expecting that that act is life-ending). As such, the common characteristics of individuals that carry out extrafamilial homicide-suicide are difficult to identify but in line with the majority of the other homicide-suicide patterns, individuals carrying out extrafamilial homicide-suicide are likely to be male and older than individuals who generally carry out just homicide or just suicide (Rice and Sher 2016).

Key Themes of Homicide-Suicide Literature

While homicide-suicide literature is relatively limited at this point in time (it is a very rare incidence of violence and distinct from both homicide literature and suicide literature), there are two key themes that can be observed within the existing literature: the gendered nature of homicide-suicide and the prospect of preventing homicide-suicides.

The Gendered Nature of Homicide-Suicide

One aspect of almost all forms of homicide-suicide that is impossible to miss (within the literature and within society) is the over-representation of women as victims and men as perpetrators of homicide-suicide. In the USA, between 2003 and 2005, 96.1% of intimate-possessive homicide-perpetrators were male (Logan et al. 2008). As the dominant form of homicide-suicide, this demonstrates the extent to which men are overrepresented as homicide-suicide perpetrators. If most forms of homicide-suicide involve intimate-possessive aggression and most of the perpetrators of this form of violence are men—and the majority of perpetrators of all the other forms of homicide-suicide (with the noted exception of infant filicide) are men—it seems fair to conclude that the gender and therefore primary profile of the typical perpetrator of homicide-suicide is male.

The incidence of homicide in intimate-possessive cases occurs usually during or after a relationship that has been marked by jealousy, verbal abuse and physical violence, which highlights that violence towards women is not a one-off event but a normalized act for these individuals and possible predictor of homicide-suicide. The male violence towards women demonstrated in homicide-suicide rates is a reflection of the violence towards women that occurs in societies globally and in all socio-economic groups. Furthermore, this finding is a reflection of the cultural legitimacy that normalizes male violence in society for whereas homicide-suicides are rare events, male violence against women and children, globally, is the norm. As gender has not been deeply explored within the homicide-suicide literature, it is a fruitful possibility for future study.[1]

The Possibility of Prevention of Homicide-Suicides

The other key theme that is evident within the literature is the possibility of preventing homicide-suicides. A study done by Saleva et al. assessed the possibility of prevention in cases of Finnish homicide-suicide to be 30%—if previous threats of suicide or homicide had led to action, or if obvious alcohol abuse/dependence had been noticed and treated (2007). While homicides and homicide-suicides may lead one to imagine rage and aggression in perpetrators of this form of violence, Roma et al.'s (2012) review of homicide-suicide research carried out over the previous sixty years in Asia, Australia, Canada, Europe and the USA highlighted that mental illness (especially depression) played a significant role in homicide-suicide cross-culturally. In this study, depression occurred in 39% of cases, substance abuse in 20% and psychosis in 17%. As discussed in the previous chapter, the prevention of suicide in those with mental illness is multifaceted and difficult but treatment related to depression and substance abuse could contribute to the prevention of many homicide-suicides. The varying rates of homicide-suicides in different regions globally highlight that the approach of some cultures and legislations to homicide-suicide is more effective than others, presenting possible opportunities for future intervention.

Saint-Martin et al. (2008) found that homicide-suicide events are more frequent in countries where guns are readily available. Guns are used in 88.2% of homicide-suicide cases in the USA, with sharp objects the next most used but only utilized in 3% of cases (Logan et al. 2008). While Zalsman et al. (2016) highlight that reducing access to firearms is generally ineffective at preventing suicides, other studies show that controlling access to guns can indeed impact homicide rates (this is echoed in other suicide prevention methods such as limited access to poisons and controlling access to areas typically utilized in life-ending acts such as bridges or shorelines). Siegel et al. (2013) highlighted that there is a strong correlation between higher levels of gun ownership and higher firearms homicide rates, which conversely shows correlation between lower levels of gun ownership and lower firearms homicide rates. This is echoed in Brown's (2017) study that observes a decline in Australian firearm suicides and homicides following the introduction of strict gun laws 1996. While it is not possible to draw a causal link between strict gun control and lowered homicide rates in these studies due to extenuating factors, there is a strong chance that limiting access to guns could lower the homicide rates in countries with limited gun control. Given that homicide-suicide, while sharing some characteristics with suicide and homicide, is ultimately a distinct behaviour, there is the possibility that reducing access to firearms could impact rates of homicide-suicide as is seen in relation to homicide (many homicide-suicides are firearm related). Further research on homicide-suicide is necessary in order to explore effective avenues of intervention.

Martyrdom Operations

The second form of suicide to be discussed within this chapter is martyrdom suicide. Martyrdom is defined by Bélanger et al. (2014, 496) as 'the psychological readiness to suffer and sacrifice one's life for a cause', with those who do so being known as martyrs. Martyrs are revered figures who gain properties of sacredness through the sacrifice of their life for their values (Flanagan and Jupp 2014). Martyrs are often also called witnesses, as they witness or testify to the truth of a statement or the importance of a value by dying (Halverson et al. 2013). A key contemporary example of martyrdom is Mohamed Bouazizi, who famously and publicly burnt himself alive in December 2010 in protest of the corrupt Tunisian regime he lived under—an act that sparked the Arab Spring, a wave of uprisings in North Africa and the Middle East protesting governmental violence and corruption (Halverson et al. 2013). Martyrdom is traditionally religious based, but can relate to political or cultural causes. Flanagan and Jupp (2014) consider that martyrdom is distasteful to many in this day and age, where growing indifference towards ideological ideals makes self-sacrifice difficult to comprehend.

While definitions of martyrdom range in inclusivity (with some perceiving those who have died being persecuted for their beliefs, such as the Jews massacred during World War II, as martyrs) (Johnson and Zurlo 2014), this chapter will focus on those acts of martyrdom that involve the choice to end one's life violently, referred to as martyrdom suicides.

While martyrdom profiles typically look at race and gender,[2] martyrdom is still often linked to religious beliefs. Most religions condone heroic self-sacrifice of some kind but Abrahamic religions deeply celebrate martyrdom. Christianity's major link to martyrdom is the crucifixion of Jesus the Nazarene, as Jesus is believed to have willingly died to provide forgiveness to sinners (Bélanger et al. 2014). Martyrdom is defensive in Christianity (not passive or voluntary) and a Christian martyr is typically killed for their faith through torturous means (Olechowicz and Matusitz 2013). Judaism celebrates martyrs with the Hebrew title *kedoshim*, which translates to Holy Ones, and views these individuals as sanctified by bringing honour, respect and glory to God. Bélanger et al. (2014) highlight that one way of sanctifying God's name is to sacrifice one's life instead of violating God's commandments not to serve idols or commit adultery, incest or murder. In Islam, martyrdom plays an important role, with martyrs being known in Arabic as *shahid* (witness). While martyrdom has become largely historical for Christians, Islam has both a long tradition and a recent history of martyrdom. Islam's definition of a martyr is one who has given up his/her life in defence of the faith (Johnson and Zurlo 2014). According to the book of Islamic scripture, the *Qur'an*, doing this will gain the martyr entrance into paradise where they will receive heavenly rewards for their actions (Olechowicz and Matusitz 2013).

Martyrdom as Altruistic Suicide

Altruistic suicide is a contentious form of suicide. Émile Durkheim defined altruistic suicide as the result of too much social integration and connected altruistic suicide with a sense of duty or honour (cited in Leenaars 2004). Durkheim further created three subcategories of altruistic suicide: obligatory, where one feels obliged to complete suicide; optional, where one doesn't feel it is a duty but it is encouraged by society; and acute, which occurs only circumstantially (cited in Leenaars 2004). While altruistic suicide was significant once as one of Durkheim's original four typologies of suicide alongside egoistic suicide, anomic suicide and fatalistic suicide, this concept has largely faded out of contemporary academia. The fading of altruistic suicide from academia has been a result of the inclusion of altruism as a motivation for other forms of suicide: martyrdom literature has strong links with concepts of altruism, but altruism is also considered as a motive for assisted suicide, euthanasia or even homicide-suicide in cases of suicide pacts of the elderly. The framing of altruistic motives for suicide within these types has largely denounced altruistic suicide as a form in itself and relegated altruism to the status of a motivation for other forms of suicide including martyrdom operations.

Forms of Martyrdom Suicides

Martyrdom has been on the global scene for centuries and was first recorded occurring in Christianity in the fourth century. Though martyrdom has a long history in relation to each Abrahamic religion (see Chapter 2), this section will focus on the contemporary forms of martyrdom that are being carried out in the world today. The most recognized contemporary patterns of martyrdom are Islamic, with suicide attacks being denoted as martyrdom by those carrying it out/supporting it and martyrdom being utilized as 'power of the people' against crooked governments during the Arab Spring.[3]

Martyrdom as the Power of the People

In opposition to the martyrdom of Christianity being primarily defensive, the martyrdom of Islam is primarily offensive. As such, Islam is said to have 're-invented' the martyr and thrust him/her onto the contemporary stage of events (Flanagan and Jupp 2014). In the political and social protests of the Arab Spring, martyrdom was a tool that aided people in opposing their governments. The Arab Spring, as was mentioned, was sparked by the martyrdom of Mohamed Bouazizi, who self-immolated to protest the corrupt Tunisian regime and he has been greatly distinguished for doing so (Halverson et al. 2013). Buckner and Khatib (2014) highlight that martyrdom was utilized during the Arab Spring to embody the struggle of the people against the state. These authors further argue that the image of a martyr in Islam developed over the Arab Spring, transitioning from being produced by the *state* (or would-be state organs) to being produced by *civilians*, becoming more personalized and representing empowerment and agency rather than victimization or strategic attack. Significantly, the martyrs of the Arab Spring transcended religious connotations of martyrdom due to their social and political causes, which invites further research in relation to the consequences of transcending religious association (Buckner and Khatib 2014).[4]

Martyrdom as Suicide Attacks

Islamic martyrdom has not been limited to self-harm in the name of a social or political cause. A major trend of Islamic martyrdom, though the terminology of martyrdom becomes contentious in such situations, is the use of offensive martyrdom to justify and carry out suicide attacks—a suicide attack involves a lethal aggressive action in which the perpetrator of the attack expects to die. This becomes contentious because the Muslims carrying out such instrumental suicide acts, namely members of Jihadist groups, do so in the name of an extreme interpretation of the *Qur'an* that is not shared or recognized by the majority of Muslims. Islam forbids one to kill oneself, kill non-combatants and kill fellow Muslims (Hafez 2010). The extremist Muslims of (for example) Islamic

State, al Qaeda or al-Shabaab (to name only three) ignore these prohibitions and argue that intention is more important than action, thus reframing their acts of suicide and homicide into martyrdom. Despite world spectaculars of suicide attacks in the West, the most common victims of extremist Islamic martyrdom operations are other Muslims.

Suicide bombings are the dominant form of Islamic martyrdom operations (Olechowicz and Matusitz 2013). Utilizing oneself, as a human weapon, is a pattern of martyrdom that has become common since its emergence in Lebanon in 1983, where an attack on the US embassy in Beirut killed 63 people (Fierke 2009). The human as weapon is not an Islamic or otherwise religious phenomenon by definition, but has become somewhat synonymous in contemporary times with acts carried out by Jihadists. Other common forms of extremist martyrdom operations involve fighting with firearms or knives, where Islamic extremists are well armed and inflict as much damage as possible on the public before being inevitably killed by security forces. A final form increasing in frequency (especially in attacks in Western countries) involves vehicular martyrdom operations—suicide attacks using cars or trucks to kill, or, infamously, in the Twin Tower attacks on September 11 in the USA, airplanes.

Themes Within Martyrdom Literature

Distinctions Between Sacrifice and Suicide

One of the key themes of martyrdom literature is the debate surrounding the classification of martyrdom as suicide, predominantly in relation to Muslim martyrs. Many academics and religious figures argue that martyrdom and suicide are distinct concepts, the *Qur'an* itself strictly prohibits suicide but encourages martyrdom—which is part of the predicament (Bélanger et al. 2014). This is a point of ongoing debate both within Islam and within academic literature surrounding martyrdom and acts of suicide. Within Islam, Islamic clerical institutions issued a *fatwa* (judicial ruling) in 2011 reaffirming that suicide is a violation of Islam even if carried out as a social or political protest (Halverson et al. 2013). This *fatwa* meant to reframe suicide within the religious tenets of Islam, but failed to be upheld in the context of the Arab Spring. In essence, the framing of martyrdom as suicide or achievement is dependent on the form of Islam that you personally subscribe to. For example, in relation to individuals in Islamic State or al Qaeda that commit suicide attacks, such actions are not seen by most outside of those groups as martyrdom due to the extreme interpretation of Islam that is used to justify their actions. Instead, as those actions kill innocent people, Muslim and non-Muslim alike, in order to send a political message, most would define this as suicide attack, not an act of martyrdom. Martyrdom thus is subjective as a social concept; one may commit suicide for a cause and believe it to be martyrdom but it may not be perceived thusly by others.

The Language of Martyrdom

The language utilized to describe martyrdom has become very important. In relation to suicide bombers for example, Fierke (2009) highlights that Western discourse predominantly uses the terminology of 'suicide terrorism' or 'suicide bombings', as opposed to the prevalence of 'martyrdom operation' utilized in Arab, Muslim and Middle Eastern discourses (in Arabic but also translated into English in both academic and media sources). In these situations, the terminology 'martyrdom' politicizes and gives moral legitimacy to an attacker (and the attack) as a pursuer (and a pursuit) of justice (Fierke 2009). In using the terminology of 'suicide terrorism', states position themselves as the protector of citizens where so-called martyrs become moral deviants, which undermines the suicide attack/martyr's message and purpose (Fierke 2009). Speckhard (2006, cited in Fierke 2009) argues that suicide bombings proliferate in situations of support and legitimacy, which creates cycles of economic and moral provision for consequent acts. It is clear throughout the literature thus that the framing and language of martyrdom are highly significant to the political context surrounding martyrdom operations and consent for acts of martyrdom often leads to future support of such acts.

The first two forms of *instrumental* suicide in this chapter have been researched and written about from academic, clinical and criminal justice points of view as well as with an intersectional and cultural lens. The amount of literature surrounding the first two types of *instrumental* suicide is significant and growing. The same cannot be said about the next, far more obscure and under-researched (in my opinion) forms: daredevil suicide and protest suicide. The first could be branded as tangential while the second can be considered fictitious or ex post facto. The second half of this chapter will attempt to unravel the particularities of these forms for consideration in future research, study and peace praxis.

Daredevil Suicide

The third type of ***instrumental*** suicide to be discussed in this chapter is daredevil suicide. Daredevil suicide can be defined as suicide occurring as a result of an individual engaging in risk-taking behaviour that could clearly lead to the end of their life.[5] Such risk-taking behaviour could range from engaging in extreme sports, to driving under the influence of substances or at excessive speed, to playing games such as Russian roulette or YouTube challenges.[6] Breivik (2007) distinguishes between three forms of risk-taking: the first is pro-social risk-taking, where risks are taken for the sake of others such as by firefighters saving individuals under dangerous circumstances; the second form is anti-social risk-taking where risks are taken in ways that can endanger other individuals, for example when burglars break into a home; and the third form is ludic risk-taking, where risk is taken for the sake of one's own interests and satisfaction, such as by extreme sportspersons (typically men) or gamblers. Daredevil suicide is related to the third form: ludic risk-taking. Baechler (cited in Shields et al. 2008) referred to daredevil suicide as ludic suicide and subdivided this type into the 'ordeal' and the 'game'. The 'ordeal' refers to an individual risking their life to prove something to themselves or to other individuals, whereas the 'game' involves an individual playing with their life solely because of the potential of a fatality.

There is limited literature available in relation to daredevil suicide, as this is a contentious type of suicide.[7,8] This contention is due to some definitions of suicide distinctly including the intent to take one's own life; Winokur and Black (1992) went so far as to state that 'suicide is the intentional taking of one's own life… it is not the unhappy result of the actions of a daredevil' (490). Daredevil suicide, as death resulting from engaging in risk-taking behaviour that has inherent potential for fatality rather than death resulting from direct intention to die, does not meet such requirements of direct intent as daredevil acts involve the element of chance. Differing definitions of suicide, however, classify that suicide is the manner of death if an individual dies from an intentional self-inflicted act that was intended to end their life *or* had an inherently high risk of this result (Collins 2010). The contentiousness of daredevil suicide[9] as a suicide form thus depends on the definition of suicide being utilized. This further complicates which deaths are classified as daredevil suicides, as deciding the degree of risk in an act that led to death is subjective and there is a fine line between a classification of suicide and accident. Daredevil suicide has been included within this chapter for the sake of comprehensiveness, but requires more research.

Patterns of Behaviour Related to Daredevil Suicide

As there is little literature on daredevil suicide as a concept, there are no patterns able to be gleaned of daredevil suicide, nor any themes of literature to be discussed. Able to be discussed, however, are the types of risk-taking behaviour that can be linked to daredevil suicides and the common characteristics of individuals that carry out such behaviour, though the term 'daredevil suicide' is not directly used within this literature. While Russian roulette, online 'challenges' (such as the Blue Whale) and participation in extreme sports are forms of risk-taking behaviour discussed within this chapter, daredevil suicides are not limited to these acts.

The first risk-taking behaviour that can be linked to daredevil suicide, and that is perhaps the most obvious example of this type of suicide, is engaging in 'playing' Russian roulette. Russian roulette is a deadly game, in which an individual spins the cylinder of a revolver loaded with one or more bullets, aims the muzzle towards their head and then pulls the trigger—to 'win' is to not be killed (Collins 2010). In a typical revolver, there are six chambers for bullets; thus, there is a one in six chance during Russian roulette that an individual will be killed. The probability of death is altered if the revolver has a different number of chambers, and increases significantly if the gun is discharged more than once after being loaded. The majority of victims of Russian roulette are men under the age of thirty who are under the influence of alcohol or other drugs and in the presence of others at the time the Russian roulette game is played (Shields et al. 2008; Stack and Wasserman 2008). Shields et al. (2008) highlight that victims of Russian roulette generally lack the typical characteristics of those that complete suicide such as depression, hopelessness and/or domestic, legal or financial difficulties, instead being driven by a group mentality or effects of drugs to thrillingly tempt fate. As such, many individuals argue that deaths by Russian roulette should be classified as accidents, particularly given that there is generally an 83% survival rate of single Russian roulette acts

(Shields et al. 2008). Other individuals see the placing of a loaded gun to the head and pulling the trigger as inherently dangerous and thus inferring sub-intent to do self-harm or accept serious injury/death (Collins 2010). This argument leads back to the contentious nature of daredevil suicide.

Numerous incarnations of contemporary risk-taking or 'challenge culture' behaviour linked to daredevil suicide highlight the increasingly fragmented and hazardous social landscape of the Internet. There are many perilous online challenges. Here are the just three:

1. The Kiki Challenge: jumping out of a moving car dancing to Drake's 'In My Feelings'.
2. The Fire Challenge: drench a part of your body in flammable liquid and set it alight.
3. The Choke Challenge (aka Pass-Out or Space Monkey Challenge): cut off oxygen via 'choking' until you lose consciousness.

What all of these challenges (and many others) have in common is that the object of the acts is to both film the actions and then post them online as proof of completion. And although the field of online challenges is crowded special mention must be made regarding the Blue Whale suicide challenge. The Blue Whale has been identified as a worldwide threat to vulnerable youths incited to life-ending acts. This 'game' has been linked to 130 deaths in Russia since 2013 and the Blue Whale has been reported in Argentina, Brazil, Bulgaria, Canada, Chile, China, Colombia, France, Georgia, Italy, Kenya, New Zealand, Paraguay, Portugal, Russian, Saudi Arabia, Serbia, Spain, the UK, USA, Ukraine, Uruguay and Venezuela (Bershidsky 2017).

> It is said that this "game" can reach a young teenager on social media sites if they endorse certain hashtags and get involved in some groups. When the player signs up for the game, she or he is assigned an administrator who provides them with a daily task to complete for 50 days, of which they must send photographic proof of completion. These tasks are initially simple enough, such as watching a horror movie or waking up at odd times but eventually they are told to inflict harm on themselves. But on the 50th and final day, they are asked to kill themselves. Those who get cold feet are threatened that the administrator possesses all their information and would bring harm to them or their loved ones. (Rathi 2017, 1)

There are very few academic sources who are engaging with this form of daredevil suicide as it is a very new cluster of phenomenon that is either poorly understood or misunderstood (online critics say that teenagers are suicidal anyway and the game is not a cause so much as an effect of suicidality in world youth). Polizzi (2017) has explored digital literacy and online harm for youth and the notion of social media as a magnet for those with mental health issues in teens and young adults. The Blue Whale challenge requires photographic evidence of acts of self-harm leading up to and including suicide that puts this form of self-killing squarely in the *instrumental* category of daredevil suicide. As has already been mentioned, daredevil suicides typically are risks taken for others (in this case peers and the online audience), that (may) endanger others (peers and watchers in the online community who then join the challenge) but for the sake of one's own interest. This form of daredevil suicide is not the only incidence of 'digital suicide' as there are increasing investigations of suicidal instigation via text or social media (where people are encouraged, even ordered, to take their own lives) but the nature of the Blue Whale suicide challenge clearly locates risk and risk-taking behaviour with the life-ending act of self-killing.

The last form of risk-taking behaviour linked to daredevil suicide in this section is participation in extreme sports. Extreme sports are differentiated from traditional sports by the amount of risk involved in participation and are defined as 'independent leisure activity where the most likely outcome of an accident is death' (Brymer 2005, cited by Lebeau and Sides 2014, 628). Such sports include but are not limited to BASE jumping, parachuting, rock climbing and bungee jumping. With extreme sports, the risks are clear to both participant and observer, to the extent that life insurance companies classify extreme sport participation for higher premiums and/or additional surcharges or outright denial of coverage (Lebeau and Sides 2014). Unfortunately, there is little research available surrounding the statistics of extreme sports fatalities and none (that I could find) that consider them deliberate suicides. But academics such as Brymer (2010) have shown that extreme sports are not solely undertaken due to a need for risk, but that in fact participants take extensive precautions in order to mitigate risks. However, the risk of death is an inextricable part of such sporting behaviour; indeed without lethal possibilities, these sports would likely be far less attractive to participants and onlookers.

Extreme sport fatalities meet the criteria of daredevil suicide by engagement in an act that is inherently dangerous, possibly lethal and typically spectacular (involving spectators either in situ or via media) but in contrast to those individuals who play the odds of Russian roulette, or partake of digital games such as the Blue Whale, participants of extreme sports bet their lives on skill and preparation and still take the risk that their actions could result in their demise. This does make the inclusion of accidents arising from extreme sports participation as suicides controversial (furthermore there are varying views of which sports are classified as extreme) but similar to other contentious forms of suicide, sometimes it is the act and sometimes it is the intention of life-ending acts that argues for inclusion.

The Protest Possibility

In this section, we will consider acts of social, cultural, economic or political protest as *instrumental suicides.*[10] Spehr and Dixon (2013) consider protest suicide 'to be meaningful social action as a purposive political act intended to change oppressive political policies or practices', and include, 'deliberate suicide action (such as self-immolation), an action that, at the time undertaken, is likely to result in suicide (such as a hunger strike), or an action where suicide is a by-product of killing others (a suicide attack)' (368–369). The purpose of the act of suicide, here, is the hopeful transformation of oppressive violence—not merely the *consequence* of such violence itself. The object of a protest suicide, as considered by Spehr and Dixon, is 'almost always an authoritative body', but also 'the general public', or in the case of great oppression, the international public via the media (2013, 369–370). To include an act of suicide in the domain of 'protest' requires a deliberate act that communicates the need for change to an audience.

Somewhat less limited is Andriolo's (2006) definition of protest suicide as 'dying with a message, for a message, and of a message' (100) which, unsatisfyingly, posits that most, '"regular" suicides include in their web of meanings and messages a strand of protest—against having been hurt, rejected, or failed by others; against devastating circumstances; against the meanness of opportunity; or against the unceasing resurgence of depression' (107) sincerely limiting our ability to comprehend the instrumentality of such acts as deliberate and communicative and potentially making all acts of suicide a form of protest. If all acts of suicide can be considered acts of protest, what distinguishes 'protest' suicide from 'regular' suicide? And, if a suicide does not perform a specific communicative (*dialogic*) aspect, does this then ask the observer to 'read' life-ending acts for specific signals and ascribe to such actions of self-killing intentions where such aims are not necessarily clear? Andriolo remarks,

> Protest Suicide attempts to draw the attention of others to something that, in the suicide's perception, constitutes a wrong of moral, political, or economic dimension, a wrong that affects the lives of many. If a protest suicide were to reach its ideal goal, attention would initiate action that, ultimately, would right the wrong. This definition, potentially, could cover two kinds of suicide: (1) a version in which the protest agenda is expressed solely by means of suicide, and (2) a version in which self-destruction is intended to kill others, as in the case in suicide bombing. (2006, 100)

Andriolo initially classifies protest suicide as 'message' but then determines that a protest suicide that seeks to draw attention to a wrong affecting many must be established *in the suicide's perception*—which cannot necessarily be determined and presents a conundrum in classifying a suicide as an act of protest, because unless clearly communicated, how do we know? From this position, 'reading' protest in a suicide means the protest goal of the suicide would need to be clearly communicated. Andriolo states that protest suicides, 'have chosen, different from so many others who have ended their own lives, to place this act in the service of a public concern' (2006, 107) but how do we know a public (protest) suicide from a non-protest suicide?

Here, the audience is the object of the act but in much of the commentary of protest suicide, such an objective is either unclear or illusory. Also, problematically, the tendency to mark suicides as acts of 'protest' may relate to where they occur, who they include and sociocultural considerations that surround suicide. As we recall from previously in this chapter, martyrdom is defined by Bélanger et al. (2014, 496) as 'the psychological readiness to suffer and sacrifice one's life for a cause', so is martyrdom a form of protest and/or is protest suicide a form of martyrdom? Can we logically separate out acts of signal-suicide (suicides that send a message), and if we could, how would we? When deciding on how to encapsulate forms of *instrumental* suicide for this chapter, I delineated thusly: where there are long-term traditions of self-sacrifice in various cultures, I have categorized such acts as martyrdom but where actions of signal-suicide appear to be divergences related to cultural trauma that deviate from established cultural norms (e.g. the historical low incidences of suicide in the Greek culture) I categorize such acts as protest.

And whereas culture is key, something must also be said about discrepancies, absences and obscurants in suicide data globally. Several years ago, Vijayakumar intoned:

> Data on suicide is not available for roughly half the countries (53%) of the world and one third (27%) of the population. Seventy-three percent of suicides in the world occur in developing countries, though data is unavailable for 73% of countries. More than half the suicides (54%) in the world occur in China and India. Considering that under-reporting of suicide is a major issue in developing countries, the enormity of the problem and the urgent need for suicide prevention is evident. (2004, 158)

Scholars have indicated the challenge of getting sound information about suicide from countries (either developed or developing) with limited capacity to monitor such forms of violence and/or cultural taboos to recognition of deliberate life-ending acts in general. This is evident in various studies of suicide that categorize acts of deliberate self-killing as acts of protest (Liu 2005; Chan and Ngai 2010; Minoo 2013; Widger 2014; Münster 2015; Davis 2015) where the threshold for inclusion is the perception that the act of suicide is experienced in an oppressive milieu. But is that enough? In this book, the notion that we need to stabilize the term 'suicide' in our scholarship by clearly defining how dissimilar acts can be distinguished means we might need to look a little closer at the idea of protest suicide from the evidence. In order to very briefly illustrate the 'is it protest?' quandary, the following section will very briefly examine 'protest suicides' in Greece and India.

Greece

Despite Greece's historically low incidences of suicide, recent scholarship on the rate of suicide mortality in Greece before and during the financial crisis confirmed increases in all age categories for males but also females aged 50–59 (Alexopoulos et al. 2019). Some have termed the increase in suicide an 'epidemic', and described 'crisis' Greece as a "morbid social environment where one of its symptoms [is] suicide" (Kermeliotis cited in Davis 2015, 1010).

The vulnerability of Greek citizens due to the economic restructuring of austerity measures led to a 40% increase in suicides in Greece in early 2011. Notwithstanding the private practices of self-killing seen in many parts and populations in Greece during and after the economic crisis, there were also 'public suicides' termed 'political suicides' or 'public protest' suicides (Kermeliotis 2012).

> A series of horrifying public suicides in Greece in 2011–2012 brought to public visibility a series of suicide notes, some published and some not, blaming the austerity measures, overwhelming debt, the wealthy and powerful classes, the Greek state, and the Troika for the victims' loss of dignity and hope for the future. In media coverage, these notes have been framed as transparent proof of the authors' intentions to commit suicide as a political act of protest. (Davis 2015, 1015)

These suicides were deliberate life-ending acts with clear communication to the public that the suicide was a result of crisis and the austerity measures put on regular Greek citizens to try to survive. To take only one example, Dimitris Christoulas was a seventy-seven-year-old retired pharmacist. His pension, his only form of income, had recently been cut, so he shot himself to death outside Parliament in Athens after shouting to all that would listen that he was not killing himself—*they* were killing him. A note, he left said the following:

> The occupation government of Tsolakoglou has literally destroyed my means of survival, which were based on a very respectable pension that I alone paid into for thirty-five years, with no help from the state. And since I'm at an age where I don't have the capacity to react actively (although if a Greek were to grab a Kalashnikov, I would be right behind him), I find no other solution than a dignified end to my life, before I find myself scrounging in the garbage for food. I believe that young people with no future will someday take up arms and hang the traitors of this country by their feet in Syntagma Square, just like the Italians did to Mussolini in the Piazzale Loreto of Milan in 1945. (Davis 2015, 1016)

Kyrios Christoulas was one of several who either attempted or successfully killed themselves publicly to protest and communicate their oppression to others. This is an unequivocal protest suicide. The aim of his actions was to end his life with a message of protest and he stated his aim clearly in person and in writing. Princeton anthropologist Elizabeth Davis remarks:

> Since the crisis, suicide has been mediated by a peculiar kind of publicity that has introduced a way for people in despair to imagine themselves, and be imagined by others, as political actors, at a moment when other forms of political action may seem exhausted or futile. (2015, 1029)

In Greece, the circumstances of austerity have led to an overall increase in suicide rates in both males and females but in particular circumstances, the act of deliberate self-killing is performed publicly as an act of political and economic protest. The 'public suicides' in Greece adhere to Spehr and Dixon's standard of a meaningful purposive social action intended to change oppressive political policies or practices but also Andriolo's criteria of protest suicide—an attempt to draw attention to something perceived by the suicide as wrong.

India

It has been reported that between 2005 and 2015, 'more than 100,000 farmers in distress...committed suicide' (Münster 2015, 1581). This demographic phenomenon is attributed to a variety of sociocultural and economic-political factors such as the realities of rising debt and diminished agricultural returns that resulted from the liberalization of the agrarian economy but also sociological issues related to social rootedness (individualization and integration). While many suicides involve females in India, the vast majority of such suicides are accomplished by males (Plewis 2017)

Mohanty (2013) states that the prevalence of farmer suicides provides an impression, 'that indebtedness and crop failure, one way or the other, pushed the farmers towards economic distress and suicide' (7), but later points out that a more detailed analysis of the suicide data 'hints that the disappointment and despair of the suicide victims, associated with loss of agricultural income and indebtedness, had its origin in growing social isolation and individualism' (Mohanty 2013, 7).

Farmer suicides are considered by many as 'public deaths' but research has indicated that they are actually private affairs that only become public 'via the enumerative and statistical practices of the Indian state and their scandalization in the media' (Münster 2015, 1580). Ethnographic work has indicated that surviving families of the farmer suicide are awarded financial compensation incentivizing many people to identify lost family members as suicides. While others categorize the 'epidemic' of farmer suicides as actions of protest, the bulk are individual and private practices of small landowners faced with financial ruin and or social/cultural shame and disgrace. In order to read these deaths as acts of protest, some form of communication from the suicides would be needed, and from the thousands said to perform this act of self-killing in India, it would seem that public communiques that challenge the economic oppression are missing.

Take the case of Kurien (pseudonym) who completed suicide by poison in 2002.

> Kurien grew up working as an agricultural labourer (*kūli*). After his marriage, Kurien moved with his wife to Pulpally and bought one acre of land. In addition to working on a daily-wage basis, he began cultivating pepper with a loan from the bank. But pepper was a complete failure for him. Although he replanted frequently, he never got any yield due to drought and diseases. Kurien borrowed more money from all available sources: banks, neighbours, moneylenders (*paliśakkāran*). Finally, he made another attempt at a new beginning: he pledged all his land to the bank and started a small furniture shop. That business, too, was a complete failure—mainly, his wife believed, because he gave away furniture on credit and his customers did not pay up. In 2002, the peak year of suicides in Wayanad, he drank Furadan, the aforementioned 'red-label' pesticide, at his shop and came home to confess to his wife, 'It is not for me to stay in this world. If I stay I will make only more debts. It is better if I leave.' He died on the way to the hospital. (Münster 2015, 1599)

Despite the 'politicization' of Indian suicides as economic protest, this story communicates a private act communicated to ethnographers via the surviving spouse. In contrast to notions of farmer suicides as forms of public suicide, Münster states that:

> Political messages have not been formulated, those who have committed suicide have not sought audiences for their self-destruction beyond domestic contexts, and expectations of exchange (with the state) did not appear to have played a significant role in the suicide. (2015, 1592)

While Indian farmer suicides must be examined for their own unique aetiology, they do not seem to adhere to Spehr and Dixon—*a meaningful purposive social action intended to change oppressive political policies or practices*—or Andriolo's criteria as acts of protest suicide—*an attempt to draw attention to something perceived by the suicide as wrong.*

To study suicide and to study suicide with an intention to impact change, eradicate self-killing and champion social and political transformation that decreases this form of violence is incredibly admirable and difficult. Scholars, of necessity, are often tasked with invading the spaces of the bereaved and engaging with the trauma of attempted or successful suicide and the wake of pain in its stead. The purpose of this section is not to deconstruct or delegitimize the admirable work of these researchers but to clearly delineate from the studies surveyed the predicament of categorizing suicide as an act of protest. From my vantage point, the notion that acts of deliberate self-killing are also acts of protest is not useful unless protest is communicated in the act. When some individuals so clearly state their intention to self-sacrifice as a message for others, it seems disingenuine to aggregate undefined suicides as acts of deliberate protest too.

This book is arguing that through a peacebuilding lens, suicides can be separated into acts that affect individuals (or on behalf of individuals) or acts that include (and mean to include) others. An authentic protest suicide would certainly be a form of *instrumental* suicide—a deliberate life-ending act that includes others—but when intention is ascribed to acts of suicide 'after the fact' this weakens our ability to include this incarnation of suicide in the typology. We can conclude that martyrdom suicides are deliberate acts of self-killing with an intention to communicate to the greater public intolerable circumstances. We can also conclude that acts of genuine protest suicide exist outside of the category of martyrdom. Despite the rarity of protest suicide (and the protest question), I include this form of life-ending act under the category *instrumental* suicide.

Protest as a Form of Instrumental Suicide

As mentioned previously, martyrdom is subjective as a social concept; one may complete suicide for a cause and believe it to be martyrdom but it may not be perceived thusly by others. Inversely, suicide may be completed for individual reasons and perceived as protest by others—*notwithstanding the actual motivation or intention of the suicide.* In considering whether or not to include protest suicide as a separate form of *instrumental* suicide in this chapter (alongside homicide-suicide, martyrdom and daredevil suicide), it became clear that intentionality was often applied to suicides as acts of protest when no such intention was communicated by the suicide themselves. The inclusion of acts that result in death that include *others* in their composition—whether *actual others* or the *audience of others*—includes protest suicide in the typology of *instrumental* suicide, but is wary of the posthumous categorization of suicide as an act of protest.

Conclusion

Homicide-suicide, martyrdom suicide (altruistic suicide), daredevil suicide and protest suicide are non-medically related forms of suicide that have been explored within this chapter. Though the incidence of these four types of suicide is much lower than that of the types discussed in the previous chapter, they are still highly important and require further research. Further research could solve some of the contentious issues that come up in relation to martyrdom operations, daredevil suicide and protest suicide related to the position that acts that deliberately lead to self-death and acts expected (or anticipated) to result in self-death are dissimilar but share characteristics that must be recognized and encompassed within the greater phenomena of suicide. For PACS pracademics to engage with the typologies of suicide presented in this book, clarity and specificity are a useful tool for defining research trajectories, identifying categories of risk and piloting programs for the nonviolent transformation of these acts. This chapter sought to delineate forms of *instrumental* suicide as acts that are not solely personal but practice acts of self-killing for a specific aim or purpose that involves others. The next chapter looks at the potential role of suicide in PACS research and practice by identifying how the interdisciplinary field of PACS can engage with *medical* and *instrumental* suicide through the spectrum of social, cultural and political violence.

Notes

1. PACS research could look at gender in homicide-suicide as a reflection of cultural, structural and not just direct forms of violence (Galtung 1990).
2. Although there are many white, female and Christian martyrs, Arab and Muslim males comprise the majority of global suicide attackers (Rae 2012).
3. The term martyrdom operations will be used to signify suicide attacks considered self-sacrifice by the perpetrators of such acts. The contemporary use of 'terrorism' is a conceptually unstable term that is frequently

used by persons or institutions (sometimes states) that seek to delegitimize and/or denounce acts of violence that could just as easily be termed 'homicides'. This section will dispense with the conceptually unstable terms of 'terror' or 'terrorism' to focus on the acts under review and not their relative social, cultural or political legitimacy or illegitimacy.

4. PACS could investigate how various personal forms of violence are used to transcend political violence in the future including acts of personal or political resistance that involve life-ending acts.
5. Canadian rapper Jon James McMurray died in such a stunt when attempting to film a music video on the wing of an airplane in 2018 (Bruner 2018).
6. YouTube pranks such as the Bird Box Challenge show participants doing blindfold challenges such as walking or driving with blindfolds on (Feldman 2019).
7. And even less literature on suicide-related Internet challenges on the darknet, the hidden part of the Internet not searchable via conventional search engines like Yahoo, Bing or Google (Mörch et al. 2018).
8. Although beyond the scope of this work, the link between daredevil or anti-social behaviour online and suicide is an important topic for future PACS suicide scholars (see Phillips and Mann 2019).
9. Would one classify, for example, those suffering from anorexia nervosa as daredevil suicides (Joiner 2010)?
10. This section will later explore how protest suicide is or is not distinct from acts of martyrdom.

References

Alexopoulos, Evangelos C., Katerina Kavalidou, and Fani Messolora. 2019. "Suicide Mortality Patterns in Greek Work Force Before and During the Economic Crisis." *International Journal of Environmental Research and Public Health* 16: 469. https://doi.org/10.3390/ijerph16030469.

Andriolo, Karin. 2006. "The Twice-Killed: Imagining Protest Suicide." *American Anthropologist* 108 (1): 100–113.

Ateriya, Navneet, Ashish Saraf, Tanuj Kanchan, Viakas P. Meshram, Raghvendra Siggh Shekhawat, and Puneet Setia. 2018. "Filicide-Suicide: An Unusual Variant of Dyadic Death." *Medico-Legal Journal*: 1–3. https://doi.org/10.1177/0025817218787392.

Bélanger, Jocelyn, Julie Caouette, Keren Sharvit, Michelle Dugas, and Laura King. 2014. "The Psychology of Martyrdom: Making the Ultimate Sacrifice in the Name of a Cause." *Journal of Personality and Social Psychology* 107 (3): 494–515.

Bershidsky, Leonid. 2017. "Why the Russian Suicide Game Went Global." *Bloomberg View*. Accessed April 26, 2017. https://www.bloomberg.com/view/articles/2017-04-25/why-the-russian-suicide-game-went-global.

Breivik, Gunnar. 2007. "Can BASE Jumping Be Morally Defended." In *Philosophy, Risk and Adventure Sports*, edited by Mike McNamee, 168–185. New York: Taylor & Francis.

Brown, Penelope. 2017. "Impact of Gun Law Reforms on Rates of Homicide, Suicide and Mass Shootings in Australia." *Evidence-Based Mental Health* 20: 25.

Bruner, Raisa. 2018. "A Rapper Has Died After Attempting a Stunt on the Wing of a Plane." Accessed March 3, 2018. http://time.com/5431849/jon-james-death/.

Brymer, Eric. 2010. "Risk Taking in Extreme Sports: A Phenomenological Perspective." *Annals of Leisure Research* 13 (1–2): 218–238.

Buckner, Elizabeth, and Lina Khatib. 2014. "The Martyrs' Revolutions: The Role of Martyrs in the Arab Spring." *British Journal of Middle Eastern Studies* 41 (4): 368–384.

Burgess, Ann, Kathleen Sekula, and Carrie Carretta. 2015. "Homicide-Suicide and Duty to Warn." *The American Academy of Psychoanalysis and Dynamic Psychiatry* 43 (1): 67–90.

Chan, Jenny, and Ngai Pun. 2010. "Suicide as Protest for the New Generation of Chinese Migrant Workers: Foxconn, Global Capital, and the State." *The Asia-Pacific Journal* 8 (37) (2): 1–33.

Collins, Kim. 2010. "Adolescent Russian Roulette Deaths." *The American Journal of Forensic Medicine and Pathology* 31 (1): 4–6.

Davis, Elizabeth. 2015. "'We've Toiled Without End': Publicity, Crisis, and the Suicide 'Epidemic' in Greece." *Comparative Studies in Society and History* 57 (4): 1007–1036. https://doi.org/10.1017/s0010417515000420.

Dayan, Hava. 2018. "Sociocultural Aspects of Femicide-Suicide: The Case of Israel." *Journal of Interpersonal Violence* 1 (1): 1–19.

du Plessis, Marna, and Khazamula Keven Hlaise. 2012. "Homicide-Suicide (Dyadic Death): A Case Study of Double Hanging." *The American Journal of Forensic Medicine and Pathology* 33 (3): 262–264.

Eliason, Scott. 2009. "Murder-Suicide: A Review of the Recent Literature." *Journal of the American Academy of Psychiatry and Law* 37 (3): 371–376.

Feldman, Brian. 2019. "YouTube Bans Dangerous Pranks Like the 'Bird Box' Challenge." Accessed March 3, 2019. https://www.theguardian.com/technology/2019/jan/16/youtube-bans-dangerous-pranks-after-bird-box-challenge.

Fierke, Karin. 2009. "Agents of Death: The Structural Logic of Suicide Terrorism and Martyrdom." *International Theory* 1 (1): 155–184.

Flanagan, Kieran, and Peter Jupp. 2014. "Martyrs and Martyrdom." *Morality* 19 (2): 105–116.

Fridel, Emma E., and Gregory M. Zimmerman. 2018. "Examining Homicide-Suicide as a Current in the Stream Analogy of Lethal Violence." *Social Forces* 71: 1–28. https://doi.org/10.1093/sf/soy071.

Friedman, Susan H., Sarah Horwitz, and P. J. Resnick. 2005. "Child Murder by Mothers: A Critical Analysis of the Current State of Knowledge and a Research Agenda." *The American Journal of Psychiatry* 162: 1578–1587.

Galtung, Johan. 1990. "Cultural Violence." *Journal of Peace Research* 27 (3): 291–305.

Gray, Richard. 2015. "How to Spot a Family Killer: Experts Discover 'Distinct Psychological' Traits in Men Who Murder Their Partners and Children." *Daily Mail*, August 27. Accessed June 29, 2017. http://www.dailymail.co.uk/sciencetech/article-3211390/How-spot-family-killer-Experts-discover-distinct-psychological-traits-men-murder-partners-children.html.

Hafez, Mohammed. 2010. "The Alchemy of Martyrdom: Jihad Salafism and Debates Over Suicide Bombings in the Muslim World." *Asian Journal of Social Science* 38 (3): 364–378.

Halverson, Jeffry, Scott Ruston, and Angela Trethewey. 2013. "Mediated Martyrs of the Arab Spring: New Media, Civil Religion, and Narrative in Tunisia and Egypt." *Journal of Communication* 63 (2): 312–332.

Johnson, Todd, and Gina Zurlo. 2014. "Christian Martyrdom as a Pervasive Phenomenon." *Society* 51 (6) 679–685.

Joiner, Thomas. 2010. *Myths About Suicide.* Cambridge: Harvard University Press.

Kermeliotis, Teo. 2012. "Austerity Drives Up Suicide Rate in Debt-Ridden Greece." CNN.com, April 6. Accessed February 4, 2019. http://www.cnn.com/2012/04/06/world/europe/greece-austerity-suicide/.

Knoll IV, James. 2016. "Understanding Homicide-Suicide." *Psychiatric Clinics of North America* 39 (4): 633–647.

Lebeau, Jean-Charles, and Ryan Sides. 2014. "Beyond the Mainstream Versus Extreme Dichotomy: A Cyclical Perspective on Extreme Sports." *Sport in Society* 18 (6): 627–635.

Leenaars, Antoon. 2004. "Altruistic Suicide: A Few Reflections." *Archives of Suicide Research* 8 (1): 1–7.

Liem, Marieke, and Frans Koenraadt. 2008. "Filicide: A Comparative Study of Maternal Versus Paternal Child Homicide." *Criminal Behaviour and Mental Health* 18: 166–176.

Liu, Si-Si. 2005. *Suicide as Protest.* China Rights Forum "Fuelling Unrest," 26–29. Accessed February 6, 2019. https://www.hrichina.org/sites/default/files/PDFs/CRF.1.2005/1.2005SuicideAsProtest.pdf.

Logan, Joseph, Holly Hill, Michele Black Lynberg, Alex Crosby, Debra Karch, Jamar Barnes, and Keri Lubell. 2008. "Characteristics of Perpetrators in Homicide-Followed-by-Suicide Incidents: National Violent Death Reporting

System—17 US States, 2003–2005." *American Journal of Epidemiology* 168 (9): 1056–1064.

Manning, Jason. 2015. "The Social Structure of Homicide-Suicide." *Homicide Studies* 19 (4): 350–369.

Marzuk, Peter M. 1992. "The Epidemiology of Murder-Suicide". *JAMA: The Journal of the American Medical Association* 267 (23): 3179.

Mirnoo, Alinia. 2013. *Honor and Violence Against Women in Iraqi Kurdistan.* New York: Palgrave Macmillan.

Mohanty, Bibhuti B. 2013. "Farmer Suicides in India." *Economic and Political Weekly*, May 25. Retrieved February 4, 2019 from. https://search-proquest-com.ezproxy.otago.ac.nz/docview/2153731012?accountid=14700.

Mörch, Carl-Maria, Louis-Philippe Côté, Laurent Corthésy-Blondin, Léa Plourde-Léveillé, Luc Dargis, and Brian L. Mishara. 2018. "The Darknet and Suicide." *Journal of Affective Disorders* 241 (1): 127–132.

Münster, Daniel N. 2015. "Farmers' Suicides as Public Death: Politics, Agency and Statistics in a Suicide-Prone District (South India)." *Modern Asian Studies* 49 (5): 580–1605.

Olechowicz, Kari, and Jonathan Matusitz. 2013. "The Motivations of Islamic Martyrs: Applying the Collective Effort Model." *Current Psychology* 32 (4): 338–347.

Phillips, James, and Leon Mann. 2019. "Suicide Baiting in the Internet Era." *Computers in Human Behavior* 92: 29–36.

Plewis, Ian. 2017. "Analyzing Indian Farmer Suicide Rates." *Proceedings of the National Academy of Sciences of the United States of America* 115 (2): E117.

Polizzi, Gianfranco. 2017. "The Blue Whale Game Paradox, Digital Literacy and Fake News." *Parenting for a Digital Future*, May 25. Accessed June 27, 2017. http://blogs.lse.ac.uk/parenting4digitalfuture/2017/05/25/the-blue-whale-game-paradox-digital-literacy-and-fake-news/.

Rae, Jonathan A. 2012. "Will It Ever Be Possible to Profile the Terrorist?" *Journal of Terrorism Research* 3 (2): 1–11.

Rathi, Nandini. 2017. "The Truth of 'Blue Whale' Challenge: A Game Said to 'Brainwash' Teens into Committing Suicides." *Indian Express*, May 9. Accessed July 4, 2017. http://indianexpress.com/article/opinion/web-edits/blue-whale-suicide-challenge-fact-or-fiction-and-a-wake-up-call-4641835/.

Rice, Timothy, and Leo Sher. 2016. "Preventing Plane-Assisted Suicides Through the Lessons of Research on Homicide and Suicide-Homicide." *Acta Neuropsychiatrica* 28 (4): 195–198.

Riedel, Marc. 2010. "Homicide-Suicides in the United States: A Review of the Literature." *Sociology Compass* 4 (7): 430–441.

Roma, Paolo, Floriana Pazzelli, Maurizio Pompili, David Lester, Paolo Girardi, and Stefano Ferracuti. 2012. "Mental Illness in Homicide-Suicide: A Review." *Journal of the American Academy of Psychiatry and the Law* 40 (4): 462–468.

Saint-Martin, Pauline, Marie Bouyssy, and Patrick O'Byrne. 2008. "Homicide-Suicide in Tours, France (2000–2005): Description of 10 Cases and a Review of the Literature." *Journal of Forensic Medicine* 15 (2): 104–109.

Saleva, Outi, Hanna Putkonen, Olli Kiviruusu, and Jouko Lönnqvist. 2007. "Homicide-Suicide: An Event Hard to Prevent and Separate from Homicide or Suicide." *Forensic Science International* 166: 204–208.

Shackelford, Todd K., and Viviana A. Weekes-Shackelford. 2012. *The Oxford Handbook of Evolutionary Perspectives on Violence, Homicide, and War.* Oxford: Oxford University Press.

Shields, Lisa, John C. Hunsaker, and Donna Stewart. 2008. "Russian Roulette and Risk-Taking Behavior: A Medical Examiner Study." *American Journal of Forensic Medicine & Pathology* 29 (1): 32–39.

Siegel, Michael, Craig Ross, and Charles King. 2013. "The Relationship Between Gun Ownership and Firearm Homicide Rates in the United States, 1981–2010." *American Journal of Public Health* 103 (11): 2098–2105.

Spehr, Scott, and John Dixon. 2013. "Protest Suicide: A Systematic Model with Heuristic Archetypes." *Journal for the Theory of Social Behaviour* 44 (3): 368–388. https://doi.org/10.1111/jtsb.12047.

Stack, Steven, and Ira Wasserman. 2008. "Social and Racial Correlates of Russian Roulette." *Suicide & Life-Threatening Behaviour* 38 (4): 436–441.

UNICEF. (2014). "Hidden in Plain Sight: A Statistical Analysis of Violence Against Children, United Nations Children's Fund" (UNICEF). Division of Data, Research and Policy. Accessed June 29, 2017. http://files.unicef.org/publications/files/Hidden_in_plain_sight_statistical_analysis_EN_3_Sept_2014.pdf.

Vijayakumar, Lakshmi. 2004. "Suicide Prevention: The Urgent Need in Developing Countries." *World Psychiatry* 3 (3): 158–159.

West, Sara G. 2007. "An Overview of Filicide." *Psychiatry (Edgmont)* 4 (2): 48–57.

Widger, Tom. 2014. "Reading Sri Lanka's Suicide Rate." *Modern Asian Studies* 48 (3): 791–825. https://doi.org/10.1017/s0026749x1200073x.

Winokur, George, and Donald Black. 1992. "Suicide-What Can Be Done?" *The New England Journal of Medicine* 327 (7): 490–491.

Zalsman, Gil, Keith Hawton, Danuta Wasserman, Kees van Heeringen, Ella Arensman, Marco Sarchiapone, Vladimir Carli, Cyril Höschl, Ran Barzilay, Judit Balazs, György Purebl, Jean Pierre Kahn, Pilar Sáiz, Alejandra Lipsicas, Cendrine Bursztein, Julio Bobes, Doina Cozman, Ulrich Hegerl, and Joseph Zohar. 2016. "Suicide Prevention Strategies Revisited: 10-Year Systematic Review." *Lancet Psychiatry* 3 (7): 646–659.

CHAPTER 6

Social, Cultural and Political Violence

A single death is a tragedy; a million deaths is a statistic. (Joseph Stalin)

This book has presented the argument that self-killing is a form of violence that can manifest in *medical* (mental illness, assisted suicide or euthanasia) or *instrumental* (martyrdom operations, protest suicide, homicide-suicide and daredevil suicide) forms. Violence (inflicting deliberate harm) and suicide (inflicting deliberate self-harm) are frequently associated with connections that view suicide as a form of self-violence but at times also a form of self-violence that is utilized as a means to additionally harm or impact others. This chapter seeks to explore the links between social, cultural and political violence and suicide. This will be approached through distinguishing the linkages between three types of violence—social, political and cultural violence—and roots of suicide. These three forms of violence are distinct but interconnected (at times reinforcing, legitimizing and obfuscating one another) but will allow us to more comprehensively consider suicidal causality. This chapter further seeks to explore connections between violence and suicide by examining how the roots of suicide relate to academic and professional standpoints explored elsewhere in the book including: sociology, social work, criminal justice, anthropology, political studies and philosophy.

K. Standish, *Suicide through a Peacebuilding Lens*,
https://doi.org/10.1007/978-981-13-9737-0_6

Defining Violence

There are numerous definitions of *violence*. For a quick dictionary survey of prevalent designations, one could consider the following:

Cambridge Dictionary: actions or words that are intended to hurt people.
Oxford Dictionary: behaviour involving physical force intended to hurt, damage or kill someone or something.
Merriam-Webster Dictionary: the use of physical force so as to injure, abuse, damage or destroy.
World Health Organization (WHO): as the intentional use of physical force or power, threatened or actual, against oneself, another person, or against a group or community, that either results in or has a high likelihood of resulting in injury, death, psychological harm, maldevelopment or deprivation.

A comprehensive and exhaustive comparison of *how* and *in what way* violence is demarcated, considered and encapsulated is beyond the scope of this chapter (or indeed this book) what follows will be a rumination on a typology of violence that considers deliberate harm in three forms: *social, cultural* and *political violence.* In many fields of the social sciences, there are detailed and deterministic categorizations of violence that name and collect instances of harm into various camps by instigator (agent), target (victim), intended audience (spectators), severity (can you walk away from it) or social level (personal, interpersonal, group or global) (Standish and Joyce 2018). In PACS, a common typology incorporates Galtung's notion of direct, indirect (structural) and cultural violence (1990), and his conceptualization is a useful interpretation of the interconnectivity of actions, systems and worldviews that can cause harm. While Galtung has done a great deal towards *making visible* forms of invisible violence (you cannot see structural or cultural violence so much as see their consequences) to understand the roots of *medical* and *instrumental* suicide, this chapter acknowledges Galtung's rubric as foundational to PACS discourse but will also introduce a typology of violence that categorizes violence as social, cultural and/or political (see Table 6.1). Galtung's model separates violence into visible and invisible forms whereas separating violence into social, cultural and political incarnations makes visible the roots and hurdles of forms that help us to

Table 6.1 Social, cultural and political violence: the basics

Social violence	*Cultural violence*	*Political violence*
Child abuse, youth gangs, bullying, sexual assault, elder abuse, intimate partner abuse	Infanticide, racism, misogyny, colonization, slavery, honour crimes, genital mutilation, genocide	Assassination, kidnapping, 'terrorism', insurgencies, civil wars, police brutality, counter 'terrorism', political torture, capital punishment

unpack the diversity of phenomena under review. As mentioned previously in this book, the goal of this study is to attend to suicide through a peacebuilding lens. With that aim, looking at how violence manifests socially, culturally and politically provides us with more nuance and breadth than notions of solely visible and invisible violence.

Whence suicide you ask? In this typology, I have reproduced a quick list of common perceptual examples of social, cultural and political violence to highlight the fact that suicide is often not considered from social, cultural or political vantage points. But it should be. In the next section, arguments and evidence for the presence of suicide in social, cultural and political violence will be presented and offered to support the emerging thesis of this chapter that suicide should be considered in all forms of violence because its presence is actually considerable.

Social Violence

Social violence is typically acknowledged as interpersonal violence and can be defined as 'acts of violence between individuals or small groups of individuals' (Fox and Hoelscher 2012, 431). The World Health Report on Violence and Health considers social violence from two subcategories: family/intimate partner violence, which occurs between family members and intimate partners, and community violence, which occurs between persons who may or may not know each other but are not related (Krug et al. 2002). Family/intimate partner violence generally occurs within the home but is not exclusive to the home environment, while community violence usually occurs outside of the home (Krug et al. 2002). Social violence normally includes, but is by no means limited to, domestic violence, assaults, homicides and rapes (Fox and Hoelscher 2012; Manning 2015).

Social Violence and Medical Suicide

A strong link can be demonstrated in the literature between social violence and suicide, and this link relates to both *medical* and *instrumental* forms. Regarding *medical* suicide, social violence has been linked to suicidal ideation and suicidal execution through mental unwellness. While mental illness alone cannot be regarded as a sole cause of suicide due to the multifactorial nature of suicide, it can attribute greatly to the decision and willingness to complete suicide (Gvion and Apter 2012). 90% of people who complete suicide are under a mental illness diagnosis of some kind when they 'succeed' in killing themselves (Phillips 2010), and studies show a connection to interpersonal (social) violence and acts of self-harm and suicide too.

There has been significant focus on the relationship between the first subcategory of social violence—intimate partner violence—and suicide, with copious research showing that intimate partner violence can be strongly related to suicide or suicide attempts (MacIsaac et al. 2017; Gulliver and Fanslow 2013; McLaughlin et al. 2012). An international review of 37 studies relating family/intimate partner violence and suicide carried out by McLaughlin et al. (2012) concluded that 35 of the 37 studies demonstrated a strong, consistent connection between family/intimate partner violence and suicidal thoughts and attempts.

The second subcategory of social violence—community violence—has also been linked to the causation of mental illness that could increase the risk of suicide. Experiencing physical or sexual violence has been shown to have links to post-traumatic stress disorder, which significantly increases the risk of suicide (Panagioti et al. 2009). Olshen et al. (2007) highlight people who experience sexual assault may develop post-traumatic stress disorder, and notably, even when post-traumatic stress disorder is not experienced, being the victim of physical and/or sexual violence has been shown to increase suicide rates (Panagioti et al. 2009).

Social Violence and Instrumental Suicide

Social violence has also been linked to *instrumental* forms of suicide, primarily homicide-suicides. In cases of homicide-suicide, family/intimate partner violence is more common than community violence. Of the five patterns of homicide-suicide conceived by James Knoll IV (2016), mentioned in Chapter 5, four involve family/intimate partner violence: *intimate-possessive*, *intimate-physically ailing*, *filicide-suicide* and *familicide-suicide*. The most dominant form of homicide-suicide is *intimate-possessive homicide-suicide*, which usually involves a man killing his female partner after estrangement (Knoll IV 2016). Such cases often have a history of domestic abuse, and the committers of these acts commonly suffer from mental illness too (Roma et al. 2012). This demonstrates a strong link between homicide-suicide and family/intimate partner (social) violence.

The fifth pattern of homicide-suicides identified by Knoll IV (2016) is *extrafamilial homicide-suicide*, which can range in scale from single-victim homicide-suicides to mass murder homicide-suicides. This is related to the subcategory of community violence and suicide, but unfortunately due to the large range of acts that this encompasses, the causation of suicide is widely varied and difficult to study (we recall that the subcategory of *community violence* occurs between persons who may or may not know each other but are not related [Krug et al. 2002]).

Further links between community violence and *instrumental* suicide include acts of martyrdom that affect other individuals, such as suicide attacks. However, a distinction is made between social violence, cultural violence and political violence in regard to the *motivation* for suicidal acts—cultural violence includes an established cultural narrative of such actions, and political violence includes a political motivation for violence. Despite motivating factors (in this instance cultural and political factors), martyrdom operations, while not necessarily linked to mental illness, are clearly forms of social violence as they involve strangers (non-family members).

While it is beyond the scope of this work to investigate the roots and hurdles of mass shootings in the USA (which are perpetrated by male individuals with mental disorders and histories of abuse), an obvious connection to acts of homicide such as school shootings where the perpetrator does not expect to survive adds another incarnation of social violence and suicide as male adolescent killers end their lives in a mass shooting of others. In these instances and with non-school-based mass shooters, a sizable amount of speculation and evidence shows homicidal ideation placing these acts squarely in the 'camp' of social violence.

Cultural Violence

The second form of violence to be explored within this chapter is cultural violence. Cultural violence in the social, cultural and political typology of violence adopts the concept conceived of by peace researcher Johan Galtung as 'aspects of culture… that can be used to justify or legitimize direct or structural violence' (Galtung 1990, 291). Direct violence and indirect (structural) violence are earlier categories of violence conceived of by Galtung; direct violence is violence that is personally committed against an individual/individuals by another individual or group, while indirect (structural) violence is committed by social structures and/or institutions via the systematic disadvantaging of individuals or groups (Galtung 1969). Cultural violence includes aspects of culture that can legitimize direct and indirect violence and includes religion and ideology, education, language, art and science (Galtung 1990).

Essentially, cultural violence is present where there is any form of violence that is normalized in communities and/or societies, and cultural violence (according to Galtung) can be the root of direct and indirect (structural) forms of violence too—indeed, he posits that cultural violence drives most forms of violence (1990). And, while different cultures have different normalized forms of violence, ALL cultures exhibit violence, albeit in either innumerable distinctive behaviours or in startlingly similar ways. An anthropological assessment of cultural violence—conflating *culture*, a shared symbolic landscape with *cultural violence*, aspects of culture that can legitimize direct and structural violence—is harmonious as long as 'legitimate violence' becomes the underlying infrastructure of culture (like kinship systems for example) not actual cultures (e.g. Latinx or Swedish) themselves (Galtung 1990).

A distinction can be made between cultural violence, social violence and political violence through the legitimization of acts of violence; social and political violence generally include acts of direct violence, whereas cultural violence is the normalization of certain forms of violence, varying between cultures, countries, states, generations and associations. To imagine how cultural violence legitimizes forms of political and social violence, one need only ponder momentarily, for example martyrdom (which occurs in relatively few cultures) versus violence against women that occurs worldwide.

Cultural Violence and Medical Suicide

Violence and suicide have been investigated by many academics confirming that the literature surrounding cultural violence and suicide links to both *medical* and *instrumental* forms. In regard to *medical* suicide, cultural violence can be linked to mental illness, euthanasia and assisted suicide. *Medical* suicide related to mental illness is present when prejudice, stigmatization and discrimination against those with mental illness is normalized (Corrigan and Watson 2002). This can be seen as those with mental illness struggle to gain jobs, safe housing, social acceptance and appropriate treatment by others and in perceptions that persons suffering bouts of mental illness are somehow less worthy of respect and dignity than those who are experiencing either physical illness or mental wellness (Corrigan and Watson 2002). Rüsch et al. (2005) highlight that stigmatization of mental illness can reinforce some aspects of illnesses in individuals through self-stigmatization and social isolation, making their symptoms worse. Not surprisingly, this self-stigmatization in combination with cultural stigmatization forms a significant barrier to seeking treatment. This demonstrates a critical link between cultural violence and suicide, particularly as treatment would likely decrease the risk of suicide in those suffering from mental illnesses through medication or therapy or both (many symptoms of depression are temporary and treatable) (Biggs and Diesfeld 1995). Mental illness additionally relates to cultural violence by making people feel like their experience of mental unwellness relates to their character or life choices—both considered in some cultures to be individual decisions that result in circumstances of life that are 'your own fault'.

Cultural violence can additionally be seen in relation to euthanasia/assisted suicide. Banović and Turanjanin (2014) highlight that euthanasia is viewed in three differing ways in criminal justice systems globally: the first is that euthanasia is considered murder just as any other form of murder and the second is that euthanasia is murder committed under privileged circumstances. Thirdly, in some states euthanasia is seen as a legal medical procedure, with requirements that are legally prescribed. While euthanasia/assisted suicide is ultimately the same in each state (barring perhaps difference in procedure), *the difference lies in the cultural legitimization* that determines whether these acts are normalized and/or legalized. Pierre (2015) perceives of these acts as culturally sanctioned murder, regardless of whether motives of unbearable pain or a wish to exercise autonomy rather than lose all dignity, are present, and some researchers and practitioners also see euthanasia/assisted suicide as a form of cultural violence that is interwoven with devaluation of disability (Golden and Zoanni 2010; Gill 2010). This is due to the normalization of the choice of death over disability or loss of dignity that is associated with euthanasia/assisted suicide. Gill (2010) highlights that this normalization has further led to the subconscious bias of some medical professionals against disabled persons in states where euthanasia and/or assisted suicide is actually legal. Further research has supported this, with Heyer (2011) demonstrating that some disabled individuals have been pressured, or continuously asked, to sign Do Not Resuscitate forms. This demonstrates that euthanasia/assisted suicide can create and reproduce cultural violence towards disabled individuals.

Cultural Violence and Instrumental Suicide

Cultural violence can also be linked to forms of *instrumental* suicide, namely martyrdom. There is a strong link between cultural violence and martyrdom, as martyrdom is justified by way of religion. In current times, martyrdom is heavily associated with Islam; thus, this is the form of martyrdom that will be discussed here. In Islam, martyrdom is viewed as a brave sacrifice and an honourable path straight to the afterlife, where multiple rewards are waiting (Pierre 2015; Speckhard 2005). On Earth, the families of martyrs are viewed with great honour within society and are often given material wealth (Pierre 2015). Hasso (2005) highlights that Muslim and Christian Palestinians frequently utilize the term 'martyrdom' as opposed to 'suicide' in relation to suicide bombings, as it shows respect and honour for the bombers and their families. There is a noted difference between martyrdom and suicide, whereas suicide is forbidden within Islam, martyrdom operations are highly praised and doctrinally sanctioned (Pierre 2015). The rewards, both religious and social, of martyrdom and the social celebration of martyrs give cultural justification to martyrdom. As cultural violence legitimizes acts of violence, martyrdom can thus be seen as a form of cultural violence.

Political Violence

The final type of violence to be explored in this chapter is political violence. Political violence is defined as sub-state violence with a political motivation to defy or challenge the authority of a state (Fox and Hoelscher 2012). Political violence can be non-lethal or lethal, and can range from, but is not limited to, street demonstrations, 'terrorism' and civil war (Sayari 2010). While some academics use the term 'political violence' to describe any violence related to political causes, current literature generally distinguishes political violence to be of a sub-state nature as opposed to state-sponsored violence. Fox and Hoelscher (2012, 433) specifically refer to political violence as challenging the authority of a state to 'monopolize the legitimate use of violence within its borders'. Political violence can be distinguished from social violence by motivation; social violence does not actively involve an attempt to challenge a state's authority, as opposed to political violence. There is a link between political violence and social violence however, as countries suffering from political violence are associated with higher levels of social violence too (Fox and Hoelscher 2012; Cummings et al. 2009).

Political Violence and Medical Suicide

In regard to *medical* suicide, there is a demonstrable link between the consequences of political violence and the causation of mental illness such as depression and disorders, such as post-traumatic stress disorder that may lead to suicide (Tol et al. 2010). The consequences of political violence can include but are not limited to human rights violations, poverty, reduced access to health care and increased family, financial and political stress (Haj-Yahia 2008). Research on the link between political violence and mental health focuses on armed conflicts as political violence highlighting the psychological effects of wars, both interstate and intrastate (Haj-Yahia 2008). In a study of Latino adults that had previous exposure to political violence, Eisenman et al. (2003) determined that political violence has significant impacts on depression and post-traumatic stress disorders. Betancourt and Williams (2008) highlight that Western labels and approaches to mental illness are inappropriate in some cultural contexts, but also underline that trauma-related mental disorders are common consequences of armed conflict that occur across cultures. Further sources of research show that children are particularly affected by political violence; Haj-Yahia's (2008) review of literature surrounding the consequences of political violence for children highlighted that while not all children have negative psychological reactions to political violence, many of them experience both short- and long-term implications including anxiety, sleep disorders and post-traumatic stress disorders. This conclusion is supported by Cummings et al. (2009), who identified similar findings in research on children and political violence experienced within Northern Ireland. Post-traumatic stress disorders have been experienced by children in varying culturally different areas, including Cambodia, Kosovo, Bosnia, Croatia, Lebanon, Palestine and Israel, demonstrating that this is a cross-cultural occurrence following political violence (Haj-Yahia 2008). As noted previously in this chapter, the multifactorial nature of suicide can make causality difficult to assert, but there is a strong link between mental illness and suicide causation. Unfortunately, while much research is available on the link between political violence and mental illness in both children and adults, there is little research available that directly connects political violence with *medical* suicide.

Political Violence and Instrumental Suicide

While there is inadequate research on the direct link between political violence and *medical* suicide, there is a convincing connection between political violence and *instrumental* suicide. Although martyrdom operations are not always political, it is commonly considered to be an act of sacrificing oneself for one's values or to draw attention to and protest an injustice (Halverson et al. 2013). While some acts of martyrdom involve only the death of the martyr, other forms of martyrdom aim to injure or kill others simultaneously. The latter form of martyrdom suicide is known as a suicide attack and intends to incite fear within another group within society with the act or threat of violence (Pierre 2015). Martyrdom in such ways can be an effective means of political violence, as there is significant drama and communicated willingness to place one's body on the line for a political cause (Hasso 2005). Cook (2002) highlights that suicide attacks are nearly always aimed at civilians rather than military targets, as this demonstrates both the inability of the victimized individuals' government to protect 'their' people from harm and perceptions from the offensive group of the legitimate targeting of out-group victims. Because civilians are generally easier to target than military individuals or compounds, there is an added benefit of the 'echo' of the attack that instils fear and suffering in people long after the attack is over. Speckhard (2005) underlines that this is a way of coercing governments into making concessions, as suicide attacks can affect peace processes, gain international media attention and create a widespread sense of dread and horror. As such, martyrdom creates strong links between suicide and political violence.

At this point, one might feel somewhat 'under it' with all the terminology and types, forms and manifestations of violence in this contemplation, but to simplify something very complex, it goes something like this: suicide, which has both *medical* and *instrumental* forms, has social, cultural and political roots. Galtung's rubric (termed his triangle shown in Fig. 6.1) shows how his types of violence (visible-direct and invisible-structural and cultural) intersect and reinforce one another.

And the typology explored in this chapter's incarnations of violence (social, cultural and political) is considered in relation to *medical* and *instrumental* suicide. If one were very complex and multifactorial, one could create a matrix of violence(s) to show how suicide relates to direct, structural and cultural violence within the rubric of direct, indirect (structural) and cultural violence and articulate both theoretical frameworks to instances of *medical* or *instrumental* suicide (and those inclined may do), but for our purposes, it is sufficient to highlight that in either Galtung's triangle of direct, indirect (structural) or cultural violence or in the social, cultural and political violence typology used in this chapter, there seems to be a pronounced connection but simultaneous lacunae of suicide—*and this is despite being the number one form of violent death in most countries*—which leads us to reflect once more, suicide, self-harm, self-killing and killing of self and others seems to be (mostly) missing.

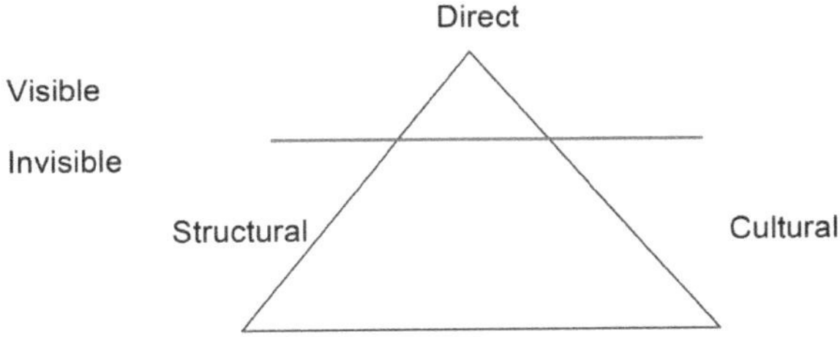

Fig. 6.1 Galtung's triangle of violence

Table 6.2 Social, cultural and political violence: including suicide

Social violence	*Cultural violence*	*Political violence*
Child abuse, youth gangs, bullying, sexual assault, elder abuse, intimate partner abuse, *medical* suicide, *instrumental* suicide	Infanticide, racism, misogyny, colonization, slavery, honour crimes, genital mutilation, genocide, *medical* suicide, *instrumental* suicide	Assassination, kidnapping, 'terrorism', insurgencies, civil wars, *instrumental* suicide

A reimagining of the table presented in the Introduction of this chapter that included suicide would look something like this (Table 6.2).

So why do we keep missing suicide? Is it something about how we look at it or just that we do not look at it at all? Like a sun that shines too bright to be observed or a shuddering spectacle we dare not attend to for fear of duplication, suicide, it seems, is absent. But what of scholar/practitioners in other social sciences, have they something that could help us in PACS to jump the gully? In the following section, a brief exploration of how suicide is considered in relation to social, cultural and political violence in the fields of sociology, social work, criminal justice, anthropology, political studies and philosophy may supplement a lack of inclusion in the study of violence and violence prevention.

Social, Cultural and Political Violence and Suicide in Six Fields

Sociology

The first field of study to be addressed in relation to the interaction of suicide and social, cultural and political violence is sociology. Sociology is a field that scientifically investigates human society and social behaviour and seeks to contextualize individual actions within societies (Lee 2016). As such, sociologists have long taken an interest in violence within societies, including suicide, though interest in suicide has waxed and waned over decades (Wray et al. 2011). The study of suicide in sociology has been heavily influenced by the prominent work of Émile Durkheim in 1897, which has also greatly impacted other fields of study (Scourfield et al. 2012). Durkheim's approach was to examine the relation between suicide rates and various social factors, namely social integration and regulation (Wray et al. 2011). Social integration is understood to be the sense of social belonging and inclusion that results from social ties, whereas social regulation is the monitoring and external restraints that also result from social ties. Both over-integration and under-integration and over-regulation and under-regulation result in additional vulnerability to suicide, which demonstrates that suicide risk is only diminished when these forces are in balance (Durkheim 1897, cited in Wray et al. 2011). Durkheim also developed a theory known as the social-environmental approach, which highlighted that change to social, political, religious or economic environmental factors could alter social roles, values and relationships and lead to a greater risk of suicide (1897, cited in Milner et al. 2013). These theories of suicide have informed and influenced much of the contemporary sociological literature on suicide, which still continues to focus on social explanations for suicide.

Sociological literature clearly highlights the role of social violence and cultural violence in the causation of suicides. In relation to social violence, sociology highlights not physical violence but violence related to social interaction. Stack (2000b) demonstrated that social isolation could be linked to increased likelihood of suicide among individuals that have become divorced and among individuals that have migrated countries. Similarly, Milner et al. (2013) highlighted that divorce, separation and widowhood result in a higher likelihood of suicide and that individuals living in rural areas have much higher rates of suicide than those in urban areas. The latter may be related to many other factors (not solely social isolation), with other possible roots such as inaccessibility of mental health services and access to lethal means being highlighted (Milner et al. 2013).

Societal exposure to suicide has also been shown to play a role in suicide causation. Hedström et al. (2008) highlighted that those who are exposed to suicide in their family or workplace are significantly more likely to complete suicide: men who were exposed to suicide in the family were seen to be 8.3 times more likely to complete suicide themselves and were 3.5 times more likely to complete suicide if exposed to suicide in the workplace. Further research has shown that there are also links between media reporting of suicide and suicide rates, which additionally underlines the effects of social exposure to suicide (Milner et al. 2013). This link between media reporting of suicide and suicide rates has also been noted by Yip et al. (2012), who highlight that this is due to the sensationalizing of celebrity suicides and the provision of information to individuals that reminds or informs them of means of completing suicide.

While social isolation and social exposure to suicide are not intentional interpersonal violence, these are linked to causes of suicide that are created by social interaction.

Sociology literature has demonstrated that suicide has links to cultural violence through the gendered causes of suicide. Statistics show that men are three times more likely than women to complete suicide (Wray et al. 2011). Shiner et al. (2009) highlight that factors of employment problems and criminal activity are more frequently associated with suicides of men, whereas isolation, mental illness and issues related to children are more frequently associated with women. Furthermore, relationship problems were shown to be a cause in twice as many male suicides as compared to female suicides. Scourfield et al. (2012) underline that problems with children being heavily associated with female suicides and problems of employment and debt being strongly associated with male suicides reflect traditional gender roles. These authors go on to suggest that, in regard to male suicides, publicly failing to live up to societal ideals of masculinity by losing a job or being in debt can be a cause of suicide. This is backed up by Stack (2000a), who highlights that the traditional primary role for men of economic success is more visible in relation to failure than the roles of women. Amitai and Apter (2012) and Stack (2000a) mention that the greater number of male suicides could also be related to difficulties in recognizing warning signs of suicide, asking for help and communicating about suicidal feelings, which again highlights the effects of gender expectations. This not only demonstrates a link between suicide and cultural violence, but also shows the consequences of gender expectations and inequality in society.

Social Work

The next field of study to be discussed in this chapter is social work. Social work is a field of study where theory leads to professional social work responses and frameworks surrounding family/intimate partner violence and community violence. Literature in this area has a particular focus on intimate partner violence and child abuse, but has comparatively had limited focus on suicide despite patients with suicidal behaviour being common in the practice of social work (Paolucci et al. 2001; Joe and Niedermeier 2006). A study carried out by Feldman and Freedenthal (2006) highlighted that social workers in America receive little, if any, training in suicide prevention or intervention, even though they have abundant interaction with suicidal individuals. While suicidal behaviour is most visible to social workers that provide mental health services, it is also seen in nearly all areas of social work (Feldman and Freedenthal 2006). The causation of suicide, as perceived within social work literature, is linked to social and cultural violence, but does not interact with political violence. The literature also considers only *medical* forms of suicide, particularly mental illness-related suicide, and has limited reference to *instrumental* forms of suicide.

The literature surrounding suicide in the field of social work has been increasing over the last two decades. A literature review carried out by Joe and Niedermeier (2006) of social work literature concerning suicide highlighted that existing literature tends to relate the causes of suicide to social violence, including both intimate partner violence and community violence. A representative sample of literature that demonstrates this link includes Benda's (2003) study that showed victims of sexual abuse and/or physical violence have significantly increased rates of suicidal behaviour; Bagley et al.'s (1997) study that also demonstrated a relationship between sexual harassment and assault with suicidal behaviour among females and Hsiao-Rei Hicks and Bhugra's (2003) research that highlighted a link between current abuse or domestic violence and suicide. These studies, along with further studies that support their conclusions (see Joe and Niedermeier 2006), underline that suicide within social work is seen as a social problem with social causes. Michailaki and Schirmer (2014) highlight that this conclusion of suicide as a social problem places social workers in a position of at least partial responsibility to prevent suicide.

Social work literature surrounding the causes of suicide also connects suicide causation with cultural violence. Though cultural violence is not mentioned by name, studies have shown that oppression, discrimination and prejudice may increase the risk of suicide, particularly of those in minority groups (Joe and Niedermeier 2006). A study of attempted suicide among Native American youth raised on a reservation highlighted that perceived discrimination had significant input into suicide attempts (Freedenthal and Stiffman 2004). There is also a strong link between transsexual individuals and suicide, with gender-based prejudice being highlighted as a major cause of suicide as well as a means of prevention if addressed (Clements-Nolle et al. 2006). Interestingly, Fernquist (2003) demonstrated a connection between perceived income inequality and increased suicide rates, particularly for men, which could denote a link between suicide and assigned gender roles. These studies highlight that reducing cultural violence relating to gender and minorities could influence suicide rates.

Criminal Justice

The third field of study that is to be explored in relation to suicide causation in this chapter is criminal justice. Criminal justice is a field that concentrates on the study of criminal behaviour and the response of society to such behaviour, seeking to create theories that explain this relationship (Bernard and Engel 2001). The literature of the criminal justice field that relates to suicide largely focuses on suicide of prisoners and ex-prisoners (Webb et al. 2011). Research has shown that within the USA and the UK, rates of suicide in correctional institutes are higher than those in the general population (Gupta and Girdhar 2012). There is also a further link between heightened rates of suicide and individuals that have been processed through the criminal justice system but remain in the community, including individuals that with non-custodial sentences and those that have been given non-guilty sentences (Webb et al. 2011). As such, Webb et al. (2011) highlight that there is a significant public health issue relating to suicide and the criminal justice system.

The field of criminal justice regards the cause of suicide among those associated with the criminal justice system, in prison or in the community, to be primarily associated with mental illness (Marzano et al. 2016; Gupta and Girdhar 2012; Webb et al. 2011; Hanson 2010). Webb et al. (2011) also proposed that the criminal offences and/or the criminal justice system might play a role in exacerbating the risk of suicide in individuals that are already vulnerable due to mental health issues. However, some literature also connects causation with social violence (Webb et al. 2011; Gupta and Girdhar 2012). Criminal justice takes a different perspective than other fields of study in regard to social violence related to suicide, as it looks at the suicides of those who commit social violence, not necessarily those who are the victims of social violence. Webb et al. (2011) underline that the risk of suicide is particularly high among individuals that commit violent crimes and venture that powerful feelings of regret may cause this ratio, particularly in cases where victims were family members or where crimes were carried out while intoxicated. There could also be an element of cultural violence to this, as women who commit violent offences have higher rates of suicide than men (Webb et al. 2011). Interpersonal conflicts within prison, including sexual abuse, are considered a chronic stressor that can aid in causation of suicide (Gupta and Girdhar 2012). Fear of, or the threat of, physical or sexual violence was also linked to suicide within prisons (Gupta and Girdhar 2012). Hanson (2010) highlights that increasing gang violence within prisons is leading to increased risk of suicide, as individuals may feel pressured to join a gang or be victimized by a gang. In such cases, suicide is seen as an option where prison protection against these activities is not sufficient. Conversely, where prison facilities exercise strict social control that removes opportunities for violence, such as in high-security prisons, suicide rates are also increased due to social isolation and inability to create social networks (Huey and McNulty 2005). Overcrowding of prisons also has been shown to significantly increase the risk of suicide (Huey and McNulty 2005).

There are hints of suicide relating to cultural violence within the criminal justice literature. This is highlighted in Hanson's (2010) study into suicides of prisoners, which mentions that prisoners may avoid seeking treatment for mental health issues due to penalization and stigma. Hanson underlined that prisoners with a history of mental health issues are less likely to be granted parole, may be transferred to easily recognizable mental health tiers within prisons and could even be stripped and placed in suicide observation cells before their mental health is assessed if they mention suicidal ideation. The aforementioned trauma of sexual abuse in prison relates to cultural legitimizers such as toxic, dominatory masculinity and contributes to increased risk of suicide for victims of sexual assault (Gupta and Girdhar 2012). Furthermore, prisoners with a history of mental health may not be allowed to participate in work schemes or be allowed to transfer to lower-security programs such as home detention if local psychiatric services are not available, regardless of the state of the inmate's mental illness. This demonstrates stigma and penalization of inmates relating to their mental illness and is shown to be a barrier to inmates seeking treatment, thus increases their risk of suicide (Hanson 2010). Further studies show that even where mental illness has been diagnosed, psychiatric treatment while in prison may not be forthcoming (Marzano et al. 2016). With the strong connections between mental illness and suicide of those in prison, cultural barriers to seeking help and lack of treatment can play a significant role in suicide rates.

Anthropology

The fourth field of study to be addressed in this chapter is anthropology. Anthropology can be defined as 'the scientific study of humanity, which describes the workings of societies around the world through comparative and cross-cultural (sometimes historical) methods' (Lee 2016, 159). Anthropologists usually, but not always, investigate cultures other than their own and aim to study cultures within the context of their historical background and perspective (cultural context) by utilizing an ethnographic methodology of meticulous and objective observation, recording and study (Lee 2016). This means of study can mean that there is limited focus on creating generalizable theories, as ethnographic studies are specific to each culture and context. Münster and Broz (2015) highlight that anthropology has been late to the study of suicide and has contributed relatively little in regard to suicidology. Studies that have been carried out into suicide are limited, but continue on the anthropological tradition of ethnography (Staples and Widger 2012).

The limited anthropological research that has been carried out on suicide has linked the causes of suicide primarily to cultural and political violence. Anthropological studies have highlighted that there is accusation or revenge inherent in most suicides and that suicide is fundamentally a communicative act (Münster and Broz 2015). This relates to suicides associated with cultural violence as well as suicides associated with political violence. Marecek and Senadheera (2012) separate suicides into dialogue suicides, defined as suicides that are expressive and intended as communication to others, and monologue suicides, which are inwardly focused acts that intend to end persistent pain. These authors put forward that cultures have acknowledged narratives of suicide, which individuals utilize to give meaning to suicide and which thus inform both perspectives on and acts of suicide. For example, suicides in European and North American contexts are generally seen as monologue suicides, where mental illness is shown to play a large role (Marecek and Senadheera 2012). Conversely, an ethnographic study of suicide in Sri Lanka highlighted dialogue suicide as the dominant cultural narrative (Marecek and Senadheera 2012). Along similar lines, other anthropologists also relate suicide to cultural violence via the link between suicide statistics and feedback loops (Münster 2015). In these situations, populations that are statically labelled to be suicide-prone, such as young homosexual individuals or farmers in India, become cyclically more likely to complete suicide (Münster 2015; Münster and Broz 2015).

In regard to political violence, anthropological studies have shown that suicides can have a political motive. According to Münster and Broz (2015), anthropology seeks to move beyond visions of political suicide as those of public self-destruction to include less spectacular suicides that may function as political acts or accusations against structural violence. As mentioned in Chapter 5, Münster (2015) carried out an ethnographic study of farmer suicides in India, where agrarian crises are creating economic crises and ultimately leading to greater rates of suicide among farmers. Münster highlights that farmer suicides in this context may be intended to be political, where suicide is caused by the desire to send a message or protest to the state. While anthropologist Karin Andriolo refers to protest suicides as 'dying with a message, for a message, and of a message' (cited in Münster 2015, 1592), Münster (2015) highlights that suicides regarded as political, in relation to the farmer suicides in India, can also have co-occurring motivations such as fear, shame and economic distress unrelated to 'messaging'. Furthermore, Münster underlines that political suicide can be framed as political by individuals other than the person who completed suicide—his ethnographic study demonstrated that the context and politicization of farmer suicides may impose this interpretation on or play a part in facilitating later suicidal situations. In India, this led to occurrences of suicides being regarded as political or public deaths, when in fact they were apolitical private acts caused by economic distress, depression, shame or other factors, and the possibility that suicides were influenced by the politicization of previous suicides. This underlines the anthropological view that suicides can be political through intention or through the influence of political contexts.

Ethnographic studies, generally carried out in developing countries, highlight that dialogue suicide is often related to aspects of cultural violence such as gender roles. An ethnographic study carried out in Sri Lanka highlighted that cultural gender norms of obedience and respect impede young women from speaking back to their parents during disputes, which can lead to young women self-harming or completing suicide as a means of registering their disagreement (Marecek and Senadheera 2012). The same study showed that suicidal behaviour in Sri Lanka is heavily associated with both the experiencing of interpersonal problems and the feeling of anger. This, combined with the idea that suicide in Western countries is generally related to mental illness, further suggests that suicidal behaviour and suicide can be an interpersonal experience rather than an intrapersonal experience and that culture tends to guide this distinction. Other anthropological studies also highlight issues of gender in causation and perceptions of suicide; Staples and Widger (2012) reference several studies demonstrating that women may utilize suicide as a form of legitimate protest where social norms do not allow for other means of objection.

Political Studies

The fifth field of study to be discussed in this chapter is political studies, also known as political science. Political studies is a field of study that investigates government and issues of power, authority and conflict at local, national and international levels. In regard to suicide, political studies' focus is on the political causes for suicide and the political effects of suicide, with literature concentrating on *instrumental* forms of suicide, in particular martyrdom suicides. Horowitz (2015) highlights that political studies, more so than other fields of study, is affected by and follows political and economic shifts within the world. Research within the field of political studies tends to focus on acts of martyrdom suicide that intend violence to other individuals, such as suicide attacks, rather than martyrdom suicides that do not. The suicide acts that intend violence to others are defined as suicide 'terrorism', where suicide is used as a tactic to commit and/or threaten violence in order to incite fear (Pierre 2015). Though academics tend to agree on the political motives of martyrdom suicides, which are often espoused by the martyrs themselves or in some cases the non-state actor that has organized suicide attacks, the cause of these suicides is disputed.

Suicides related to political violence intend to undermine the authority of a state by making a political statement and/or creating fear within the general population, utilizing death to show the extent of their commitment (Pierre 2015). Robert Pape (2003) further puts forth that suicide attacks primarily intend to coerce governments to alter their policies. There are differing causes for martyrdom suicides in each situation, but generalized causes have been highlighted within the literature. Moghadam (2006) highlights that one act of suicide is likely to have several associated causal factors. Humiliation, desire for revenge, despair or identity issues can be a personal motivation for carrying out these acts (Moghadam 2006). Kruglanski and Orehek (2011) also underline humiliation as a cause and add further causes of social rejection and exclusion, personal loss and trauma, injustice and poverty. These causes are echoed too by Speckhard (2005), who disagrees only with the aspect of poverty and proposes instead relative deprivation, underlining that suicide bombers in particular have been found to be socioeconomically better off and just as well educated, if not more, than peers. Speckhard explains that consequently, suicide bombers are more likely to be educated and socially aware but are lacking in opportunities in their communities to legitimately address injustices; suicide bombing then becomes a viable option.

Not all motivations to commit martyrdom suicides are negative however, as Moghadam (2006) and Speckhard (2005) demonstrate that these acts can bring a sense of purpose and social belonging, heightened social status and empowerment, particularly if the individual concerned is part of a 'terrorist' organization. Being part of an organization can initiate further causes however of social pressure (Speckhard 2005). Pape's (2003) prominent study on suicide 'terrorism' found that a main objective of suicide bombing was to stop foreign occupation and gain control of areas that non-state groups considered their home territories. This is backed up by Braun and Genkin (2014), but has been disputed by several other academics based on varying definitions of foreign occupation and many suicide attacks that are unrelated to foreign occupation (see Horowitz 2015). Regardless of other causes, individuals that commit martyrdom suicides tend to live in contexts of relative deprivation where there are few economic opportunities, which could be the basis of many of the other causal factors (Horowitz 2015).

Causation of martyrdom suicides has also been heavily explored at an organizational level within political studies, as violent martyrdom suicides are often coordinated by 'terrorist' organizations. Moghadam (2006) underlines that causation at the individual and organizational level can be intertwined; belonging to a 'terrorist' organization for example can lead to positive feelings of social belonging, purpose and empowerment. At an organizational level, there are several factors suggested for the causation of suicide. Horowitz (2015) highlights that sending members to commit suicide attacks demonstrates commitment to the relevant cause and can attract new members to organized groups. In situations where several groups are competing for members, this is stated to be 'outbidding' for new members (Horowitz 2015, 76). Moghadam (2006) also included several more causes of martyrdom suicides: the level of attention that is drawn to suicide attacks which thus draws attention to the group's motivations; creation of extreme fear in other populations; increasing morale within the group; strengthening support in the international arena; invoking a harsh response from other states that increases support for the group's cause; and finally the strategic advantages of suicide attacks, which are highly lethal, cost-efficient and don't require an escape plan.

Political studies' academics also highlighted religion as a cause or facilitating factor of martyrdom suicides, at both an individual and group level (Speckhard 2005; Horowitz 2015; Kruglanski and Orehek 2011). While this is still related to political violence given the political motivations of such an act, there is also a link to cultural violence. This is due to the legitimization of martyrdom that religion offers, in particular Islam. The interaction of Islam and martyrdom has been discussed previously in this chapter, thus will not be detailed here, but this highlights that cultural violence can legitimize forms of political violence.

Philosophy

The final field to be discussed in relation to the causes of suicide within this chapter is philosophy. Within philosophy, literature on suicide has mainly surrounded the ethics of suicide and the rationality, or irrationality, of committing suicide. This has resulted in very few studies on the roots of suicide, with causes of suicide being mentioned mostly in discussions of what is and is not morally permissible. Those causes that do exist within the literature emphasize personal causes for suicide, rather than those that relate to social, cultural or political violence. During his denial that suicide is ever morally permissible, Kant suggests that suicide can be motivated by grief, anxiety and depression (cited in Cholbi 2010). Another study within philosophy attributes the causation of suicide to mental illness and highlights that the psychological effects of mental illness have not been taken into account in earlier philosophical debates surrounding the permissibility of suicide (Cholbi 2002). Velleman (1999) highlights that unbearable pain or loss of dignity associated with illness could cause suicide. Velleman's association of loss of dignity with death, particularly morally permissible death, could be related to cultural violence. This is due to the cultural acceptance of death due to loss of dignity that suggests that disability is a fate worse than death, which devalues those who are disabled within our society and may lead to direct or structural violence against such individuals which this study would include as acts of cultural violence (Golden and Zoanni 2010). As philosophy's focus is on the questions surrounding suicide and not the reasons

Table 6.3 Social, cultural and political violence in six fields

Field	*Social violence*	*Cultural violence*	*Political violence*
Sociology	✓	✓	
Social work	✓	✓	
Criminal justice	✓	✓	
Anthropology		✓	✓
Political studies		✓	✓
Philosophy	✓	✓	

for suicide itself, there are few other causes that can be drawn out from the literature but the location of mental illness and cultural legitimization of discrimination against individuals in society experiencing disability connects these considerations to both social and cultural violence.

Perhaps unsurprisingly, these fields focus on various forms of violence while ignoring or obscuring others. A graphic illustration of the entertainment of suicide in these six fields would look like this (Table 6.3).

This brief exploration of how various fields treat suicide in regard to social, cultural and political violence lays open a pathway for future researchers to supplement the existing (although often meagre) attention to acts of self-killing in relation to their apertures of investigation. To suggest that there is a social aspect to suicide would benefit political studies and anthropology (for example) as would a conceptualization of the political aspects of violence in sociology, social work, criminal justice and philosophy.

Conclusion

This chapter has explored not only the links between suicide and social, cultural and political violence, but also the role that these forms of violence play in regard to causation of suicide in differing fields of study. The fields of study that were examined here—sociology, social work, criminal justice, anthropology, political studies and philosophy—each had differing views on the causation of suicide, with some fields offering much greater amounts of research on the topic. The distinctions between social, cultural and political violence and the way that these forms of violence were related to suicide causation also demonstrated the breadth of difference between the fields of study, as fields addressed differing forms of violence dependent on their research focus. This exemplifies the range of perspectives relating to causation of suicide and highlighted the relevance that is placed on the topic of suicide within different fields of study. With this range of perspectives on causation, it may be possible to problematize suicide further and if these fields all encounter suicide from one vantage point or another (none had 'none'), it remains to be answered why the number one cause of violent death in most nations gets so little focus in Peace and Conflict Studies.

This chapter explored the links between *medical* and *instrumental* suicide and social, cultural and political violence in PACS and six adjacent disciplines. The next chapter will alter our angle of investigation through a consideration of how *medical* and *instrumental* suicide related to intention, motivation and intervention.

References

Amitai, Maya, and Alan Apter. 2012. "Social Aspects of Suicidal Behavior and Prevention in Early Life: A Review." *International Journal of Environmental Research and Public Health* 9 (3): 985–994.

Bagley, Christopher, Floyd Bolitho, and Lorne Bertrand. 1997. "Sexual Assault in School, Mental Health and Suicidal Behaviors in Adolescent Women in Canada." *Adolescence* 32 (126): 361–366.

Banović, Božidar, and Veljko Turanjanin. 2014. "Euthanasia: Murder or Not—A Comparative Approach." *Iranian Journal of Public Health* 43 (10): 1316–1323.

Benda, Brent. 2003. "Discriminators of Suicide Thoughts and Attempts Among Homeless Veterans Who Abuse Substances." *Suicide and Life-Threatening Behavior* 33 (4): 430–442.

Bernard, Thomas, and Robin Engel. 2001. "Conceptualizing Criminal Justice Theory." *Justice Quarterly* 18 (1): 1–30.

Betancourt, Theresa, and Timothy Williams. 2008. "Building an Evidence Base on Mental Health Interventions for Children Affected by Armed Conflict." *Intervention* 6 (1): 39–56.

Biggs, Hazel, and Kate Diesfeld. 1995. "Assisted Suicide or People with Depression: An Advocate's Perspective." *Medical Law International* 2: 23–37.

Braun, Robert, and Michael Genkin. 2014. "Cultural Resonance and the Diffusion of Suicide Bombings: The Role of Collectivism." *Journal of Conflict Resolution* 58 (7): 1258–1284.

Cholbi, Michael. 2002. "Suicide Intervention and Non-ideal Kantian Theory." *Journal of Applied Philosophy* 19 (3): 245–259.

Cholbi, Michael. 2010. "A Kantian Defense of Prudential Suicide." *Journal of Moral Philosophy* 7 (4): 489–515.

Clements-Nolle, Kristin, Rani Marx, and Mitchell Katz. 2006. "Attempted Suicide Among Transgender Persons: The Influence of Gender-Based Discrimination and Victimization." *Journal of Homosexuality* 51 (3): 53–69.

Cook, David. 2002. "Suicide Attacks or 'Martyrdom Operations' in Contemporary Jihad Literature." *Nova Religio: The Journal of Alternative and Emergent Religions* 6 (1): 7–44.

Corrigan, Patrick, and Amy Watson. 2002. "Understanding the Impact of Stigma on People with Mental Illness." *World Psychiatry* 1 (1): 16–20.

Cummings, E. Mark, Marcie Goeke-Morey, Alice Schermerhorn, Christine Merrilees, and Ed Cairns 2009. "Children and Political Violence from a Social Ecological Perspective: Implications from Research on Children and Families in Northern Ireland." *Clinical Child Family Psychological Review* 12 (1): 16–38.

Eisenman, David, Lillian Gelberg, Honghu Liu, and Martin Shapiro. 2003. "Mental Health and Health-Related Quality of Life Among Adult Latino Primary Care Patients Living in the United States with Previous Exposure to Political Violence." *Journal of the American Medical Association* 290 (5): 627–635.

Feldman, Barry, and Stacey Freedenthal. 2006. "Social Work Education in Suicide Intervention and Prevention: An Unmet Need?" *Suicide and Life-Threatening Behaviour* 36 (4): 467–480.

Fernquist, Robert. 2003. "Perceived Income Inequality and Suicide Rates in Central/Eastern European Countries and Western Countries, 1990–1993." *Death Studies* 27 (1): 63–80.

Fox, Sean, and Kristian Hoelscher. 2012. "Political Order, Development and Social Violence." *Journal of Peace Research* 49 (3): 431–444.

Freedenthal, Stacey, and Arlene Rubin Stiffman. 2004. "Suicidal Behavior in Urban American Indian Adolescents: A Comparison with Reservation Youth in a South-Western State." *Suicide and Life-Threatening Behavior* 34 (2): 160–171.

Galtung, Johan. 1969. "Violence, Peace and Peace Research." *Journal of Peace Research* 6 (3): 167–191.

Galtung, Johan. 1990. "Cultural Violence." *Journal of Peace Research* 27 (3): 291–305.

Gill, Carol. 2010. "No, We Don't Think Our Doctors Are Out to Get Us: Responding to the Straw Man Distortions of Disability Rights Arguments Against Assisted Suicide." *Disability and Health Journal* 3 (1): 31–38.

Golden, Marilyn, and Tyler Zoanni. 2010. "Killing Us Softly: The Dangers of Legalizing Assisted Suicide." *Disability and Health Journal* 3 (1): 16–30.

Gulliver, Pauline, and Janet Fanslow. 2013. "Exploring Risk Factors for Suicidal Ideation in a Population-Based Sample of New Zealand Women Who Have

Experienced Intimate Partner Violence." *Australian and New Zealand Journal of Public Health* 36 (6): 527–533.

Gupta, Anju, and N. K. Girdhar. 2012. "Risk Factors of Suicide in Prisoners." *Delhi Psychiatry Journal* 15 (1): 45–49.

Gvion, Yari, and Alan Apter. 2012. "Suicide and Suicidal Behavior." *Public Health Reviews* 34 (2): 1–20

Haj-Yahia, Muhammad. 2008. "Political Violence in Retrospect: Its Effect on the Mental Health of Palestinian Adolescents." *International Journal of Behavioural Development* 32 (4): 283–289.

Halverson, Jeffry, Scott Ruston, and Angela Trethewey. 2013. "Mediated Martyrs of the Arab Spring: New Media, Civil Religion, and Narrative in Tunisia and Egypt." *Journal of Communication* 63 (2): 312–332.

Hanson, Annette. 2010. "Correctional Suicide: Has Progress Ended?" *Journal of the American Academy of Psychiatry and the Law* 38 (1): 6–10.

Hasso, Frances. 2005. "Discursive and Political Deployments by/of the 2002 Palestinian Women Suicide Bombers/Martyrs." *Feminist Review* 81 (1): 23–51.

Hedström, Peter, Ka-yuet Liu, and Monica Nordvik. 2008. "Interaction Domains and Suicide: A Population-Based Panel Study of Suicides in Stockholm, 1991–1999." *Social Forces* 87 (2): 713–740.

Heyer, Katharina. 2011. "Rejecting Rights: The Disability Critique of Physician Assisted Suicide." *Studies in Law, Politics and Society* 54 (Special Issue): 77–112.

Horowitz, Michael. 2015. "The Rise and Spread of Suicide Bombing." *Annual Review of Political Science* 18: 69–84.

Hsiao-Rei Hicks, Madelyn, and Dinesh Bhugra. 2003. "Perceived Causes of Suicide Attempts by U.K. South Asian Women." *American Journal of Orthopsychiatry* 73 (4): 455–462.

Huey, Meredith, and Thomas McNulty. 2005. "Institutional Conditions and Prison Suicide: Conditional Effects of Deprivation and Overcrowding." *The Prison Journal* 85 (4): 490–514.

Joe, Sean, and Danielle Niedermeier. 2006. "Preventing Suicide: A Neglected Social Work Research Agenda." *The British Journal of Social Work* 38 (3): 507–530.

Knoll IV, James. 2016. "Understanding Homicide-Suicide." *Psychiatric Clinics of North America* 39 (4): 633–647.

Krug, Etienne, Linda Dahlberg, James Mercy, Anthony Zwi, and Rafael Lozano, eds. 2002. *World Report on Violence and Health*. Geneva: World Health Organization.

Kruglanski, Arie, and Edward Orehek. 2011. "The Role of the Quest for Personal Significance in Motivating Terrorism." In *The Psychology of Social Conflict and Aggression*, edited by Joseph Forgas, Arie Kruglanski, and William Kipling, 153–166. New York: Psychology Press.

Lee, Bandy. 2016. "Causes and Cures V: The Sociology and Anthropology of Violence." *Aggression and Violent Behaviour* 27: 158–163.

MacIsaac, Michael, Lyndal Bugeja, and George Jelinek. 2017. "The Association Between Exposure to Interpersonal Violence and Suicide Among Women: A Systematic Review." *Australian and New Zealand Journal of Public Health* 41 (1): 61–69.

Manning, Jason. 2015. "The Social Structure of Homicide-Suicide." *Homicide Studies* 19 (4): 350–369.

Marecek, Jeanne, and Chandanie Senadheera. 2012. "'I Drank It to Put an End to Me': Narrating Girls' Suicide and Self-Harm in Sri Lanka." *Contributions to Indian Sociology* (1–2): 53–82.

Marzano, Lisa, Keith Hawton, Adrienne Rivlin, E. Naomi Smith, Mary Piper, and Seena Fazel. 2016. "Prevention of Suicidal Behavior in Prisons: An Overview of Initiatives Based on a Systematic Review of Research on Near-Lethal Suicide Attempts." *Crisis* 37 (5): 323–334.

McLaughlin, Jennifer, Ronan O'Carroll, and Rory O'Connor. 2012. "Intimate Partner Abuse and Suicidality: A Systematic Review." *Clinical Psychology Review* 32 (8): 677–689.

Michailaki, Dimitris, and Werner Schirmer. 2014. "Social Work and Social Problems: A Contribution from Systems Theory and Constructionism." *International Journal of Social Welfare* 23 (40): 431–442.

Milner, Allison, Heidi Hjelmeland, Ella Arensman, and Diego De Leo. 2013. "Social-Environmental Factors and Suicide Mortality: A Narrative Review of Over 200 Articles." *Sociology Mind* 3(2): 137–148.

Moghadam, Assaf. 2006. "The Roots of Suicide Terrorism: A Multi-causal Approach." In *Root Causes of Suicide Terrorism: The Globalization of Martyrdom*, edited by Ami Pedahzur, 81–107. London: Routledge.

Münster, Daniel. 2015. "Farmers' Suicides as Public Death: Politics, Agency and Statistics in a Suicide-Prone District (South India)." *Modern Asian Studies* 49 (5): 1580–1605.

Münster, Daniel, and Ludek Broz. 2015. "The Anthropology of Suicide: Ethnography and the Tension of Agency." In *Suicide and Agency: Anthropological Perspectives on Self-destruction, Personhood and Power*, 1st ed., edited by Ludek Broz and Daniel Münster, 3–23. London: Ashgate.

Olshen, Elyse, Katharine McVeigh, Robin Wunsch-Hitzig, and Vaughn I. Rickert. 2007. "Dating Violence, Sexual Assault and Suicide Attempts Among Urban Teenagers." *Archives of Pediatrics & Adolescent Medicine* 161 (6): 539–545.

Panagioti, Maria, Patricia Gooding, and Nicholas Tarrier. 2009. "Post-Traumatic Stress Disorder and Suicidal Behaviour." *Clinical Psychology Review* 29 (6): 471–482.

Paolucci, Elizabeth, Mark Genuis, and Claudio Violato. 2001. "A Meta-Analysis of the Published Research on the Effects of Child Sexual Abuse." *Journal of Psychology* 135 (1): 17–36.

Pape, Robert. 2003. "The Strategic Logic of Suicide Terrorism." *American Political Science Review* 97 (3): 343–361.

Phillips, Michael R. 2010. "Rethinking the Role of Mental Illness in Suicide." *American Journal of Psychiatry* 167 (7): 731–733.

Pierre, Joseph. 2015. "Culturally Sanctioned Suicide: Euthanasia, Seppuku, and Terrorist Martyrdom." *World Journal of Psychiatry* 5(1): 4–14.

Roma, Paolo, Floriana Pazzelli, Maurizio Pompili, David Lester, Paolo Girardi, and Stefano Ferracuti. 2012. "Mental Illness in Homicide-Suicide: A Review." *Journal of the American Academy of Psychiatry and the Law* 40 (4): 462–468.

Rüsch, Nicolas, Matthias Angermeyer, and Patrick Corrigan. 2005. "Mental Illness Stigma: Concepts, Consequences, and Initiatives to Reduce Stigma." *European Psychiatry* 20 (8): 529–539.

Sayari, Sabri. 2010. "Political Violence and Terrorism in Turkey, 1976–80: A Retrospective Analysis." *Terrorism and Political Violence* 22 (2): 198–215.

Scourfield, Jonathan, Ben Fincham, Susanne Langer, and Michael Shiner. 2012. "Sociological Autopsy: An Integrated Approach to the Study of Suicide in Men." *Social Science & Medicine* 74 (4): 466–473.

Shiner, Michael, Jonathan Scourfield, Ben Fincham, and Susanne Langer. 2009. "When Things Fall Apart: Gender and Suicide Across the Life-Course." *Social Science & Medicine* 69 (5): 738–746.

Speckhard, Anne. 2005. "Understanding Suicide Terrorism: Countering Human Bombs and Their Senders." In *Towards a Transatlantic Consensus on the Nature of the Threat*, vol. 1, edited by Jason Purcell and Joshua Weintraub, 1–22. Washington, DC: Atlantic Council Publication.

Stack, Steven. 2000a. "Suicide: A 15-Year Review of the Sociological Literature Part I: Cultural and Economic Factors." *Suicide and Life-Threatening Behavior* 30 (2): 145–162.

Stack, Steven. 2000b. "Suicide: A 15-year Review of the Sociological Literature Part II: Modernization and Social Integration Perspectives." *Suicide and Life-Threatening Behavior* 30 (2): 163–176.

Standish, Katerina, and Janine Joyce. 2018. *Yogic Peace Education*. Jefferson, NC: McFarland & Company Inc.

Staples, James, and Tom Widger. 2012. "Situating Suicide as an Anthropological Problem: Ethnographic Approaches to Understanding Self-Harm and Self-Inflicted Death." *Culture, Medicine and Psychiatry* 36 (2): 183–203.

Tol, Wietse, Brandon Kohrt, Mark Jordans, Suraj Thapa, Judith Pettigrew, Nawaraj Upadhaya, and Joop de Jong. 2010. "Political Violence and Mental

Health: A Multi-Disciplinary Review of the Literature on Nepal." *Social Science and Medicine* 70 (1): 35–44.

Velleman, J. David. 1999. "A Right of Self-Termination?" *Ethics* 109 (3): 606–628.

Webb, Roger, Ping Qin, Hanne Stevens, Preben Mortensen, Louis Appleby, and Jenny Shaw. 2011. "National Study of Suicide in All People with a Criminal Justice History." *Archives of General Psychiatry* 68 (6): 591–599.

Wray, Matt, Cynthia Colen, and Bernice Pescosolido. 2011. "The Sociology of Suicide." *Annual Review of Sociology* 37 (1): 505–528.

Yip, Paul, Eric Caine, Saman Yousuf, Shu-Sen Chang, Kevin Chien-Chang Wu, and Ying-Yeh Chen. 2012. "Means Restriction for Suicide Prevention." *The Lancet* 379 (9834): 2393–2399.

CHAPTER 7

Intention, Motivation and Intervention

> In my view people die by suicide because they have both the ability and the desire to do so. (Joiner 2010, 5)
>
> Imagine if someone had a heart attack of a stroke—let's imagine that it's your loved one—and the public policy was essentially, "why bother intervening? They'll just have another". (Joiner 2010, 152)

Peacebuilding aims not only to recognize violence but also to find means of transforming violence into nonviolence. This chapter seeks to explore the processes of intention, motivation and intervention in relation to suicide, and how these processes can inform transformative considerations and practices in peacebuilding. With the WHO predicating a global suicide rate of 1.53 million suicides in 2020 with a further 10–20 times more individuals attempting suicide, transforming suicide and suicidal behaviour into nonviolence is highly important (cited in Gvion and Apter 2012). This chapter will begin by describing the processes of *intention, motivation* and *intervention* that relate to *medical* and *instrumental* suicide. As these processes may differ greatly for *medical* and *instrumental* suicides, these will be discussed separately in each section. Finally, this chapter will consider how these processes can inform peacebuilding in transforming suicide as a form of violence. As the literature on suicide is dominated by research surrounding suicide due to mental illness, there will likely be a greater amount of information regarding this form of suicide within this chapter compared to other forms of suicide.

K. Standish, *Suicide through a Peacebuilding Lens*,
https://doi.org/10.1007/978-981-13-9737-0_7

Intention and Suicide

The first process of suicide that is to be explored within this chapter is intention in relation to suicide. In this context, intention is outlined as the goal, aim or outcome of carrying out a suicide attempt. Due to the lack of information that can be gained from those who are successful in suicide attempts (for obvious reasons), many studies focus on non-fatal suicide attempts in order to attain knowledge surrounding suicide. While it may seem obvious that the intention of suicide is death, there are further factors within suicidal intentions that can impact on this goal. These factors can be dependent on the type of suicide that is being carried out, thus the need to separately address *medical* and *instrumental* suicide. And, while many studies have addressed intention and motivation in relation to *medical* forms of suicide, homicide-suicide and martyrdom there is limited research and therefore few conclusions that can be drawn surrounding the *instrumental* forms of daredevil and protest suicide. Due to the fact that most daredevil suicides can be considered 'accidents' and not acts of deliberate self-killing and due to the fact that there is contention and disputation surrounding acts labelled 'protest' suicides, this chapter will focus on *medical* suicide and the *instrumental* suicide forms of homicide-suicide and martyrdom.

Intention and Medical Suicide

In regard to *medical* suicide, discussion of intention must be separated into suicide related to mental illness and euthanasia/assisted suicide. In both cases, the principal intention of suicide is *to die*, yet there are additional factors of these intentions that need to be taken into account. In regard to suicide related to mental illness, the motivations for completing suicide can be split into intrapersonal and interpersonal motivations (May and Klonsky 2013; Gvion and Apter 2012). While this will be discussed further in the following section on *motivations* of suicide, it has an impact on intent relating to suicide. Intrapersonal motivations for suicide, comprising internal reasons associated with a distressed state of mind, are much more strongly driven by a desire, and intent, to die (May and Klonsky 2013). Conversely, individuals with interpersonal motivations for suicide, which are related to the desire to communicate with or influence other individuals, displayed less intent of wanting to die and had a greater likelihood of being found (May and Klonsky 2013).

De Leo and Krysinska (2017) argue that the intention of suicide is not necessarily *to die*, but can be *a cry for help*. This demonstrates that suicides include varying levels of desire to die, which can affect the intention and lethality of suicides. Furthermore, statistics show that following approximately 90% of attempted suicides the individual involved does not end up dying by suicide, demonstrating a shift in the desire to die (Barber and Miller 2014). This underlines that intentions can vary not only between individuals but also within them.

A factor that may complicate the notion of intent is impulsivity, which is acknowledged as a common risk factor for suicidal behaviour (May and Klonsky 2013). Studies have shown a link between individuals suffering from depression and high levels of impulsive behaviour (Gvion and Apter 2012). Suicide attempts are frequently impulsive, with impulsivity measured by the length of time between an individual deciding to attempt suicide and actually attempting suicide. Studies have shown that the interval between decision and attempt for 24–74% of suicide attempts is ten minutes or less, with nearly one quarter of survivors of near-lethal suicide attempts considering their attempt for less than five minutes (Barber and Miller 2014). In such cases, the lethality of methods that are easily available tends to dictate the likelihood of a fatal suicide attempt, rather than the strength of intent. Gvion and Apter (2012) highlight that impulsive suicides have a lower likelihood of success and lower expectation of death as opposed to planned suicides, which are more likely to succeed. This underlines that outcomes of suicide attempts can be affected by impulsivity.

In regard to euthanasia/assisted suicide, impulsivity is limited as a factor due to the legal requirements of these procedures being carried out. While the legalities differ between states (and even within states as demonstrated in the USA), there are organizational barriers that prevent immediate access to euthanasia/assisted suicide (Emanuel et al. 2016). The intention of suicide in cases of euthanasia and assisted suicide is not just to die, but also to die in an autonomous and painless manner (Pierre 2015). Within the USA, around 75% of individuals utilizing assisted suicide have terminal cancer with a further 15% or so having neurodegenerative diseases (Emanuel et al. 2016). Individuals that seek euthanasia/assisted suicide generally suffer from terminal illnesses, unbearable pain or limited abilities to enjoy life due to disease, leading to this intention of dying in an autonomous, painless way (Fischer et al. 2009).

Intention and Instrumental Suicide

The intention of *instrumental* forms of suicide differs from *medical* forms of suicide, as by definition these suicides aim to have impact outside of ending mental or physical pain. Forms of *instrumental* suicide with such impactful intentions are homicide-suicide and martyrdom. In regard to homicide-suicide, the five different forms of homicide-suicide as identified by Knoll IV (2016) can lead to wide variance of intentions for suicide. It must be highlighted firstly that the victims of homicide are not suicidal, and thus are victims of homicidal/suicidal urges (Salari and LeFevre Sillito 2016). The most dominant form, *intimate-possessive homicide*, has most likely the intention of *homicidal intent* as perpetrators of these cases often have histories of domestic violence and jealousy within their relationship with the victim (Salari and LeFevre Sillito 2016). These homicide-suicides are typically committed after estrangement from a partner (overwhelmingly female), who becomes their victim (Knoll IV 2016). Conversely, intimate-physically ailing homicide-suicides have an intention of *mercy*, as these are motivated by the perpetrator trying to spare one or more close dependents from deprivation or shame (Manning 2015). The typical perpetrators are elderly men with poor health and/or ailing spouses (Knoll IV 2016). Familicide-suicide, in which the senior male of the household is characteristically the perpetrator, can also occur with intentions of mercy or despair following marital, financial or employment issues, in an effort to *avoid* their family facing sustained *suffering* (Knoll IV 2016). Filicide-suicide, the killing of a child by a parent followed by the parent's suicide, is proven to be connected to a range of intentions from *mercy* to *revenge*, and thus intent cannot be categorically determined (Knoll IV 2016). The final type of homicide-suicide, extrafamilial homicide-suicide cannot be determined in terms of intention. This is due to the wide range of cases that come under this heading, from single-victim homicides to mass murders, and the wide range of intentions that escort these cases. Further study is necessary in order to categorize extrafamilial homicide-suicides and to investigate further the intentions of extrafamilial homicide-suicide, particularly as homicide-suicides are distinct in characteristics from both homicides and suicides (Manning 2015).

In contrast, there is abundant information on the intentions of martyrdom forms of suicide. The intentions of suicide via martyrdom can vary depending on context but can be broadly split into martyrdom that does not harm others and martyrdom that seeks to commit violence towards others, generally regarded as suicide 'terrorism' or 'terrorist' martyrdom (Pierre 2015).[1] In cases of martyrdom where no harm is intended to others, the intention of martyrdom is to *sacrifice oneself* for their values or to draw attention to a particular cause (Halverson et al. 2013).[2] This intention also applies to cases where martyrdom does seek to commit violence towards others, but additional intentions also factor into these martyrdom suicides. Such intentions generally include the intention of *injuring and killing other individuals* as to *incite fear* within another group within society, hence why this is referred to as suicide 'terrorism' within the literature (Pierre 2015). This intention of inciting violence and fear on another group in society is usually linked to an intention of supporting a political and or social cause (Brym and Araj 2012).[3] Compared to other forms of suicide, both *medical* and *instrumental*, the desire to die may not be as important to the carrying out of martyrdom suicides due to the commitment individuals are showing to their cause (Brym and Araj 2012).

Motivation and Suicide

Following intention related to suicide, it is important to discuss the motivation behind such intentions. *Motivation* in this context can be defined as the reasons behind suicide. Motivation is distinct from intention in this manner: *intention* is the goal or objective of an act whereas *motivation* is the reasons intent is held. In simplistic terms, intent is *connected but subsequent* to a motivation whereas motive (reason) is *why* intent (objective) is fashioned. Due to the multitude of factors that can be included in the causation of suicide, there are frequently several co-occurring motivations for completing suicide in relation to both *medical* and *instrumental* forms of suicide.

Motivation and Medical Suicide

An estimated 90–100% of individuals that complete suicide suffer from mental illness, yet only a fraction of the number of individuals that suffer from mental illnesses attempt or complete suicide (Bertolote and Fleishman 2002; Joiner 2010; Gvion and Apter 2012). This demonstrates that there must be motivations while suffering a mental illness that cause, or don't cause, suicidal ideation and behaviour. In regard to suicide related to mental illness, motivations for suicide can be divided into two common categories: intrapersonal and interpersonal motivations

(May and Klonsky 2013). Intrapersonal motivations are those motivations that come from within an individual, and include hopelessness, a need to escape from an unbearable state of mind and ending intolerable emotional pain (May and Klonsky 2013). Mental pain is a key motivational factor in suicide and has been expanded on and coined as 'psychache' by Shneidman (1985, cited in Gvion and Apter 2012). According to Shneidman, *psychache* results from frustrated or thwarted essential needs that lead to a range of negative emotions such as guilt, shame, rage, hopelessness, disgrace, and defeat. This is said to lead to a state of unbearable mental pain, which can become so intense that suicide becomes a viable option. Once an individual conceives of the idea of suicide, the risk of completing suicide within one year increases by approximately 170 times (Kliem et al. 2017). More recent studies have also demonstrated the link between mental pain and experiences such as hopelessness and suicide (Gvion and Apter 2012) making a release of suffering a major motivator for *medical* suicides related to mental illness.

Interpersonal motivations for suicide related to mental illness include motivations that are related to the desire to communicate with or influence other individuals (May and Klonsky 2013). Such motivations can include *loneliness, isolation* and *difficulty in communicating with other individuals*, which has been demonstrated to increase the risk of suicide (Gvion and Apter 2012). Having few social supports and a *lack of ability to discuss personal problems* can be a motivation for suicide, while conversely having strong support systems can protect against the risk of suicide (De Leo and Krysinska 2017). Joiner's theory of interpersonal suicide further highlights that suicide can result from a *sense of not belonging* and *being a burden* on others, which can then lead to intrapersonal motivations such as mental pain (2005, cited in Gvion and Apter 2012). As suicide is multifactorial it is likely that individuals suffer both intrapersonal and interpersonal motivations of suicide, and that these motivations can influence each other.

Euthanasia and assisted suicide have perhaps the most well-documented motivations in regard to suicide. This is due to the extensive processes that are required for individuals to access euthanasia/assisted suicide services, through which such information is gathered. The dominant motivations for euthanasia and assisted suicide are *loss of autonomy*, *loss of dignity* and the *diminishment* of ability to enjoy life's activities (Emanuel et al. 2016). In a study done by Fischer et al. (2009) surrounding the motivations of individuals who seek assisted suicide in

Switzerland, over one-third of individuals identified the importance of controlling the circumstances of their death, as well as their loss of dignity. Loss of dignity was shown to be a motivation for 61% of cases in the Netherlands, and 52% of cases in Belgium (Emanuel et al. 2016). Experiencing unbearable pain is also a key motivation of suicide via euthanasia/assisted suicide, though data from the USA highlighted that less than a third of those who complete suicide in this way have inadequate pain control (Emanuel et al. 2016). This figure is higher in Belgium as 50% of these suicide cases were motivated by pain (Emanuel et al. 2016), and higher still in Switzerland where it was accounted to 58% of assisted suicide cases (Fischer et al. 2009). Mental illness may also play a role in motivation for euthanasia/assisted suicide: patients are four times more likely to ask for euthanasia if depressed, but the chance of having a request granted due to depression was significantly lower than physical diseases (Emanuel et al. 2016). More research is required regarding motivations-mental illness and euthanasia/assisted suicide, particularly as mental illness can co-occur with physical illnesses.

Motivation and Instrumental Suicide

Motivations for homicide-suicides can include those motivations outlined in relation to mental illness, with Bourget et al. (2010) highlighting that mental illness, in particular depression, is common in perpetrators of homicide-suicide. However, there are further motivations that are specific to homicide-suicide. Motivations for homicide-suicides, like the intentions of homicide-suicides, are dependent on the type of homicide-suicide that is being discussed. The first type of homicide-suicide to be discussed is intimate-possessive homicide. The motivations for the homicide aspect of this act can vary, but may be related to a *feeling of possessiveness* or *jealousy*, particularly given that most cases involve estrangement prior to the act of homicide-suicide (Knoll IV 2016). These acts tend to be motivated by homicide rather than the suicide (Salari and LeFevre Sillito 2016). While it is a common assumption that *guilt* is the motivating factor for the following suicide, Manning (2015) highlights that these suicides can be a means of *protesting injustice, avoiding an enemy* or justice or of seeking *revenge*. Conversely, intimate-physically ailing homicide-suicide commonly has the same motivation guiding murder and suicide. In these cases, which involve suicidal individuals killing one or more dependents so that they are spared from shame or deprivation, the motivation is *mercy* or *despair* (Manning 2015). This motivation typically stems from financial difficulties resulting from poor health or depression, and perpetrators are most often elderly men with poor health and/or spouses with poor health (Knoll IV 2016). Recent *health problems* and *mental illness* can also act as motivation (Bourget et al. 2010). Familicide-suicide has similar motivations, with *marital, financial or employment issues* leading to a perpetrator killing their family and then committing suicide to avoid their family facing sustained suffering (Knoll IV 2016). The senior male of a household usually perpetrates these cases, with *depression* being a frequent motivation. The next type of homicide-suicide is filicide-suicide, which is extremely rare (Knoll IV 2016). As such there is little research that has studied motivations in these cases, but mental illness may play a significant role (Bourget et al. 2007). The final type of homicide-suicide, extrafamilial homicide-suicide, faces the opposite issue with the same result in that there are so many variations of these cases that there is no standard motivation. With cases ranging from single-victim homicide-suicides to plane-assisted suicide, motivations of extrafamilial suicide can vary greatly and thus are difficult to expand on in this space.

In regard to martyrdom, motivation is linked first and foremost to *religion*. This chapter will discuss only Islamic martyrdom, as this is currently the most dominant form of martyrdom. Suicide within Islam is forbidden and rates of suicide in Muslim countries are among the lowest in the world (Pierre 2015). However, suicide is culturally differentiated from martyrdom in Islam, and martyrdom is viewed as a pathway to the afterlife that promises immortality in the presence of and with the approval of Allah (Pierre 2015). This provides ideological motivation and cultural support for martyrdom. Acts of martyrdom are motivated by *perceived injustices*, and the act of carrying out martyrdom is intended to draw attention to these injustices as a form of protest (Kruglanski and Orehek 2011). *Protesting injustice*, gaining access to *paradise* and bringing *honour* to family are key motivations for martyrdom, both in contexts of martyrdom where individuals do not seek to harm others and in situations of martyrdom attacks. For perpetrators of martyrdom attacks, additional motivations are suggested such as *resistance* to foreign occupation, desire for emotional and social *support* and a feeling of *belonging*, social *status, vengeance, prior humiliation, resentment* and *relative deprivation* (Kruglanski et al. 2009). As with other forms of suicide, the motivation behind martyrdom is multifactorial. While some academics argue that suicide attackers are motivated by mental illness, Pierre (2015) underlines that not only are the vast majority of the perpetrators of suicide attacks free of mental illness (though not necessarily psychological stress), but those that recruit suicide attackers specifically avoid individuals with mental health issues. This is the reason that martyrdom suicides have been excluded from being linked to the motivations of suicides related to mental health within this chapter.

Intervention and Suicide

In recent decades, suicide has come to be viewed as a public health issue in many countries, which has stimulated much conversation and research into effective methods of intervention (Yip et al. 2012). However, due to stigmatization and comparably low levels of public health focus, suicide remains one of the most important and least discussed public health issues (Toronto Public Health 2014). Rates of suicide and suicidal behaviour have remained relatively stable over time but are estimated to rise significantly in coming decades, underlining the need for greater consideration of and commitment to prevention and intervention (Nock et al. 2008). In order to lower suicide rates, intervention strategies need to be undertaken simultaneously and systematically at individual and societal levels (Krysinska et al. 2016).

Intervention in Medical Suicide

While the importance of preventing suicide is becoming increasingly clear, suicide is a rare event and high-risk factors such as mental illness are common, which increases the difficulty of suicide intervention (Yip et al. 2012). This has resulted in interventions taking place at both an individual and a societal level in order to prevent suicide in as many individuals as possible, focusing on those with mental illnesses. There are two major methods of suicide intervention that dominate the literature surrounding suicide. The first method is *gatekeeper training*, which is the education of physicians, teachers and social workers in identifying mental illnesses and/or suicidal behaviour so that medical treatment can be undertaken, and the second is the *restriction of* access to *means* of suicide. In both of these instances, there is a territorial approach to intervention that surrounds the individual and/or limits suicidal resources in the surrounding environment. In both of these instances, the actual 'completer' of suicide (the individual who imagines, attempts or succeeds at ending their own lives)

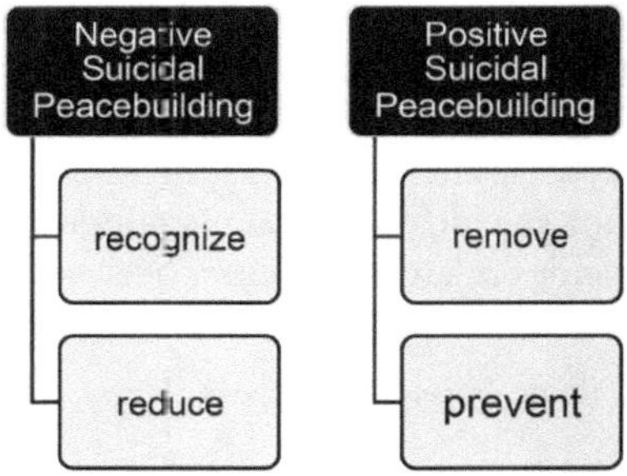

Fig. 7.1 Negative and positive suicidal peacebuilding

is the by-product of intervention not the specific target. In both of these instances, the surrounding environment (trainers and lethal methods) is used to identify persons at risk and/or modify/deny resources to an otherwise suicidal individual. From a peacebuilding perspective, this means that these interventions (gatekeeper training and restriction of means) do not eradicate the violence so much as dampen or dull the opportunity for this form of violence to occur. The peacebuilding arc attempts to recognize, minimize, remove and prevent violence. Along these lines, these two methods can be considered 'negative' suicidal peacebuilding as opposed to 'positive' suicidal peacebuilding (Galtung 1990, 1996).[4]

Negative suicidal peacebuilding *acknowledges* and *minimizes* suicidal violence whereas positive suicidal peacebuilding seeks to do this but also *eradicate* and *inhibit* suicidal violence (see Fig. 7.1). Positive suicidal peacebuilding would eliminate more than the number incidences of this form of violence but also the motivations of such violence as well.

Individual Level Intervention

At an individual level, the dominant method of suicide intervention includes educating gatekeepers (gatekeeper training), such as physicians, teachers and social workers, in recognizing mental disorders and suicidal behaviour that can be a major factor in the causation of suicide, and referring affected individuals for appropriate treatment (Cerel et al. 2012). Gatekeepers are people that come in contact with high-risk individuals, and are not restricted to the professions mentioned (Toronto Public Health 2014). There is a particular focus on the training of primary-care physicians as gatekeepers, as research has shown that 25–50% of women who display suicidal behaviour visited a healthcare provider in the month prior to attempting or completing suicide (World Health Organization 2014). Nock et al. (2008) highlight that primary-care physician education and training programs can reduce suicide rates by 22–73% for individuals that do attend a medical appointment while engaging in suicidal behaviour. Once individuals at risk of suicide are identified, treatments such as medication and therapy have been shown to reduce suicide risk (Zalsman et al. 2016). The education of gatekeepers, including increasing their understanding of suicide and its warning signs, and increasing their knowledge on how to intervene and refer individuals to receive help, is highly important to increasing the knowledge base surrounding suicide within both the general public and the healthcare sector (Toronto Public Health 2014).

Societal Level Intervention

At a societal level, a main strategy of suicide intervention is restriction of the means of completing suicide. Otherwise known as means restriction, this strategy is viewed as decidedly effective as highly lethal and common methods of completing suicide are removed or restricted within a country (Toronto Public Health 2014; Yip et al. 2012). Means restriction can occur in three ways: by physically impeding access to methods of suicide, such as building bridge barriers at popular suicidal jumping spots; by reducing the lethality of some methods, for example reducing the carbon monoxide content of vehicle exhaust or access to pesticides; and by reducing the appeal of certain methods of suicide, largely by discouraging media coverage of suicide methods (Barber and Miller 2014). The first two methods of means restriction in particular have seen much-recorded success. In Sri Lanka, where pesticides are the leading method of suicide, restrictions on pesticide sales in the 1990s have seen overall suicide rates drop by 50% (Barber and Miller 2014). In another example, legislation to restrict the quantities of analgesics such as paracetamol (acetaminophen) in a packet in the UK as to hinder overdosing has been shown to reduce this form of suicide by 43% (Zalsman et al. 2016). The third aspect of means restriction includes discouragement of media surrounding the reporting of suicide. Studies have shown that publicizing suicide methods can create a copycat or contagion effect, whereby particularly vulnerable individuals are moved towards publicized methods of suicide rather than others (Daigle 2005). Media can also sensationalize celebrity suicides, inform or remind individuals of particular means of suicide, and complicate intervention efforts (Yip et al. 2012). Due to the nature of this aspect of means restriction and the influence of online social media, there is little research on the success of limiting media suicide reporting within societies.

The effectiveness of means restriction is due to preventing individuals from utilizing their preferred method, or common methods, of suicide (Yip et al. 2012). This forces individuals to either use less lethal methods of suicide, increasing the chances of survival, or rethink suicide. Studies have shown that restricting one method of suicide does not necessarily lead to a rise in other forms of suicide, suggesting that removing the desired method can prevent suicide (Yip et al. 2012). Barber and Miller (2014) highlighted that around 30% of individuals who had seriously contemplated suicide in the past found that the strong suicidal urge lasted for under an hour. In these cases, limiting the accessibility of lethal methods of suicide can be life-saving, as this limits impulsive suicides. Means restriction can also be enacted on an individual level, whereby clinicians or family members remove means of suicide from the immediate environment of individuals who are at risk of completing suicide (Bryan et al. 2011). While means restriction can be a very effective method of suicide intervention, it depends on an accurate understanding of preferred methods of suicide within different groups within society. Such understanding requires in-depth data collection on the method of suicides, which is not carried out in every country (World Health Organization 2014). Furthermore, effective means restriction at a society level depends on cooperation and collaboration between multiple government and community divisions, which can be difficult to achieve particularly where little public health attention is given to suicide (World Health Organization 2014).

There is currently little research regarding intervention in euthanasia/assisted suicide, as literature focuses on the legalization of and requirements for these procedures in lieu of intervention. Intervention in this sense is done at an individual level where doctors can accept or deny requests for euthanasia/assisted suicide and at a state level, where states set regulations for these procedures if legalized. While pain levels, indicated as a motivation for these procedures, may be able to be managed by modern medicine, the loss of autonomy and dignity that are key motivators for euthanasia are unlikely be satisfied by more medication or improved hospice situations. Interventions in the context of euthanasia and assisted suicide are therefore complex, and this topic could benefit from further research attention.

Intervention in Instrumental Suicides

Compared to medical suicide intervention, there has been a lesser focus on intervention of forms of instrumental suicide. Homicide-suicide in particular has few planned or researched intervention strategies, possibly due to the rarity of these events occurring. As homicide-suicide is distinct from homicide or suicide, it can be difficult to specifically discourage but may be impacted by suicide intervention programs. Salari (2007) identifies a strategy for intervention in the case of intimate partner homicide-suicides similar to the idea of gatekeepers—professionals could be trained to recognize domestic abuse and offer advocacy without dominating the victim. This however is recognized to be ineffective in situations where homicide-suicide occurs without a history of domestic abuse. As Roma et al. (2012) and Knoll IV (2016) have highlighted that mental health plays a significant role in homicide-suicide, intervention programs aimed at suicide related to mental illness such as the training of gatekeepers and restricting means of suicide could be effective in reducing homicide-suicide rates too. Restricting access to guns in particular could be effective, as guns are utilized in 88.2% of homicide-suicide cases in the USA (Logan et al. 2008), and as homicide-suicide cases are more frequent in countries where guns are readily available (Saint-Martin et al. 2008). Furthermore, as Knoll IV (2016) has underlined—men killing their female partners dominate homicide-suicide cases, so logically addressing cultural violence in regard to violence against women could potentially decrease the rate of homicide-suicides as could intervention that protects women and children from these instances of homicide (intimate partner or familial or both). In any case, further research is necessary to determine effective ways of intervening in homicide-suicide cases and with such limited levels of existing support for intimate partner-related violence (let alone intimate partner violence that includes mental illness and homicide-suicide) it is unlikely that 'more research' is sufficient to address at-risk individuals.

Intervention in martyrdom suicides is very complex, due to the cultural sanctioning and celebration that martyrdom receives within Islam. Due to the entrenchment of the practice of martyrdom within Islam, academics have suggested that suicide intervention strategies should focus not on individual behaviour, but on addressing the issues that lead individuals to martyr themselves (Pierre 2015). This in turn could save lives, not just in terms of those committing martyrdom but also in regard to the victims of martyrdom attacks. Pierre (2015) suggests strategies such as reducing military retaliation and racial profiling as to avoid escalation of violence, avoiding demonizing of Muslims and aiding in building an economic infrastructure and opportunities for those who feel oppressed. Speckhard (2005) also highlights the importance of encouragement of reform of repressive governments for the purpose of economic growth and increased opportunities for youth and supports the notion that all ethnic and religious groups must be treated with respect so that there is no need for support in 'terroristic' activities. Speckhard additionally underlines that human rights abuses must not be tolerated, even within the pursuit of 'terrorists', as this ultimately undermines efforts and continues the cycle of encouraging negative values. These strategies, as compared to other strategies for suicide prevention, involve significant political and cultural shifts both nationally and internationally. This reflects the realities and complexities of preventing martyrdom and cross-cultural investigations that look at acts of political suicidal and political suicide-homicides from more than just the Islamic cultures.

The Transformation of Violence: Possibilities for Peacebuilding

The nonviolent transformation of violence is at the core of peacebuilding. In order to transform suicidal violence into nonviolence, more than the intention, motivations and interventions of suicide need to be understood, the roots of suicide causation need to be examined and action undertaken to address these roots. In regard to *medical* suicide related to mental illness, the roots of suicide causation lie primarily in mental health and lethal opportunity restriction at the population level. Nock et al. (2008) underline that while effective suicide intervention programs exist, many suicidal individuals do not receive any attention or treatment, demonstrating that further public awareness and prevention efforts are necessary. It is a problem that continues to challenge us globally as population levels rise just as social service initiatives and scope diminish. Transformative measures need to go further than training gatekeepers to identify and refer cases of mental illness and suicidal behaviour; they need to include an approach to mental illness that begins at the cultural/societal level not just the cultural/individual level.

Mental illness is stigmatized in both developing and developed countries, which can reinforce aspects of some illnesses, lead to self-stigmatization and social isolation and act as a significant barrier to seeking treatment (Rüsch et al. 2005) and until mental illness is considered alongside physical illness (much of which is temporary and treatable too) there will continue to be barriers and obstacles placed in the path of individuals and their loved ones who struggle to experience mental wellness.

Mental health stigma can take place as direct, indirect (structural) and cultural violence—forms of violence examined in greater detail in Chapter 6—but if stigma can be reduced, it is likely that rates of treatment for mental illness would increase and suicide rates would be decreased. Rüsch et al. (2005) highlight that protesting negative portrayals and stereotypes, increased education and contact with those stigmatized are three common strategies of fighting stigma have had varying results in regard to stigma surrounding mental illness. Studies have shown that both increased education and contact with those stigmatized have had positive effects on reducing stigma, with education being a more effective strategy with adolescents and contact being a more effective strategy with adults (Corrigan et al. 2012). To reduce cultural violence and stigmatization around mental illness, and in turn reduce rates of suicide, communities and states need to carry out long-term anti-stigma campaigns (Rüsch et al. 2005). This is one way in which violence, not just of suicide but also violence experienced by those suffering from mental illness, could potentially be transformed. Considering that suicide is the number one cause of violent death in most countries it is surprising that there is not a more coordinated and sustained effort to intervene in suicidal violence worldwide—but it must be noted that in the competitive lethality Olympics (if such a macabre association ever existed) suicide lags far behind other public health concerns such as cardiovascular disease, cancer, respiratory diseases, diabetes, dementia, diarrhoea, liver disease, tuberculosis, kidney disease, digestive diseases and HIV/AIDS (IHME 2016). By way of comparison, in 2016 there were 817,148 suicide deaths and 17.65 million deaths related to cardiovascular disease. While it makes sense for medical professionals to focus on health-related death, violent death, deaths that are deliberate acts of harm that are also preventable should be a substantial focus of peacebuilding. And it isn't—not even close (see Chapter 1).

The transformation of violence in regard to *instrumental* suicide should be based on identifying and addressing the roots of suicide. For homicide-suicides, these roots can be varied but are often related to mental illness. There is another root issue that needs to be addressed within homicide-suicide however: violence against women. Men typically carry out intimate-possessive homicide-suicides, which account for 50–75% of all homicide-suicides, with their female partner or ex-partner as the victim. In these homicide-suicides, women are nearly always the victims, and a history of domestic abuse is typical (Knoll IV 2016; Bourget et al. 2010). Furthermore, men are the typical perpetrators of most other forms of homicide-suicide, with women or children the typical victims in these cases (Knoll IV 2016). Homicide-suicide is one of the most extreme forms of intimate partner violence, and both the acts of homicide-suicide and the typical histories of domestic violence highlights the gender-based violence that is so often legitimized by cultures. There is an opportunity to transform violence in the form of homicide-suicide by investigating and addressing gender-based violence both within the context of intimate partner violence and within society in general. If cultural norms surrounding violence towards women can be altered, then rates of homicide-suicide may transform in turn.

Transformation of violence in relation to martyrdom is complex but may take place in both national and international domains. Grimland et al. (2006) highlight that a suicide attack is incomparable to suicide in important aspects and is more comparable to killing in a war or as a military/political strategy. As such, the best strategy to transform violence may be to address martyrdom suicides as a political issue but also as a social issue. In cases of martyrdom suicide, where religious and cultural norms have sanctified the practice of martyrdom, concentrating on the root causes for martyrdom is the more likely means of transforming martyrdom suicides into nonviolent acts such as dialogue or nonviolent protest/resistance. At a state level, addressing root causes of martyrdom could include lessening military retaliation, supporting struggling states in economic development and creating opportunities for oppressed individuals and groups, as identified by Pierre and discussed previously (2015). At a societal level, addressing root causes could include diminishing cultural violence that normalizes racism, including racial profiling, towards Muslim individuals and those in other ethnic and religious groups to increase social cohesion and limit further alienation (Speckhard 2005). These solutions of political and cultural change are not simple, but may be an opportunity to effectively transform violence and prevent future acts of martyrdom suicide.

Conclusion

The transformation of violence is a core goal of peacebuilding. With the differing intentions, motivations and interventions that exist in relation to *medical* and *instrumental* suicide, there is much to inform the transformation of violence, and many possibilities for transforming the violence of suicide into nonviolence. Such possibilities include addressing stigma against mental illness, addressing gender-based violence that coexists with many forms of homicide-suicide and addressing the root causes of martyrdom suicides. Ultimately, opportunities for the transformation of violence in relation to suicide, both *medical* and *instrumental*, should be based in addressing the root causes of suicide. This would allow for greater likelihood of cultural and political changes that reinforce outcomes of nonviolence. In the next chapter, this book turns to the notion that as we have many forms of suicide (this book theorizes *medical* and *instrumental* suicide) we might need to step back from the declaration that 'suicide is always wrong' and problematize the phenomenon from the position of those who would advocate for 'more' suicide, not less.

Notes

1. As mentioned in Chapter 5, the terms 'terrorist' and 'terrorism' are discursively employed to refer to legitimate and illegitimate acts of aggression. While I prefer the descriptor of martyrdom many academics use the term 'suicide terrorism' or 'martyrdom terrorism' and I acknowledge their terminology while endeavouring to minimize such discursion in my own writing.
2. As mentioned in Chapter 5, there are similarities between acts of martyrdom and protest suicide (and some acts of martyrdom are quite obviously and clearly acts of protest) but as too little research exists to reasonably attribute intention and motivation in martyrdom operations to non-martyrdom protest suicides (such as in Greece), I will focus only on the form of *instrumental* suicide with adequate commentary—martyrdom.
3. This is distinct from the intention of an act of purely protest suicide (see Chapter 5) where the intention is to transform oppressive violence but not to incite fear utilizing deliberate violence (Spehr and Dixon 2014).
4. Galtung distinguishes between negative peace (the absence of violence) and positive peace (the absence of structural and cultural violence) *and* presence of pro-social life qualities that permit the full expression of one's humanity (1990, 1996).

References

Barber, Catherine, and Matthew Miller. 2014. "Reducing a Suicidal Person's Access to Means of Suicide: A Research Agenda." *American Journal of Preventative Medicine* 47 (3): 264–272.

Bertolote, José Manoel, and Alexandra Fleischmann. 2002. "Suicide and Psychiatric Diagnosis: A Worldwide Perspective." *World Psychiatry* 1 (3): 181–185.

Bourget, Dominique, Jennifer Grace, and Laurie Whitehurst. 2007. "A Review of Maternal and Paternal Filicide." *Journal of the American Academy of Psychiatry and the Law* 35 (1): 74–82.

Bourget, Dominique, Pierre Gagné, and Laurie Whitehurst. 2010. "Domestic Homicide and Homicide-Suicide: The Older Offender." *Journal of the American Academy of Psychiatry and the Law* 38 (3): 305–311.

Bryan, Craig, Sharon Stone, and M. David Rudd. 2011. "A Practical, Evidence-Based Approach for Means-Restriction Counselling with Suicidal Patients." *Professional Psychology Research and Practice* 42 (5): 339–346.

Brym, Robert, and Bader Araj. 2012. "Are Suicide Bombers Suicidal." *Studies in Conflict & Terrorism* 35 (6): 432–443.

Cerel, Julie, Jason Padgett, Vestena Robbins, and Barbara Kaminer. 2012. "A State's Approach to Suicide Prevention Awareness: Gatekeeper Training in Kentucky." *Journal of Evidence-Based Social Work* 9 (3): 283–292.

Corrigan, Patrick, Scott Morris, Patrick Michaels, Jennifer Rafacz, and Nicolas Rüsch. 2012. "Challenging the Public Stigma of Mental Illness: A Meta-Analysis of Outcome Studies." *Psychiatric Services* 63 (10): 963–973.

Daigle, Marc. 2005. "Suicide Prevention Through Means Restriction: Assessing the Risk of Substitution. A Critical Review and Synthesis." *Accident Analysis and Prevention* 37 (4): 625–632.

De Leo, Diego, and Karolina Krysinska. 2017. "Suicide and Self-Directed Violence." In *International Encyclopedia of Public Health*, 2nd ed., edited by Stella Quah and William Cockerham, 115–123. Amsterdam: Academic Press.

Emanuel, Ezekiel, Bregje Onwuteaka-Philipsen, John Urwin, and Joachim Cohen. 2016. "Attitudes and Practices of Euthanasia and Physician-Assisted Suicide in the United States, Canada and Europe." *Journal of the American Medical Association* 316 (1): 79–90.

Fischer, Susanne, Carola Huber, Matthias Furter, Lorenz Imhof, Romy Imhof, Christian Schwarzenegger, Stephen Ziegler, and Georg Bosshard. 2009. "Reasons Why People in Switzerland Seek Assisted Suicide: The View of Patients and Physicians." *Swiss Medical Weekly* 139 (23–24): 333–338.

Galtung, Johan. 1990. "Cultural Violence." *Journal of Peace Research* 27 (3): 291–305.

Galtung, Johan. 1996. *Peace by Peaceful Means: Peace and Conflict, Development and Civilization*. London: Sage.

Grimland, Meytal, Alan Apter, and Ad Kerkhof. 2006. "The Phenomenon of Suicide Bombing: A Review of Psychological and Nonpsychological Factors." *Crisis* 27 (3): 107–118.

Gvion, Yari, and Alan Apter. 2012. "Suicide and Suicidal Behavior." *Public Health Reviews* 34 (2): 1–20.

Halverson, Jeffry, Scott Ruston, and Angela Trethewey. 2013. "Mediated Martyrs of the Arab Spring: New Media, Civil Religion, and Narrative in Tunisia and Egypt." *Journal of Communication* 63 (2): 312–332.

Institute for Health Metrics and Evaluation (IHME). 2016. *Share of Deaths by Cause*. Retrieved from https://ourworldindata.org/what-does-the-world-die-from.

Joiner, Thomas. 2010. *Myths About Suicide*. Cambridge: Harvard University Press.

Kliem, Sören, Anna Lohmann, Thomas Möble, and Elmar Brähler. 2017. "German Beck Scale for Suicide Ideation (BSS): Psychometric Properties from a Representative Population Survey." *BMC Psychiatry* 17 (1): 389–397.

Knoll IV, James. 2016. "Understanding Homicide-Suicide." *Psychiatric Clinics of North America* 39 (4): 633–647.

Kruglanski, Arie, and Edward Orehek. 2011. "The Role of the Quest for Personal Significance in Motivating Terrorism." In *The Psychology of Social Conflict and Aggression*, edited by Joseph Forgas, Arie Kruglanski, and William Kipling, 153–166. New York: Psychology Press.

Kruglanski, Arie, Xiaoyan Chen, Mark Dechesne, Shira Fishman, and Edward Orehek. 2009. "Fully Committed: Suicide Bombers' Motivation and the Quest for Personal Significance," *Political Psychology* 30 (3): 331–357.

Krysinska, Karolina, Philip Batterham, Michelle Tye, Fiona Shand, Alison Calear, Nicole Cockayne, and Helen Christensen. 2016. "Best Strategies for Reducing the Suicide Rate in Australia." *Australian and New Zealand Journal of Psychiatry* 50 (2): 115–118.

Logan, Joseph, Holly Hill, Michele Lynberg Black, Alex Crosby, Debra Karch, Jamar Barnes, and Keri Lubell. 2008. "Characteristics of Perpetrators in Homicide-Followed-by-Suicide Incidents: National Violent Death Reporting System—17 US states, 2003–2005." *American Journal of Epidemiology* 168 (9): 1056–1064.

Manning, Jason. 2015. "The Social Structure of Homicide-Suicide." *Homicide Studies* 19 (4): 350–369.

May, Alexis, and E. David Klonsky. 2013. "Assessing Motivations for Suicide Attempts: Development and Psychometric Properties of the Inventory of Motivations for Suicide Attempts." *Suicide and Life-Threatening Behaviour* 43 (5): 532–546.

Nock, Matthew, Guilherme Borges, Evelyn Bromet, Christine Cha, Ronald Kessler, and Sing Lee. 2008 "Suicide and Suicidal Behaviour," *Epidemiology Review* 30 (1): 133–154.

Pierre, Joseph. 2015. "Culturally Sanctioned Suicide: Euthanasia, Seppuku, and Terrorist Martyrdom." *World Journal of Psychiatry* 5 (1): 4–14.

Roma, Paolo, Floriana Pazzelli, Maurizio Pompili, David Lester, Paolo Girardi, and Stefano Ferracuti. 2012. "Mental Illness in Homicide-Suicide: A Review." *Journal of the American Academy of Psychiatry and the Law* 40 (4): 462–468.

Rüsch, Nicolas, Matthias Angermeyer, and Patrick Corrigan. 2005. "Mental Illness Stigma: Concepts, Consequences, and Initiatives to Reduce Stigma." *European Psychiatry* 20 (8): 529–539.

Saint-Martin, Pauline, Marie Bouyssy, and Patrick O'Byrne. 2008. "Homicide-Suicide in Tours, France (2000–2005)—Description of 10 Cases and a Review of the Literature." *Journal of Forensic Medicine* 15 (2): 104–109.

Salari, Sonia. 2007. "Patterns of Intimate Partner Homicide Suicide in Later Life: Strategies for Prevention." *Clinical Interventions in Aging* 2 (3): 441–452.

Salari, Sonia, and Carrie LeFevre Sillito. 2016. "Intimate Partner Homicide-Suicide: Perpetrator Primary Intent Across Young, Middle and Elder Adult Categories." *Aggression and Violent Behavior* 26 (1): 26–34.

Speckhard, Anne. 2005. "Understanding Suicide Terrorism: Countering Human Bombs and Their Senders." In *Towards a Transatlantic Consensus on the Nature of the Threat*, vol. 1, edited by Purcell, Jason, and Joshua Weintraub, 158–175. Washington, DC: Atlantic Council Publication.

Spehr, Scott, and John Dixon. 2014. "Protest Suicide: A Systematic Model with Heuristic Archetypes." *Journal for the Theory of Social Behaviour* 44 (3): 368–388. https://doi.org/10.1111/jtsb.12047.

Toronto Public Health. 2014. *Suicide Prevention in Toronto.* Toronto: Toronto Public Health.

World Health Organization. 2014. *Preventing Suicide: A Global Imperative.* Geneva: World Health Organization.

Yip, Paul, Eric Caine, Saman Yousuf, Shu-Sen Chang, Kevin Chien-Chang Wu, and Ying-Yeh Chen. 2012. "Means Restriction for Suicide Prevention." *The Lancet* 379 (9834): 2393–2399.

Zalsman, Gil, Keith Hawton, Danuta Wasserman, Kees van Heeringen, Ella Arensman, Marco Sarchiapone, Vladimir Carli, Cyril Höschl, Ran Barzilay, Judit Balazs, György Purebl, Jean Pierre Kahn, Pilar Alejandra Sáiz, Cendrine Bursztein Lipsicas, Julio Bobes, Doina Cozman, Ulrich Hegerl, and Joseph Zohar. 2016. "Suicide Prevention Strategies Revisited: 10-year Systematic Review." *Lancet Psychiatry* 3 (7): 646–659.

CHAPTER 8

Why Not Suicide?

> Suicide is the worst of all human tragedies. (De Leo 2004, 155)
>
> Having the choice at the end of my life has become incredibly important. It has given me a sense of peace during a time that otherwise would be dominated by fear, uncertainty and pain. (Brittany Maynard, November 19, 1984–November 1, 2014)

An assumption in many (most) people's minds is that suicide is a tragedy, a great disaster and calamity that must be prevented, avoided, prohibited and, in a perfect world: absent and/or obsolete.[1] But, as we have seen in this exploration—there is no (1) kind of suicide, so there can also be no (1) solution to the problem of suicide. The fact we are required to be particular and focused (targeted is too violent a word) in our peacebuilding does not mean we do not entertain the magnitude and interconnectivity of the phenomena included under the term *suicide* but that we appreciate that in order to do *something* you cannot do *everything*. Peacebuilding is an intervention, an action that stands in between harm and the foci of harm. And it is a moral and ethical endeavour undertaken without guarantee of success. I recollect an op-ed I read in a paper last year delegitimizing Peace and Conflict Studies that said '*the field is ineffectual, it does not work, there is still war and violence everywhere!*' which made me consider the fact that the enduring presence of death, illness and injury has not shuttered global health centres and medical programmes. Doctors and nurses cannot completely cure the human

K. Standish, *Suicide through a Peacebuilding Lens*,
https://doi.org/10.1007/978-981-13-9737-0_8

condition—but they still try. And so should we. We peacebuilders, like the healers and social workers and sociologists and anthropologists and artists that seek to understand what it means to be human (there are many, many others) and the myriad other contributors that seek to support living systems such as gardeners, peacemakers, builders, storytellers, musicians, caregivers and food makers (there are many, many more) should keep trying too. But one of the foundational requirements of effective peacebuilding is that it addresses one form of violence while not also supporting or resulting in another kind of violence. In the consideration of suicide, is the *zero suicide* initiative, positive and nonviolent if it results in forcing people to continue to live who rationally and authentically seek to end their lives? This is the question that drives this chapter, the notion that we might need to step back from the 'suicide is always wrong' conclusion and once more problematize the phenomenon.

Suicide is an emotionally charged topic. It can be considered from philosophical, ethical, historical, cultural, moral, legal and biological points of view. The realities of a life ending (by deliberate choice) when we normalize the sacredness of humanity and strive for a world where our mortality is considered and cherished from all points along the life cycle are juxtaposed in the contemplation of suicide with logical reflections that easily find arguments for the act of suicide as moral and reasonable—even kind. The emotional dimension of mourning and perceptions of illegitimate (and preventable) death can impair our ability to conceptualize suicide as a rational, personal and at times compassionate act. So then, if we ordinarily view suicide as a catastrophe to be averted at all costs, how can we conceive of suicide as adaptive, compassionate, honourable and ultimately humane? To investigate the cognitive/emotional responses to suicide, we perhaps can start by asking what arguments are commonly made *for* suicide? This simple question 'why not suicide?' shapes this chapter's inquiry to identify ongoing conversations that address the 'why and why not' of suicide. In this chapter reason, faith, culture and biological heredity are examined to investigate the rational, religious, relativist and genetic perspectives of suicide that support this books' argument for the critical importance of viewing suicide through a peacebuilding lens.

Aspects of suicide intersect one other; while the decision to complete suicide may be an individual matter, it has implications for family, friends and the responsible bodies who are left to deal with the material repercussions of that 'personal' decision. And while death is the inevitable ending to all life (therefore normal), suicide is considered abnormal to most and to some it is an abomination. 'Rational suicide' and the 'right to die' are symbiotic concepts that relate to notions of the humaneness of ending suffering and that we should be entitled to dignity in death (Simmons 2018). But as we approach the question 'why not suicide?' we realize that answers can come from diverse and not necessarily congruent vantage points. Medical and psychological professionals have therapeutic ethics that engage with facets of this debate and in oaths to sustain life or relieve suffering struggle to reach consensus on right conduct in all circumstances—ask an intensive care doctor or nurse where he or she stands on such an issue and you will find a variety of responses that relate to practice, ideology and personal choices.[2] There is an understandably fragmented professional accord from medical professionals tasked with caring for those who no longer seek to (or no longer have the physical capacity to) stay alive (Anderson and Caddell 1993; Bulmer et al. 2017). There are religious traditions that weigh into the discussion with everything from ruminations of the start of life (attached to the right to prevent or terminate pregnancy) and the ending of life with companion ramifications on a perceived spiritual afterlife encoded in dogma and ritual devised hundreds if not thousands of years ago (Larson and Amundsen 1998; Lester 2006; Gearing and Lizardi 2009; Witztum and Stein 2012). Additional bodies such as the modern nation-state (Szasz 2011) and international laws (Hunter 2015) engage with this conversation from yet further afield and to these multitudinous inquires we can add the instrumental human level of existence (not merely the social/intellectual/spiritual realms) to ask ourselves about species-level dynamics such as biological inheritances and biotic maxims[3] to ask if there is such a thing as a *suicide gene* in our DNA (leading to evolutionary suicide) (Parvinen 2005) just waiting to be *triggered by the environment.*

There is no reason to assume that suicide has not always been a part of the human tradition. In the absence of information from archaeology sociology and worldwide historical records, we can still see that suicide has been with us for a long time. In various contexts from various civilizations, the act of ending life via auto-homicide cannot be ignored. We see it in ancient Greece, where hemlock was used to end life (Matzo 1997; Clarke 1999). We see it in ancient Rome where suicide was a sanctioned and legal act (Melton 1991; Clarke 1999). We see it in the Middle Ages from the Judeo-Christian writings of Augustine (Melton 1991) and Aquinas (Melton 1991; Pilpel and Amsel 2011) who made suicide a solemn social taboo. And though it remained a sin for devout

Christians during the Renaissance and Enlightenment eras, more secular members of society began to view it and consider it with increasing tolerance (Melton 1991). This tolerance was not without philosophical debates on its rationality by such notable thinkers as Kant, who saw suicide as an irrational act (Melton 1991; Clarke 1999; Cholbi 2000; Pilpel and Amsel 2011; Cooley 2013; Ho 2014), and Hume, who believed suicide, was entirely reasonable (Melton 1991; Cholbi 2000) to name but two discordant sentiments.

Moralist, Libertarian and Relativist Suicide

There are three common perspectives from which suicide is ordinarily viewed. The moralist view, such as the Judeo-Christian view seen in Job 1:21 (God is the giver of life. He gives, and He takes away) is that all life, as a divine gift, is sacred (*life belongs to God*). The libertarian view is that suicide is not an immoral act, can be entirely rational and that individuals, by rights, possess personal autonomy over their own lives (*life belongs to each individual*) (Schramme 2013). The relativist view is that the decision to complete suicide is generally governed and corralled by various cultural norms (that can change) that take into consideration a cost-benefit analysis to maximize its social utility and therefore acceptability (Ho 2014) that, of course, varies according to each cultural group. These views help shape our understanding of this very complex issue, but they also look at the act of suicide as an entitlement that is contingent on relevant concepts of 'ownership' or 'utility'. From a peacebuilding lens, we need to broaden this conceptualization somewhat and encounter these opinions from the position of harm, violence and prevention of violence. As we will see, that is no easy feat. It is, quite frankly, a consideration that emerges from *the peacebuilding mind* that finds limited provision (though not none) in existing scholarship about suicide.

A recent literature search of the library database at my institution using the term 'suicide' yielded 300,171 peer-reviewed articles published in the last 17 years. When the phrase 'rational suicide', a way of describing *intentional* and *deliberate suicide*—suicide done on-purpose—yielded 26,886 articles. Randomly selected article titles and abstracts were reviewed. Those that were deemed relevant—addressing rational suicide, dignity in death, right to die and biotic maxims—were then used to develop a picture of the commonest views presented by the debate. The research related here reflects those articles that share a common voice.

Reason

The large number of articles on suicide reveals that this topic is highly debated and highly challenging. To move forward with this review, it would be useful for us to attain a definitional understanding of which types of suicide are being considered in what parts of the discourse, and luckily, Werth and Holdwick (2000) give us a framework with which to understand the different types of suicide we are discussing here. *Rational suicide* refers to a decision to complete suicide through a sound decision-making process, without coercion by others. This form of rationalization often comes in response to terminal illness with unbearable suffering. *Aid-in-dying* (termed assisted suicide in Chapter 4) is the enabling of patients to self-administer their own cause of death. *Hastened death* is a general term referring to acceleration of the process of dying by acts that can include rational suicide and aid-in-dying that relate to clinical treatment. It can also include the withholding of life support systems with the patient's consent (Werth and Holdwick 2000).

In Thompson's assessment of the debate (2014), proponents of suicide argue that legal suicide affords personal autonomy and allows the dying to retain their dignity. Opponents say that is just a legal way of allowing someone to be put to death (Thompson 2014). The two positions are characterized by central themes: (1) suicide is a personal matter in which personal autonomy and dignity are key components; (2) legality is problematic because even the best-intentioned laws have unintended consequences (Thompson 2014). The legality issue is complicated and not universally applied. Due to its complexity, we will not delve into the law. What is safe to say is Thompson is correct in that legality is problematic. It is good to keep in mind that what was law and an accepted norm hundreds of years ago may not be under contemporary laws.

(Ir)Rational Suicide

Two major camps contribute to the rational suicide debate: those who believe suicide is a rational act and those who do not. The idea of rational suicide is a feature of the personal and humane aspects of the debate. Rationality intertwines with the legal and political debate on the ideas of the right to die and dignity in death. In her chapter entitled 'Rational Suicide', Deborah Gould (2008) gives an overview, presenting the two sides of the rational suicide argument. On the one hand are the proponents, who believe suicide is a personal right and individuals should be allowed to exercise this right as they see fit (Gould acknowledges that this is a position most likely to be taken in the face of a lethal and painful illness that cannot be treated). Opponents of rational suicide hold that suicide is not acceptable under any circumstances and that while suicide may not always be considered irrational it is, nonetheless always immoral (Gould 2008). To focus on the (ir)rational positions should give us an aperture from which to view this debate adequately.

Rationalists in this debate (with few exceptions) hold that, barring those suffering from a psychiatric disorder,[4] individuals may come to a decision to end their suffering through a logical decision-making process (Werth and Holdwick 2000; Schramme 2013; Ho 2014). Schramme posits that rational suicide 'is not based on a metaphysically dubious comparison between the actual life of a person and the supposed state of being dead' (Schramme 2013, 484) and Cooley (2013) adds that we should not stray too far into pure reason or the metaphysics of reason, but that we should be able to see that we have a duty to ourselves. And, concomitantly, that this duty may entail taking one's life. It is not a reflection of pure reason, 'but rather it stems from how emotion and reason would be expressed by an embodied, empathetic person' (Cooley 2013, 373).

There is an ongoing debate between Cooley and Cholbi on the Kantian view of suicide and such arguments demonstrate 'intellectual' positions that may be of interest as we grapple with ageing populations that are growing in many parts of the world. Cooley, who is a bioethicist, has made the argument that it may be a *requirement* to commit suicide. This view is based on what he sees as one's duty as a moral agent. He claims that those who in certain danger of losing their moral integrity (presumably the aged) have the responsibility to commit suicide before they lose their dignity (*life as dignity*). Morally reprehensible agents such as rapists and murderers are what bring him to this conclusion; Cooley argues that such agents should have killed themselves before committing such heinous crimes (Cooley 2007). Cholbi counters Cooley by arguing that Cooley's analysis is far too 'coarse' and compares people suffering from dementia (impaired mental processes) with individuals who commit heinous crimes. To Cholbi, those who commit heinous crimes are morally corrupt and undignified and therefore unable to maintain moral integrity. In contrast, those who have dementia are neither undignified nor dignified but have a mental condition that prevents them from making choices that can be classified as dignified (Cholbi 2015). In this debate, the moral position that one *should* commit suicide if one is in danger of losing one's moral integrity is nuanced by the argument that the default position of humanity is not 'morality' but vivacity—not dignity but anime.

Their arguments indicate a progression of thinking on suicide reflecting, not absolute ideological positions (always *wrong* or always *right*), but explorations about the idea of suicide as a form of obligation (Battin 2005; Corlett 2001), or not (Tong 2000a; Drebushenko 2000) based on circumstances and responsibilities. Regardless of pro or con positions, all of these authors can envision a case—such as terminal illness—in which the sufferer may wish to complete suicide. It is in the notion of what duty means and whether one has a moral duty to complete suicide that they differ. It is safe to say that our central question 'why not suicide?' remains unanswered by these different positions. As this philosophical debate did not directly address the peacebuilding position, perhaps the religious debate can abet our inquiry.

Religion

It is generally accepted that the act of suicide is condemned in most major religions (see Chapter 2). And while an analysis of the *degree* of acceptance within each religion is not the aim of this section, it is important to understand the role religion plays in shaping discussions around suicide. To engage with religion, it may be useful for us to begin with sociology: the social science of societal discord. Suicide, as a social problem, was first entertained in the West by Durkheim in his 1897 work *Suicide: A Study in Sociology* (Hassan 1998). Durkheim's work took an empirical look at the role of religion in suicide by comparing suicide rates in Protestant and Catholic regions in Western Europe. Durkheim's comparison showed that there was a higher degree of suicide among Protestants than Catholics. He did not conclude that religion 'caused' suicides nor that religion 'prevented' suicide but that tendencies were visible in the data to quantify which confessional group exhibited higher rates of self-killing. Durkheim, did, however, find that it was the integration and power exerted on the congregation through shared religious beliefs as well as a sense of intimacy and fellowship that affected the various suicide rates in the groups. To simplify, Protestants are taught about freedom and free will; Catholics are taught that suicide is mortal sin (there is a difference between mortal sins and venial sins in Catholicism; a venial sin is a minor infraction that does not result in separation from God whereas a mortal sin results in eternal damnation to Hell).

For Durkheim, this understanding was an essential component. Durkheim concluded that Catholics had fewer suicides due to stronger religious affiliations (Hassan 1998) and Durkheim's assessment is a framework for continued inquiries in sociology over a century later. In 2007, Helliwell made a comparison of Durkheim's results with his own (120 years after Durkheim) and concluded that Durkheim's argument that 'the more religion encouraged independent thought, the less integrated was the church and the community it served' (Helliwell 2007, 460) did explain the difference in the number of suicides between Protestants and Catholics, but once Helliwell conducted empirical testing with more robust data sets and variables, he found that, though religion may be a factor, economics played an equally prominent role. The integration in social groups was not merely spiritual and doctrinal but financial as well. Helliwell, similar to Durkheim, saw living in an integrated society, with close familial (and religious ties), as the best defence against suicide. The 'net' of an integrated society here is not merely a predictor of ones' propensity to complete suicide (or the ramifications of such acts on individual souls) but an insulation against acts of self-death via community.

In 2014, Torgler and Schaltegger recreated Durkheim's Protestant and Catholic comparisons and found that theological and social differences between the two groups have now empirically greatly decreased. They found that the two religious groups now share more commonalities than Durkheim's study found but still conclude that Catholics are still less prone to completing suicide or accepting suicide as an alternative to life's struggles. They also found that attendance at church (possibly as an indicator of adherence to religious discipline) is an essential factor; Catholics are more likely to attend religious services than Protestants are. Unsurprisingly, the authors found that the stronger the religious commitment, the more pronounced disapproval of suicide becomes (Torgler and Schaltegger 2014) and frequency and regularity of attendance at religious services were directly correlated to an abhorrence of suicide (Gearing and Lizardi 2009; Kleiman and Liu 2014). As have been seen elsewhere in this book, injunctions against suicide don't simply relate to religious dogma but the urge to conceal or mislabel life-ending acts by loved ones' who gain or lose stature through acts considered religious abominations. Our understanding of how religion can be an effective barrier against suicide is demonstrated in data that shows increased religious practices as *inhibitors* of suicide. But there is another way of considering religions' connection to suicide that relates to the notion of suicide as a practice of the religious: sacred suicide.

Sacred Suicide

To call a group a 'cult' or a 'religion' is an act of discourse that contemplates a number of parameters in order to categorize a group of believers. While a short conclusion is that all religions started as cults (due to size), another framework considers that to be a religion a group of followers must share:

- Belief in some kind of supreme being or principle (such as God).
- Belief in the importance of certain books as a source of spiritual truth (such as the Bible, Qur'an, Bhagavad Gita).
- A set of principles to guide living members.
- Membership in a religion tied to ancestry or bloodline (such as the Druze).
- An established organization, often with a hierarchy of priests.
- The geographical existence of holy places to visit (Pettinger 2017, 1).

While Hinduism, Buddhism, Christianity, Islam, Sikhism and Taoism are commonly considered 'religions', there are other spiritual groups that consider suicide in meaningful ways that can also be considered religious. While the term 'cult' is increasingly used in a pejorative sense, there is little difference between the basic tenets of both cults and religions.

> The term cult is often used to describe new religious movements or alternative religious movements by those who wish to stereotype the movement in a negative way. These new religious movements involve a wide diversity of different groups/movements/sects. But often involve: a new spiritual movement and different teachings to established religions. (Pettinger 2017, 1)

The notable category of 'alternative' religions, for our purposes, involves the so-called suicide cult. In the book, *Sacred Suicide* (2014), editors Lewis and Cusack encounter religious suicide from historical and contemporary perspectives. As history, the mass suicide of Jews at Masada in 73CE and mass suicides of Orthodox Christians in Russia in the eighteenth century are reviewed as are contemporary suicide cults including the Jonestown Massacre (1978), the Order of the Solar Temple (1994–1997) and the 1997 Heaven's Gate suicides (among others). Included in this scholarly work is the role of martyrdom as a religious practice (related to both Buddhist immolation and Islamic Jihad) that firmly places the act of self-death into religious custody. In each of these instances, suicide, deliberate self-killing, had a doctrinal role in religious adherence. There are disputes surrounding whether many of these instances amounted to homicide-suicides (clues that poke holes in the 'purity' of such mass suicides abound) but it cannot be denied that at least *some* of the suicides in each of these so-called sacred suicide cults, where bona fide acts of self-death related to religious dogma and perceptions of divinity and the human relationship to divinity. As we can see from this short rumination, while the orthodox religious conclusion is that suicide is *morally* wrong some religious/cult groups, both historically and in the contemporary world, both sanctioned and operationalized suicide as a sacred act. Moving from the philosophical debate to divine arguments, we have one more view to consider before we inject this argument with the peacebuilding position: genetics.

Relativist

The relativist view is the 'it depends' view that sees acceptability and frequency of suicide in various cultural mores and values (Ho 2014). From a biological and not merely sociological perspective, there exists an additional form of relativistic perspective that relates to DNA. That of our genes and a genetic 'it depends'. As a global review of various relativistic perspectives on suicide to address the central research question 'why not suicide?' seemed unmanageable, perhaps we can appreciate a biological suggestion. While the notion of evolutionary suicide in humans (via biotic maxims) seems largely theoretical (Vitale and Kisdi 2018; Parvinen 2005), this segment will focus on an empirical advance in the genetics of suicide that fits squarely into the relativist camp: suicide in our genes.

The Suicide Gene

Do we humans have a suicide gene? Placing the content within the relativist camp, some geneticists believe we do. The long answer to this question is no: scientists have not proved the existence of a suicide gene beyond a doubt, *but* there is some evidence of special evolutionary suicide that can be considered in our contemplation of 'why not suicide?' As we try to evade absolutes (the conclusion that ALL suicide is catastrophe and ALL suicide must/should/needs to be eradicated), the idea that it isn't up to us but rather is up to our genes to drive the instinct of our 'human animal' to self-death gives one pause.

The complexity of the science behind this view is daunting, unless one has a background in genetics (and I don't) but evidence exists.

Consider the following gem from our friends studying the genetics of suicide:

> The concept that genetic factors contribute to the complex trait of suicidal behaviour has stimulated much work aimed at identifying susceptibility genes. So far molecular genetic studies focused on the serotonergic pathway as the intent to die and the lethality of suicide acts were related to the serotonergic system. Two genes have so far emerged as being involved in the vulnerability for suicidality: first, the intronic polymorphisms (A218C or A779C) of the tryptophan hydroxylase 1 (TPH1) gene, which was suggested as a quantitative risk factor for suicidal behaviour; second, the insertion/deletion polymorphism of the serotonin transporter gene (5-HTTLPR), which does not seem to be involved in general suicidal behaviour, but in violent and repeated suicide attempts. The data have further shown that the MAOA gene, which is consistently associated with impulsive-aggressive personality traits, is not related to suicide but might induce violent methods in subjects with other suicide risk factors. (Bondy et al. 2006, 36)

It is estimated that we may inherit up to 55% of the genes that cause us to be prone to suicide (Roy 1993; Roy et al. 1995; McGuffin et al. 2001; Voracek and Loibl 2007). Bring in environmental factors, and a depth of discussion and complexity is added to our understanding. Halldorsdottir and Binder (2017) posit that environmental factors act as triggers for genes. Their explanation of G × Es (genotypes and environmental influences) is complex but provides a distinctive way to understand why we may indeed be predisposed to suicide. The authors caution about the limitations of the studies thus far that more research is needed to validate the multitude of possible environmental connections (Halldorsdottir and Binder 2017) but that there is a possible connection between our genes, the environment and suicide.

Balestri et al. (2017) concur that while the gene hypothesis is sound, associations between genetics and suicide should be interpreted with great caution. They aver that 'several lines of evidence indicate that suicidal behaviour is partly heritable, with multiple genes implicated in its aetiology [and that] … neurotrophic gene variants, in particular EFEMP1 and PTPRR, may have a role in the pathogenesis of suicidal behaviour' (98). This finding echo's Antypa et al.'s conclusion from 2013 that,

> Since genes can only partially explain suicidal risk, several studies during the past decade have tried to incorporate environmental factors in the susceptibility model. Studies to date show that variation on the 5-HTTLPR, MAOA and HTR2A gene can interact with stressful life events to increase risk for suicidal behavior. (1125)

I am not a geneticist and don't presume to understand the intricacies of this particular evidence regarding genes and the environment but one can clearly comprehend from this that there is something in our genes that might also factor into the propensity to conduct self-killing. The dizzying (to me) data suggests a possibility that might need to be pondered when we consider the role of the environment (surroundings that include nature and the human community) in suicide. To conclude this section, the short answer to the 'is there a suicide gene?' question is yes, but it is not that simple. Science is advancing, but we may be years away from a definitive answer on the subject of a suicide gene, how we isolate it and what factors inhibit its expression. Having explored reason, religion and relativist/genetics (the 'it depends' position) in this exploration of 'why not suicide?' we now turn to an argument that relates to the overarching thesis of this book: the PACS field teaches us to look at life through a peacebuilding lens, a lens that urges us to both recognize conflict, transform violence nonviolently and eradicate harm via intervention. So, what are the arguments for or against 'why not suicide?' from a peacebuilding lens? In a dialogue with a front-line intensive care doctor, this next section asks about the intricacies of viewing suicide as an act of nonviolence.

The Peacebuilding Position?

> Imagine being told you have less than six months left to live. On top of that horrific news, you experience excruciating pain every single day that is far more atrocious than anything you could have possibly imagined. Now imagine being unable to move or perform basic daily tasks, being completely dependent on others, losing your dignity, and facing the terror of contemplating the impending process of a slow and painful death. You have zero control over your life and the pain of grief, stress, and fear coupled with the incredible physical pain you endure day in and day out is more than any human should endure. (Ullman 2017, 1)

The empathetic reader has no choice but to imagine what such an existence would be like. The griever, someone who has had to watch loved ones suffer, endures just such an experience or the constant companion to end of life suffering seen in medical and palliative care units all over the world feels this. There are three dehumanizing forms of suffering in situations such as this, great pain, loss of autonomy and loss of dignity. Each of these forms of suffering is unique but universal to those who bear end of life passage accompanied by terminal illness and intolerable and unbearable pain. The famous 'doctor death' Jack Kevorkian responded to criminal charges against him for assisting 54 years old Janet Atkins who suffered from Alzheimer's to die with,

> If I'm a criminal then, then you can look at me and say, 'you're a criminal' and then throw me in jail. But keep me there because if I get out I'll do it again. I want this to be a medical service that can be controlled. Now it's all hit or miss. People are shooting each other, suffocating each other, poisoning each other, and drowning each other. (MacNeil 2011, 1:20–1:40)

As I mentioned in the front matter of this chapter, the PACS field teaches us to look at life through a peacebuilding lens, a lens that urges us to recognize conflict and transform violence nonviolently. The directive of this position includes the preclusion of behaviour (where at all possible) that contributes to harm. This is not a position that can be held in total: to be human is to eradicate life in eating, breathing and moving, so death is a part of the experience of our organism (even for the Jains whose faith eschews all violence). Violence, as a deliberate and unnecessary act (optional act), is the ballast that holds the nonviolent tenet up for the peacebuilding position: were there a maxim (and there is not, the field is too large and interdisciplinary) it would go something like this '*be aware, impede violence and be non-harming in thought, word and deed*'.

The following dialogue took place in 2018 with an experienced clinician (of over 40 years) working in intensive care in a hospital setting. My goal in speaking to this individual was to glean some understanding of the authentic action of deciding care that could lead to death. In my opening remarks, I explain the position of my field and ask, somewhat naively I suppose, if there is a clear directive for professionals regarding these acts. We established prior to this interview that this medical professional (represented in this exchange by R*) had frequently contributed care that hastened death in appropriate circumstances and that the complete preservation of life was not a position held by this individual. I learned a lot about the actual practice of life-ending action in this exchange.

KS: I'm approaching this chapter from the perspective that through a peacebuilding lens it can be a moral decision to intervene in suffering. If someone was being tortured it would be unproblematic for us to decide to intervene and stop their experience of being tortured. In assisted-dying, hastened death, euthanasia or other such terms that relate to actions that result in ending life the person is not being tortured by an outside agent rather an internal circumstance of pain.

*R**: In the premise where you say I have an agent torturing another and I am morally obliged to intervene I think we can all agree that that is clear-cut. In the scenario of a person who is, if you like, tortured by pain from their cancer or something like that, the first additional thing I think you need to add is ambiguity. So if you are absolutely certain this person is going to die then it is reasonably clear cut, in that case, you should work to relieve their suffering and that if in doing so you shorten their life so-be-it but there is no ethical or legal debate around that in Australia or New Zealand at the moment. So that is a done deal. The questions start to arise in the two circumstances where 1. You have ambiguity about the chance of recovery—so, I might be able to stop you being tortured if we push on trying to treat you and you recover and go on to have quality and meaning in your life for many years, but to achieve that we would need to persist with treatments which are unpleasant or distressing, and you will need to put up with your disease until then. The chance that the treatment will work is small, and if it fails then you will have gone through additional suffering without getting the quality of life we hoped for. Alternatively, we could say that the chance of a treatment working is so small that the high likelihood of a prolonged unpleasant death outweighs the possible benefit of recovery, in which case the focus of care becomes solely on relief of suffering, and an acceptance that death is imminent. In that environment you get marked disparity of opinion between treating clinicians and to my mind the principal driver of the disparity is a combination of the perception of the intrinsic value of life, um, and to some degree individual beliefs how much value life holds, and how bad the disease and treatments are …The patient has this cancer, the treatment for this cancer is X, I'm focused on treating with X as opposed to pull back and say, oh, uh, actually X isn't working. I have no more things up my sleeve, I need to recognize that now maybe I am doing more harm than good with X and I should move to a more, um, to a treatment based around comfort with fewer side effects but maybe a hastening of death. So there are personal, individual clinician things, that come into that matter. Does that make sense?

KS: Yes.

*R**: So, what was I saying, there is the personal, the personal perception of ambiguity I don't know what your chances are of surviving this…or your chances of surviving this are slim…but not zero. It's very rare that we have a zero chance of surviving something. (It is unusual that we have a zero chance it is usually just very small.) So how do you as a person, as a clinician weight the cost of suffering attributed to disease and treatment versus the small but unknown probability of recovery?

KS: its sounds like, it is not about whether it is right or wrong it is whether it works….

*R**: I think that is fair, yeah. And it is about the perception about the likelihood of whether it is going to work. And whether or not that likelihood is sufficiently large.

KS: in instances where there is ambiguity that decision is much more challenging to make.

*R**: yes. Where there is no ambiguity and you have a patient who is suffering that is not a decision that is at all difficult to make either ethically or legally but it just doesn't get called assisted suicide or euthanasia at the moment it falls under a thing called the Doctrine of double effects.

KS: Can you clarify the Doctrine of double effects?

*R**: yes, if for example I administer morphine to a patient with severe pain that is a reasonable thing because morphine is a painkiller right?

KS: right.

*R**: if I have to give that person very large doses because the pain is very severe and they have already been exposed to a fair bit of it that is acceptable because I am still treating their pain. If in the process of doing that I give that person so much morphine that it is highly likely I will shorten their life or terminate their life—that is ok.

KS: and that is the Doctrine of double effects if in treating pain the outcome could be the ending of life?

*R**: yes but the important comment is that you have to be treating the suffering and that the death is an acceptable side effect of the treatment as opposed to death is the principal goal of the treatment.

KS: what is your opinion on the position that says 'it is never rational to ask for assistance in dying?'

*R**: I think that that comes from a set of personal beliefs that are usually predicated on coming from often a somewhat moralistic sometimes-religious viewpoint. I fear that those who have very clear and unambiguous views of what is normal behavior for somebody else, and they disagree with that person and therefore label their view as "abnormal" may be coming from a perspective of not truly understanding that person. For example, somebody who has never had significant suffering in their own life may struggle to understand how a rational person might see that death is superior to suffering. Personally, I believe that the rational individual ought to have autonomy over [their] own life. And, that if from a rational perspective you say I have been suffering it is intolerable, I want it to end because the only end is for me to die then that is, to my personal belief that is a reasonable and valid perspective.

However I do understand the competing argument and if I was going to represent the competing argument I would say that it is very hard to dissect out purely rational thought from reactive thought in somebody facing either intractable pain or severe suffering and specifically when it comes to depression, within the context of depression, many people wish to die. Depression also has as one of its hallmarks the inability to see the way out. So you say you have pain, I can't measure that in any way and if you are actually depressed you might give all the signs to say you have pain because that might be an acceptable way out whereas depression would not be.

KS: you would distinguish between types of pain?

*R**: From my personal practice, it is very uncommon that I am faced with requests for dying with imminent death and the palliation of people with principally psychiatric illness. (That is my personal job I'm an intensivist). That is not to say that patient group does not exist. The question of whether or not distinction between psychological suffering vs. physiological suffering is a meaningful one is part of the euthanasia debate that our society has not yet been prepared to deal with, but it is one which has been faced by some nations which have had assisted suicide laws in place for some time. In our current society, and within the confines of the current debate, a request for euthanasia would only be considered for those who are deemed to be psychiatrically competent. That is not to say that there are no untreatable psychiatric diseases which result in severe suffering, merely that we don't want to include those patients in the current discussion because they are much more ethically challenging.

KS: There are people that would delegitimize the notion of someone rationally requesting assistance to end their life because their position is that the individual must be mentally incapable of making that decision to even ask that. But as you experience pain, depression is part of that so it must be very challenging to separate that out.

*R**: It often is. And, I think we also need to understand the current legal and ethical constructs that we function in whereas clinicians are bound to both care for an individual as an individual understanding their own individual needs and wants in their life so generally speaking with that in mind we do our best to adhere to patient requests with the important exception of mental illness. So when you become mentally incapacitated, society says there are certain circumstances where it is appropriate for the state or the clinician to simply take charge of your life and remove your decision making capacity because you have demonstrated you are incapable of making decisions or do anything other than harm you or others.

KS: is there a personal repercussion for you in this work?

*R**: most of my patients are not autonomous…some are but most aren't because they are otherwise incapacitated so that they cannot make meaningful decisions. So in those environments the most common decision I can make is after having sat with either the notes and reading what their perceived directions and values in life are or sitting down with the whanau[5] and saying 'tell me about your mom' so I tell the family or patient what is wrong with them and the family or the patient tell me about them and based on that we come to the conclusion, for example "look I tell you what, this disease is bloody awful, the chances of recovery are very slim, as an individual, this patient is at the point, they are ready to see the end of their life coming and a treatment which prevents significant suffering would be preferable to a protracted treatment course with a slim chance of return to recovery.

KS: so it involves consultation with themselves and the family?

*R**: as a clinician you are duty bound to do your best to work out what you think that person wants and who they are. How you source that information is variable but you first see if they have an advance directive that is relevant.

KS: what would an advance directive be?

*R**: so, if I am in an accident that leaves me with significant brain injury I would not want to survive that illness if I was unable to return to work and unable to care for my family. Or if there was good likelihood I was unable to do that.

KS: how would a clinician know an advance directive exists?

*R**: the challenge with an advance directive is someone has to go through and write it with a primary care physician whom they have a reasonable amount of contact with. A common example would be I know that I have end stage lung disease, if I get to the point where I need to be put on a breathing machine to keep me alive I would rather you didn't and just let me go.

KS: that would be a conversation that took place with a caregiver or…

*R**: yes, and ideally they record it and that written record would be available for all clinicians who subsequently would need to treat that patient. For it to work, the system must be underpinned by a good IT system.

KS: going back to the first thing I mentioned regarding the peacebuilding position you spoke about ambiguity and it is very easy to say 'you should act' but are you acting in the patients interest? The support of their community or whanau and is that inevitably even your decision… it seems to come from a variety of sources that lead to your course of care that may hasten someone's death.

*R**: the official position is that the choice to offer a type of treatment is the decision of the treating clinician, while the decision to accept or refuse that treatment is the choice of the competent patient or when the patient is incapacitated the choice must be made by the clinician, and the clinician is responsible for taking certain steps to ascertain what they believe the person would want. It should be noted that this is a legal position in New Zealand, which is not shared in some other jurisdictions, including most states of Australia.

KS: and if the patient already has communication that says don't put me on a machine, for example, that narrows the possibilities of care the clinician can decide to use.

*R**: When patients are incapacitated it does become greyer…and for the initial parts of this discussion we should probably say…well we already established that incapacity can exist in a mental way as opposed to you are drugged up or brain injured or something like that…this is just psychologically ill…when you get to the mentally incapacity group it starts to get very, very, grey because let's say that even if you have when clearly mentally capable, written in advance directive the clinician still has the right to override that advance directive if they believe that advance directive is not relevant to the circumstances.

KS: so the notion of care still relates to whether or not it is going to work?

*R**: it is whether or not it is going to work or in the particular case of the advance directive, whether the advance directive is significantly informed to be applicable to the current circumstances.

KS: so in a way you could make grey matter out of anything.

*R**: correct so you can make it grey if you wish to make it grey anything can be grey.

KS: I guess what I am hearing is that it is a case-by-case situation but that it is all underneath the rubric of care.

*R**: I think that is correct.

KS: so I am trying to draw parallels between info I have been looking at regarding suicide and genetics surrounding the idea of genetic factors contributing to traits associated with suicide.

*R**: so when you say a suicide gene to do you mean a suicide profile or a psychiatric profile? Is it a genetic profile towards psychiatric illness or a profile towards suicide?

KS: suicide.

*R**: as depending on how you wish to interpret the comment around a genetic profile towards suicide I think it is quite important to dig a little deeper. With regard to the association between suicide and psychiatric illness. Let us say that most who complete suicide have some psychiatric illness. So to say that genetic profiles cause suicide without causing mental illness is a big leap because the majority of people who have committed suicide have mental illness. And you could make the argument that it was the mental illness that made them commit suicide and the genetic predisposition made them have the mental illness and the reason that that is important is that the treatment strategies change. When you say I have identified you at risk of depression I am going to teach you coping strategies and have a low threshold antidepressant medication for you vs. my genetic profile identifies you at risk of suicide I am going to put you in a safe environment.

KS: can I echo that back to you Dr?

*R**: yes.

KS: were someone identified at risk of mental illness, for example: depression, care would include preventative tactics such as coping strategies and medication?

*R**: yes.

KS: and, were someone identified at risk of suicide preventive measures would include external factors that surround the individual?

*R**: yes, putting someone in a safe environment.

Throughout this book, I have tried to learn about the phenomena of suicide in order to appreciate this form of violent death through a peacebuilding lens. While I don't see PACS professionals working on the front lines of the battle against depression via cognitive training and therapeutic pharmacology, I do think we can logically place ourselves in Dr R*'s concluding prescription: *if someone is at risk of suicide, they need a safe environment.* I learned a lot about the actual practice of life-ending actions in this exchange and how incredibly difficult it must be to arrive at the notion of assisted death (for purely the autonomous and the rational) as simplistic because magnifying factors related to psychological stress must make a surface assessment unsophisticated and naïve at best and at its worse meagre and obtuse. But is it the question of assisted dying that seems challenging or the question of dying overall that is at issue? Can we encounter death as non-violence if we have not also considered death as natural, normal and desired?

Serrano del Rosal and Heredia Cerro (2018) in their study of Spanish attitudes towards Euthanasia and Physician-Assisted Suicide state that 'death is not only a biological occurrence, it is also a social event…so, discussing the right to die…[is] not actually referring to the right to die in itself, but rather, the right to die with dignity' (104).

> To dignify the process of dying, so as to ensure that it takes place with the same autonomy and freedom that one has in life, since in fact, the process of dying cannot be separated from the process of living, being merely the final part of the same. (Serrano del Rosal and Heredia Cerro 2018, 104)

It is the final act of life, unquestionably, yes, but does this 'natural' happenstance hide a puzzling and troubling reality that needs to be considered? In contemplation of the increasing *ageing* of Western society, Serrano del Rosal and Heredia Cerro state the following:

> [Aging in the West] has far from reached its peak, continuing to grow over time. So, while the moment of death has been delayed, the process of dying has extended, becoming less accidental and more controlled and medically controllable…the greatest concentration of healthcare expenses per capita occurs over the final years of life, increasing considerably as of the age of 75…[while] there is a tendency to deny death, assuming that it is not real or certain, and avoiding its study within a social context due to this attempt to separate, hide and reject it, even though this is clearly a ridiculous and socially ineffective approach. And so, death and the process of dying continue to be almost invisible, external, unknown and even spurned in contemporary Western societies. These societies declare that "to be dead is an unthinkable anomaly. No place, space or time is assigned to the dead" (Marí-Klose and De Miguel, 2000: 116); this would be turning our back on the reality in which we live. (2018, 104)

Asking 'why not suicide?' means delving into a topic that is contentious, emotionally triggering and 'unthinkable'. Death, to say nothing of deliberate life-ending seems to resist inquiry for a variety of prevalent but troublesome reasons. In a world where the *cannon of death* (ideal death circumstances) refers to dying:

1. In one's sleep
2. Quickly
3. Surrounded by loved ones
4. At an advanced age
5. At home (Serrano del Rosal and Heredia Cerro 2018, 104).

Many human exits are unintentional or medicalized (an accident or during hospitalization), many have prolonged illness, are alone when they die or surrounded by strangers and are nowhere near their own homes. Is it any wonder we do not comfortably make arguments surrounding intentional suicide? Are we comfortable speaking of death at all more than to resist or reject the notion of the end of life? I am not a philosopher but as a peacebuilder I see how good intentions (relieve suffering and respect wishes) are far more complex than ethical notions of always 'right' or never 'wrong'.

Sprung et al. (2018, 1) list five reasons for rejecting physician-assisted suicide-Euthanasia:

1. **Slippery slopes:** There is evidence that safeguards in the Netherlands and Belgium are ineffective and violated, including administering lethal drugs without patient consent, absence of terminal illness, untreated psychiatric diagnoses and nonreporting;
2. **Lack of self-determination:** Psychological and social motives characterize requests for PAS-E more than physical symptoms or rational choices; many requests disappear with improved symptom control and psychological support;
3. **Inadequate palliative care:** Better palliative care makes most patients physically comfortable. Many individuals requesting PAS-E don't want to die but to escape their suffering. Adequate treatment for depression and pain decreases the desire for death;

4. **Medical professionalism:** PAS-E transgresses the inviolable rule that physicians heal and palliate suffering but never intentionally inflict death;
5. **Differences between means and ends:** Proeuthanasia advocates look to the ends (the patient's death) and say the ends justify the means; opponents disagree and believe that killing patients to relieve suffering is different from allowing natural death and is not acceptable.

They conclude that 'physicians have a duty to eliminate pain and suffering, not the person with the pain and suffering' (Sprung et al. 2018, 1). And, a very important part of this discussion surrounding notions of the right to die that should be amplified again when we consider all of these notions of rational/irrational, autonomy and dignity in death is that it may disproportionately impact persons living with physical disability and for a very specific reason, those who live with physical disabilities have a greater chance of suffering from mental illness as well because of their environment/circumstances. To quote Khazem (2018),

> The presence of a PD [physical disability] may lead to difficulties in activities of daily living (ADL) including cooking, cleaning, or tasks associated with employment. These individuals also report lower employment rates and are more likely to experience negative social outcomes including workplace discrimination and harassment, stigmatization, loneliness, and lower life satisfaction due to disability-related discrimination … The presence of PD has been associated with other various concerning mental health-related outcomes including depression, anxiety and posttraumatic stress disorder, all risk factors for suicide. (2018, 18)

Asking 'why not suicide?' resists parsimony and for good reason. When we look at this question through a peacebuilding lens, it can be considered sensible. For example, the care aspect of the notion of relieving suffering for those at the end stage of life when it is desired is completely congruent with the peacebuilding position that seeks to recognize and ameliorate violence and anguish wherever possible (if we consider the harm coming from within a person's body). And, from a peacebuilding perspective, there is also no counter position that I can see in Dr R*'s communicated medical practice wherein addressing an experience of suffering the intervention may lead to death—where due to the 'doctrine of double effects' the result (though not the intention of the act) is death. But I can see how support for deliberate life-ending acts that relate to medical conditions could also become violence, could become a license for harm and from a peacebuilding perspective, this would not be tolerable. I suppose the question is, in relation to suicide, could we, as peacebuilders stomach addressing one form of violence by enabling or excusing another form? Medical professionals use the term 'triage' to assign degrees of urgency to patients. Would supporting suicide be a form of violence triage—erasing a form of harm (internal but still pain) via harm?

Conclusion

Despite my attempt in this chapter to reply to the central question 'why not suicide?' the content does not answer the question so much as problematize it further. The answer may depend on where you look and whom you ask. A rationalist may answer that suicide is acceptable under the right conditions or that it may be rational but not moral. For a devoutly religious person, the answer is that suicide is wrong and a mortal sin. For a member of a suicide cult, the answer is that suicide is a practice of faith. A libertarian may say it is everyone's right; we all have the autonomy to do what we want to do with our life and that includes ending it for any reason, not simply because we are dying of a known disease. Those with a terminal illness, deep in pain, may say it would be a humane act to let them end their life. Medical professionals, who have taken the Hippocratic Oath, may differ in their answers. What is wrong with suicide is that it is complex; there is no absolute, no global right or wrong. Cultural differences, societal norms and individual needs (and apparently individual genes) all play a part in deciding what is wrong or right with suicide. Based on the literature, it is safe to say the debate that has been going on since Ancient Greece will continue well into our future.

From a peacebuilding perspective, it is moral and ethical to stand in the way of harm when it is recognized and endeavour not to cause harm or suffering whenever possible. When it comes to the notion of aiding someone in pain to end their life, grey areas abound. The bulk of research surrounding life-ending acts asks 'why suicide?' and 'where suicide?' and 'who suicide?' and 'how much suicide?' and some of it looks at things that work to 'prevent suicide', 'decrease suicide' and 'understand suicide'. Still others propose arguments that surround suicide the 'should/must/needs to' content that leads to perceptions that there is a way of grasping the phenomena of deliberate end of life actions under one tent. This chapter has sought to entertain the question 'why not suicide?' Perhaps, just as there are so many ways and circumstances, we come into this world—and grow and live in the challenge and turbulence of many points within the life cycle—there is more than one way to exit our humanity too.

Notes

1. With a goal of eradication, the *Centre for Suicide Prevention* launched the *Zero Suicide Initiative* (ZSI) in hospitals in 13 nations to reduce and eliminate suicidal deaths and in institutions where ZSI has been implemented, they have seen a 65% decrease in suicide see *Centre for Suicide Prevention* at https://www.suicideinfo.ca/resource/ie23-aiming-perfection-zero-suicide-movement/.
2. Remembering that physician and nurse suicide is both 'hidden' and on the rise (like many forms of suicide) with professional groups grappling with the institutional inhibitions surrounding 'care ethics' for medical providers. See Davidson et al. (2018) and Wible's January 1, 2018 article in the *Washington Post*: What I learned from my tally of 757 doctor suicides.
3. Biotic maxims refer to the view that humans are not special but merely members of a biotic community who's DNA can suddenly cause the population to go extinct. This 'evolutionary suicide' (Parvinen 2005, 241) posits that self-extinction is a natural potential in genetic adaptation.
4. Although recent scholarship does identify euthanasia and physician-assisted suicide for people suffering from psychiatric disorders. See Evenblij et al. (2019).
5. *Whanau* is a te reo Māori word that means family/community.

References

Anderson, James G., and David P. Caddell. 1993. "Attitudes of Medical Professionals Toward Euthanasia." *Social Science & Medicine* 37: 105–114.

Antypa, Niki, Antonio Drago, and Alessandro Serretti. 2013. "The Role of COMT Gene Variants in Depression: Bridging Neuropsychological, Behavioral and Clinical Phenotypes." *Neuroscience and Biobehavioral Reviews* 37 (8): 1597–1610. https://doi.org/10.1016/j.neubiorev.2013.06.006.

Balestri, Martina, Concetta Crisafulli, Luigi Donato, Ina Giegling, Raffaella Calati, Niki Antypa, Barbara Schneider, Dragan Marusic, Maria Eugenia Tarozzi, Dorjan Marusic, Metka Paragi, Annette M. Hartmann, Bettina Konte, Agnese Marsano, Alessandro Serretti, and Dan Rujescu. 2017.

"Nine Differentially Expressed Genes from a Post Mortem Study and Their Association with Suicidal Status in a Sample of Suicide Completers, Attempters and Controls." *Journal of Psychiatric Research* 91: 98–104.

Battin, Margaret Pabst. 2005. *Ending Life: Ethics and the Way We Die*. New York: Oxford University Press. Accessed April 15, 2017.

Bondy, B., A. Buettner, and P. Zill. 2006. "Genetics of Suicide." *Molecular Psychiatry* 11 (4): 336–351. https://doi.org/10.1038/sj.mp.4001803.

Bulmer, Maria, Jan R. Böhnke, and Gary J. Lewis. 2017. "Predicting Moral Sentiment Towards Physician-Assisted Suicide: The Role of Religion, Conservatism, Authoritarianism, and Big Five personality." *Personality and Individual Differences* 105: 244–251.

Cholbi, Michael J. 2000. "Kant and the Irrationality of Suicide." *History of Philosophy Quarterly* 17 (2): 159–176.

Cholbi, Michael J. 2015. "Kant on Euthanasia and the Duty to Die: Clearing the Air." *Journal of Medical Ethics* 41 (8): 607–610.

Clarke, David M. 1999. "Autonomy, Rationality and the Wish to Die." *Journal of Medical Ethics* 25: 457–462.

Cooley, Dennis R. 2007. "A Kantian Moral Duty for the Soon-to-Be Demented to Commit Suicide." *American Journal of Bioethics* 7 (6): 37–44.

Cooley, Dennis R. 2013. "A Kantian Care Ethics Suicide Duty." *International Journal of Law and Psychiatry* 36 (5–6): 366–373.

Corlett, J. Angelo. 2001. "Is There a Moral Duty to Die?" *Health Care Analysis* 9 (1): 41–63.

Davidson, Judy, Janet Mendis, Amy R. Stuck, Gianni DeMichele, and Sidney Zisook. 2018. "Nurse Suicide: Breaking the Silence." NAM Perspectives. Discussion Paper, National Academy of Medicine, Washington, DC. https://nam.edu/nurse-suicide-breaking-the-silence.

De Leo, Diego. 2004. Suicide Prevention Is Far More Than a Psychiatric Business. *World Psychiatry* 3 (3):155–156.

Drebushenko, David. 2000. "How Could There Be a Duty to Die?" In *Is There a Duty to Die?*, edited by James M. Humber and Robert F. Almeder, 159–176. Totowa, NJ: Humana Press.

Evenblij, Kirsten, Roeline W. H. Pasman, Rosalie Pronk, and Bregje D. Onwuteaka-Philipsen. 2019. "Euthanasia and Physician-Assisted Suicide in Patients Suffering from Psychiatric Disorders: A Cross-Sectional Study Exploring the Experiences of Dutch Psychiatrists." *BMC Psychiatry* 19 (74): 1–10. https://doi.org/10.1186/s12888-019-2053-3.

Gearing, Robin E., and Dana Lizardi. 2009. "Religion and Suicide." *Journal of Religion and Health* 48 (3): 332–341.

Gould, Deborah. 2008. "Rational Suicide." In *Encyclopedia of Aging and Public Health*, edited by Sana Loue and Martha Sajatovic, 696–697. Boston: Springer.

Halldorsdottir, Thorhildur, and Elisabeth B. Binder. 2017. "Gene × Environment Interactions: From Molecular Mechanisms to Behavior." *The Annual Review of Psychology* 58: 215–241.

Hassan, Riaz. 1998. "One Hundred Years of Emile Durkheim's Suicide: A Study in Sociology." *Australian and New Zealand Journal of Psychiatry* 32 (2): 168–171.

Helliwell, John F. 2007. "Well-Being and Social Capital: Does Suicide Pose a Puzzle?" *Social Indicators Research* 81: 455–496.

Ho, Angela Onkay. 2014. "Suicide: Rationality and Responsibility for Life." *The Canadian Journal of Psychiatry* 59 (3): 141–147.

Hunter, Jane. 2015. "Suicide Bombings: What Does the Law Actually Say?" *Action on Armed Violence.* https://aoav.org.uk/2015/suicide-bombings-what-does-the-law-say/.

Khazem, Lauren R. 2018. "Physical Disability and Suicide: Recent Advancements in Understanding and Future Directions for Consideration." *Current Opinion in Psychology* 22: 18–22.

Kleiman, Evan M., and Richard T. Liu. 2014. "Prospective Prediction of Suicide in a Nationally Representative Sample: Religious Service Attendance as a Protective Factor." *The British Journal of Psychiatry* 204 (4): 262–266.

Larson, Edward J., and Darrel W. Amundsen. 1998. *A Different Death: Euthanasia and the Christian Tradition.* Downers Grove, IL: Inter-Varsity Press.

Lester, David. 2006. "Suicide and Islam." *Archives of Suicide Research* 10 (1): 77–97.

Lewis, James R., and Carole M. Cusack. 2014. *Sacred Suicide.* London: Routledge.

MacNeil, Robert. 2011. "Dr. Jack Kevorkian on the Assisted Suicide of Janet Adkins." YouTube, *PBS NewsHour*, June 3. youtube.be/OJsbefxfVsg.

Matzo, Marianne LaPorte. 1997. "The Search to End Suffering: A Historical Perspective." *Journal of Gerontological Nursing* 23 (3): 11–17.

McGuffin, Peter, Andrej Marusic, and Anne Farmer. 2001. "What Can Psychiatric Genetics Offer Suicidology." *Crisis: The Journal of Crisis Intervention and Suicide Prevention* 22 (2): 61–65.

Melton, J. Gordon. 1991. *The Church Speaks Out on Euthanasia: Official Statements from Religious Bodies and Ecumenical Organizations.* Detroit, MI: Gale Research.

Parvinen, Kalle. 2005. "Evolutionary Suicide." *Acta Biotheoretica* 53: 241–264.

Pettinger, Tejvan. 2017. "Religions and Cults." Oxford. www.biographyonline.net, January 10, 2013, accessed January 18, 2018. Retrieved from https://www.biographyonline.net/spiritual/articles/difference-religion-cult.html.

Pilpel, Avital, and Lawrence Amsel. 2011. "What Is Wrong with Rational Suicide." *Philosophia* 39 (1): 111–123.

Roy, Alec. 1993. "Genetic and Biologic Risk Factors for Suicide in Depressive Disorders." *Psychiatric Quarterly* 64 (4): 345–358.

Roy, Alec, Nancy Segal, and Marco Sarchiapone. 1995. "Attempted Suicide Among Living Co-Twins of Twin Suicide Victims." *The American Journal of Psychiatry* 152 (7): 1075–1076.

Schramme, Thomas. 2013. "Rational Suicide, Assisted Suicide, and Indirect Legal Paternalism." *International Journal of Law and Psychiatry* 36 (5): 477–484.

Serrano del Rosal, Rafael, and Adrián Heredia Cerro. 2018. "Spanish Attitudes Towards Euthanasia and Physician-Assisted Suicide." *Revista Española de Investigaciones Sociológicas* 161: 103–120.

Simmons, Kevin M. 2018. "Suicide and Death with Dignity." *Journal of Law and the Biosciences* 5 (2): 436–439.

Sprung, Charles L., Margaret A. Somerville, Lukas Radbruch, Nathalie Steiner Collet, Gunnar Duttge, Jefferson P. Piva, Massimo Antonelli, Daniel P. Sulmasy, Willem Lemmens, and E. Wesley Ely. 2018. Physician-Assisted Suicide and Euthanasia. *Journal of Palliative Care* 33 (4):197–203.

Szasz, T. 2011. The Shame of Medicine: Is Suicide Legal? *Freeman* 61 (July): 30–31. Retrieved from https://search.proquest.com/docview/876179754?accountid=14700.

Thompson, Tamara. 2014. *The Right to Die: At Issue*. Farmington Hills, MI: Greenhaven Press.

Tong, Rosemarie. 2000a. "Duty to Die." In *Is There a Duty to Die?*, edited by James M. Humber and Robert F. Almeder, 133–157. Totowa, NJ: Humana Press.

Tong, Rosemarie. 2000b. "Dying in America." *Theory Medical Bioethics* 21 (6): 601–611.

Torgler, Benno, and Christopher Schaltegger. 2014. "Suicide and Religion: New Evidence on the Differences Between Protestantism and Catholicism." *Journal for the Scientific Study of Religion* 53 (2): 316–340.

Ullman, Kerry E. 2017. "The Necessary Right of Choice for Physician-Assisted Suicide." Gettysburg College Student Publications, 574. Retrieved from http://cupola.geysburg.edu/student_scholarship/574.

Vitale, Caterina, and Eva Kisdi. 2018. "Evolutionary Suicide of Prey: Matsuda and Abrams' Model Revisited." *Bulletin of Mathematical Biology*. http://dx.doi.org.ezproxy.otago.ac.nz/10.1007/s11538-018-0472-9. Retrieved from https://search-proquest-com.ezproxy.otago.ac.nz/docview/2089854819?accountid=14700.

Voracek, Martin, and Lisa Mariella Loibl. 2007. "Genetics of Suicide: A Systematic Review of Twin Studies." *Wien Klin Wochenschr* 119 (15): 463–475.

Werth, James L., and Daniel J. Holdwick Jr. 2000. "A Primer on Rational Suicide and Other Forms of Hastened Death." *The Counselling Psychologist* 28 (4): 511539.

Witztum, Eliezer, and Daniel Stein. 2012. "Suicide in Judaism with a Special Emphasis on Modern Israel." *Religions* 3: 725–738.

CHAPTER 9

Peacebuilding Suicide

> The World Health Organization estimates that by the year 2020 at least 1.5 million human beings could die by suicide and for each suicide there might be between 15 and 20 suicidal attempts. It represents a suicide every 40 seconds and a suicidal attempt every 1 or 2 seconds. (Aldridge and Pérez Barrero 2011, 46)

Thus far, this book has sought to amplify the reality of suicidal violence left unexamined by my field by establishing the suicide gap. It has attempted to illuminate, scrutinize, clarify and organize various understandings of phenomena relevant to self-killing while locating the relevance and rationale for concern and attention from the field of Peace and Conflict Studies (PACS) in accordance with the Seville Statement on violence. This book has delved into a cross-discipline appreciation of suicide from geographic, cultural, temporal and spatial perspectives and sought to locate life-ending acts among a broad scope of incarnations. This breadth has led to a theorization of forms of suicide that can be considered under the rubric of *medical* or *instrumental* forms and include mental illness, assisted suicide, euthanasia, homicide-suicides, martyrdom (altruistic) operations, daredevil and protest suicides. The book has sought to appreciate suicidal phenomena from the perspective of direct, indirect and cultural violence as well as in relation to intention, motivation and intervention. The book has then endeavoured to critique, problematize and challenge notions and assumptions that surround suicides as voluntary and rational acts.

K. Standish, *Suicide through a Peacebuilding Lens*,
https://doi.org/10.1007/978-981-13-9737-0_9

This final chapter reiterates the case for suicide research in the interdisciplinary field of PACS and offers an original meta-theory of peace praxis termed *Encounter Theory*. The chapter then suggests a theoretical and empirical way to incorporate suicidal violence into our work via the Encounter Theory of *relationship*. There are seven forms of suicide identified in this work and overwhelmingly, by an immense margin, the majority of suicides can be characterized as *medical* and categorized as forms of mental illness. In Chapter 1, three approaches to suicide were discussed which could inhibit, decrease or eradicate the violence of self-killing including: (1) awareness raising, gatekeeper training and means restriction, (2) medication and therapy and (3) *relationship building* (Fig. 9.1).

By exploring the four facets of *relationship* (connection, reciprocity, interconnection and friendship), this final chapter will posit to peacebuild suicide related to mental illness.[1] This work concludes with an echo of the Seville Statement of 1986 entreating people from all life paths and disciplines to bring violence to light wherever it is found.

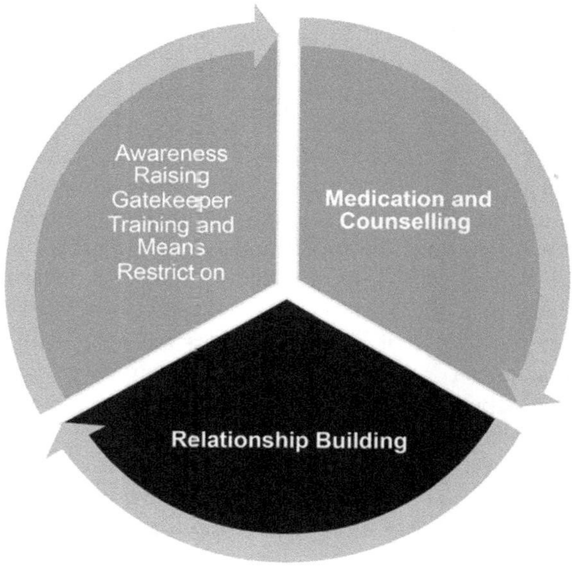

Fig. 9.1 Relationship approach to peacebuilding suicide

Fig. 9.2 Negative and positive suicidal peacebuilding

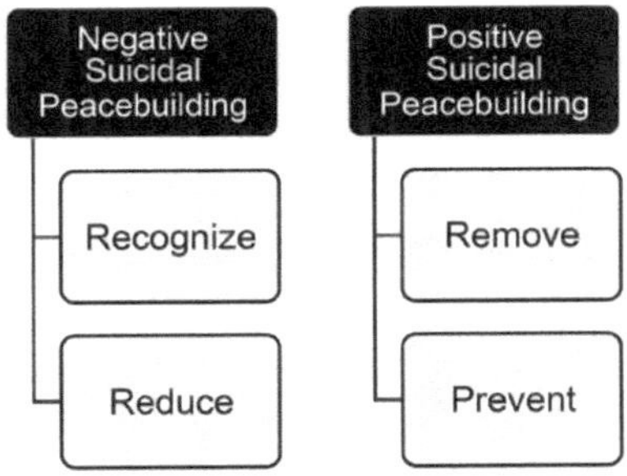

Peacebuilding seeks to recognize, reduce, remove and prevent violence. Despite some success in addressing suicide, the global violence of self-killing remains. It is clear that gatekeeper training and restriction of the means of suicide have made some inroads to diminish the opportunity for form one (mental illness) of *medical* suicide to occur but has had less success in diminishing *instrumental* forms of suicide. As posited in Chapter 7, an overarching trend in addressing suicide (whether *medical* or *instrumental*) can be conceptualized along the lines of negative and positive peace (Galtung 1996). Turning to suicide, creating the conditions of negative or positive peace can be conceived here as 'negative' suicidal peacebuilding and 'positive' suicidal peacebuilding (Fig. 9.2).

The utility of defining efforts that acknowledge and minimize vs. efforts that eradicate or prevent relates to our ability to grasp fully the differences and nuances so that we do not collapse the terms into an unclear or imprecise usage. Negative peace, as per Galtung, stops direct violence and positive peace stops cultural and structural violence. In this rubric, negative suicidal peacebuilding recognizes and reduces—one level of impact—whereas positive suicidal peacebuilding removes and prevents, an altogether more comprehensive and hopefully sustainable impact. In this instance, negative does not mean bad or detrimental but rather refers to a level of intervention Galtung recognized as minimums with positive peace referring to more-than-minimums. It can be useful, for our purposes, to perceive that both negative and positive forms of peacebuilding (and in this instance suicidal peacebuilding) comprise levels of intervention (they are not doing nothing) but methods termed *positive* are more impactful that methods termed *negative*.

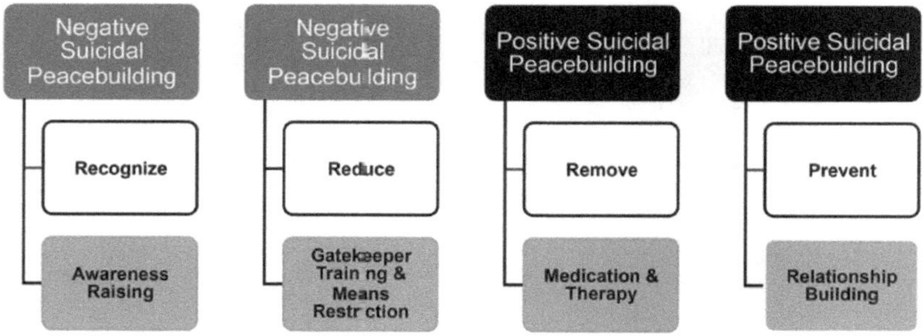

Fig. 9.3 Negative and positive suicidal peacebuilding and relationship

When Fig. 9.3 incorporates, the three approaches to suicide identified in this study: (1) awareness raising, gatekeeper training and means restriction, (2) medication and therapy and (3) *relationship building*. A metaphysics of suicidal peacebuilding emerges.

Peacebuilding Suicide?

In *Building Peace: Sustainable Reconciliation in Divided Societies*, John Paul Lederach, a seminal and inspirational pracademic whose work is pivotal and instrumental in the field of reconciliation and peacebuilding, wrote that as PACS scholars we need to be 'descriptive before we can be prescriptive. We must increase our capacity to describe situations, identifying the key dilemmas around issues and relationships, before we jump into solutions' (1997, 137). Then, a few years later, in *The Moral Imagination, The Art and Soul of Building Peace*, he wrote that you can only simplify once you have complexified, 'once the full complexity is understood, you can then make a choice about what particular thing to do in a given setting' (2005, 33). This book has been my attempt to unravel and unpack the '…messiness of ideas, processes and change' of suicide, 'and from such a place speculate about the nature of….' peacebuilding suicide (Lederach 2005, x).

Peacebuilding is an action. It is an action with an intention to affect change, to alter a landscape of negativity and endangerment and buttress our capacity for nonviolent conflict transformation; it is also a method of skill-building, aptitude training, future visioning, planning, preparation and anticipation that builds personal and interpersonal resilience, skill competency and emotional and cognitive comfort. The metaphor of *firefighting* vs. *housekeeping* is well known in the medical world where the argument goes—it is better to housekeep (maintain health) than to firefight (manage illness) and the same could be said for peacebuilding. What if, instead of concentrating our peace research and praxis[2] on conflict (the disease) we instead looked at ways to maintain wellness amidst conflict, recognizing that the world is full of conflict (or *germs* in the medical metaphor) but that we can do many things to maximize our well-being and work to maintain our wellness as individuals, families, communities and cultures? The following section will explore the notion of peacebuilding as housekeeping (resilience amid and wellness among conflict) by presenting a philosophy of peace praxis I have termed *Encounter Theory*. An appeal for the development of a 'positive PACS' is presented followed by a proposal to peacebuild suicide via the Encounter Theory of *relationship*.

Encounter Theory

My field (Peace and Conflict Studies or PACS) is a discipline that seeks to disentangle and deeply comprehend the interconnecting facets and facilitations of violence. We are committed to the normalization of 'conflict' as a human form of discord that can be creative, critical and productive but also the delegitimization of violence (in all its forms) as address. To us, violence is optional, conflict is not.

Social science has long been concerned with the 'why' of things and has created and contained distinct but complementary disciplines to formulate, cogitate and conclude the 'why' of conflict. We are far from being able to fully understand and collaborate our knowledge with one another in order to share answers and knowledge (instead of spinning in circles merely critiquing the questions and methods). There are not enough hours or research assistants in the world to 'comprehend' the totality of knowledge in the world—to fully appreciate the deluge of voices, the subaltern, the outliers, the 'other' or the inaudible—either those whose languages we do not comprehend or those who know much and would have much to say but do not communicate it via elite or popular forms of communication and broadcast their knowledge outside their intimate circles. The aim to understand our humanity, in any other way but partially, is impossible and in the social sciences we delimit our inquiries so we can at least draw some knowledge from our research to share with others.

Social scientific theories are constructs of understanding that seek to explain, describe or calculate something. They come from particular conceptualizations of reality (ontology) and the nature of knowledge (epistemology) and they delimit, define and divine outcomes based on previous findings or well supported speculations. There are hundreds of 'theories' that seek to illuminate human actions and reactions but also to predict or prophesize future scenarios based on past understandings or sophisticated deductions. In this regard, PACS has been no different, seeking to procreate knowledge of 'why' conflict and violence happen to understand and transform it. The diversion or fork in the road I am suggesting is to amplify the orientation of our research and work away from the *why*, a term, that is both a question of cause and its elucidation because with *why*—both the *how-come* and the *because*—the outcome is always (and only) an explanation whereas in peace praxis we go further and ask 'where to from here?' and then *peacebuild* whatever incarnation of harm is under review seeking transformation. But much peace praxis begins at the problem[3] (the conflict) or exists along a conflict temporality which could be looked at another way.

Many PACS theories seek to understand the 'why' of conflict and violence, to partially or potentially glimpse the underlying motivations, intentions and practices that lead persons or people to harm themselves or others. Causal theories are ideas that seek to understand and explain 'why' conflict occurs. The aim is to comprehend in order to destabilize the conditions leading to conflict and/or alter the circumstances that give rise to conflict in the first place (this intention excludes *intellectual* PACS scholarship—see Standish and Joyce 2018—whose sole ambition is to comprehend, not impact, affect or intervene). The objective for most is to eliminate conflict so that *conflict transformation* is unnecessary. The underlying goal—cogently—in many PACS causal theories is to use knowledge to eradicate the conflict.

Chapter 3 looked at the history of the PACS movement to include functional practices of PACS such as Alternative Dispute Resolution (ADR), Conflict Management, Conflict Analysis and Resolution (CAR) and Conflict Transformation. This section seeks to add an appreciative conceptualization of the conflict transformation succession in PACS to include *Encounter Theory*. In our peace praxis, the PACS world has historically and typically packaged techniques of communication and confrontation such as mediation, negotiation, third-party intervention, structured dialogue and various forms of interaction and cooperation as ways of addressing conflict. What many of these peacebuilding technologies or mechanisms share, what underlies them (yes, the transformation one too), is a sensibility that conflict is an obstacle, problem, crisis or dilemma—and therefore, is the part that needs to be focused on first—that conflict is bad, and that conflict needs attention. I propose that these mechanisms need not consider conflict a problem to engage with it (to recognize, remedy or repackage it) to foster the conditions for its absence and prevention (the endgame of positive peacebuilding). We can, instead of focusing on conflict, simply acknowledge, as Elise Boulding did (2000) that 'conflict is' and then focus our attention on creating the conditions of positive peace via mechanisms of encounter. This does not mean ignoring conflict or blinding ourselves to conflict or accepting conflict—this means fortifying ourselves with training, discipline and awareness so that in instances where we seek, are obliged or are driven to engage with conflict (either systems or symptoms of conflict such as racism or misogyny) we are ready, resilient and impactful in our responses and above all, conduct our peace praxis with compassion and nonviolence.

An Appeal for a 'Positive' PACS

Peace praxis as housekeeping means learning how to support and communicate positive humanity skills and practising personal and interpersonal custodianism (taking care) not because conflict might happen, but so we are instantly aware and able to engage with one another to maximize our well-being *normally*—if we normalize discord, friction and diversity, we will cease dehumanizing others (we often dehumanize people that think differently than we do) and become competent and comfortable in practices of personal wellness and interpersonal outreach. Humans have always had cultural mechanisms and mannerisms that seek to maximize wellness and community well-being. After more than sixty years of focusing on 'the problem' in PACS, I support the evolution of 'positive PACS' to focus on positive peace, peace praxis, peaceteaching, peacelearning and peace practice.

We would not be the first discipline to do this either, the positive psychology movement has striven to focus on what works in human thinking and community instead of what is not. As a response to psychology's traditional focus on 'mental illness' and barriers to well-being in 1998 Martin Seligman, Mihaly Csikszentmihalyi, Christopher Peterson and Barbara Fredrickson began to flip the focus of the field into *eudaimonia*—a good life and what makes it worth living. The new and complementary direction I propose for PACS does not seek to eradicate the focus of conflict and violence cessation as important aims but, similar to positive psychology, in positive PACS we could focus on what deters, deflects and averts conflict though inter-group, community and personal peacebuilding and infuse our peace praxis with peace-abilities that lead to conflict avoidance instead of conflict management, resolution or transformation. Many of us do this type of work already but frequently find ourselves sitting at the table with people whose vision, intentions and scope are enormously dissimilar to our own. I sincerely believe there is a need for a PACS that focuses on 'bottom of the cliff' realities but I think we also need a PACS that prevents us from ever going over the edge in the first place. The recognition and fortification of existing 'positive' PACS work and the generation of new peace praxis will provide an ingathering of many able and committed peacebuilders as well as people working on 'positive' understandings in other fields too. We can make ourselves more resistant to conflict if we recognize, mobilize, activate and maintain our ability to enthusiastically and nonviolently encounter the world. Indeed, we can turn our energies to a more harmonious way of living via nonviolent communication and supportive and compassionate humanity.[4]

Encounter Theory in Action

In my teaching, I often use OSCEs to scaffold my grad students' confidence in their ability to use peace praxis in their everyday lives. OSCEs (objective structured clinical examinations) are used in medical training and are 'tests' that evaluate a student's ability to perform a task. Think about learning, as a nursing student, how to take blood from a patient. You can read about it, listen to someone explain the procedure and even have your own blood taken but none of these will give you the confidence to take blood from someone yourself. PACS OSCEs, in my class, work exactly the same. I have two OSCE units in my class, one on civility and one on bystander intervention.[5] In each, students craft an active scenario for their classmates where a particular facet of the focus is practised. For example, in one civility OSCE students were asked to speak about what they did the night before (1 on 1) for several minutes—but at the same time! The room was a cacophony of two-sided monologues and laughter ensued at the ridiculousness of speaking non-stop about yourself without listening. The next part of the unit asked the A of each group (each had an A and a B participant) to relate to the class what the other person did the night before. It was then B's turn. As you can imagine, the students (all groups) were unable to do more than minimally explain what their conversation partner had done as they had spent the time (as instructed) also talking about their night. The unit was a great example of how ineffective interaction is without the critical art of listening. The students instantly understood that the purpose of civil interaction is to engage in dialogue with equal emphasis on sharing their information and listening to others. Students were then asked to do it again, but this time they took turns and each was relieved and relaxed at the chance to absorb the other's story and relate it to the class. Practising civil interaction might seem silly but you would be surprised how often people engage in conversation without listening to the other person.

The bystander OSCE is more challenging because this is about intervening when you see potential violence in front of you. Many, if not most of the students are trepidatious of this aspect of peace praxis because for both personal and cultural reasons, intervening in the business of other people is considered rude, makes you a possible target of aggression or can be the result of a misunderstanding which can lead to anger from the person you might be trying to help. Many bystander OSCEs that the students come up with in my classes relate to a form of intervention that utilizes *distraction*. If someone is being bullied on a bus (for example), the quickest way to deescalate bullying behaviour is to focus on the person being bullied and break the bond between the person using bullying behaviour and the person experiencing the bullying behaviour (bullying is a repeated act of verbal or physical aggression meant to subordinate, intimidate, humiliate or harm someone and is a common form of dehumanization). If you imagine an invisible bond that is created between the two poles of experience you need to 'break' the bond. You cannot change a syndrome of aggression as a bystander but you can, simply by being present in the space, break or at least weaken the directional aggression you see. It sounds easy, but is actually really hard and student OSCEs repeatedly engage with this difficulty: At what point do you intervene? Is there a signal you send to other potential (one would hope) bystanders that 'you got this one!'? How do you intervene? With your body? With your words? Do you fake a heart attack to take the attention your way? Do you confront the person bullying? Do you pretend you know (you may indeed actually know them) the person who is the target? What language do you use? The answer to all of these questions is the reason that most people don't intervene—they get stuck in a cognitive loop of potential action and consequences and it leads them to freeze. My students typically highlight a best (peace) praxis, where you completely ignore the person utilizing the bullying behaviour and focus on the person who is the target. Simply walking up to them and beginning a conversation will break the bond. It can be a simple comment on something observable like 'I think I have the same backpack (handbag, jacket, sneakers) as you, did you get them at (name a store)?' This sends three important signals: to the person engaging in bullying behaviour you are signalling that their behaviour won't be tolerated, to the person experiencing the behaviour, you are signalling your allyship and to other potential bystanders, you are signalling to them that it is safe to join you which may lead to others joining the intervention too. In one of my favourite class OSCEs, each student came up with a personal catchphrase to use and each practised it during role play until it became second nature. Both of these OSCEs are incarnations of positive encounter—they don't attempt to erase conflict but each focuses on perfecting a technique of engagement that leads to more congenial relationships and support. And both of these operationalize Encounter Theory.

Lederach avers,

> Theory is not writing perfectly defined but intangible explanations of social realities. It is about the common sense of how things are connected, how they influence each other, and how they may relate to desired change. Theory is our best speculation about how complex things work. (2005, 125)

Encounter Theory is my sense of how things are connected and an umbrella or gathering space for the 'work' of peace praxis. It recognizes that our vocation is about engaging with others and has led me to speculate about the complexities of enacting and maintaining social change. If a theory is a construct of understanding undergirding a social phenomenon, then the meta-theory of peace praxis is *Encounter Theory*. The theory does not just include 'others' as people or peoples but engaging (and confronting and resisting and comprehending) other cultures, other ways of living and other ways of thinking about our humanity. It is 2019 as I write this and in the current cultural landscape, we are increasingly confronted with perceptions of 'difference as dangerous', 'difference as less than' and 'difference as violence'. Encounter Theory seeks to support peace praxis to include both encountering other people but also other ways of thinking and perceiving from a position of accomplished compassion and proficient nonviolence. Staying in our echo chambers is no longer possible, we are not savanna dwellers with social networks that tap-out at 150 individuals. We are global humans living in spaces as small as a microchip and as large as the Internet. We live constantly in a space of encounter and this means that we would do well as humans to start curating the skills and practices of encounter not because there might be 'conflict' but because there simply, always, is.

Encounter Theory rejects the notion of healthful isolation, dislocation, marginalization, disconnection, segregation and loneliness and posits that human nonviolence is only sustainable through sustained humanization of others. Encounter Theory appreciates conflict but amputates violence through encounter technologies: engagement, support, empathy, affection and humanization. Put simply, Encounter Theory undergirds peace praxis—it underpins, upholds and sustains the enactment of engaging mindfully, nonviolently and compassionately with difference. It is the 'how' that the field practices and I believe it has something to offer as an intervention in life-ending acts.

Peacebuilding work needs vision, it needs a sense of hopefulness, pathways thinking and enough agency to get you there. It also needs collaboration and an interconnectivity of knowledge, practice and understanding. As Lederach says, 'the great challenge of peacebuilding [is]…to build creative responses to patterns of self-perpetuating violence' (2005, 33) via *capacity* the combination of 'understanding, ability, and discipline…*capacity* is empowerment at its most primordial essence: "I am able and committed"' (2005, 96). So far, this book has endeavoured to provide an understanding of suicide from a PACS perspective to increase our fields' ability to encounter suicide and contribute to our disciplinary capacity. We are *committed* to transforming conflict and eradicating violence, in terms of the violence of suicide, through this offering I have hoped to make us more *able*.

This book is a disciplinary call for peacebuilders (from all disciplines) to pay attention to the number one cause of violent death in the developed world. It has also investigated and envisioned a multidisciplinary approach (via peacebuilding) to connect and contemplate how suicide can be collectively considered. It has contributed a cultural and historical survey deliberating suicide and ruminated on the position of PACS to engage with suicide with the mindful and contextual consideration that can emerge from our unique positionality. It has offered a new theory of life-ending-acts as *medical* or *instrumental* and then presented conceptualizations of suicide via intention, motivation and intervention and social, cultural and political violence. In the previous chapter, this book asked key questions and proposed substantial challenges regarding acts of suicide to further problematize the term and its 'catch all' conundrum. In this final chapter, I would like to offer a *peacebuilding prescription* for *medical* suicide from this important PACS perspective: *relationship*.

Relationship

A relationship, in simplest terms, is a connection. It is the condition of being in 'relation' with another and can be categorized as an individual holding a bond with someone else. You may have affinity for music or art or sports or any other facet of culture but you have relationships with people. We all have consanguineal (blood) and affinal (by association) relationships and such bonds or alliances can be characterized by levels of intimacy, antagonism or indifference. What positive PACS and Encounter Theory seek to foster is positive relationships, the opposite of dehumanization, disunion, intolerance and discrimination and relations comprised of empathy, affection, support, positive reciprocity and care.

There are many peace technologies encompassed in Encounter Theory but this section will consider 4 facets of positive relationships that can be considered in suicidal peacebuilding: *connection*, *positive reciprocity*, *interconnection* and *friendship*. Relationships are not necessarily positive—there are all kinds of negative human associations and some are much more than distasteful and inconvenient, they are roots of violence and traumatizing victimhood. Peacebuilders have termed conflict a breakdown in or absence of relationship (Lederach 2003, 2005); a circumstance where 'trust' is not possible due to non-existent bonding (Boulding 2000); a lack of *humane*ness in relations (Reardon 1995, 1988) or hostile or destructive relations (Jeong 2011). But there are human practices that create and buttress human connectivity, that seek to establish and reinforce relationships and also to support and sustain them. In this section, four techniques of positive peacebuilding will be considered that can potentially ameliorate suicide: *connection*, *positive reciprocity*, *interconnection* and *friendship*.

Humans need relationships the same way they need air, water, food and rest—to survive, human living needs to include others. In a positive social environment, relationships are beneficial, warm and supportive, in conflictual or traumatic social environments relationships can be destabilizing, destructive and violent. Humans don't live articulated but isolated lives, they are collective creatures whose wellspring and well-being emerge and rely on social interactions—to thrive, human living needs *positive* interactions with others. When Durkheim discovered that suicide related to social integration, he learned that there was an inverse relationship between social enmeshment and self-killing. The looser or more limited your social obligations the greater your chance of suicide. He famously looked at religious groups (Protestants vs. Catholics) but also social relations in 'domestic society' to discover that the people most likely to kill themselves were those living alone. This has not changed. But, what has changed is the society around us. Countless people feel detached and marginalized and this has led many to feelings of isolation and disconnection. The 'peacebuild' for disconnection is reconnection via relationships. The outcome of strong relationships is not just suicide risk-reduction 'having strong social relationships strengthens the immune system, extends life...speeds recovery from surgery, and reduces the risks of depression and anxiety' too (Haidt 2006, 133). This book has identified three approaches to suicide: (1) awareness raising, gatekeeper training and means restriction, (2) medication and therapy and (3) *relationship building*. It is to this third remedy that this chapter will turn now.

The goal of the following section is to establish a platform of understanding for positive relationships but also an architecture or underlying strata to comprehend both what positive relationships are comprised of and how to form them. As Lederach says, relationships are 'both the context in which cycles of violence happen and the generative energy from which transcendence of those same cycles bursts forth' (2005, 34) (Fig. 9.4).

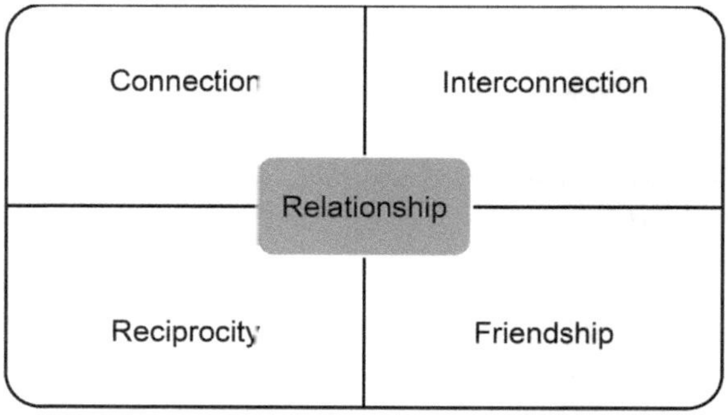

Fig. 9.4 Four aspects of relationship

In this chapter, I would like to deconstruct the peace praxis of *relationship* into four divergent but interrelated components to contribute a creative response to the patterns of suicide. In my research, I have found all four of these distinct (to me) forms of relation termed 'relationship' but when seeking to mobilize, manifest and sustain relationships it is necessary to take apart the soup (challenging but not impossible) surrounding our assumptions about what relationships are and are comprised of. And, I do this as a PACS scholar/practitioner, not a psychologist or philosopher or social worker so I humbly submit my own understandings of these terms to establish clearer bounds (not borders) surrounding their domains.

A persons' relationship can include all or some of these four strains of relation but I am going to suggest (later in this chapter) that the greater insulation against suicide will not be from what I theorize as negative suicidal peacebuilding but from positive suicidal peacebuilding. I also will need to tweak (apologies) some of the established terms used by scholar-practitioners in my own field, not to ignore their own sense-making but to delineate and then differentiate forms so that I can then treat them operationally as distinct forms of peacebuilding.

Definitions

Connection: Connection in human interactions is also called bonding, bonding is a process of encounter and intimacy between people. It is the interpersonal development of connectivity and closeness and it gives individuals a sense of belonging, a trust in others, a feeling of being supported and a sense of identity (Miller and Rodgers 2001). Whereas *bonding* is often considered something innate to familial connections (think of parental bonding with newborns) that forms attachments, *connection* is something all humans, regardless of association, can do to nurture closeness (Rossi and Rossi 1990). Human bonds are moulded through interactions with others and new relationships typically result from shared experiences, shared goals, proximity to others and investments where you deliberately contribute to the goals of others (Bowlby 1990). Bonds are not actions so much as outcomes of continued interactions with others but there is a point of first (or mindful)[6] contact that is necessary to begin the process of bonding and that starting point I term *connection*.

Reciprocity: reciprocity is a social medium that exchanges aid (actions or resources) in the present for cooperation in the future (Molm 2010). Through reciprocity, social ties between strangers become stronger and reciprocity becomes an 'art', the goal of which is to secure for the self (or others) favours, resources or privileges that benefit the individual, group, society or the world at large. In laypersons terms and game theory scholarship reciprocity is called a 'tit for tat' or 'you scratch my back and I will scratch yours' methodology (Fudenberg and Tirole 1991) but there is more to the art of reciprocity in social functions than merely being a social medium of exchange, gratitude, indebtedness and obligation. Reciprocity breeds reciprocity. Social psychology illumines that the role of reciprocity in social interactions actually creates the conditions for the return of behaviours and attitudes (Larson 1998). An end in itself, the art of reciprocity uses an exchange of benefits to secure and stimulate future interaction. Once a reciprocal bond is created a relationship results and, as the foundation of human social interaction, reciprocity not only fosters constructive interaction in the present but it may act to inhibit destructive relations in the future.

Interconnection: interconnection signals a mutual connection between two or more things. In human interconnection, an initial (and mindful) connection has occurred and bonds of human relatedness have been established via acts of reciprocity. Mutuality differentiates *interconnection* from *connection* because the bond is two-way and does not simply indicate an avenue of potentially unreciprocated affiliation. Interconnection is a *relationship* or the state of being connected with others (Berscheid and Peplau

1983) and can relate to a number of different types of interconnection including: acquaintances, family relationships, interpersonal relationships, associations, neighbourhoods, community, lifestyle or cultural groups and nations. Interconnections can include interpersonal interactions rooted in feelings of commitment, support, solidarity, loyalty and sometimes affection but are manifested and maintained via repeated interactions.

Friendship: friendship is a particular kind of interconnection that has affective bonds. Friendships are relationships characterized by warmth, intimacy, sharing, tolerance and reciprocity (Devere 2018). They are voluntary and beneficial and are rooted in the values and actions of trust, care, empathy, support and affection (Devere and Smith 2010). Friendship can exist between peoples (in friendship treaties for example), communities (in various peacebuilding initiatives) as well as between persons but each type of friendship involves mutual fondness, affinity and custodianship (Austin 2012). Between non-romantic partners, friendship is the highest level of affective intimacy and interconnection and is second only to the bond between parents and children in giving satisfaction and meaning to a person's life.

In the following section, I would like to posit and progress the peace praxis of relationship by examining these four relational stages as aspects of either negative peace praxis or positive peace praxis. In Chapter 3, Galtung's premise of negative and positive peace was explored. Galtung established that negative peace was comprised of nonaggression or the cessation of direct violence whereas positive peace included the absence of cultural and structural forms of violence as well as the maximization of conditions needed to attain full humanity. In this section, I will propose that the first two forms of relationship (connection and reciprocity) can be considered forms of negative peace praxis whereas the inclusion of the latter two forms (interconnection and friendship) is positive peace praxis.

If we recall the rubric of negative and positive suicidal peacebuilding from earlier in this chapter (see Fig. 9.2), we see the separation between interventions that *recognize*, *reduce*, *remove* and *prevent* self-killing (Fig. 9.5).

These four aspects (*recognize*, *reduce*, *remove* and *prevent*) identify interrelated but distinct facets of peacebuilding that can be considered forms of either negative or positive peacebuilding. In the next section, I would like to explore four interrelated but distinct facets of relationship (see Fig. 9.6) as avenues of either negative or positive peace praxis.

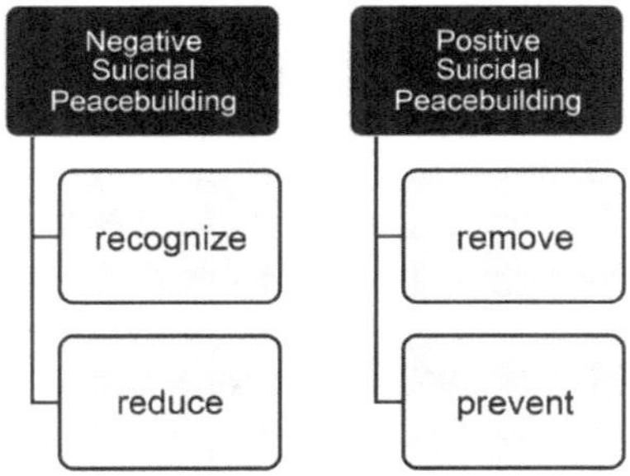

Fig. 9.5 Negative and positive suicidal peacebuilding

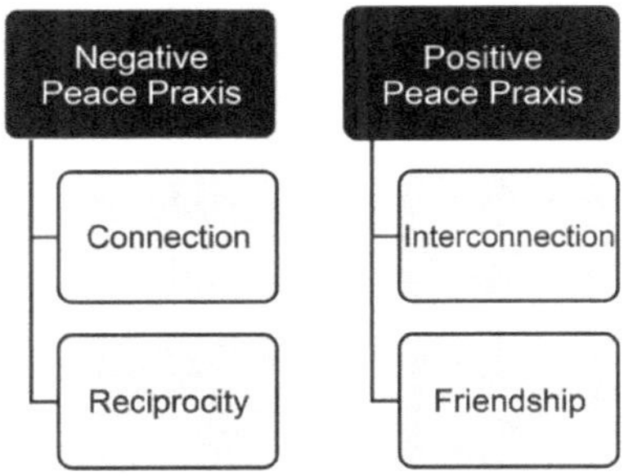

Fig. 9.6 Negative and positive peace relationship praxis

The reason I position my understandings thusly is that while making connections and engaging with reciprocal exchanges are certainly parts of relationships they lack mutuality and warmth, conditions I think are necessary to attain positive relationship status and circumstances that are vital in suicidal peacebuilding. In the next section, I would like to more fully explore the four facets of the relationship under review here. I will consider them within the rubric of negative and positive peace, and later, articulate these facets of relationship to notions of peacebuilding *medical* suicide related to mental illness.

Connection

The first step in relationship building as peace praxis involves making contact. This is something that many of us don't think about strategically because most of us think of making connections as happenstance not deliberate actions. In fact, some of us (introverts but extroverts who are spread very thin too) dread 'new' connections and actively avoid them. Think about it, when was the last time you made a new connection and what were the circumstances that surrounded that connection? Odds are you 'met' in pre-organized or structured environments (work or school pick-up, for example), lesser chance (but entirely possible) you met someone laughing at a YouTube video on the subway or in a café and struck up a 'like-minded' conversation. If we are in the world (in real life but also online), there are all kinds of ways we interact with others that are potential sites of connection. But there are all kinds of things that problematize connection in our world too including:

- Gender—is the person you are seeking to connect with a potential romantic partner or think you might be (or want to be)?
- Age—many of us live in age ghettos where we don't interact with youth, the elderly or young children unless they are our own.
- Past experience—did your last three attempts end up as 'toxic' relationships and/or do you hold prejudices about certain 'types' of people?
- Intention—what do you want? And what do they think you want?

There are 'transactional' ways of thinking about connection that involve getting something that you want, or that you have been told is beneficial, and those involve notions of acquiring people like things. Books with subtitles like *how to get more friends or dates* or the *art of seduction or attraction* abound in book stores and TED talks, where your life circumstances are success markers for others to judge you by and the idea of networking and connecting with others is pretty mercenary. In negative peace praxis, this is exactly what connection is comprised of, strategic contact that may provide future beneficial outcomes.

There is another way of thinking about connection that flows into positive peace praxis and that involves the notion of connection as *reconnection* (Feuerstein 2001; Hari 2018). There are two ways of thinking about the reconnection concept. The first is related to philosophical non-dualism or the notion that we are all connected anyway and we need only to become aware of our inherent and manifest connectivity to others and nature to be in attachment with them (Feuerstein 2001). The second involves the 'actions' of reconnection to include anti-isolation practices that reconnect a marginalized, secluded or unwell person (defined as socially, psychologically and biologically unwell) with people, nature and positive values to form meaningful attachments (Hari 2018). Atomization of individuals considers our humanity as discrete incarnations of our species that bond with family first (in infancy and childhood) and then with strangers after maturity is gained. Holistic notions of humanity perceive humans as inherently in connection but with obstructions or veils obscuring this truth. The obstacle to 'reconnection as recognition' lies within the individual (Feuerstein 2001) but the obstacle to 'reconnection as restoration' (Hari 2018) lies within the rest of us.

Reciprocity

The second step in relationship building as peace praxis involves *reciprocity*. Haidt and other psychologists consider reciprocity a 'tool for getting along with people' and an underlying code or explanation for how humans interact and what motivates us (2006, xi). There are several forms of reciprocity including: negative and positive reciprocity, direct and indirect reciprocity and instrumental and symbolic reciprocity. The following section will briefly define the six types of reciprocity then focus on the final aspect: symbolic reciprocity, and its connection to negative and positive peace praxis.

Along the lines of the 'tit for tat' mentality, negative reciprocity is punitive and includes acts 'of harming those who wrong us' whereas positive reciprocity is cooperative and kind and includes gifts or benefit exchanges to those who 'do right' by you in the past (Friedman and Singh 2003, 155). In a direct reciprocal relationship, the primary parties exchange and benefit from a closed circle of prosperity while in indirect relationships the recipients can include outside individuals too (Molm et al. 2007). While direct reciprocity can be seen to stimulate relationships between individuals, indirect reciprocity has a wider pool of beneficiaries and may benefit extended networks of individuals as well. Indirect reciprocity can be considered a way of broadening relationships of direct reciprocity to impact, include and encounter others.

Instrumental reciprocity refers to the intrinsic 'value' of a benefit (Molm et al. 2007). Assessed monetarily or in terms of its utilitarian quality, the 'benefit' in instrumental reciprocity can alternately be reciprocated with exchanges more or less generous than the original benefit or equal to the original benefit whereas Symbolic reciprocity refers to the value conveyed by the act of reciprocity itself (Molm et al. 2007).

Symbolic Reciprocity

The symbolic value of a reciprocal benefit is important because although instrumental reciprocity is valuable and can create a 'space of recognition' (Lederach 2005, 35) between parties, symbolic reciprocity carries along with it significance 'over and above the instrumental value of the benefits provided' (Molm et al. 2007, 201) creating 'high levels of trust, mutual regard, and feelings of commitment' (Molm et al. 2007, 200). Symbolic reciprocity adheres to important cultural traits of understanding that see positive gestures as valuable and perhaps even more valuable than the item of exchange itself echoing the maxim that 'it is the thought that counts' not a particular instrumental manifestation.

In order for a reciprocal benefit to be considered symbolic, it requires three qualities: it has to be a long-term exchange of benefits, there must be a sense of uncertainty regarding a return of benefits and it must be deliberate (Molm et al. 2007). When exchanges are uncertain, voluntary and occurring over a period of time reciprocal benefits obtain *symbolic* value resulting in solidarity, affective regard and social bonding. That 'uncertainty' becomes a tool of mutability wherein parties' can increase positive affection through action and the possibility of future beneficial interaction strengthens the bond of beneficial relationship.

Obviously, negative reciprocity, the return of bad actions or items with other bad actions or items, is not a part of negative peace because it signals an ongoing transfer of violence via exchange. The remaining forms of reciprocity aid in relationship building via an interaction of exchanged benefits. The human practice of recognizing generosity and returning the favour is a mechanism of interaction that can be strategically employed to create association and interaction. However, only symbolic reciprocity can lead to genuine affective bonding and therefore can be considered advantageous in positive peace praxis.

Interconnection

The third step in relationship building as peace praxis involves interconnection. In this section, I am going to talk about interconnection as webbing or yoking that results from repeated interactions. Many scholars term interconnection as 'relationship', but as I see it, there are steps or platforms in relationship building that do not stop or apex at, what I term, interconnection and so I will reframe what others term 'relationship' as interconnection.

If we consider that connection is the point of contact, and reciprocal exchange is the next step of potential bonding, we can then progress to the state of interconnection which is a mutual state of repeated exchange leading to security and trust. We are, 'social creatures that have the capacities to identify and recall the earlier behavior of specific individuals, and to reward or punish them contingent on earlier behavior' (Friedman and Singh 2003, 156). In this regard, interconnection in the future is contingent on interactions in the past. As previous social interactions contribute to future social confidence positive voluntarily interactions, overtime and deliberately exchanged lead to a two-way or mutual connection. Instigating (at first) and then sustaining positive reciprocity is critical to forming and maintaining relationships that lead to feelings of duty and trust and practices of mutual aid and protection.

Because positive reciprocity is a direct contributor to the creation of affective social bonds and stronger relationships, peacebuilders focus on relationships because 'it connotes the potential of transformation by changing the way people interact—by focusing on the interaction itself' (Saunders 1999, 33). One way to see the importance of interconnection in social life is in comprehending how it functions to root and tether us and what an absence of interaction breeds.

> When relationships collapse, the center of social change does not hold. And correspondingly, rebuilding what has fallen apart is centrally the process of rebuilding relational spaces that hold things together. Paradoxical by their very nature, relational spaces create social energy that is simultaneously centripetal and centrifugal. But rather than anarchy, which is like exploding into a million pieces, peacebuilding understands that relationships create and emanate social energy and are places to which energy returns for a sense of purpose and direction … In our social world, a family typically has this characteristic. It sends us out into the world, yet we return to it for a sense of identity, direction, and purpose. Faith communities, chosen families, and even geographic locations provide a sense of identity and also have this centrifugal/centripetal capacity. In each of these examples, there exists a force that pushes out and pulls in, and in so doing creates a 'center that holds'. (Lederach 2005, 75–76)

The centripetal and centrifugal nature of social interconnections does several things, it bolsters our identity, insulates us from insecurity and permits us to assume and predict positive and useful future interactions based on our lived experience of mutual aid and protection. And it goes both ways, we both receive and provide this mutuality holding the 'centre' relational space for others. This history of mutual aid and protection can perpetuate itself and become sustaining: if we know that our actions count, that they go into an 'interaction bank' where they colour regard and reflect our inner values—we act with others in mind—such practices can then become avenues of self-esteem, well-being and both personal and communal benefit.

Friendship

The fourth step in relationship building as peace praxis involves friendship. In this rubric of relationship as peace praxis the apex of relationship is not romantic love (although that is a very common form of affective bonding that can lead to families) but filial love. Friendship, as previously defined, is a relationship characterized by warmth, intimacy, sharing, tolerance and reciprocity (Devere 2018). For our purposes, an individual can connect with others, forge and fashion reciprocal bonds with others and exist in webs or networks of interconnection that produce mutual aid and protection but in friendship, these relational spaces are occupied by more than beneficial resources and support, they are filled with love. In connection, reciprocity and interconnection, the outcome of the relationship is a benefit (either to the individual or group) but in friendship, the outcome *is the relationship itself.*

Devere (2011, 2014, 2018) classifies friendships as associations of empathy, support, attachment and closeness. Relationships 'based on emotion, cognitive awareness, social conscience and trust' and comprised of love, affection and compassion but also respect, tolerance, care, forgiveness, generosity, empowerment, reliability and trustworthiness (2018, 62–63). The distinction between interconnection and friendship relates to the presence of emotional warmth. A close connection can include helpfulness and confidence but a friendship cannot exist without love.

Friendships are simple, they are close relationships of mutual fondness, caring and trust, they involve cooperation, they endure overtime and they protect you from life stress. Denworth (2017) considers friendship like three-legged-stool. Remove one of the legs and you fall over! The first leg of friendship involves time, the more time you spend on your friendship, the stronger it is. The second leg is positivity, friends who make you feel good make you more resilient and positively disposed (happy). The final leg is being helpful, when you are there for someone else, and they are there for you when *you* need it, you have friendship (Denworth 2017). If you look for information about friendship you will find rubrics of the seven pillars of friendship, the 13 basics of friendship or the (yikes) 25 components of a great friendship! But the science of friendship really relates to three identifiable qualities: friendships are a mix of empathy, support and reciprocity—*I understand you, I will help you and by being there for you, long-term, you will also be there for me.*

Instinctively, we know that friendships are good but scientific studies have proven their beneficial qualities can extend to our very survival as individuals. Friendship scholar Daniel Perlman (2017) lists five benefits of friendship that impact human vivacity:

1. Having more and better relationships is associated with better physical health and greater odds of survival,
2. There exists strong epidemiological evidence of a directional effect of relationships on health—being socially connected can be protective,
3. Having a larger number of friends improves physical and mental health,
4. The overall magnitude of the [social connectedness] effect on risk for mortality was comparable with and in many cases exceeds the effect of many well-established risk factors for mortality. For instance, lacking social connectedness carries a risk equivalent to smoking up to 15 cigarettes per day, and is greater than alcohol abuse, physical inactivity (sedentary lifestyle), obesity, and air pollution, among others, and
5. Close friendships give meaning in our lives and make us happier (289).

The most beneficial form of relationship, the one that will give you the most protection, the greatest social and personal benefit and the type of relationship that will provide you with social and personal resilience and well-being is friendship. Knowing (connection) and being in beneficial (reciprocity) and mutual association (interconnection) have positive impact on our humanity. These three 'steps' in the relationship ladder provide great strides towards wellness and are vital parts of engaging with the social world so necessary for human wellness. As potential networks of strategic support, these three aspects of relationship are crucial signposts on the road to reducing life stress and unwellness and building networks

Fig. 9.7 Negative and positive peace relationship praxis

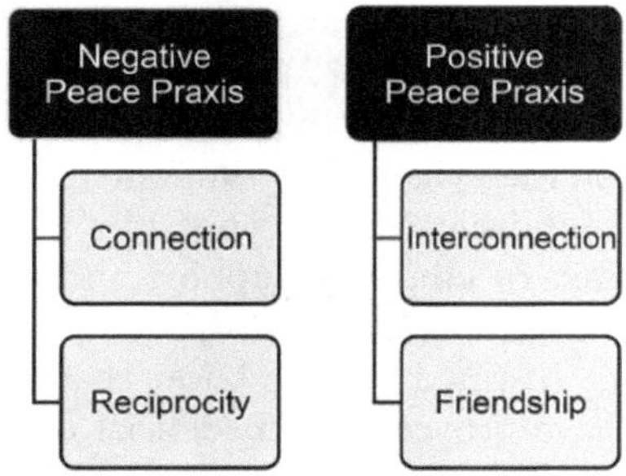

of maintenance and interchange. However, the benefit of well-being and fortitude fostered in long-term, supportive friendship comprised of emotional warmth, empathy, compassion and dependable assistance both amplifies and surpasses the social benefits of interaction and inclusion.

Earlier in this chapter, the following rubric was introduced to reflect the PACS perception of negative and positive peacebuilding in relationship (Fig. 9.7).

This chapter posits that there are benefits from negative and positive peace praxis in peacebuilding suicide. There are hundreds of training programs worldwide for peacebuilding such as conflict resolution, mediation, structured dialogue processes and negotiation—what if there were thousands of training programs, worldwide for building relationships? Meeting the human need for others, that for millennia was a part of the way we lived, has been eroded, erased and increasingly undervalued. As Johann Hari has discovered in his work on understanding the roots of depression and anxiety, we (a global 'us') have, somehow, dismantled our tribes and in doing so, lost vital support, succour and social solidarity (2018, 90).

Many of us think of ourselves as individuals (not of collectives) whose life is 'what we make' of it and when we don't find satisfaction or meaning in our worlds have no one to blame (so the self-help scribes assert) but ourselves. But I agree with Mr. Hari, if disconnection is the main driver of the circumstances that lead to suicide 'we need to find ways to reconnect' (2018, 161). Mr. Hari, a journalist and best-selling author, discovered that 'you could fill a toy airplane with the research into reconnection' but I think the field of PACS, via processes of Encounter Theory, have been working parallel to this aim for decades. I hope that this contribution can at least rest underneath that toy airplane and someday, maybe help it to fly.

Who Should Peacebuild Suicide?

Peacebuilding suicide related to mental illness involves interventions that foster and strengthen relationships. However, an important point must be made regarding the identity or identities of people who seek to *recognize*, *reduce*, *remove* and *prevent* suicidal violence. The 'work' of peacebuilding suicide is not the work of the individual or individuals who are facing and experiencing mental illness but those that surround such a person or persons. Medical professionals and various disciplinary onlookers may be able to identify 'at risk' individuals in the system of care (from the receptionist to the social worker to the nurse, etc.) but all of us, or at least those of us with the intention and awareness, can spot people who are untethered and alone and seek to encounter and engage them in relationship. I repeat, the work of peacebuilding suicide is not for people who are experiencing mental unwellness rooted in biological, psychological and social causes it is for those with the wherewithal and resources to aid them. Though a potential suicide is considering enacting life-ending violence on themselves, the work of peacebuilding suicide falls to the rest of us.

And this is not a new approach so much as a paradigm shift in how to address violence in society (Potter and Moynihan 2011). In looking at bystander intervention, the focus on individuals who are either experiencing violence or behaving violently (in suicide the individual is one and the same) is altered to the people that surround them. And, when individuals are 'trained' to be comfortable and assured bystanders they show 'improved efficacy or confidence about being a prosocial bystander, increased intention to help as bystanders, and greater sense of responsibility' to actually *do something* when situations of potential violence arise (Moynihan et al. 2011, 712). What works for bystander intervention training can potentially work for suicide related to mental illness and it doesn't have to be formal and institutionalized either, it can just be a set of circumstances, intentions and characteristics that are mindfully curated such as the ones I witnessed in Dunedin, New Zealand at the Hope Centre.

The Hope Centre

I met a woman in 2017 named Corinda Taylor. She has lost a son to suicidal violence and had started a collective that (from my perspective) peacebuilds suicide. She started the *Life Matters Suicide Prevention Trust*, a place for training volunteers to assist in the prevention of suicide but also a support space for those in bereavement. One of my first, and incredibly impactful, interactions with Corinda involved her delivery of a workshop on preventing suicide. It was an all-day affair filled with dozens of insightful and iterative units that helped us understand suicide and our appreciations of suicide but also, crucially, what to do. Spotting those in need was part of the peacebuild and involved looking with new eyes at those who are around us but one part of the workshop was like fireworks in my mind and echoes in my brain to this day; the single great take away from the whole day of education and training could be summed up (to me) in one single directive: if you think someone is going to harm themselves, *don't leave them alone.*

The workshop was designed to be a peer-based acute response training for regular people to hand off persons at risk of suicide to professionals (imagined as the medical community). But to me, the directive was not only something that could be done at the critical pre-suicide phase but well in advance of notions of self-harming or self-killing to prevent the risk altogether. There will be people who say you cannot stop a suicide, that if someone wants to kill themselves, they will. But as research in this book has shown, many incomplete suicides are relieved they did not die, that they did not accomplish violent self-death and certainly those left behind, like Corinda, are certain that preventing suicide is possible and will save lives (Joiner 2010).

The Hope Centre is a drop-in space for people who feel alone. Part of the Life Matters Suicide Prevention Trust[7] is a (as much as they can) discreet and very small office space with a couch and a table and a few chairs that you can go to, if you are contemplating suicide. The person who walks in wants help but what they receive when they enter (and I have seen this with my own eyes so I am not relating something from the website) is love. They are connected with, they are spoken to as friends dropping by, provided with hospitality (can I get you a meal, a drink, a hot coffee?), and they are asked about their lives and plans. They are treated with friendship and told to come back whenever they can. They can make appointments to come back or drop in but they are welcome and they are treated like an old friend who matters. Their lives matter to Corinda and all the other volunteers and the exercise, the *peacebuild*, is a living, breathing intervention of affective bonding. And it is saving lives.

The paradigm shift you see in support settings such as the Hope Centre and in bystander and civility training is environmental and empowering. As Hari concludes in his essential work finding a human

Fig. 9.8 The relationship as pyramid

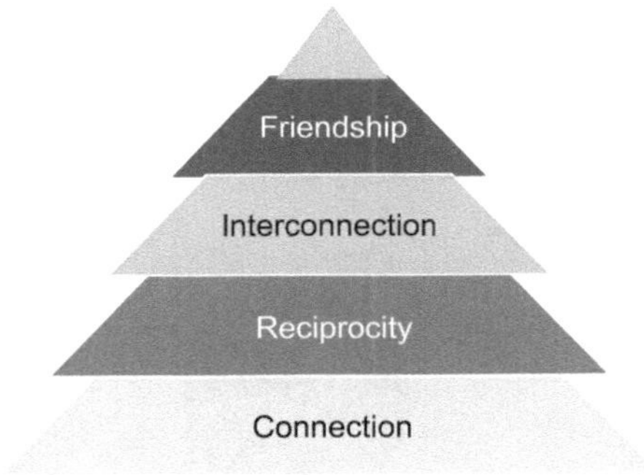

(non-pharmaceutical) anti-depressant, 'the self isn't the solution', (2018, 183) *it is the rest of us*. So okay, how? We can instinctively and decently know that something is wrong or potentially damaging and do nothing (such as when we see bullying or sexual harassment) or we can unpackage and skill build a difficult situation to enable positive change (Moynihan et al. 2011). Relationship peacebuilding, like bystander intervention training, is possible, and in the next section, I want to graphically present this peacebuilding method. Two visual representations will be offered (1) as a pyramid with 'steps' but also, (2) a circle with continuous processes because it may be useful to think of 'first steps' for the model (certainly my description that follows is 'stepped') but in reality, this is a continual and circular process that resists discreet categories and instead, overlaps and reinforces connection and reconnection in relationship (Figs. 9.8 and 9.9).

Relationship as Peace Praxis

Connection is mindful and deliberate contact with another human. Mindfulness is a practice in engagement or 'way of being' that combines observation with compassion (Williams and Penman 2011). You are a human, if you are self-aware and acting with nonviolent intention to 'meet' another person (whether an infant, child, youth or grown-up) the first step in connection is being open to the other's humanity by watching and being present for an opening or invitation to engage. This can be eye contact it can be assistance or it can be solidarity, it can be recognition or acknowledgement that says 'I see you' or a signal or action that 'my humanity is of service to your humanity'.

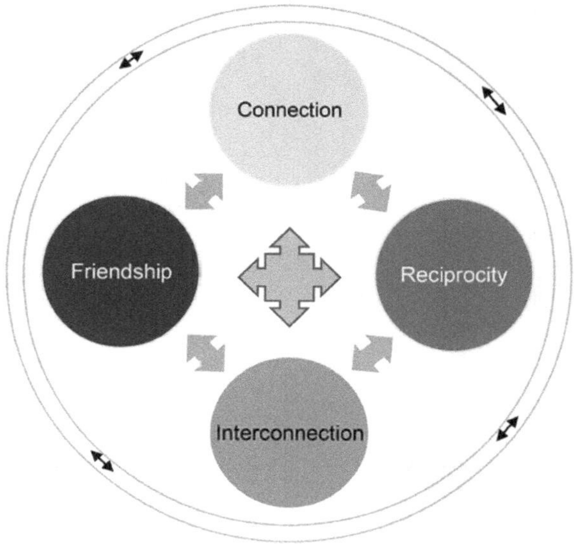

Fig. 9.9 The relationship as cyclic

Reciprocity undergirds the social fabric of life. It is an exchange of benefits between people that encourages cooperation in the future because reciprocity breeds reciprocity. As reciprocity (in this case positive reciprocity) creates the conditions for the return of behaviours and attitudes going forward that are beneficial, any positive exchange (of objects or actions) begins the dance of social reciprocity. Following or in tandem with the act of connection, this facet of relationship requires a generosity where a reciprocal relationship is established through the act of giving (something of some kind to someone). Simply put, to engage in reciprocity, give something to someone without expectation of return, and in time, your generosity should be returned. And, as the value of symbolic reciprocity is higher, indicating that the act of giving is more important than the inherent value of said thing or action, acts of reciprocity should include a long-term exchange of benefits, a sense of uncertainty regarding the return of benefits and it should be deliberate. The positive reciprocity formula is simple: give something positive, beneficial and non-harming (a gift, a token of appreciation, your attention or assistance etc.) without expectation of return, and keep doing it, over and over again.

Interconnection is a two-way or mutual state of repeated exchange that results in security and trust. Because our lived experience of mutual aid and protection colours our future actions interconnection occurs when positive reciprocal exchanges happen overtime. As we both receive and provide these benefits mutual aid and protection can perpetuate itself and become sustaining. The result of these interactions is the assumption of security—that what was experienced in the past will work to form what happens in future. For strategic networkers, this is the end goal of social interaction—a strategic arithmetic of past offers as guarantors of future outcomes. This can be considered transactional generosity and interconnections are maintained via repeated interactions. Prolonged and mutual acts of positive reciprocity lead to interconnections. If you want to create interconnections, go back to the 'how' of reciprocity and when it becomes mutual (two-way) you have interconnection.

Friendship is a mutual interconnection characterized by warmth, affection and love. It is an interpersonal avenue of assistance, understanding and positivity and it is cooperative and kind. If you read many PACS publications (as I have), they will frequently talk about how interactions can become friendships or how strategic networking and acts of reciprocal benefit lead to lifelong relational bonds. Indeed, the reality of peacebuilding is that you are partnering with others in the transformation of violence which can create vast and robust bonds of fidelity and fondness. But, if you ask most grownups how to make 'friends' (devoid of life and death circumstances), they will blink into the twilight even though most of us know on an instinctive level how our own friendships were created. But for those who feel disconnected and alone, the techniques of making and keeping friendships can seem intangible, overwhelming and impossible.

I am not going to say making friends is easy because it is not. I have progressed through the previous three facets of relationship in this section on peacebuilding suicide with words such as *connect*, *give*, *mutual benefit*, and these terms belie the emotional challenge of trying to make contact unsuccessfully, giving without return or seeking to build relationships when social interactions feel like an off-ramp to nowhere. That is why the work of relationship peace praxis is for those that surround the disconnected, the alone, that is why it is our job to contact, give, interconnect and befriend, so that people do not feel isolated, abandoned and hopeless.

The making friends intervention:

Be mindful—notice and recognize when someone is isolated,
Make contact—reach out and make a connection,
Provide benefit—be generous and giving without expectation of return,
Keep it up—when you receive attention, support, stuff or assistance return the favour,
Invest—make time for interconnections and then make *more* time for them,
Upvest—be positive and make people feel good, and
Collaborate—join in, work together and be there for them when they need help.

I reiterate that relationship peace praxis is not the work of individuals who feel disconnected and alone, these are not self-help tools for people to utilize in order to maximize their social networks or build beneficial connections. This is for the rest of us, to stop rushing by people who need us, get out of our bubbles that separate us and be of service to others so that they don't feel disconnected, so that they don't feel alone and so they don't feel hopeless. And this means connecting with ourselves, connecting with others and then building the insulating and shielding bonds that make us healthier, more resilient and more hopeful. As Hari avers potentially suicidal people 'aren't a machine with broken parts. [They] are an animal whose needs are not being met. [They] need to have a community' (2018, 256) which is where the rest of us come in. We are the community that is needed, we are the connections that need to be reconnected and we are the tribe that needs to come back together.

For those who hear this call as work for organized individuals like Corinda Taylor from the Hope Centre (and there are countless other groups who seek to address mental unwellness and suicide all over the world), I would like to suggest an additional custodial direction: there are roughly seven billion people in the world. Some are in spaces of vulnerability that make it challenging or impossible to be a life raft for others. But, if each of us could simply decide to befriend one person, then the impact would be staggering. I cannot tell you how many people Corinda and her team have helped. It is likely hundreds if not thousands (her work is never-ending and occupies every waking minute of her day). I can tell you how many suicides I have definitively prevented: one.

Just one. In a world of seven billion people where 800,000 to 1 million individuals successfully accomplish this form of violence every year, and we recall that number does not include attempts, or suicidal ideation or so-called accidents that are really suicides or suicides that loved ones or those left behind or government functionaries characterize as 'other', one may not seem very impressive

Suicide happens worldwide and affects 'approximately one hundred people per hour' (Baudelot and Establet 2008, 1). And, although the average suicide was previously said to impact an average of six people, recent scholarship has shown that up to 135 people are affected by each individual suicide (Cerel et al. 2018). If you calculate 135 people by 800,000 successful suicides last year, the number of people affected by suicide is 108 million. That also means that globally, out of 7.5 billion people, 1 in 69 will be a suicide. 1 in 69. That is staggering. If we were still in tribes, then there could be 2–3 people you knew intimately who could die by suicide.

It is said that most of us have 3–5 'real' friends, and the average Facebook user has 338. If you don't know someone who has died by suicide yet, you will, the odds favour it. Many of us have been touched by suicide or will be in our lifetime. This reality might fill you with dread or despondency, it might seem impossible to face much less ameliorate, but permit me to motivate you with a reasonable assumption: you cannot save everyone from this form of self-directed and lethal violence (certainly not all 800,000), but out of the 2–3 that you know, could you save one? I think you can. Hopefully this book has inspired you to try and hopefully this chapter has shared with you a method to do so.

A Book Summary and a Predictable, Inevitable and Indisputable Call for More

Suicide through a Peacebuilding Lens is a serendipitous journey into understanding. What the phenomena of suicide includes, how suicide incarnates, how the field of PACS entertains this form of violent death, how it is understood and how it can be ameliorated. In Chapter 1, this book sought to amplify suicide, urge my field to bridge the suicide gap and engage with suicidal violence in our work. In Chapter 2, this book delved into a cross-discipline appreciation of suicide from geographic, cultural, temporal and spatial perspectives and sought to contemplate understandings of these phenomena relevant to self-killing in the past, the present and along the lines of culture, gender and space. In Chapter 3, the field of PACS was described introducing the essential directive, to many of us, shared in the Seville Statement on violence: that it is our duty as scholars to reveal and attend to the reduction of violence wherever we see it. In Chapters 4 and 5, this interdisciplinary exploration led to a theorization of forms of suicide that can be considered under the rubric of *medical*—mental illness, assisted suicide, euthanasia—or *instrumental*—homicide-suicides, martyrdom (altruistic) operations, daredevil and protest suicides. In Chapter 6, this book sought to appreciate suicidal phenomena from the perspective of social, cultural and political violence and in Chapter 7 grasped suicide in relation to intention, motivation and intervention. Chapter 8 challenged notions of suicide as 'tragedy' as well as problematique that surround suicides as voluntary and rational acts. Finally, this chapter has introduced Encounter Theory and offered a peacebuilding prescription for suicide via the Encounter Theory of relationship.

This book has made the substantiated claim that suicide, the leading cause of violent death in most countries in the world is being ignored by PACS. It has presented a dearth of information that I am optimistic will be of use to future PACS scholar/practitioners and anyone with an aim to peacebuild suicide. As so many people are looking at suicide in their disciplinary cubicles, I encourage all of us to take a view from the top and share, mostly I encourage my field to add this form of violence and peacebuilding to our work in the world. I have learned a great deal about suicide in this study and along the way gained some valuable insight into topics and evidence that many other people are professionally committed to both understanding and sharing beyond my expertise and ability. I am grateful for the chance to learn about this and seek to invite suicide scholarship into the PACS world. Would this book begin a framework of study into suicide in PACS I would be incredibly gratified but even if this just becomes a footnote in larger studies about violence and peacebuilding at least I have put the ladder up the wall if to only reach the first rung. There is so much further to do, more to consider and much to understand.

One of the purposes of this book was to establish some conceptual knowledge of suicide and to find something relevant in this material to the uptake of suicide as a theme of attention in PACS. A recognizable trend can be identified via this material that relates to a state of dislocation—whether psychological or physical—that seems to correlate to self-killing. By living in Aotearoa/New Zealand, I learned that in the Māori world (similar to many other Indigenous worldviews) a person born in his or her familial land is considered *rooted*, to their birthplace, ancestors and spirits. Those of us who are migrants or displaced (physically or culturally), marginalized or disconnected, for any number of reasons related to violence, economy or culture are called *seeds in the wind*—they have no soil, no sense of connection to place and cannot form roots. There is a logic in the Māori perception of humans in space that seems to relate to this investigation—seeds in the wind commit suicide—much more than people who are rooted by religion, socio-economic status, group prestige, personal well-being or, critically, social bonding. Being dislocated, as has been shown in the previous content supplied in this chapter, is not simply a matter of geography (many different Indigenous groups still live in places where their ancestry is embedded) but to cultural connectivity, social assembly and interpersonal rootedness. But it does seem to be hitting one group of victims harder than another, by a landslide: men.

Gendering Suicide

In this work, I could not help but notice something that I hope others have spotted too. *Disconnection* is a large part of what makes us susceptible to suicide but the 'us' is overwhelmingly, and importantly, not really an 'us' it is males—boys and men of all ages—and therefore, gender-neutral terms like 'majority' or 'most' should immediately be scrutinized because when the stats show incidences of suicide they often hide the vitally important fact that they really mean 'male' suicide. This is not to dispute the reality that girls and women also complete suicide and attempt to do so in numbers we do not even know, but the fact that just one country: China, has a higher female to male suicide ratio[8] signals something that relates to our capacity to peacebuild suicide—*relationships* may be a key to suicide resilience for women. As proposed by Saint-Laurent et al., 'women's resistance to committing suicide may be explained by the strong role they play in family life, even if they work outside the home; their tasks prevent them from becoming socially and emotionally isolated' (2003, 792). Vijayakumar, too, connects the social environment of women to lower incidences of suicide and these 'protective' factors directly relate to the four facets of relationship peace praxis presented in this chapter. She writes that in addition to pregnancy and motherhood as protective factors,

> Women may also be protected against suicide because they are more willing to ask for, and more likely to be offered, help for emotional problems. They may more often have family support, social networks, good social skills, and be more likely to use telephone help lines, visit family doctors, discuss their problems with others, and have better opportunities to access social and health services. Because women tend to have better verbal and social skills than men, they may respond better than men to psychological and cognitive-behavioral therapies for depression. (2015, 237)

Saint-Laurent's and Vijayakumar's declarations bear repeating, *women's resistance to committing suicide may be explained by the strong role they play in family life*, and, *women tend to have better verbal and social skills than men*—both of which contribute to their ability to support and sustain relationships. This is an inference echoed by Chang et al. (2019) who intone that although 'women face a variety of social disadvantages, suicide rates are generally lower in women than in men [which] could be an indication of women's resilience in responding to stress and crises…as women are in general more, adaptive and are survivors' (300). Could women's resilience be social and not individual? Does female resilience to suicide (in comparison with males worldwide) relate to women's greater ability to manifest and maintain social networks? Is it not worth looking a little closer at the link between *relationship* and suicide? I agree with Chang, Yip and Chen that 'how women develop strengths to survive hardships are areas that need in-depth exploration, and this kind of inquiry would complement suicide prevention in men' (2019, 303). After all that I have learned in this study, I think *relationships*, connection, reconnection, interconnection, friendship and positive affective bonding presents a peacebuilding avenue for addressing, minimizing and preventing suicide.

To recap just some of the scholarship presented in this book individuals are more at risk of suicide if they are:

Indigenous (Leenaars 2006),
Migrants (Hjern and Allebeck 2002),
Divorced, separated or widowed (Milner et al. 2013),
Have relationship problems (Shiner et al. 2009),
Experience discrimination and social marginalization (Spallek et al. 2014),

Struggle with more than one form of mental illness (Effinger and Stewart 2012),
Have limited social support (De Leo and Krysinska 2017),
Have a history of committing violence (Ilgen and Kleinberg 2011),
Live in remote areas (Milner et al. 2013),
Have an internal locus-of Hope (Wagshul 2018),
Grow up with authoritarian parenting (Singh and Behmani 2018),
Have *psychache* (Shneidman 1985, cited in Gvion and Apter 2012),
Struggle with masculinity (Scourfield et al. 2012),
Have an unmet need to belong (Joiner 2005, 2010),
Grapple with addiction (Colpe and Pringle 2014)
Won't ask for help (Amitai and Apter 2012),
Have 'suicide' within their cultural framework (Pierre 2015),
Are undergoing serious interpersonal problems (Rajalin et al. 2017),
Have experienced childhood trauma (Manthorpe and Iliffe 2011),
Experience unemployment (Hanna et al. 2011),
Have no children (Baudelot and Establet 2008),
Are exposed to suicide via media (Scherr and Steinleitner 2017).
Are incarcerated (Gupta and Girdhar 2012),
Perceive that they do not fit in (Gvion and Apter 2012),
Are socially isolated (Huey and McNulty 2005), and
Are men (Wray et al. 2011).

And, in addition to the predominant form of suicide addressed in this chapter (*medical* suicide related to mental illness) four types of *instrumental* suicide were identified in this study—homicide-suicide, martyrdom, daredevil and protest suicide. While mental illness can play a significant role in *instrumental* suicide (Roma et al. 2012) of the five patterns of homicide-suicide, the major perpetrators of:

Intimate possessive homicide-suicide (Knoll IV 2016) are men,
Intimate-Ailing homicide-suicide (Manning 2015) are men,
Filicide homicide-suicide (Liem and Koenraadt 2008) are men,
Familicide homicide-suicide (Riedel 2010) are men,
Extrafamilial homicide-suicide (Rice and Sher 2016) are men,
Most martyrs (Rae 2012) are men,
Most daredevil suicides (Breivilk 2007) are men and
Most protest suicides (Alexopoulos et al. 2019; Plewis 2017) are men.

The gendered aspect of suicide is an important aperture of inquiry for all social scientists but considering how the protective factor of social bonding is a key peacebuilding praxis it may be a vital new line of investigation linking the Encounter Theory of relationship to preventing suicide.

Protective factors are insulators against suicidal violence and they include a number of different qualities that limit or reduce the incidence of self-harming and suicide. As Lester and Krysinska (2012) relate,

> On the individual level, these include hopefulness, reasons for living, resilience, problem-solving and coping-with-stress skills, plans for the future, and constructive leisure time…on the interpersonal level are the availability and suitability of social support from family and others, involvement in stable and significant relationships (including marriage), responsibility for children and parenthood, especially having children under the age of 18 living at home. (562)

While individuals who attempt and ultimately succeed in suicidal acts come from all walks of life, all over the globe, this so-called heterogeneity cannot mask the fact that men are overrepresented in this form of violence at a rate of 3–4 times that of women (Ludwig and Dwivedi 2018).

> In the vast majority of countries, three to four times fewer women commit suicide than men. In itself, that observation tells us nothing about suicide. But in leading us to ask why women are less vulnerable, it forces us to explore what it is about the social conditions of women and men that is so different as to produce this behavioural difference. (Baudelot and Establet 2008)

In looking forward, I hope we begin to do more than explore social conditions and their various protective factors related to suicide, I hope we peacebuild them and start the promising practice of building the value and practice of relationship into our social/cultural worlds.

As I mentioned in the first chapter of this book, the Seville Statement from UNESCO (1986) states that violence and war are human creations. If that is true (and I believe wholeheartedly that they are), then the work of nonviolence (which many term peace) is also human bound. We recognize that there is nothing in our nature that leads to violence and war but plenty in our *cultures* that do (cited in Adams 1989). We are a planet of many people and for those of us whose human vulnerabilities permit us to do so, we must act as individuals and as groups to recognize, reduce, ameliorate and prevent violence. While suicide is not directly mentioned in the Seville Statement, we need to cease to ignore this form of violence and both seek to understand it (in its many incarnations) and where appropriate and possible to eradicate it. Suicide, similar to other forms of violence, is not an inherent biological behaviour. As the Seville Statement notes, if individuals believe that violence is biologically determined then there is less likelihood that they will engage in activities that encourage peace (1986, cited in Adams 1989). We know that suicide is optional and as peacebuilders, we cannot join the fight against suicide unless we understand what suicide(s) is.

As mentioned in Chapter 3, the Seville Statement emphasizes that it is the obligation of scientists within academic disciplines to address the *most dangerous and destructive* activities of our species (1986, cited within Adams 1989). This includes the responsibility of studying issues that are contentious or complicated to navigate, such as suicide. PACS academics and practitioners have a duty to engage in suicide research. Given the strong link between research, theory and practice within PACS, a focus on suicide could lead to the transformation of this form of violence via the peace praxis of *relationship* (Lederach 2005). Suicide affects between 800,000 and 1 million individuals and their families a year. It is a global and pressing issue and there is not a moment to lose.

Notes

1. As we have learned, the majority of suicides relate to mental illness. Despite the rarity and unique circumstances that surround the remaining six forms of suicide identified in this book, I feel strongly that attention and exploration from a PACS perspective would be beneficial and productive and I wholeheartedly support and encourage further and future inquiry along those lines.
2. As we have learned, the majority of suicides relate to mental illness although the empirical analysis presented in the first chapter of this book demonstrated that PACS has almost exclusively ignored this form. Despite the rarity and unique circumstances that surround the remaining six forms of suicide identified in this book, I feel strongly that attention and exploration of these more rare forms of suicide from a PACS perspective is needed, would be beneficial and productive and I wholeheartedly support and encourage further and future inquiry along those lines.
3. The goal of much PACS scholarship is to put the knowledge gained from academic inquiry into action (Freire 2003). This process is described as

praxis—when information becomes a foundation for accomplishing something transformative and the experience of that action forms a feedback loop.
4. This study included.
5. For a glimpse at the budding field of positive suicidology see recent scholarship by Kelliher Rabon, Hirsch and Chang (2018) *Positive Psychology and Suicide Prevention: An Introduction and Overview of the Literature.*
6. Bystander Intervention, such as '*Bringing in the Bystander*' (BITB), is a method of violence reduction and/or elimination that focuses on those that surround a potential victim/perpetrator (see Potter and Moynihan 2011 or Moynihan et al. 2011).
7. Mindfulness is be more clearly defined shortly.
8. For more information about the *Life Matters Suicide Prevention Trust* and the *Hope Centre* and to donate to their incredibly important work look here, https://www.lifematters.org.nz/donate.
9. Recent scholarship suggests that Bangladesh may also join China (see Arafat, S.M. Yasir, 2018. "Females Are Dying More Than Males by Suicide in Bangladesh." *Asian Journal of Psychiatry*, https://doi.org/10.1016/j.ajp.2018.10.014).

References

Adams, David. 1989. "The Seville Statement on Violence: A Progress Report." *Journal of Peace Research* 26 (2): 113–121.

Aldridge, David, Barrero Pérez, and Andrés Sergio. 2011. *A Comprehensive Guide to Suicidal Behaviours: Working with Individuals at Risk of Suicide and Their Families.* London: Jessica Kingsley.

Alexopoulos, Evangelos C., Katerina Kavalidou, and Fani Messolora. 2019. "Suicide Mortality Patterns in Greek Work Force Before and During the Economic Crisis." *International Journal of Environmental Research and Public Health* 16: 469. https://doi.org/10.3390/ijerph16030469.

Amitai, Maya, and Alan Apter. 2012. "Social Aspects of Suicidal Behavior and Prevention in Early Life: A Review." *International Journal of Environmental Research and Public Health* 9 (3): 985–994.

Arafat, S. M. Yasir. 2018. "Females are Dying More Than Males by Suicide in Bangladesh." *Asian Journal of Psychiatry*, https://doi.org/10.1016/j.ajp.2018.10.014. Accessed March 20 from https://ac-els-cdn-com.ezproxy.otago.ac.nz/S1876201818307834/1-s2.0-S1876201818307834-main.pdf?_tid=0adc89b8-f8f2-43db-9b3c-f0eab4766c32&acdnat=1553039169_44b93b499362912ae8b5c818b9a5a293.

Austin, Wendy J. 2012. "Relational Ethics." In *The Sage Encyclopaedia of Qualitative Research Methods*, edited by Lisa M. Given, 749–753. Thousand Oaks, CA: Sage.

Baudelot, Christian, and Roger Establet. 2008. *Suicide, the Hidden Side of Modernity*. Malden, MA: Polity Press.

Berscheid, Ellen, and Peplau Letitia A. 1983. "The Emerging Science of Relationships." In *Close Relationships*, edited by Harold H. Kelley, Ellen Berscheid, Andrew Christensen, John H. Harvey, Ted L. Huston, George Levinger, Evie McClintock, Letitia A. Peplau, and Donald R. Peterson, 1–19. New York: W.H. Freeman.

Boulding, Elise. 2000. *Cultures of Peace: The Hidden Side of History*. Syracuse: Syracuse University Press.

Bowlby, John. 1990. *The Making and Breaking of Affectional Bonds*. London: Routledge.

Breivik, Gunnar. 2007. "Can BASE Jumping Be Morally Defended." In *Philosophy, Risk and Adventure Sports*, edited by Mike McNamee, 168–185. New York: Taylor and Francis.

Cerel, Julie, Margaret M. Brown, Myfanwy Maple, Michael Singleton, Judy Venne, Melinda Moore, and Chris Flaherty. 2018. "How Many People Are Exposed to Suicide? Not Six." *Suicide and Life Threatening Behavior*. https://doi.org/10.1111/sltb.12450.

Chang, Qingsong, Paul S. F. Yip, Ying-Yeh Chen. 2019. "Gender Inequality and Suicide Gender Ratios in the World," *Journal of Affective Disorders*, 243: 297–304.

Colpe, Lisa, and Beverly Pringle. 2014. Data for Building a National Suicide Prevention Strategy: What We Have and What We Need. *American Journal of Preventive Medicine* 47 (3): 130–136.

De Leo, Diego, and Karolina Krysinska. 2017. "Suicide and Self-Directed Violence." In *International Encyclopedia of Public Health*, 2nd ed., edited by Stella Quah and William Cockerham, 115–123. Amsterdam: Academic Press.

Denworth, Lydia. 2017. *The Three Basics of Friendship*. Retrieved February 27, 2019 from https://www.psychologytoday.com/us/blog/brain-waves/201703/the-three-basics-friendship.

Devere, Heather. 2011. "The Resurrection of Political Friendship." In *Varieties of Friendship, Interdisciplinary Perspectives on Social Relationships*, edited by Bernadette Descharms, Eric Anton Heuser, Caroline Krüger, and Thomas Loy, 17–42. Göttingen: V&R Unipress.

Devere, Heather. 2014. "The Many Meanings of Friendship." *AMITY: The Journal of Friendship Studies* 2 (1): 1–3.

Devere, Heather. 2018. Exploring Relationships for Positive Peace. *Factis Pax* 12 (1): 59–79.

Devere, Heather, and Graham M. Smith. 2010. Friendship and Politics. *Political Studies Review* 8 (3): 341–356.

Effinger, Jenell, and David Stewart. 2012. "Classification of Co-occurring Depression and Substance Abuse Symptoms Predicts Suicide Attempts in Adolescents." *Suicide and Life Threatening Behaviour* 42 (4): 353–358.

Feuerstein, Georg. 2001. *The Yoga Tradition: Its History, Literature, Philosophy and Practice*. Prescott: Hohm Press.

Freire, Paulo. 2003. *The Pedagogy of the Oppressed*. New York: Continuum.

Friedman, Daniel, and Nirvikar Singh. 2003. "Negative Reciprocity: The Coevolution of Memes and Genes." *Evolution and Human Behavior* 25: 155–173.

Fudenberg, Drew, and Jean Tirole. 1991. *Game Theory*. Cambridge: The MIT Press.

Galtung, Johan. 1996. *Peace by Peaceful Means: Peace and Conflict, Development and Civilization*. London: Sage.

Gupta, Anju, and N. K. Girdhar. 2012. "Risk Factors of Suicide in Prisoners." *Delhi Psychiatry Journal* 15 (1): 45–49.

Gvion, Yari, and Alan Apter. 2012. "Suicide and Suicidal Behavior." *Public Health Reviews* 34 (2): 1–20.

Haidt, Johnathan. 2006. *The Happiness Hypothesis*. New York: Basic Books.

Hanna, Morid M., Etemad A. A. El-Shereef, and Azza H. Griew. 2011. "Study of Pattern and Outcome of Suicidal Methods Used in Benghazi City–Libya." *Egyptian Journal of Forensic Sciences* 1 (3): 124–132.

Hari, Johann. 2018. *Lost Connections: Uncovering the Real Causes of Depression—And the Unexpected Solutions*. New York: Bloomsbury.

Hjern, Anders, and Peter Allebeck. 2002. "Suicide in First-and Second-Generation Immigrants in Sweden A Comparative Study." *Social Psychiatry and Psychiatric Epidemiology* 37 (9): 423–429. https://doi.org/10.1007/s00127-002-0564-5-12242618.

Huey, Meredith, and Thomas McNulty. 2005. "Institutional Conditions and Prison Suicide: Conditional Effects of Deprivation and Overcrowding." *The Prison Journal* 85 (4): 490–514.

Ilgen, Mark, and Felicia Kleinberg. 2011. "The Link Between Substance Abuse, Violence and Suicide: Implications and Interventions." *Psychiatric Times* 28 (1): 25–27.

Jeong, Ho-Won. 2011. *Understanding Conflict and Conflict Analysis*. New York: Sage.

Jessica Kelliher, Rabon, Jameson K. Hirsch, and Edward C. Chang. 2018. "Positive Psychology and Suicide Prevention: An Introduction and Overview of the Literature." In *A Positive Psychological Approach to Suicide: Advances in Mental Health and Addiction*, edited by J. Hirsch, E. Chang, and J. Kelliher Rabon, 1–15. Cham, Switzerland: Springer.

Joiner, Thomas. 2005. *Why People Die by Suicide*. Cambridge, MA: Harvard University Press.

Joiner, Thomas. 2010. *Myths About Suicide*. Cambridge: Harvard University Press.

Knoll IV, James. 2016. "Understanding Homicide-Suicide." *Psychiatric Clinics of North America* 39 (4): 633–647.
Larson, Deborah. 1998. "Exchange and Reciprocity in International Negotiations." *International Negotiation* 3: 121–138.
Lederach, John Paul. 1997. *Building Peace: Sustainable Reconciliation in Divided Societies*. Washington, DC: United States Institute of Peace.
Lederach, John Paul. 2003. *The Little Book of Conflict Transformation: Clear Articulation of the Guiding Principles by a Pioneer in the Field*. Intercourse, PA: Good Books.
Lederach, John Paul. 2005. *The Moral Imagination: The Art and Soul of Building Peace*. Oxford: Oxford University Press.
Leenaars, Antoon A. 2006. "Suicide Among Indigenous Peoples: Introduction and Call to Action." *Archives of Suicide Research* 10 (2): 103–115.
Lester, David, and Karolina Krysinska. 2012. "Suicide." In *Encyclopedia of Human Behavior*, 2nd ed., edited by, S. Ramachandran Vilayanur, 558–563. London: Academic Press.
Liem, Marieke, and Frans Koenraadt. 2008. "Filicide: A Comparative Study of Maternal Versus Paternal Child Homicide." *Criminal Behaviour and Mental Health* 18: 166–176.
Ludwig, Birgit, and Yogesh Dwivedi. 2018. "The Concept of Violent Suicide, Its Underlying Trait and Neurobiology: A Critical Perspective." *European Neuropsychopharmacology*, 28: 243–251.
Manning, Jason. 2015. "The Social Structure of Homicide-Suicide." *Homicide Studies* 19 (4): 350–369.
Manthorpe, Jill, and Steve Iliffe. 2011. "Social Work with Older People—Reducing Suicide Risk: A Critical Review of Practice and Prevention." *British Journal of Social Work*, 41 (1): 131–147.
Miller, Warren B., and Joseph L. Rodgers. 2001. *The Ontogeny of Human Bonding Systems: Evolutionary Origins, Neural Bases, and Psychological Manifestations*. New York: Springer.
Milner, Allison, Heidi Hjelmeland, Ella Arensman, and Diego De Leo. 2013. "Social-Environmental Factors and Suicide Mortality: A Narrative Review of Over 200 Articles." *Sociology Mind* 3 (2): 137–148.
Molm, Linda. 2010. "The Structure of Reciprocity." *Social Psychology Quarterly* 73 (2): 119–131.
Molm, Linda, David Shaefer, and Jessica Collett. 2007. "The Value of Reciprocity." *Social Psychology Quarterly* 70 (2): 199–217.
Moynihan, Mary, Victoria L. Banyard, Julie S. Arnold, Robert P. Eckstein, and Jane G. Stapleton, 2011. "Sisterhood May Be Powerful for Reducing Sexual and Intimate Partner Violence: An Evaluation of the Bringing in the Bystander In-Person Program with Sorority Members." *Violence Against Women* 17 (6): 703–719.

Perlman, Daniel. 2017. "Conclusion: Friendship: An Echo, a Hurrah and Other Reflections, 283–300." In *The Psychology of Friendship*, edited by Mahzad Hojjat and Anne Moyer, 283–300. Oxford: Oxford University Press.

Pierre, Joseph. 2015. "Culturally Sanctioned Suicide: Euthanasia, Seppuku, and Terrorist Martyrdom." *World Journal of Psychiatry* 5 (1): 4–14.

Plewis, Ian. 2017. "Analyzing Indian Farmer Suicide Rates." *Proceedings of the National Academy of Sciences of the United States of America* 115 (2): E117.

Potter, Sharyn, and Mary Moynihan. 2011. "Bringing in the Bystander In-Person Prevention Program to a U.S. Military Installation: Results from a Pilot Study."*Military Medicine* 176 (8): 870–875.

Rae, Jonathan A. 2012. "Will It Ever Be Possible to Profile the Terrorist?" *Journal of Terrorism Research* 3 (2): 1–11.

Rajalin, Mia, Tatja Hirvikoski, Ellinor Salander Renburg, Marie Asberg, and Jussi Jokinen. 2017. "Family History of Suicide and Interpersonal Functioning in Suicide Attempters." *Psychiatry Research* 247: 310–314.

Reardon, Betty A. 1988. *Comprehensive Peace Education: Educating for Global Responsibility*. New York: Teachers College Press.

Reardon, Betty A. 1995. *Educating for Human Dignity: Learning About Rights and Responsibilities*. Philadelphia: University of Pennsylvania Press.

Rice, Timothy, and Leo Sher. 2016. "Preventing Plane-Assisted Suicides Through the Lessons of Research on Homicide and Suicide-Homicide." *Acta Neuropsychiatrica* 28 (4): 195–198.

Riedel, Marc. 2010. "Homicide-Suicides in the United States: A Review of the Literature." *Sociology Compass* 4 (7): 430–441.

Roma, Paolo, Floriana Pazzelli, Maurizio Pompili, David Lester, Paolo Girardi, and Stefano Ferracuti. 2012. "Mental Illness in Homicide-Suicide: A Review." *Journal of the American Academy of Psychiatry and the Law* 40 (4): 462–468.

Rossi, Alice S., and Peter, H. Rossi. 1990. *Of Human Bonding: Parent-Child Relations Across the Life Course*. New York: Aldine de Gruyter.

Saint-Laurent, Danielle. 2003. "Suicide and Gender." In *Macmillan Encyclopedia of Death and Dying*, edited by Robert Kastenbaum, 792–795. New York: Macmillan Reference.

Saunders, Harold. 1999. *A Public Peace Process: Sustained Dialogue to Transform Racial and Ethnic Conflicts*. New York: Palgrave.

Scherr, Sebastian, and Anna Steinleitner. 2017. "Between Werther and Papageno Effects: A Propositional Meta-Analysis of Ambiguous Findings for Helpful and Harmful Media Effects on Suicide Contagion." In *Media and Suicide: International Perspectives on Research, Theory, and Policy*, edited by Thomas Niederkrotenthaler and Steven Stack, 1–14. New York: Routledge.

Scourfield, Jonathan, Ben Fincham, Susanne Langer, and Michael Shiner. 2012. "Sociological Autopsy: An Integrated Approach to the Study of Suicide in Men." *Social Science & Medicine* 74 (4): 466–473.

Shiner, Michael, Jonathan Scourfield, Ben Fincham, and Susanne Langer. 2009. "When Things Fall Apart: Gender and Suicide Across the Life-Course." *Social Science & Medicine* 69 (5): 738–746.

Singh, Vijeta, and Rakesh K. Behmani. 2018. "Parenting Style and Adolescent Suicide Ideation: A Review." *International Journal of Academic Research and Development* 3 (2): 1245–1252.

Spallek, Jacob, Anna Reeske, Marie Norredam, Signe Smith Nielsen, Jessica Lehnhardt, and Oliver Razum. 2014. "Suicide Among Immigrants in Europe—A Systematic Literature Review." *European Journal of Public Health* 25 (1): 63–71.

Standish, Katerina, and Janine Joyce. 2018. *Yogic Peace Education*. Jefferson, NC: McFarland & Company.

Vijayakumar, Lakshmi. 2015. Suicide in Women. *Indian Journal of Psychiatry* 57: 233–238.

Wagshul, Yitzchok. 2018. "Effect of External Locus-of-Hope on Acquired Capability for Suicide." Walden Dissertations and Doctoral Studies. Accessed March 16 from https://scholarworks.waldenu.edu/dissertations/5145/.

Williams, Mark, and Danny Penman. 2011. *Mindfulness: A Practical Guide to Finding Peace in the Frantic World*. London: Piatkus.

Wray, Matt, Cynthia Colen, and Bernice Pescosolido. 2011. The Sociology of Suicide. *Annual Review of Sociology* 37 (1): 505–528.

INDEX

K. Standish, *Suicide through a Peacebuilding Lens*,
https://doi.org/10.1007/978-981-13-9737-0

Kolibri 360 GmbH
Ferdinand-Jühlke-Straße 7
99095 Erfurt, Deutschland
produktsicherheit@kolibri360.de